Understanding
Learning
Disabilities

Tanis H. Bryan

AND

James H. Bryan

Understanding Learning Disabilities

Alfred Publishing Co., Inc.

Published by Alfred Publishing Co., Inc.
75 Channel Drive, Port Washington, N.Y. 11050

© Copyright 1975 by Alfred Publishing Co., Inc.

Library of Congress Cataloging in Publication Data

Bryan, Tanis H   1937–
Understanding learning disabilities.

Bibliography: p.
Includes index.
1. Learning disabilities. 2. Minimal brain dysfunction in children. I. Bryan, James H., 1933-
joint author. II. Title. [DNLM: 1. Learning disorders. LC4661 B915u]
LC4704.B79   371.9'28   75–1215
ISBN 0–88284–023–1

To our parents, who have provided us moral and financial support beyond their call to duty; and to our children who have contributed by their sacrificing some time, and (through their development) some knowledge and much joy.

CONTENTS

Contents

Contents

Contents

Contents

Contents

PREFACE

Many parents find they have one, and all teachers at one time or another have at least one. This is a child who experiences great difficulty surviving our educational system and meeting his peer group's requirements for achievement. In the past few years a new field has developed to help such children. Through parental and professional pressures, legislation, funds and teacher training, theories and interventions (corrective programs) have evolved to help these youngsters. This is a book written for students and professionals working with children suffering from learning disabilities.

In writing this book, we have attempted to integrate what we have learned from clinical and research studies, but have been biased towards emphasizing the products of research. It is our belief that systematically gathered information is better than casually collected data and thus greater stress has been placed on the former. Indeed, in making judgments about "truth," we have been cautious about relying on clinical data, not because we know that such data are wrong, but rather because we do not know whether the observations on which the data are based are totally correct.

The reader will note that the learning-disabled child has been defined in a variety of ways. He is the brain damaged, the poor reader, the poor speller and the poor mathematician. In other words, the learning disabled are a melange of children with a variety of academic problems. Clearly, all of these children are not really alike in important elements, but they all fall within the scope of the learning disability specialist. How they will be grouped, viewed and otherwise treated in the future remains to be seen. More information is needed on the similarities and differences which exist among children labeled as learning disabled. But that information is not available, or we have not been skilled enough to detect it, so that in writing this book, we talk about a variety of problems and children.

We have been critical of the field, as we saw this as our role. It is a field of imperfect knowledge, imperfect programs and imperfect progress. But yet, so are all fields studied. We trust that our criticism will not dim the enthusiasms of students, but will rather provide them with freedom from the many dogmas which seem to guide some members of the field.

Finally, no book is written without help from others. We are particularly grateful for the efforts of Jean E. Slater and Roslyn Wheeler, who served as right-hand women in tasks which required both hands. Time and support were provided by the Illinois State Pediatric Institute, for which we are quite grateful. Lastly, our thanks to those reviewers who offered valuable suggestions concerning the organization, style and substance of the text.

Tanis H. Bryan
James H. Bryan

Understanding
Learning
Disabilities

CHAPTER
1
INTRODUCTION

This is a book about children who have problems learning in school. It is concerned with how we define such children, what we believe we know about their problems, the characteristics we associate with these problems and the diagnostic and remedial procedures developed to help these children. This book is about the child with learning disabilities and the field of learning disabilities.

Who is the child with learning disabilities? The current working definition of this child, reached by consensus, is that developed by the National Advisory Committee on Handicapped Children. The definition is:

Children with special learning disabilities exhibit a disorder in one or more of the basic psychological processes involved in understanding or in using spoken or written language. These may be manifested in disorders of listening, thinking, talking, reading, writing, spelling, or arithmetic. They include conditions which have been referred to as perceptual handicaps, brain injury, minimal brain dysfunction, dyslexia, developmental aphasia, etc. They do not include learning problems which are due primarily to visual, hearing, or motor handicaps, to mental retardation, emotional disturbance, or to environmental disadvantage (Clements, 1966).

The definition is not precise, as it includes many different types of problems. It is difficult for any diagnostician to be even reasonably certain of judgments concerning a child with learning problems. By what criteria does one define a disorder of listening, thinking, talking or reading? Just what is a perceptual handicap? How might one recognize such a symptom? And how can one ever demonstrate the absence of an emotional disturbance when it is so difficult to diagnose its presence?

Problems of definition aside, there are many children failing to learn who are not blind, deaf, or dumb. A new profession devoted to serving the needs of these children has blossomed during the last ten years. It has now reached the point where it espouses and hopes for its own technology, jargon, institutional support and fee structure. It has, to a considerable extent, achieved these initial hopes. The newness of the profession does not imply that the problems it confronts are new problems. Rather, it is the importance of these problems to our society and the perspectives by which their origins and solutions are viewed which have changed dramatically. Although views of the causes of learning problems were once very narrow and similar to beliefs in witches and demons as causes of deviant behavior, research and education have had a profound effect on our understanding of the learning-disabled child. The views of children with learning problems today are not associated with a few "eggheads" or disgruntled parents, but are presented by spokesmen, learning disability specialists, who have received specialized training and the status associated with that training.

Current State of the Field

What factors precipitated the development of this new field? One can only speculate as to their nature, but three forces seem to be particularly relevant. The first is the rapid advance of technology in the United States; the second is the advance made in educational technology during and after World War II; the third is recent medical advances.

Since 1947 one's survival in the modern world has become increasingly dependent upon his ability to understand technological advances. Learning how to use new home appliances or how to analyze a computerized billing or bank statement can present problems to the illiterate or poorly educated. The requirements for existing jobs have become increasingly tied to educational achievements, even though it is likely that many of the functions of the job do not require advanced training. The college diploma, whether relevant or not, has become a prerequisite for many jobs. Perhaps for this reason alone, the percentage of Americans 25 years or older who have completed four years of high school more than doubled during the decade of the sixties and jumped to 52.5% of the population. Likewise, the percentage of this age group who completed four years of college more than doubled, rising from 4% to 10.7%. A child failing to acquire academic skills can no longer be viewed with equanimity by a middle-class parent. The future of a child within this society who cannot read is very dim. Difficulties in school are serious ones indeed for the concerned parent. How can a child who is unable to read complete high school or receive a college degree and compete in the open job market? Such parental and national concern for literacy is evidently much more intense within the United States than in other countries of the world. Downing (1972) reports that children in Finland and France may also have difficulty in learning, but this is of no great concern in these nations. Apparently, the American family is particularly worried about school failure, and well they should be, given this highly technical society.

Forces of Change

Educational technology and changes in educational perspectives are likely sources for nourishment to the field of learning disabilities. As a result of the national crisis in World War II, new techniques were developed for teaching complex skills to soldiers and basic skills to illiterates so they could become soldiers. Since the war, the results of many workers, such as Grace Fernald, B. F. Skinner, and A. A. Lumsdaine, to name a few, filtered down to the educational system in the forms of individualized and

5

programmed instruction and behavior modification. The emphasis within these views was upon the principles of learning and task analysis, not the personality of the child. These developments have permitted us to view individuals in more discrete and specific categories regarding their ability to meet the demands of the learning task. No longer can global judgments of children as lazy, stupid or bad suffice. On the contrary, the field of learning disabilities has been free to develop lists of specific behavioral and learning characteristics viewed as relevant to school failure.

Finally, advances in medical technology have resulted in the appearance of increased numbers, and perhaps types, of developmental disabilities. Infants who once might not have survived gestation, or who suffered anoxia, low birth weight, birth injury or condemning maternal infections like rubella are now more likely to survive. These infants become "high risk" children, as they are more likely to suffer developmental and learning problems than infants who did not suffer these traumas (Graham, Ernhart, Thurston and Craft, 1962; Werner, Honzik and Smith, 1964).

In addition, and perhaps because of advances in medical technology, researchers within the learning disabilities area began to view failure to learn in terms of physical malfunctioning rather than familial retardation or emotional disturbances, labels associated with considerable stigma within our society (Nunnally, 1961). The discovery that failure to learn could be caused by brain damage rather than genetic deficiencies or some failure of the parents to help their child grow emotionally and socially has relieved many concerned parents. Until these developments they were reluctant to publicly express their fears; and they were hesitant to press schools and legislatures for assistance.

What effect might these social forces have had upon the field of learning disabilities? Clearly, there are different variables by which one can measure the development of a field. One measure is the number of professionals still needed. The number of college students pursuing learning disabilities as a career is such that the number of professionals in one major organization, the Council for Exceptional Children, more than doubled in two years (D.C.L.D. *Newsletter*, 1970). Twenty-nine states now have certification requirements which specify the courses and hours which must be completed by future learning disability teachers. There appears to be growing concern for a tightening of the standards governing the conduct and training of the learning disability specialist (D.C.L.D. *Newsletter*, 1973).

Meeting the Challenge

Another reflection of professional growth is the estimate of the number of children who require learning disability programs and the cost of such programs. Illinois, for example, estimated that $18,330,400 in nonfederal funds was to be spent on learning disability programs and that an additional $9,000,000 was needed. In 1971 these figures of nonfederal spending for learning disabilities in Illinois increased to $15,500,000 to be expended and an additional $22,000,000 needed to provide adequate and appropriate services. It was estimated that within Illinois 9,900 children would be served in 1970, but that an additional 15,000 should but would not receive such help. By 1971 these figures increased to 12,500 children to be served and an additional 17,500 who should but would not receive aid. More recently the federal government has been increasing its assistance. One source, Title IV, G of the Model Demonstration Program for Children with Specific Learning Disabilities, has programmed more than $3,000,000 for fiscal year 1974–75 and has increased the figure to $5,000,000 for fiscal year 1975–76. According to the National Information Center for the Handicapped (also called CLOSER LOOK), part "B" of the Education of the Handicapped Act for 1975 allocates $10,000,000 for programs, agencies and teacher training curricula in learning disabilities. Twenty million dollars is the projected allocation for 1976. Although we recognize the distinction between what is allocated and what is actually appropriated, this kind of federally based concern and legislation is a good indicator of the catapulting interest and concern for learning disabilities research and remediation.

Introduction

It is estimated that as much as 28% of the elementary school population within the United States suffers from a learning disability (Clements, 1966; Bruinincks, Glaman and Clark, 1971). One research study, however, reported that 41% of the kindergarten and first-grade children within their school district were categorized by teachers as exhibiting characteristics associated with learning disabilities and in need of the services of trained personnel (Rubin and Balow, 1971).

The problem of learning disabilities has drawn increased attention from federal and state legislatures. Federal and state agencies have played two major roles. The first has been encouraging, by funding and legislation, universities and state departments of public education to establish teacher training programs and intervention programs for children with learning disabilities. The second has been establishing laws specific to the provision of services to children. Thus, the legal profession has become involved in problems of labeling and placement of children in special education settings.

State and national agencies became active in defining the field of learning disabilities in the mid-sixties. The National Society for Crippled Children and Adults, in part supported by the National Institutes for Health, organized three task forces to study the status of the field. Task Force I (Clements, 1966) reported on definitions and terminology used to describe learning-disabled children; Task Force II defined educational, medical and health related services relevant to these children; Task Force III (Chalfant and Scheffelin, 1969) focused on related research data. These three short publications encapsulated the directions, interests and problems in the field.

In 1966 Congress passed legislation which created Title VI of the Elementary and Secondary Education Act. This established programs of funding grants to state departments of education and funds for the establishment of the Bureau of Education for the Handicapped.

In 1969 Senator Ralph Yarborough, Chairman of the Committee on Labor and Welfare, reported that between 500,000 and 1,500,000 children were in need of learning disability intervention programs and that only 18% of these children were estimated to be receiving this help. Yarborough introduced a bill, passed by the 91st congress, entitled the Children with Learning Disabilities Act. This act mandated the federal government to facilitate the development of the field of learning disabilities as a separate entity within special education. The act led to the authorization of experiments, surveys, demonstrations and professional training for education personnel either teaching or preparing to teach learning-disabled children. Model centers to develop special educational treatments and make these treatments available to other programs for learning-disabled children were authorized.

The states have met the challenge of learning disabilities in a variety of ways and with varying speeds. Legislatures in some states (*e.g.,* New York) define the type of child to receive help and demand that public schools render appropriate services; others (*e.g.,* Maryland) provide the funds and allow the departments of public education to make these funds available to those school problems which they deem particularly urgent. In recent years twelve states have proposed legislation which refers specifically to learning disabilities. Four states, Connecticut, Florida, Hawaii and Massachusetts, used the term *learning disabilities* in their legislation. Nevada used the term *perceptual impairments,* Pennsylvania used *brain damage,* while California and Colorado adopted the term *educationally handicapped* (Kass, Hall and Simches, 1969). Whatever the predilection of the state, two-thirds had legislated services directly or indirectly to learning-disabled children by 1969.

The legislation boom is not over. Virginia estimated that 3% of the school population has learning disabilities and mandated that programs be effective for these children by 1972; Georgia will have programs by 1976. Illinois instigated legislation which provided for the establishment of programs by July, 1972, for several categories of developmental disabilities. These included learning disabilities, emotionally disturbed, speech defective, educable and trainable mentally handicapped children. The critical feature of this particular legislation is that services are to be available for ages 3 to 21.

The School Code of Illinois as amended may be exemplary

of trends in legislation for handicapped children. This act specifies that school districts must screen, identify and locate all handicapped three- and four-year-old children, make appropriate in-depth studies of these children, make plans to deliver noncategorical services and involve parents and community agencies in such efforts. The act incorporates the lowering of the age for which services are to be provided, specifies what schools must do to establish these programs, indicates the date by which school districts must be in compliance and explicates the standards which must be used for hiring teachers in order to get state reimbursement.

State certification requirements for teachers of learning-disabled children vary from state to state. Some have stringent criteria. Minnesota requires the teacher to have 24 hours of college credit in learning disability courses. Twenty-nine states now have explicit certification requirements for the learning disability teacher (D.C.L.D. *Newsletter,* 1973). Other states have not established any requirements, either because of indifference or because of a noncategorical approach to learning problems (*e.g.,* Massachusetts).

The passage of laws does not guarantee conformity or success. There have been a number of landmark court cases in which aggrieved parents, unhappy with the decision or procedures by which their children have been labeled and placed in special education programs, have brought their problems before the judiciary system. Since 1967, the courts have been increasingly active in intervening in the affairs of school districts. In 1967, Judge Skelly Wright, in the Hobson vs. Hanson case, ruled that the method used by school personnel in Washington, D.C., to test ability and achievement for the purpose of class placement was illegal. The result of this decision was that the school district was ordered to eliminate this tracking system of school placement on the basis that it created de facto segregation.

Litigation for damages is currently under way against a school district of San Diego, California, for conspiring to deprive citizens of equal protection under the law. An injunction has been sought to stop all special education placements until the procedures for placements are altered. Cases are being heard in Massachusetts brought by parents who claim they had not had an adequate opportunity to participate in the placement processes involving their children. Complaints revolve primarily around the issues of labeling, of diagnosis, of placement and of the parents' opportunity to be heard in the decision-making process (Cruickshank, 1972). A new twist is being added in a number of pending cases. Parents are suing for damages because their child did not receive an appropriate education; that is, the child failed to achieve to the level the parents believed he should have achieved. In one case a child was labeled as having a learning disability in the first grade, received special help from a learning disability teacher for one year and was then discharged from the remedial program. When the child reached junior high school, she started to receive failing grades in her academic courses. The parents argue that the school failed to adequately remediate the child's problem and dismissed the child from the remedial training program prematurely.

One can only agree with Cruickshank's belief that for the judicial system to have to specify for educators what is good and bad is an "awful indictment of educational leadership at the local level" (1972, p. 387). There is no question that the indictment has been issued, nor is there any question that the manner in which school districts respond and the degree to which they can respond will be a critical issue in special education and learning disabilities in the coming years.

Public concern about handicapped children is sufficiently aroused to have supported a publication entitled *Your Rights as Parents of a Handicapped Child.* The school district's responsibility in the evaluation and placement of children is outlined in this paperback book. State and nationally defined rights of these parents and their children are included. Other manuals are available so that parents may educate themselves on how to lobby, form groups, change laws, raise money and make headlines, and even how to develop their own private special education school or class.

The field of learning disabilities is firmly entrenched in the laws, if not yet the customs, of this country. It is unfortunate that the already overburdened judicial system is required to define and enforce the provision of services to children. But their involvement, along with that of the legislature, virtually guarantees the maintenance and growth of services to children. In all likelihood, our judges, lawyers, parents and school administrators have benevolent aims, which may far exceed the capacities of the learning disability specialist to deliver; the goals have outstripped the available technology.

CHAPTER
2
HISTORICAL BACKGROUND AND THEORETICAL MODELS

To understand this newly developed profession and its methods of assessment and remediation, one must examine the roots from which it sprang. The more recent influences upon the development of the field of learning disabilities arose from two parallel sources. Like most births, it took two progenitors. One parent was Kurt Goldstein, a German physician. He begot the pioneers Alfred Strauss and Heinz Werner. They in turn begot a whole school of American professionals, among them Laura Lehtinen and William Cruickshank. Their students and colleagues spread across the country and planted the roots of the study of learning disabilities. The second parent was the founder of Gestalt psychology, Max Wertheimer. He begot Wolfgang Kohler and Kurt Koffka, who developed a view of human behavior which was adopted by Goldstein, among others, and strongly influenced the direction in which the field of learning disabilities developed. The bonds of matrimony tying these parents was their mutual interest in relating brain activity to behavior and, what is particularly important to the student of learning disabilities, to learning processes.

Pioneer Research

In the beginning (middle 1800s), notions of phrenology dominated perspectives of the causality of normal and abnormal behavior. Phrenologists believed that one could achieve considerable predictive and explanatory precision by studying and mapping the bone structure of a person's skull. The phrenologist's ability to feel bumps would unlock the secret of man's complexity to science. Needless to say, this venture was not spectacularly successful. It was not a total failure either, since it set up a perspective that could be and was challenged.

Broca and Wernicke

A particularly important antagonist to the phrenologists was the physician Paul Broca. He rejected the bump-feeling method of diagnosis, but retained the position that specific parts of the brain were related to specific human processes. Of particular importance was that Broca had two patients who had lost the ability to talk during their middle years. Broca labeled this symptom *aphemia.* Alas for the two patients, but to the advantage of science, the two men died during Broca's lifetime. Broca performed autopsies on the two brains and reported both had suffered atrophy of a section of the brain, the third frontal convolution in the left side of the frontal hemisphere. Ultimately, this finding became part of contemporary jargon; the loss of the ability to speak is called *Broca's aphasia* or *expressive aphasia.* More important, for the first time there had been an empirical demonstration that there was a relationship between damage to a particular section of the brain and an observable symptom in man.

During the same period (1860–80) more than one investigator rejected the phrenologists' perspective and devoted their efforts to the study of the relationship of brain structures to motor behaviors. Fritsch and Hitzig (1870) mapped the motor cortex of dogs through the use of galvanic currents, cut out parts of the brain in an ablation procedure and demonstrated alterations in the dogs' motor movements. Monk (1881) performed ablation experiments with dogs and monkeys focusing upon the brain locale for the visual system. Monk was successful in demonstrating that blindness, partial or total, could be induced through physical assaults upon the occipital lobe of the cortex. Ablation of one side of the occipital lobe would produce partial blindness so that the visual field of both eyes was limited (homonymous hemianopsia), whereas ablation of both sides was necessary to produce total blindness.

By 1874 so much progress had been made in the study of the relationship of parts of the brain and aphasia, loss of the power of speech, that one investigator, Karl Wernicke, declared that "everything was known that was necessary for the understanding of aphasia" (Schuell, Jenkins and Jimenez-Pabon, 1965). This statement may carry the errors associated with overenthusiasm; nonetheless, it is safe to say these scientists made discoveries which still stand as "truths" today.

Optimism was not Wernicke's chief contribution to science. It was his refinement and extension of Broca's position on aphasia which was very significant. Wernicke believed that Broca's aphasia was one type of loss of speech, a loss in the motor ability to produce words. He demonstrated another type of aphasia, the inability to understand the speech of others. This was not a defect in hearing, nor stupidity, but rather that speech which was formerly comprehensible could no longer be understood. The loss of the comprehension of speech became known as *Wernicke's aphasia* or *receptive aphasia.* Wernicke asserted that the location of brain damage which would result in the loss of speech comprehension was the temporal lobe of the cerebral cortex. Wernicke also hypothesized that there are neural connections between the temporal lobe, Wernicke's area, and the frontal lobe, Broca's area. In essence, there is a connection between the front and left sides of

15

the brain. Damage to this connection would result in another type of aphasia, now called *conduction aphasia*. Symptoms typically include neologisms, nonspecific vocabulary and jargon. Wernicke was apparently correct and his observations refined our knowledge of speech disorders.

The pioneering efforts of these scientists influenced investigations of the causes and treatments of aphasia and made significant contributions to our understanding of this malady (Geschwind, 1968), and also influenced perspectives and techniques employed by the learning disability practitioner. Hundreds of thousands of children are being exposed to diagnostic procedures which involve analyses of *receptive, expressive* and *integrative* processes irrespective of whether the child has speech, writing or arithmetic learning problems. The model originated by Karl Wernicke for the analysis of aphasia was adopted by modern psychoeducational specialists and applied to the study of virtually all types of learning problems not associated with obvious emotional turmoil. Even those investigators who turned away from the hope that brain dysfunction could be correlated with learning problems in young children apply this process of analyzing skills within this trichotomous classification scheme.

The major assumption implicit in the efforts of Broca and Wernicke was that specific centers localized within the cerebral cortex governed particular activities. In spite of the multitude of important contributions made by these men, their assumptions did not go unchallenged.

Jackson and Head

John Hughlings Jackson (1864) was a great clinician who criticized localization theory. His argument was that words were not speech; therefore, ablation or destruction of brain centers which destroyed speech did not necessarily mean the brain area responsible for speech was affected. The search for the spot responsible for speech was seen as futile because speech is not saying individual words. Speech was controlled by the whole brain rather than a segment of cortex. Jackson anticipated modern linguistics by his emphasis on the sentence as a major unit for the communication of ideas.

Jackson viewed the human brain as the most advanced model on the evolutionary continuum. Various brain processes increase in complexity, specialization and integration as one ascends the phylogenetic scale. The most numerous interconnections among parts of the brain are found at the highest level of brain development. Man's brain is not simply a collection of locales, each independent of the other, but parts of the brain are intimately linked. Jackson reasoned that any defect, whether it affected speaking, reading, writing or conceptual tasks, would not be identified by localizing a single cortical point. Many segments of the brain in various ways and to varying degrees would be involved. Destruction or damage to any one part of the brain would reduce a man's skills on a general level. Later we will see how this work affected another pioneer in this field, Kurt Goldstein.

Sir Henry Head, a student of Jackson, devoted his life to fulfilling Jackson's notion that empirical data on aphasic subjects should be collected. The Golden Rule, voiced a great deal today, was to assess what a person could and could not do but to avoid attaching labels to the person. Above all, he was an empiricist who vigorously followed this Golden Rule, demanding that careful observations, not quick categorization, direct the investigator. Head undertook an extensive clinical research program. He produced two volumes which reported his clinical observations of aphasics and standardized tests of aphasia. He tested and later retested 26 World War I veterans who had suffered some type of brain damage which resulted in aphasic conditions.

By modern day psychometric standards, Head's test is woefully inadequate. Nonetheless, a systematic observational technique had been generated. Spurious clinical observations and inferences would be replaced by more reliable techniques. On the basis of his observations Head devised a classification scheme for aphasic symptoms which included four categories. These categories were *verbal defects,* difficulty forming words; *syntactical defects,* saying words with an incorrect emphasis or joining words inappropriately; *nominal defects,* difficulty understanding the meaning of words; and *semantic defects,* difficulty stringing words together in a logical way.

This categorical system did not prove to be viable because there was too much overlap among the categories. Aphasics did not suffer one or another of these defects, but demonstrated symptoms from more than one category. As is frequently the case, pure types were hard to find.

Head's radical contributions did not end with the development of a test of aphasia, a category system or extensive data collection. It extended to one more issue, one very much with us today. This is the nature of intelligence and the relationship between intelligence and language. Contrary to his contemporaries, such as Paul Pierre Marie, Head believed that aphasics did not suffer generalized intellectual impairment. They were not stupid because they suffered brain damage; they were unable to demonstrate their intellectual capacities because of their language difficulties. Clearly, the direction of therapeutic intervention would be, and still is, very much affected by the side of this controversy a clinician, school administrator or politician takes.

The work of two investigators, Theodore Weisenburg and Katherine McBride, a neurologist and a psychologist, should be included in a review of "ancient history." Weisenburg and McBride made two contributions, one substantive and the second methodological. Substantively, they developed a classification scheme wherein aphasia was divided into four categories: *predominantly expressive,* problems in speaking and writing; *predominantly receptive,* problems in understanding the speech of others; *expressive-receptive,* all types of language performance is affected; and *amnesic,* difficulty evoking words. This classification system was used in the pioneering work of Helmer R. Myklebust to describe aphasia in young children. On the methodological side these investigators were the first to compare in a systematic rather than intuitive way the performances of aphasics with nonaphasic subjects. The development of a standardized test for abnormality now had a control or comparison group incorporated.

Goldstein

Last, but certainly not least, is the very important work of Kurt Goldstein, a German physician who treated brain-injured soldiers in World War I. Goldstein was a significant worker within Gestalt psychology. In this framework, it was believed that patients did not suffer separate losses of functions as a result of brain damage induced by war wounds. Goldstein described their problems as reflecting a de–differentiation, a systematic reduction of all abilities. Segments of abilities were not affected; whole systems were affected. He viewed aphasia as reflecting brain damage, never mind that the damage might be undetectable, in which a disintegration of the nervous system resulted in a wide variety of symptoms. One symptom was difficulty in discriminating between foreground and background, a major tenet of Gestalt psychology. The experimental tests of this ability are typically visual in nature, such as discriminating one important feature in a visual display from the background in which it is shown. Goldstein felt that aphasic patients do hold such problems; but he employed the terms, "foreground" and "background" not only to refer to visual processes, but to other processes as well. He used the terms in a metaphorical—not literal sense. It was Goldstein's view that brain-damaged subjects had difficulty separating the important from the unimportant, the necessary from the trivial. The implication of this analysis was that brain-damaged patients suffered *perceptual impairments.* Goldstein speculated that brain-damaged patients suffered decreased receptivity and increased reaction time because of a disintegration of the nervous system. This resulted in an abnormal spread and duration of stimulus influences within a person. Today this is known as *perseveration.* In addition, these patients were described as being abnormally affected by external stimuli. Today this is known as *distractibility.*

It should be noted that within this frame of reference it was, and still is, suggested that brain-injured people pay too much attention to stimuli, perseverate, and yet are highly distractible. Until we know which stimuli, at what intensity, and in which sequence evoke which response we are faced with an impossible contradiction.

Goldstein went on to describe brain-damaged patients as exhibiting emotionally disabling reactions. The brain-damaged were viewed as lacking in initiative and rigid in their responses. They failed to have either the energy or the creativity to engage in new action and were presumed tied to a fixed pattern of responses in order to govern their daily existence. A shift in these fixed patterns or environmental arrangements resulted in their undergoing a catastrophic reaction that is great anxiety and behavioral disorganization. The patient's daily activity, rigidity and lack of initiative were construed as reflecting, in part, an attempt to avoid a catastrophic reaction which would result from excessive stimulus input. Goldstein thus introduced concepts of psychic processes into the study of brain damage.

Because of the rise to power of Hitler, two of Goldstein's contemporaries, Heinz Werner and Alfred Strauss, migrated to the United States in 1937. They spread Goldstein's views to colleagues and students in America and this resulted in the development of the field of learning disabilities. A specific and direct outcome of the substance of Goldstein's viewpoint is that area of learning disabilities known as "perceptual handicaps."

Recent Research

In covering the period from the 1850s to about 1925 we focused upon those individuals whose work germinated critical substantive topics for the field of learning disabilities. Broca and Wernicke stimulated interest in brain localizations and the relationship of the brain to language; John Hughlings Jackson greatly influenced the bases of modern linguistics and clinical practices; Sir Henry Head designed a systematic analysis of aphasia; and from Kurt Goldstein emanated the foundations for the study of perceptual handicaps. All were giants in their time and still appear to be so today. Some ideas were correct, some incorrect, some were not carried far enough. But all were sufficiently provocative and explicit to challenge the status quo of their generation, to generate new ideas and new data and to inspire their students and colleagues, who carried their work forward. It is hard to overestimate their contributions and easy to trace their influences on learning disabilities today.

Strauss and Werner

Alfred Strauss and Heinz Werner located at Wayne County Training School near Detroit, Michigan, collaborated in studies of brain damage in mentally retarded children. By focusing upon children rather than adults, upon the intellectually incompetent rather than the competent, they brought about a courtship, if not a marriage, of the fields of neurology and education. The implication of their work was that learning might be inhibited by brain damage as well as character flaws or emotional turmoil. Educators were thus alerted to those cues which might be associated with brain damage in children, cues like hyperactivity and distractibility. In time, children who could be described as hyperactive, distractible or disinhibited were labeled as suffering from the "Strauss syndrome." The views of Strauss and Werner, and later collaborators Laura Lehtinen and Newell Kephart, all under the influence of Kurt Goldstein, were to be widely disseminated in two volumes, both entitled *Psychopathology and Education of the Brain-injured Child.* Through these vehicles, probably the most influential books written in the field of learning disabilities, they argued that dull, or mentally retarded, children who exhibited hyperactivity, distractibility and disinhibition and those characteristics associated with brain-damaged adults as described by Goldstein, also suffered brain damage. Strauss and Lehtinen (1947) and Strauss and Kephart (1955) argued that children with learning problems may have suffered brain damage and that learning problems could therefore be organic rather than just genetic. In addition, children with brain damage will demonstrate a variety of behavioral symptoms.

21

As time passed, this view was perverted by many clinicians to the position that any child who exhibited these symptoms was likely to be suffering from some brain defect. Hence, competent but active, bright but distractible and adequate but disinhibited children came to be viewed as brain-damaged. This position is far removed from that originally advocated by Strauss, Lehtinen and Kephart.

The Wayne County group was revolutionary in a variety of ways. They introduced the idea of comparable problems across developmental spans. Children, as well as adults, who suffered an insult to the brain could be hyperactive, distractible and so forth. Because of their concern with individual differences among children of similar intellectual abilities, they greatly facilitated the concern with the development of methods of remediation tailored to meet the educational requirements of a learning problem. The assumption was now challenged that school competence was highly predictable on the basis of general intelligence, and questions were raised as to how one might tailor a specific educational program to meet the needs of the particular child. Further refinements were now introduced into category systems used to place a handicapped child. Intelligence alone as a categorical system would no longer suffice. New programs and new institutions were born, bred to be particularly suitable to the needs of brain-damaged children. If a child is unable to read, what were his perceptual skills? If a child is distractible, what is the effect of rearranging the furniture? If a child is hyperactive, what is his response to motor activities designed to be educational in and of themselves? The broad category of intelligence was replaced with a new perspective as to etiology (origin of causes) and remediation. The recommendations were not taken lightly. Sharp discriminations as to educational techniques with normal and learning-disabled children were initiated, and educators are, to this day, greatly influenced by them.

Orton

During approximately the same period, 1925 to 1948, the work of Samuel T. Orton, Professor of Psychiatry at the University of Iowa, played a very influential role in laying the foundation for the field of learning disabilities. Orton studied language problems, laterality of motor skills, and brain dominance in children. He described the problems of children with *strephosymbolia* in reading, speech and writing. Orton observed that children with these problems had difficulty remembering the order of letters and sounds. He theorized that these disturbances were related to specific brain locations, reasoning that one side of the brain was dominant, while the other side was dormant and useless. His particular theories of brain processes have not stood the test of advances in knowledge, but Orton's procedures for remediating the severe learning problems in children were brilliant, effective and used in a variety of teaching methods today.

Orton's (1937) method of teaching can be described as a slow-motion phonics approach. We shall see later that this method has been demonstrated more effective than other methods in teaching reading to normal and deficit children, irrespective of the "type" of child (Bateman, 1964). Orton also developed an approach in which discriminations were made as to the defective styles of children. For instance, a child who cannot write may have difficulty because of very slow motor movement, or be unable to form the letters properly. This close examination of the separate movements needed to perform a given task is known as "task analysis" (Johnson, 1967).

In addition to devising effective remedial methods for teaching children with severe reading, writing and speech problems, Orton made a number of other significant contributions. He related reading problems to language deficits. This set the stage for a viewpoint of learning-disabled children quite distinct from that of Strauss, Lehtinen and Kephart. The emphasis was upon language and not upon perception skills. A society was created and named after him. This organization, the Orton Society, is active today, holds conferences and publishes *The Bulletin of the*

Orton Society, and generally supports all efforts to improve research and study of language problems.

Fernald

Meanwhile on the West coast at the University of California at Los Angeles, Grace Fernald developed a remedial clinic for a wide range of children. Fernald developed a remedial reading approach which could be used with severely retarded children or children with normal intelligence who were experiencing reading problems. The Fernald method is discussed further in the chapter on remediation.

The field of learning disabilities is a young one and the professionals trained by professors and colleagues associated with the Wayne County Training School, the Orton group or the Fernald clinic are very active today. People like William Cruickshank, Newell Kephart, Samuel Kirk, Helmer Myklebust, Laura Lehtinen, all influenced to some extent by the efforts of Strauss, Orton, and Fernald, defined and shaped the field of learning disabilities as we know it today. This second generation of pioneers are our contemporaries.

Disability Models

Whatever differences in theories and practices have separated these first- and second-generation learning disability pioneers, one similarity existed. They all generally held a perspective of man which was an analogue of the *medical model.* Because of this perspective, the discipline of learning disabilities, until the very recent past, can be characterized as one holding a medical model of man.

The development of a discipline, such as learning disabilities, is structured around the acceptance of a basic core of concepts and assumptions. Persons trained in this discipline use these concepts and assumptions as a frame of reference by which to view the world (Mercer, 1968). Measures, tools and vocabulary develop around this common core of concepts, which the practitioners then use to solve the problems of their discipline. Practitioners come to believe and accept these concepts as self-evident.

There have been two dominant models which have served to guide the development and perspectives assumed within the field of learning disabilities. One is the disease model of medicine; the second is the statistical or psychometric model. These models have been so influential in shaping the field of learning disabilities they warrant some discussion.

Medical Model

While there are many different medical models within the field of medicine (London, 1972), the disease model has shown great influence upon clinical practices of psychologists and educators. The disease model provides the practitioner an approach to a problem which focuses upon the person with the problem, rather than upon the social milieu of that person, in searching for the source of the difficulty. The assumption is made that if the problem can be removed from that person he will be immune to that problem, irrespective of the social context in which it might occur.

Historically, the medical disease model developed as a conceptual tool to interpret the nature of biological disease processes in order to cure persons afflicted with disease. Historically, and legally, physicians are concerned with the elimination of abnormal functioning. The physician's emphasis is upon the study, detection and cure of such abnormalities. In the medical model perspective, normal becomes defined as that which has no "abnormal" signs. The patient is viewed in terms of a bipolar continuum in which placement at one end represents normal and at the other end represents being abnormal. Emphasis in this perspective is placed upon the identification and cure of characteristics of abnormality, not upon the identification and facilitation of

25

normal functions. Persons are labeled by what is wrong with them, and not what is right. In addition, the medical disease model focuses upon biological explanations for problems, and biological functions deemed important are those intrinsic to the patient. Pathology now becomes an integral part of a person. Social and cultural factors which may be related to etiology are ignored in this framework; organic malfunctioning is primary. The disease model regards its methods and findings as transcending social or cultural systems (Mercer, 1968). By and large, this is a heuristic model for physicians dealing with physical disturbances. Considerable question has been raised about this model when it has been extended from physical problems about which there is general consensus to other problems for which a physiological basis is unknown and technically beyond our ability to know.

Virtually all of the assumptions underlying the medical disease model have been challenged. Justified or not, these are some of the objections to this model. There is little evidence relevant to the biological foundations of many personality and educational problems. While a virus produces syphilis, does a virus produce reading difficulties, hyperactivity or suicide? Is it reasonable to assume that the causes of problems transcend situations so that they can survive in the context of many varying social contexts? And, even if there is a physical base to whatever ails the student, patient or client, does the disease model yield cures for these ailments? Finally, if a disease is "cured," how immune is the patient from further behavior problems if he is placed back into the same social system?

Concern with the application of the medical model to psychological and educational problems is not limited to the fear that this perspective will lead the technician astray. Concern extends to the fear that this perspective may create more problems than it cures (Scheff, 1966). This fear is based upon two factors, the conservative strategy correlated with the medical model and the stigma often associated with diagnostic labeling.

The medical disease model induces in its practitioners a concern about the elimination of abnormality. The safest strategy is to assume that a client or patient is somehow and somewhere pathological. Generally, an appropriate diagnosis is time consuming and, for most personal and social problems, rather unreliable. If a practitioner is to commit an error of diagnosis, it is best to commit a safe one, to diagnose the presence of illness which is not there rather than to diagnose the presence of health when there might be pathology. If the diagnostic error is on the safe side, all a patient may lose is a little time and a lot of money. On the other hand, if the practitioner commits a diagnostic error and concludes the patient is healthy when he is ill, the cost to the patient may be his life. Hence, the medical model tends to be associated with a conservative strategy, one that dictates the diagnosis of illness unless proven conclusively otherwise. This particular strategy is reasonable when one is dealing with a physical illness. But is this strategy reasonable when applied to school, social and emotional problems? The answer to this question is critically dependent upon the laws and stigma surrounding the particular problem. To be labeled as mentally ill by a physician will frequently and with appalling rapidity result in a citizen's loss of freedom and civil rights (Scheff, 1966). To be labeled learning disabled will mandate a school system to institute an appropriate educational program, often in a self-contained classroom. This will considerably alter the nature of an important aspect of a child's life. An adoption of the conservative strategy is based upon a diagnosis which in itself is based upon rather primitive guesswork; yet it can have significant life consequences for the labeled individual. In addition, the degree to which the label is associated with stigma, as is the case with diagnosis of mental illness (Goffman, 1961; Nunnally, 1961) and mental retardation (Jones, 1972; Christoples and Renz, 1969) is the degree to which the conservative strategy may produce long lasting, damaging effects for the patient.

Most of the initial conceptions of learning-disabled children have been based upon the disease model of medicine. Early workers in this field have perceived the locus of a child's problem within the child, and the cure for the child's ailment rested in changing the child. Children were described as having symptom complexes parallel to those observed in brain-injured adults. Children having school problems were seen as hyperactive, like the brain-injured adult; to experience perceptual problems, like the brain-injured adult; to perseverate, like the brain-injured adult; to show emotional lability, like the brain-injured adult. The search was on to locate the site and dynamics of the brain damage experienced by the child. The search has proved to be a failure, as there has been little success in finding that children with learning disabilities are brain damaged (Myklebust, Boshes, Olson and Cole, 1969; Owen, Adams, Forrest, Stolz and Fisher, 1971). It may well be that brain-injured children have learning disabilities, but that is considerably different from the assumption that children with learning disabilities have suffered an assault to the brain. As the empirical evidence yielded disappointing results in the search for damage, many professionals began to believe it foolish to invest so much time, energy and resources arguing about which part of the brain might be damaged or underdeveloped. No doubt the search for brain–behavior correlates will continue, as it should, but the efforts will be concentrated within medical research centers rather than educational sites. The medical disease model will no longer be the only perspective in town.

Statistical or Psychometric Model

A second model developed as a response by those disenchanted with the medical model is the statistical model, in which the definition of normal is based upon the statistical concept of the normal curve. Whether one is normal or abnormal depends upon where a person's score falls on the distribution of scores from a population. Both ends of the curve are abnormal, as such scores occur infrequently. The score that falls toward the middle or mean of the distribution is not abnormal, because it occurs most often. Transposing the score to a person means that an abnormal person is one who stands out, has visibility due to being different. The normal person is one who cannot be differentiated from most members of that population, a person who is in effect invisible. The statistical model is presumed to be nonevaluative. An abnormal score means an infrequently occurring score. To make the inference that a person who obtains an abnormal score is, therefore, abnormal relative to his peers is based upon an arbitrary criterion. But tests are given to determine the status of some function or trait of importance to the person or to society, to describe and define socially valued characteristics. Evaluations of abnormality become impossible to avoid. Thus, it is bad to have a low IQ score and good to have a high one, even though both scores are equally deviant from the average IQ score. While descriptive statistics operate in a moral vacuum, individuals cannot.

Mercer (1968) has suggested that these two models, the statistical and medical, have become fused into the "clinical perspective." Practitioners who apply the clinical definition to troubled persons use the statistical model to define the existence of a problem and the medical model to diagnose and understand the dynamics of the problem. Children who obtain a score which is infrequent and which reflects a state or trait deemed undesirable are then investigated as if the score were symptomatic of some underlying physiological malfunction. The transposition of a low, undesirable score into a sign of pathology carries with it all the implications of the disease model of medicine. This occurs in the absence of any evidence that this sign has any function or important relationship to that person's biological functioning.

The importance of this perspective is that it has determined the allocation of our resources into limited types of research programs congruent to the model. Data are lacking with respect to the learning disabilities field, but there is little reason to assume that it would differ in significant respects from the field of mental retardation. In the field of mental retardation, more than 50% of the population are described as having types of mental retardation which have no known biological involvements. Research funds, however, have been almost exclusively channeled into the study of organic factors in mental retardation. Thus, 99% of the resources have been directed toward the study of the biology of mental retardation, while funds have been very limited for the study of the emotional and social factors affecting the diagnosis of mental retardation (Mercer, 1973). Insofar as the remediation of the learning-disabled child might be facilitated by a diagnostic-remedial scheme emphasizing task analysis, social factors affecting the child and his labelers and the emotional or motivational states of the child, an adherence to the medical model in learning disabilities is likely to be less than optimal in advancing the current status of knowledge about these children.

As we describe the knowledge and practices related to the field of learning disabilities in subsequent chapters the reader will surely become sensitive to the impact these models have had upon this field. These models are important, as they determine the approach we take and attempts we make to understand the child failing in school. Since their applications have such significant and enduring effects upon the immediate and future lives of the children we are trying to help, the importance of these models must be recognized.

CHAPTER
3
DEFINITIONS
AND
CLASSIFICATION
SYSTEMS

As a new discipline is developed its practitioners devise terminology and classification systems to facilitate communication among those concerned with that field. The terminology and typologies are used to describe persons and procedures which appear to share common characteristics. For instance, the verbal skills of persons who score high on tests of intelligence may be of concern, whereas their height, weight and eye color would not be. Classifications based upon the shared characteristics of a large population lead to the development and use of labels to categorize these characteristics, which, in turn, permits practitioners to make predictions and provisions for those so labeled. Sometimes a special language fosters better communication; sometimes it obscures and confuses.

Establishing Standards

A variety of labels have been generated to describe learning disabilities. A number of diagnostic classification systems have been devised and employed but remain untested. However, an overview of the labels used to describe learning disabilities leads one to conclude that virtually any child with any problem falls within the domain of the learning disability specialist. Any combination of characteristics, particularly socially undesirable ones, have been included as part of some syndrome. These laundry lists of socially maladaptive traits reflect both a wide variety in the types of difficulties included and great differences in the severity of the problems. Categories of dysfunction in learning disabilities thus range from severe organic deficits (*e.g.,* choreiform syndrome, aphasoid syndrome, association deficit, cerebral dys-synchronization syndrome) to perceptual and behavioral problems (*e.g.,* hyperkinetic impulse disorder, perceptual motor handicaps, attention disorder) (Clements, 1966). There is apparent consensus that such problems have been observed in some children, but that not all children will exhibit all or even many symptoms. One might assume that everyone is talking about the same behaviors when the identical terms are used or talking about different behaviors when different words are used, but studies to objectively define terms or investigate the reliability and validity of the nomenclature are rarely conducted.

An example of the types of problems we run into when we fail to have well-defined terminology and typologies can be seen in estimates of the incidence of learning disabilities. Estimates are required in order to know how many teachers to train and employ and how many facilities and resources will be needed. This is a critical administrative problem which must be solved well in advance of the appearance of problem children at the school door. But the estimate of incidence of learning problems is related to the definition which is used, and has varied from 1% to 30% of the school population. This very wide range exists because estimators have used different samples, defining criteria, instrumentation and methods (Bruinincks, Glaman, and Clark, 1971, p. 5).

The difficulties in establishing consensually agreed upon definitions of learning disabilities stem from the application of varied theoretical and philosophical approaches to normal and atypical children. Some taxonomies have been developed from a perspective which emphasizes etiology and organically related problems (Johnson and Myklebust, 1967). Others have developed from a psychometric or psychological theoretical construct (Bateman, 1964; Kirk and Kirk, 1972). Some taxonomies have been the products of program development or the translations of what is known about controlling children's symptomatic behavior into their educational objectives (Cruickshank, Bentzen, Ratzeburg, and Tannhauser, 1961; Hewett, Taylor, and Artuso, 1969; Hewett, 1970). Others, which have nothing directly to do with learning disabilities, are nonetheless very much a part of the field. These represent systems to describe a theoretical viewpoint of child development and an educational program devised on the basis of this construct (Barsch, 1967; Doman, Spitz, Zucman, Delacato and Doman, 1967). As Keogh has suggested, the psychoanalytic psychologist focuses on psychodynamic and personality functions, the general psychologist on perceptual functions, and the cognitive psychologist on intellect and cognitive style. "Disturbance, like beauty, may be in the eye of the beholder" (Keogh, 1971, p. 545).

Each of these taxonomies has resulted in educational programs, although claims regarding the success of these methods have not been adequately tested. The few which have been put to the test have not yielded encouraging results as to the soundness of the typology or the educational methods which stemmed from it. In spite of such shortcomings, professionals have struggled to improve their services to children experiencing school difficulties.

Definitions of Learning Disabilities

Several definitions specific to learning disabilities have been used to delineate the boundaries of school services. There are many dangers involved in labeling children, as labels have been found to carry stigma while carrying little implication for remedial treatments (Scheff, 1966; Rosenthal and Jacobsen, 1968; Seaver, 1973). However small or great the dangers involved in labeling children as learning disabled, it is necessary, indeed critical, to set limits to the population to be studied and assisted. With limited resources, limited numbers of children can receive assistance. Attempts to define learning disabilities reflect attempts to devise a categorization system which aids in the development and the implementation of therapeutic efforts. Although children have stubborn ways of avoiding a clean fit into even the most narrowly limited categorization system, legislators must still provide funds and legislation to protect children who need additional assistance and give direction to the kinds of children to be favored by remedial services. Additionally, such systems are intended to assist professionals to make sense out of their dealings with a heterogeneous group of children by narrowing interest to particular rather than to all children.

Task Force I, 1966

Several definitions of learning disabilities have evolved since 1962 (Kass, 1969). The most critical evolutionary change was the shift from a definition of cerebral malfunctioning as "minimal cerebral dysfunction" to a definition which made no reference to organic etiology. Nevertheless, both definitions perpetuated the assumption that the locus of damage or dysfunction was internal to the child. The first formal definition, government agency sponsored, was advanced by Task Force I cosponsored by the National Society for Crippled Children and Adults and the National Institutes of Neurological Diseases and Blindness of the National

Institutes of Health (Clements, 1966). This definition linked learning problems and minimal cerebral dysfunction and described a group of children who shared the common characteristic of minimal, often physiologically undetectable, brain damage. This definition read:

> The term "minimal brain dysfunction syndrome" refers in this paper to children of near average, average, or above average general intelligence with certain learning or behavioral disabilities ranging from mild to severe, which are associated with deviations of function of the central nervous system. These deviations may manifest themselves by various combinations of impairment in perception, conceptualization, language, memory, and control of attention, impulse, or motor function (1966, pp. 9–10).

Specialists were unhappy with this definition because it placed on them the burden of detecting brain dysfunction. While gross damage may be relatively easy to detect, minimal dysfunction is not. The implication of organic distress presented the diagnostician with grave difficulties. The problem is that the educational diagnostician is limited to evaluation of intellectual and social behavior. The stronger the direct evidence for brain damage, such as seizures or paralysis, the less likely the diagnostic conclusion is to be "minimal" damage. The less direct the medical evidence, the more the reliance upon social and academic performance, and the more likely the diagnosis of "minimal brain dysfunction." By definition, the linkage of brain damage with learning disabilities through direct evidence becomes an impossibility.

The dilemma was resolved by the generation of another definition which makes no reference to organic etiology. The specification of central nervous system damage and the inference of the presence of minimal cerebral dysfunction were eliminated. In their stead was a reliance upon psychological variables as the criteria to distinguish learning-disabled children.

Children with Specific Learning Disabilities Act, 1969

The National Advisory Committee to the Bureau of Education for the Handicapped, Office of Education, recommended the following definition, which subsequently became used for federal legislation concerning funding of services for learning-disabled children. The 1969 Children with Specific Learning Disabilities Act defined this group:

Children with special learning disabilities exhibit a disorder in one or more of the basic psychological processes involved in understanding or using spoken or written language. These may be manifested in disorders of listening, thinking, talking, reading, writing, spelling, or arithmetic. They include conditions which have been referred to as perceptual handicaps, brain injury, minimal brain dysfunction, dyslexia, developmental aphasia, etc. They do not include learning problems which are due primarily to visual, hearing, or motor handicaps, to mental retardation, emotional disturbance, or to environmental disadvantage.

Children with Specific Learning Disabilities Act of 1969, PL 91-230, The Elementary and Secondary Amendments of 1969.

This definition removed the burden from the professional to establish the presence of minimal brain dysfunction for purposes of remedial efforts for children with learning problems. No doubt it also lessened the stigma or anxiety of parents and their children so diagnosed. Essentially, children who evidenced some difficulty with the development or use of language and related skills were to be perceived as reflecting something other than emotional or intellectual deficits. In effect, children who showed these language-related problems, if they were not otherwise socially or intellectually impaired, were to be within the purview of the learning disability specialists.

Advances in knowledge are often the result of narrowing the population studied, devising ideas or theories concerning that population and generating applicable remedial techniques. While the 1969 definition of learning disabilities provided a means to limit the population to specifiable characteristics, the definition was very broad. Investigators subsequently developed means to further limit the populations to be defined by using their own perspectives and theoretical interests. These definitions range from exclusions of other types of handicaps to inclusions of children with certain psychometrically defined characteristics.

Psychoneurological Learning Disabilities

Two important contributors to the field of learning disabilities are Doris Johnson and Helmer Myklebust (1967). They advanced a definition of learning disabilities based on their research of psychoneurological problems; and they incorporated an emphasis upon neurological dysfunctions. As a result of their specific concentration in these areas however, their definition does not account for children who are retarded or have problems resulting from or compounded by socioeconomic conditions. This means that the child's achievement and behavior have been disturbed as a result of some dysfunction within the brain which results in altered processes, but not a generalized incapacity to learn (1967, p.8). This definition incorporates the philosophy that the brain and behavior are significantly intertwined in a way which can be specified by careful diagnostic evaluation and corrected by appropriate teaching techniques. By this view, the learning disability represents a shift in brain processing of information which affects a child's achievement, but not his potential to achieve.

Maturational Lag

Another definition specifies normal potential in light of academic failure, but incorporates the idea that this reflects a maturational lag (Bender, 1938). The concept of the brain and its relationship to behavior is again included, but rather than believing that this is a result of a shift in the way the brain works, it is suggested that parts of the brain mature at different rates. If one part is slower in development than others, the result will be a strange array of skills and deficits as observed in learning-disabled children. A "maturational lag" refers to a time lag in the development of certain skills relative to others (deHirsch, Jansky and Langford, 1966).

Discrepancy Definition

The above-mentioned definitions take as their focus the connection between brain and achievement. But others have dropped this focus altogether, proposing yet different emphases. Bateman (1964) has proposed that learning disabilities are reflected by large discrepancies between what has been achieved and what the child is potentially able to achieve. For children in the early school years, this discrepancy is often defined as academic performance six months below grade level as determined by academic achievement tests, while at grade three and above the discrepancy should reflect a year and a half lag. In this definition, the learning-disabled child attains a score on an intelligence measure which is within the normal range, yet evidences scores on measures of school achievement below grade level or otherwise violates authorities' (be they psychologists or educators) expectations of that child's performance. Thus, potential is defined by performance on an intelligence test, and performance is assessed by scores on an achievement test.

There are several problems associated with discrepancy definitions of learning disability. First is the concept of potential. When one argues that a child has potential, does he mean for mastering the particular content being taught at that moment, for mastering substantive materials in related areas of concern or for always being able to master any material? Second, how, in fact, is potential assessed? Potential is typically assessed by a child's performance on some kind of intelligence test. But performance on intelligence tests is quite variable for individual children and such performances are affected by the atmosphere of testing, the nature of the tester, the child's motivation and other external and basically irrelevant factors (Masland, 1969). Moreover, while intelligence test scores are reasonably stable for many children, some children show wide variations from year to year (Honzik, Macfarlane, and Allen, 1948). Since 9% of the children will show variations of IQ scores of 30 points or more from one testing to another, how is one to know which particular score reflects the "true self"? Because of these and other factors, intelligence test scores are not particularly powerful predictors of school performance, although perhaps they are the best criteria currently available. Given the variations in motives and interpersonal relationships which might facilitate or inhibit a high score on an intelligence test aside from simple "pure intellectual abilities" (whatever that might mean), a prediction of potential school achievement on the basis of such scores becomes particularly hazardous. Any estimates of actual intelligence, not to mention potential ability, are open to serious and frequent errors and such errors have repercussions on both the research and diagnostic-remedial efforts within the field of learning disabilities.

Definition by Exclusion

Learning disabilities have also been defined on the basis of the exclusion of other possible problems (Lerner, 1971). If a child is not deaf, blind, severely retarded or very poor, yet is having learning problems, he must have a learning disability. This definition reflects the first stage in the diagnostic evaluation whereby other explanations and associated treatments are excluded. It permits further delineation of the responsibilities for intervention by professional groups into the affairs of children and schools. But, school problems may be associated with a variety of situational conditions and children may share few characteristics aside from the "symptom" of school difficulty. This definition allows a most heterogeneous array of children to be grouped as similar while they are likely to be no more similar to one another than to any same aged peer.

Characteristics of Children with Learning Disabilities

Task Force I (1966) was concerned with the development of a consensually agreed upon definition of learning disabilities, then called *minimal cerebral dysfunction.* In addition, this group set about trying to describe the symptoms and signs by which such children could be identified. The problems in so doing were admittedly great. Systematically gathered information as to which signs and symptoms were associated with each other and with particular types of children were not, and are still not, available. Some of the terms being used, such as poor school achievement, are so general or vague they have virtually no value. In other cases, there are many terms which describe the same behavior or many behaviors covered by one term (*e.g.*, excessive motor behavior and hyperactivity). In an attempt to categorize all of the symptoms cited in the literature, preliminary categories of signs and symptoms were established. These are included with accompanying examples (Clements, 1966, pp. 11–13).

A. Test Performance Indicators
    1. Poor geometric figure drawing.
    2. Poor performance on group tests.
    3. Scatter on the subtests of the WISC.

B. Impairments of Perception and Concept-formation
    1. Impaired discrimination of size.
    2. Impaired discrimination of right-left and up-down.
    3. Impaired judgment of distance.

C. Specific Neurologic Indicators
    1. Many "soft," equivocal, or borderline findings.
    2. High incidence of left and mixed laterality.
    3. Hyperkineses (hypokineses).

D. Disorders of Speech and Comprehension
    1. Impaired discrimination of auditory stimuli.
    2. Slow language development.
    3. Mild hearing loss.

E. Disorders of Motor Function
    1. Frequent delayed motor milestones.
    2. General clumsiness or awkwardness.
    3. Frequent tics and grimaces.

F. Academic Achievement and Adjustment
    1. Reading disabilities.

    2. Spelling disabilities.

    3. Poor printing, writing or drawing ability.

G. Disorders of Thinking Process
1. Poor ability for abstract reasoning.
2. Difficulties in concept-formation.
3. Poor short-term and long-term memory.

H. Physical Characteristics
1. Excessive drooling in the young child.
2. Food habits often peculiar.
3. Easy fatigability.

I. Emotional Characteristics
1. Reckless and uninhibited.
2. Poor emotional and impulse control.
3. Low tolerance for frustration.

J. Sleep Characteristics
1. Body or head rocking before falling into sleep.
2. Sleep abnormally light or deep.
3. Excessive movement during sleep.

K. Relationship Capacities
1. Poor group relationships.
2. Socially bold and aggressive.
3. Frequently poor judgment in social and interpersonal situations.

L. Variations of Physical Development
1. Frequent lags in developmental milestones (*e.g.*, language).
2. Physically immature.
3. Physical development normal or advanced for age.

M. Characteristics of Social Behavior
1. Social competence below average for age and measured intelligence.
2. Behavior often inappropriate for situation and consequences apparently not foreseen.
3. Possibly antisocial behavior.

N. Variation of Personality
　　1. Overly gullible and easily led by peers and older youngsters.
　　2. Frequent rage reactions and tantrums when crossed.
　　3. Excessive variation in mood and responsiveness from day to day and even hour to hour.

O. Disorders of Attention and Concentration
　　1. Short attention span for age.
　　2. Motor or verbal perseveration.
　　3. Impaired ability to make decisions, particularly from many choices.

Obviously, not all children with learning disabilities will experience all, many or even several of these problems, and if they experience them, evaluations will vary according to the child's age and the predilections of the labelers. Moreover, it is highly unlikely that any of these characteristics are specific only to the learning-disabled child, however defined. At any rate, certain of these characteristics are more frequently cited than others in labeling children learning disabled. These characteristics appear to have been generated through clinical observation, a notoriously weak procedure for obtaining precise measures, rather than through systematic measurement of a large and well-defined sample of children. It appears that most people assume the presence of some or all of these characteristics, along with school difficulties, to be associated with the population termed learning disabled. It is important to note that the inappropriateness of other explanations for the behavior in question, explanations such as mental retardation or emotional disturbance, is assumed when weighing the significance of these characteristics. The ten characteristics most frequently mentioned are:

1. Hyperactivity (motor behavior which is not demanded by the situation or the task involved and which is disruptive to the group or to the expectations of observers).

2. Perceptual-motor impairments (difficulty in coordinating a visual or auditory stimulus with a motoric act, such as copying letters of the alphabet).

3. Emotional lability (emotional outbursts which are not reasonably expected by observers on the basis of knowledge concerning the situation or the immediate past history of the child).

4. General coordination deficits (clumsiness).

5. Disorders of attention such as: *distractibility,* behavior which reflects the child's interest in things other than those on which he should be concentrating; *perseveration,* behavior which reflects the child's inability to change the focus of his attention even when the reason for his interest has changed.

6. Impulsivity (behavior which appears to reflect little thinking concerning its consequences).

7. Disorders of memory or thinking (difficulty in recalling material which should have been learned, or difficulty in understanding abstract concepts).

8. Specific learning disabilities (inability to learn or remember reading, writing, arithmetic, or spelling).

9. Difficulty in comprehending or remembering spoken language, deficits in articulation of speech or in expressing self verbally using appropriate grammar and vocabulary.

10. Equivocal neurological signs (neurological signs which are are not clearly associated with particular neurological problems but which are not clearly within the normal range of functioning).

Taxonomies of Learning Disabilities

Initial models constructed to describe learning-disabled children were nested in the notion that these children had minimal cerebral dysfunction. Within this structure, there were two primary, but divergent, paths of model building. One focused upon the language development of the disabled child, while the second concentrated upon perceptual and motor development. These emphases led to ever finer observations, more discrete categories of behaviors and new terms to describe the phenomena. Within these structures diagnostic labels became equivalent to shorthand communications among proponents of these models. It has often been the case that the utility of the scheme was unknown, or known but limited; nonetheless, the system has been absorbed by our profession.

We now review examples of taxonomies of learning disabilities in children. Systems based upon remedial techniques are discussed elsewhere in this text. In this section we are concerned with attempts to classify types of learning problems. The examples offered do not exhaust the efforts which have been made to describe learning-disabled children, but represent primary models. The systems which are reviewed include the psychoneurological model (Johnson and Myklebust, 1967); the psychometric model (Kirk and Kirk, 1972); an attentional deficit syndrome perspective (Dykman, Walls, Suzuki, Ackerman and Peters, 1970); varieties of the perceptual-motor construct (Kephart, 1960; Barsch, 1967; Cratty, 1969) and a behavioristic paradigm (Hewett, 1970).

Psychoneurological

In the case of early models based upon language deficits, an analogy was made between adult and childhood aphasia. Aphasia in adults represents the loss of the ability to speak and is usually the result of a cerebrovascular accident (a stroke) or injury to the brain. Aphasia in children, however, is the absence of the development of language. The dynamics of brain injury were considered analogous insofar as it was believed that particular parts of the brain were malfunctioning and that malfunction was reflected in the language behavior of both child and adult. One of the most influential theorists in the field of learning disabilities has been Helmer Myklebust. His descriptions of children experiencing language development delays or disturbances reflected one model used to describe adult speech deficits (Schuell, Jenkins, and Jimenez-Pabon, 1965). Myklebust, adopting the Weisenburg and McBride classification system used to describe adult aphasics, categorized children on the basis of whether they had difficulty in processing language inputs, producing language or a combination of both. Children, like adults, could be classified as having language problems which were predominantly receptive, predominantly expressive, mixed aphasia and central aphasia. Children who were classified as having *receptive aphasia* evidenced difficulty in comprehending spoken language. These children failed to respond appropriately to the spoken words of others. Such children could hear, they responded to sounds, but the meaningfulness of the sounds escaped them. Examples given by Myklebust included the lack of responsiveness to a door bell or telephone, and difficulty executing simple commands. *Expressive aphasia* described children who could understand and respond appropriately to others' speech, but were unable themselves to express an idea, make requests and otherwise engage in age-appropriate language behaviors. There are different forms of expressive aphasia. Some children may be unable to recall a particular word, some may be unable to use grammar properly and others may have difficulty voluntarily executing the motor pattern involved in speech even though no paralysis of any kind is present. *Receptive aphasia* is considered a more severe problem because it has reciprocal effects on expression. A child unable to connect meaning with sounds is going to have difficulty figuring out how to express feelings, events and ideas. *Mixed aphasia* was used to describe children who demonstrated problems in both comprehension and expression of language. When the language deficit interferes with a child's ability to use language for cognitive processes, such as thinking to oneself or dealing with abstract concepts, the child is said to have *central aphasia.* Language problems were thus viewed as reflecting difficulties coping with stimuli or with the adequate production of responses.

In addition to the dimension receptive-expressive, Myklebust added another. He suggested that the nature of the stimulus was critical to the required response. Stimuli were catalogued as either auditory or visual. Hence, receptive aphasia could be further categorized on the basis of whether the problem was more or less related to dealing with auditory stimuli, such as understanding someone's speech, or visual, such as comprehending the written word. As in the case of mixed receptive and expressive problems, children could have difficulty with auditory and/or visual stimuli. The following table outlines this classification system with examples of the types of problems evidenced.

STIMULUS CHARACTERISTICS

	Visual	*Auditory*	*Combined*
Receptive	Reading	Comprehending of spoken language	Severe language problems
Expressive	Writing	Talking	Talking and writing
Mixed	Reading and writing	Talking and understanding	

The 1954 Myklebust model was the product of a study of preschool-aged children who were failing to develop language. The purpose was to delineate how such children could be separated into primary diagnostic categories of aphasia, deafness, mental retardation and emotional disturbance. Each of these categories were subject to diagnosis on the basis of developmental and behavioral data, but the category of childhood aphasia was most notable as a definition by exclusion. If the child was not deaf, retarded or emotionally disturbed, the lack of language development was assumed to be the result of brain damage. The model of childhood aphasia was subsequently expanded by Johnson and Myklebust (1967) to describe children who were failing to achieve academically. This later model carried forward the hypothesis regarding the assumed relationship of the brain processing of information as a cause for the failure of some children to learn to read, write, spell and do arithmetic. The terminology used to describe these academic deficits incorporated the brain-deficit emphasis plus the auditory/visual and receptive/expressive dichotomies. The category of childhood aphasia became "psychoneurological learning disorders" and the role of the diagnostician was to specify the exact nature of this disorder.

Failure to learn to read in spite of adequate intelligence and instruction was labeled *dyslexia,* a term which carries the implication of an organic cause for the failure. This term had been used since the 1800s, but almost exclusively by members of the medical profession. *Auditory dyslexia* suggested the child had difficulty because of inability to adequately process information heard. *Visual dyslexia* referred to a failure resulting from difficulty in comprehending stimuli presented visually. In school talk, difficulty learning to read by a phonics approach would be indicative of a possible auditory dyslexia, while difficulty when taught by a whole-word approach might indicate visual dyslexia. *Receptive dyslexia* would be indicated if the child had difficulty comprehending what he read (word caller) and *expressive dyslexia* if the problem were related to writing.

Not all problems could be interpreted as the result of language deficits. Some appeared to be related to motor movements of the child. When a child had difficulty learning to ride a bicycle, manipulate a pencil, use scissors, or tie shoelaces, in the absence of any paralysis, the child was described as *apraxic.* Praxic problems were associated with poor eye-hand coordination, difficulty carrying on purposeful movement and inability to make use of objects (Waugh and Bush, 1972). The delineation of the breakdown in learning was further refined, or expanded, to analyze the ability to execute the specific skills each learning task required. For instance, a written language problem, *dysgraphia,* could be a function of difficulty manipulating writing utensils, inability to master syntactic principles of English or inability to remember what was to be written. The expansion integrated a number of other symptoms, or behavioral characteristics, associated with dyslexia. The "dyslexia syndrome" involved more than difficulty learning to read, as such children were observed to have difficulty developing concepts about space and their position in space, concepts of time and memory deficits. This translates to problems learning left from right; how to tell time; reversals in letters, words and numbers; and resulting difficulty in developing the necessary associations between sounds heard and letters seen.

There are certain inadequacies in this taxonomy. One problem is to what degree any complex set of stimuli can be classified as purely auditory or visual. Reading, for instance, is defined by Johnson and Myklebust as a "visual symbol system superimposed on auditory language" (1967, p. 148). If it is not possible to separate the stimuli, implied by the use of the term "predominantly," to what degree can and must one aspect predominate over another for a child to be viewed as failing as a result of a breakdown in that system? Most children cannot be easily labeled as having exclusively receptive or expressive problems. And most stimuli cannot be easily categorized as exclusively auditory or visual. To the degree that people, processes and tasks cannot be so classified, the taxonomy breaks down.

Irrespective of the limitations of this classification system, Johnson and Myklebust made important contributions to perspectives of language and school difficulties. They specified dimensions of language which may be critical to remediate school-related problems as well as how to implement such remediation. They brought diagnosis out of the clinic and into the classroom, therapy away from affect and familial relations to innovative intellectual training of both children and learning disability teachers.

Attentional Deficits

According to Dykman, Ackerman, Clements and Peters, children with learning disabilities "or the medical equivalent,

alking for a purpose, that is to move from one spot to
The shift in the acquisition of motor patterns to the
on of motor patterns represents a giant step in the infant's
ment. In Kephart's typology four motor patterns are
to be particularly significant. One pattern is *balance and
ce of posture.* This demands the child to maintain himself
ly in space. Ability to maintain posture under varying
ns permits the infant freedom within his environment;
orely limits exploratory behavior. The second pattern is
, which includes moving the body through space; walk-
ping and running. The third category is *contact* or *motor*
which describes the child's manipulation of objects. As
l learns to reach, grasp and release objects, he develops
rception and figure-ground relationships. *Receipt* and *pro-*
the fourth basic motor pattern. This is typified by con-
movements which incorporate familiarity of movements
ts simultaneous with body movements. The example off-
hrowing and batting a ball. At this point the child must
o integrate extensive information regarding the nature of
sical environment, his relationship to this environment
effects of the movements of himself and objects within
vironment. When a child has this type of information
ed into his repertory of knowledge regarding himself and
ronment, he can begin to explore the stationary, percep-
rld. Ocular and tactile motor control result in *perceptual-*
tch, a stabilization of the child's world as he knows it
ally, visually and through the integration of both of these
s. These patterns of motor activity are the components of
r-spatial system.*

Kephart believes that the child must also develop the
poral system,* the integration of one's movements within
ameters of time. Higher learning is considered critically
ent upon the management of information within the time
m. The degree to which a child has difficulty executing
neous movements *(synchrony),* anticipating or committing
ertain orders *(sequence)* or executing a sequence of acts with
iate time intervals *(rhythm)* is the degree to which he is
experience difficulties in academic achievement.

minimal brain dysfunction" (p. 56) share a common syndrome characterized by a deficit in attention. Attention is defined as consisting of four components: alertness, stimulus selection, focusing and vigilance. Difficulties children display in language, perception or motor skills are interpreted as reflections of attentional problems, in particular those aspects of attention which require a child to get ready to do something *(becoming alert)* and concentrate on the relevant information for the appropriate length of time *(focusing).* It is believed that attention is physiologically controlled by the reticular activating system, a diffuse network of fibers which begins in the spinal cord, enlarges in the brain stem and connects with many other parts of the brain. Dykman et al. reason that if the reticular activating system controls attentional skills, a deficit in attention reflects malfunctioning in the reticular system. These authors have contributed some excellent laboratory research studies of learning-disabled and normal children, using a number of physiological and behavioral measures in their attempt to test their ideas concerning this etiology of learning disabilities. The differences so far reported between subject groups do not yet constitute a typology of learning disabilities, but the resulting group differences shed light on the direction this type of research may lead us in specifying behavioral and physiological correlates of learning disabilities.

Dykman and his colleagues have conducted a number of impressive experiments concerning the attentional deficit hypothesis. For example, in a study of impulsivity (1971), they found that children 6 to 12 years of age diagnosed as having minimal brain dysfunction were slower than comparison children to match appropriate motor movements (pressing one of two telegraph keys) to appropriate signals (green or white light flashes). The two groups of children did not differ in the number of incorrect responses, simply the speed with which they responded. A question remained, however, as to whether this difference in response is a function of some deficit in motor abilities or in attention. The same children were subsequently tested on a tone discrimination task in which they had to indicate which of two tones was higher or lower in pitch. A difference between the performance of the two groups was found, with the minimal brain dysfunction group committing more errors of judgment. Apparently, many of these errors were the result of this group's failure to remember one tone for the 30-second period prior to the onset of the second tone. Finally, each child was given a differentiation task in which he was required to pull a cord attached to a coin dispenser to the appropriate tone stimulus. This response was reinforced for one tone, but not the other. Thus, there was an attempt to condition the child to pull the cord to the tone stimulus associated with reward more frequently than to the one associated with no reward. Prior to and during this task, physiological measures of the child's skin resistance, heart rate and muscle action potentials were obtained. While these two groups of children were equally alert prior to the experimental task, it was the nondamaged children who maintained their physiological arousal during the task, not the minimally brain-damaged ones. Additionally, the latter group failed to show conditioning. The authors interpreted their results as indicating that minimally brain-damaged children suffer an "inability to persist in attentive efforts, the vigilance aspect of attention" (p. 62).

In a second series of experiments employing children who were experiencing school achievement difficulties, Dykman et al. (1971) replicated and extended their previous findings. Again, learning-disabled children committed more errors on a discrimination task, took longer to initiate and terminate a motor response, and demonstrated less electrical brain activity associated with initiating actions than did the control subjects.

There does seem to be support, then, for the position that learning disabilities are associated with deficits in maintaining attention to the environment. The characteristics which would appear likely to discriminate learning-disabled children from their nondisabled counterparts would be their adequacy in responding to instructions, their ability to persist on a task, the number of errors committed in the task and the speed with which the child can initiate a motor movement. The outcroppings of these problems within the school would be the child's inability to comprehend and/or follow instructions, to memorize material and to determine what is or is not relevant to reinforcements

within his environment. The work
ticularly important for two reason
and the results obtained are derive
atic observations and experimental
acteristic behaviors being describe
ent circumstances than is usual, b
found are significant and appear c
plaints about these children. While
methods used may seem a strange
room difficulties, the results repo
profound implications for teacher

Perceptual-Motor Development

Other researchers have addre
development of children and have
along quite different dimensions. T
Kephart, Raymond Barsch and E
theorists may use different termi
observations, it should be noted th
and motor skills, the behaviors bei
same: namely, the execution of mo
children. The major difference bet
be in what they observe, but in
observations.

Kephart. Newell Kephart (196
children come to school unable to
because they have not assimilated
time, space and movement. In this
ment is intimately connected wit
makes distinctions between muscl
the primary acquisition of a skill
represents a learned pattern. Usir
walk, Kephart describes how walk
infant in the developmental period
basic locomotor pattern is establis

Kephart's classification scheme was extended to diagnosis and remediation techniques used with learning-disabled children. Children are assessed (and thus categorized) and treated on the basis of: balance and posture, body image, perceptual-motor match, ocular control and form perception. Specific techniques are discussed in a subsequent chapter on remediation. To summarize, Kephart believed that difficulties observed in children's school performance are fundamentally related to defects in the development of basic motor activities. Without adequate development of the motor-temporal and motor-spatial systems, children are particularly vulnerable to learning problems in school.

Kephart's classification system and the associated diagnostic and remedial procedures emphasize motor movements and ignore language-related skills. While Kephart recommends the inclusion of language-related evaluative and therapeutic exercises, these tasks are of limited importance in his general approach.

The strength of Kephart's program rests not in teaching verbal or strictly academic subjects, but in the concrete programming advice it provides for teachers to assist children in extra-academic problems, which can be defined as the inability to master the process of learning. Methods and materials are provided to improve skills which are not verbal or academic in the strict sense, but are skills which the child must master before he can perform academic tasks. For instance, Kephart suggests a program of progressive relaxation for the hyperactive child in which the child is taught to control his own movements. Or, noting the difficulties in sequentializing materials when reading, a problem noted in research studies of learning-disabled children, Kephart suggests how teachers might assist children to overcome this type of difficulty. One method he suggests is by using patterns to give the child an experience which will require him to progress from one stimulus demand to another. An exercise he found useful required only poker chips as materials. The teacher would lay out several chips in a line, alternating colors from red to blue. The teacher would then help the child learn to read the line of chips. (Kephart, 1971, p. 306). As such, the Kephart approach provides invaluable activities for difficult-to-solve problems.

Barsch. Raymond Barsch developed a theory concerned with

the maturation of movement outside the learning disabilities field (Lerner, 1971), which has been adopted by learning-disability specialists. The curriculum derived from the theory has been incorporated into many classrooms for learning-disabled children across the country. Barsch's theory, "movigenics," is a conceptualization of child development, particularly motor development.

There are ten ideas which form the foundation of "movigenics."

1. Movement efficiency is the key to life. To help a child learn to move adequately is a major goal of instruction.

2. Movement efficiency is required for man's survival. "The more efficient the movement of the individual—social, economic, academic, and physiological—the greater his survival chances." . . . "Learning is movement" (Gearheart, 1973, p. 39).

3. Movement occurs in an energy surround (Lerner, 1971, p. 100). As a person moves he must select from his environment information that helps him to survive (Gearheart, 1973, p. 39).

4. The percepto-cognitive system is the means by which man acquires information. Information is obtained through six channels: sight, hearing, touch, feeling, smell and taste—the "sensitivity system" (Barsch, 1967). To learn well requires an efficient percepto-cognitive system.

5. The terrain of movement is space. Movement and, therefore, learning occur in space. Man must learn to control his movement in physical and cognitive space.

6. Developmental momentum thrusts the learner toward maturity. According to Barsch, maturity ("developmental momentum") continues till age 50 or so and then there is a slow descent.

7. Movement efficiency is developed in a climate of stress. Man exists in a constant state of stress with more or less discomfort depending upon the efficiency of his percepto-cognitive system. Stress is seen as a necessary part of man's life, with distinctions made in degree and type experienced.

8. Human efficiency requires feedback. Man's "feedback system" permits him to know if he is performing effectively. The better the feedback system, the better the learning.

9. "Development of movement efficiency occurs in segments of sequential expansion" (Gearheart, 1973, p. 40). Development patterns move from simple to complex so that constant movement results in increasing complexity. A slowdown of any of the continuous segments affects the entire organism.

10. "Movement efficiency is symbolically communicated through the visual-spatial phenomenon called language" (Gearheart, p. 48). The ultimate criterion of movement is language.

Barsch developed curriculum guidelines for teachers which permit them to evaluate a child's performance on movement patterns and the degree to which the child is "performing in an increasingly complex manner in processing information through these channels from various distances in space and regardless of directionality of movement" (Gearheart, 1973, p. 40).

Barsch has had a great deal of experience working with physically and neurologically handicapped children as well as with learning-disabled children (Gearheart, 1973). This approach and accompanying viewpoint of children and education appear more applicable to young children and those who are more handicapped physiologically.

Cratty. An outstanding example of how a perceptual-motor approach to classification and remediation can be used with children with learning disabilities has been developed by Bryant Cratty (1969). Like Kephart's, the strength of this program is related to its guidance for behaviors described as problematic for learning-disabled children which are not specifically academic in nature. Cratty declares that the first kind of learning is motoric, that this is critically related to learning through the visual modality and that there are relationships between motor output and children's skills within the classroom. More specifically, he suggests that motor movement is the means by which we express intellect. One such example is the need for a child to be able to write down answers to a test or thoughts on some subjects. The translation, or expression, of learning and of intelligence is made through the motor mode of writing. Another specifically related example is that children are evaluated in school on tests which are timed. Not only must the child be able to perform the required motor task to demonstrate adequate learning, but must be able to do so in a limited time span. Speed of response is a factor which has been demonstrated to differentiate learning-disabled from academically successful children (Dykman et al., 1971). Thus, integrating motor skill learning with movements under timed conditions is an important adjunct to a learning disability paradigm. Cratty integrated the attentional problem noted in learning-disabled children to motor movements, suggesting that attention can be controlled by appropriate levels of motoric arousal, which is best achieved through moderate levels of physical exercise. Furthermore, Cratty suggests that using physical exercise and a games approach may alleviate motivational problems experienced by learning-disabled children. There is a side benefit, as children who are adept at playing games, particularly boys, are more likely to be valued by peers.

Cratty acknowledges the difficulty of expecting generalizations to remain valid from one type of learning to another. It cannot be guaranteed that teaching gross or fine motor movements to children will result in improved academic performance by learning-disabled children. While the empirical data are lacking, the observation is made that generalization of types of learning across situations will not occur automatically, but needs to be taught. For these reasons, particularly the approaches offered to assist children in pre-academic skills of arousal and attention, and the realization that generalization of learning will not be automatic, it is believed that Cratty's program offers a valuable approach to defining learning disabilities and to subsequent programming of intervention.

A Behavioristic Model

Frank Hewett's model reflects a marriage of the theory of child development and the technology of behavior modification applied to the needs of special education. Johnson and Myklebust (1967) based their taxonomy on the basis of a medical model. Children's auditory and visual processing capacities and these sensory processes' interventions with each other provided the vantage point from which one might conceptualize the learning-disabled child. Hewett, relying upon our knowledge of child development and the responses necessary for the child to function adequately in school, has proposed a sequence of the development of skills and responses necessary for continuing educational mastery. The model thus presents a number of developmental stages through which diagnosis and treatment might be made. The first stage that must be reached by the child in order to learn is that development which enables the child to *attend*. Attention is defined as "the ability to focus on relevant cues in the environment" (1970, p. 48). The child's attention is assessed by means of rating scales; the behaviors which are thought to be critical by this assessment are:

1. The child's focusing upon tasks presented by school authorities.
2. The child's preference for attending to external events rather than internal ones (*e.g.*, lack of day-dreaming).
3. The absence of repetitive behavior which interferes with learning (*e.g.*, self-stimulation, rituals or compulsive behaviors).
4. The absence of bizarre or "immature" beliefs.
5. The child's focusing upon the teacher at appropriate times.
6. The child's demonstration reflecting profits from instructions (*e.g.*, retains and employs the instructional material given).

The second capacity that must be evident to produce learning is *response*, obviously not entirely independent of attentional abilities. Hewett writes, "Noticing something starts the learning process; the child must next do something, that is, make a response, in order to learn" (p. 49). The behaviors of note within this response category include ratings of:

1. The child's failure to make a response.
2. The child's showing repetitive errors under conditions where change of response should occur.

3. The child's range of interest, his willingness to try new or different tasks.
4. The child's willingness to interact with teacher or peers within a learning context.
5. The child's willingness to respond in different settings, *e.g.*, the regular classroom, special education classrooms.

The third development necessary to produce learning within the classroom is the child's capacity to understand *order*. A "child must follow directions and develop order in his attending and responding" (p. 50). This means that the child, once he pays attention and is ready to respond, must learn that behaviors, such as bicycle riding or reading, represent sequential acts in which one thing is done before another. Hewett suggests the importance of the following observations in assessing the child's understanding of order:

1. Does the child follow instructions?
2. Is the child uncontrolled in learning? Is he impulsive?
3. Does the child disrupt the group?
4. Does the child finish his learning tasks?

The fourth prerequisite to learning consists of *exploratory* activities. Hewett writes, "Multisensory exploration provides the child with the raw material, the basic facts which he needs in learning" (p. 51). Ratings are obtained with regard to:

1. Children's exploratory activity of their environments.
2. Children's dependency on others for choices of interests or activities.
3. Children's deficiency in learning because of motor, physical, sensory, perceptual or intellectual difficulties.

According to Hewett, once the child masters the first four levels of this hierarchy, he will also be a member of a group. During the period of the first four levels, the child is "given, shown, and told" by others. At the fifth level, the child must orientate himself to others, becoming sensitive to the means by which he may gain social praise and avoid social censure. Thus, *social* responses are thought critical in the development of adequate academic performance. Two items on which the child is rated are:

1. Does the child gain approval from others?
2. Is the child overly dependent on attention or praise from others? Will he only work with constant supervision and attention?

The sixth level within the learning hierarchy is that of *mastery*. This level of development is assessed by means of the child's attainment of the traditional academic and adjustment skills. Reading, writing and arithmetic are part of the mastery level, but so are learning to tell time, avoid dangerous situations and self-care habits. Thus observations are made as to the child's functioning in:

1. Self-care behaviors.
2. Intellectual tasks, relative to his capacity.

Finally, the seventh level refers to *achievement* functions. "This is the enrichment level where self-motivation in learning is developed and where pursuit of intellectual and adaptive skills in depth is important" (p. 54). At this level, the child learns for the joy of learning, participates in class activities beyond the point of just following directions to do what one is told. Now the child becomes a participant in learning by such acts as "asking questions, volunteering for extra work, and researches out additional facts" (p. 54).

Hewett, incorporating a behavior modification paradigm into this sequence, also defines and assesses reinforcements for the child. Reward refers to "a positive consequence which tends to maintain or increase the strength or frequency of behavior associated with accomplishing tasks related to the achievement of educational goals on the developmental sequence" (p. 65). The child needs some kind of reward for the work in school to be worth doing. A smile from the teacher or a gold star pasted on a completed work sheet may provide such a reward. Children who have experienced failure are less likely to experience such rewards. Hewett thus includes an estimate of the child's responsiveness to reinforcements in his analysis of the child's developmental stage. These are rated according to an estimate of their occurrence as "always, sometimes or rarely."

1. Child not rewarded by tangible rewards (*e.g.*, food, money) in learning.
2. Child not rewarded by social attention in learning tasks.
3. Child not rewarded by finishing learning tasks.
4. Child not rewarded by multisensory experiences in learning.
5. Child not rewarded by gaining approval and avoiding disapproval for learning.
6. Child not rewarded by doing learning tasks correctly.
7. Child not rewarded by acquiring knowledge and skill.

Assessments of the child, according to the classification scheme proposed by Hewett, rely primarily upon rating scales completed by parents, teachers or others familiar with the child. Hewett, however, has added further requirements for the evaluator, which appear particularly useful and needed. First, multiple observations or ratings of the child should be made. That is, rather than assuming that any rating reflects a stable trait or condition of the child or his world, an implicit burden is placed upon the diagnostician that assessment be made again after certain elapsed times. Changes of important functions to learning are recognized as possible and adequate diagnosis demands that the evaluator monitor the possibility of such alterations. Second, the diagnostician is obliged to specify the instructional implications of his findings. Whatever Hewett's intent, this particular burden is likely to greatly diminish the number of vacuous statements offered by the diagnostician, those statements which sound impressive but which fail to help the practicing teacher one iota. Both of these requirements are surely likely to improve the services rendered to the disabled child, his teachers and his parents.

This model was employed in the development of an education program, labeled an engineered classroom for educationally handicapped children (California's term for learning-disabled and emotionally disturbed children). The Santa Monica Project was an experiment to obtain data to assess the efficacy of this educational design. The program was presumed to have several distinguishing and important features. One was that the children in various activities were separated spatially in accordance with their developmental levels as conceived within the model. Second was the systematic use and monitoring of social and material rewards contingent upon children's behaviors. Finally, an attempt was made to train children to be reinforced by symbolic rewards, such as grades, rather than by tangible goods. Children were assigned to one of six classrooms. One classroom was exposed to the educational innovations of the engineered program for one school year, while a second classroom was in a non-Hewett type of educational instruction for one school year. Two classrooms began with the control type of educational program and switched to the engineered classroom at midyear. The remaining two classrooms started the year with the Hewett plan and switched to the control program at midyear. Classes used for the control condition were permitted to have features of the engineered classroom with the exception of the use of tangible rewards for appropriate classroom behaviors. The behavior studied to assess the efficacy of the experimental design was the time spent by a student maintaining eye contact with the task or assignment given him by the teacher, that is, the child's attentional skills. If eye contact was irrelevant to the task or the observer could not see the child's eyes, body and head orientation were assessed as indicative of task attention. Two observers coded behaviors of children in each of the six classes for the project's year duration. In addition, achievement tests in spelling, reading and arithmetic were administered to all of the participating children at the initial screening, at midyear and at the end of the school year.

The results of the Santa Monica project indicated that the engineered classroom (when compared to the control classroom) resulted in significant improvement in arithmetic fundamentals and increasing task attention. The results were not significant for spelling and reading. The significant effects were explained as the result of the procedures followed during the arithmetic lessons in the experimental program. Students had to put things in their places, follow directions, have all work corrected each fifteen minutes and count their daily check marks. It was observed that in the engineered program the students were able to work more independently and persistently than the comparable group of children in the non-Hewett program, where teachers were observed to spend relatively more time controlling student behavior. Hewett fails to provide clues as to the failure of the engineered classroom to have effects on reading and spelling achievement. At least for the learning of arithmetic, the engineered program was effective. Whether it was effective because of the systematic use of tangible rewards, the differential use of space within the classroom or the teacher's or children's enthusiasm for a novel educational experience was not determined.

The second major finding in this study is related to the role of tangible rewards. It was found that most students within the Hewett program did not need to be given tangible rewards to continue work efforts once these efforts or habits had been established. Most children were ready for other types of rewards by the end of the first semester and many were evidently ready to respond to symbolic rewards (*e.g.,* approval, grades, etc.) after several weeks. The progression of rewards took students from the receipt of tangible rewards to check marks, to privilege time and finally to graphing check marks somewhat similar to receipt of traditional grades.

The benefit of an engineered classroom, or of this typology, is that it incorporates a theoretical viewpoint from child psychology and special education, integrating into programming for children who deviate from expectations that which is known about normal development. Furthermore, various approaches to treatment are defined as acceptable and integrated into theoretical and practical ideas and procedures. Theory was thus translated into an educational design which both clinicians and teachers can implement. It smiles upon, and uses to its advantage, an experimental approach to evaluate the theory and the educational design.

There are some caveats regarding this model of which the student should be aware. The model has not been adequately tested, the Santa Monica project being a multidimensional one. The adequacy of Hewett's theorizing is not yet known; causes and effects have not yet been determined. Additionally, in terms of diagnostic assessments, it is not known that the items used to rate children tap those functions which they are presumed to test or whether the items are measuring other aspects of development. The items do not appear to correspond to their assessment functions in terms of their content and there are no data presented to indicate either their reliability or validity.

Caveats aside, Hewett did take an important social problem, developed a model which attempted to integrate psychology and special education, translated this model into an educational program and then, most importantly, has begun to test the validity of the model on the basis of empirical results. No doubt, data will prove him wrong on some points, correct on others. But as long as there is a continuing attempt to test empirically the model and its educational implications, corrections will be made.

This chapter covered a great deal of material and ideas developed by persons in their attempts to provide organization and structure to conceptualization and treatments of children evidencing learning difficulties. It is notable that the field has advanced from the 1969 collection of terms used to describe the characteristics of the learning-disabled children to the development of more sophisticated medical, psychological and educational models to incorporate in a meaningful and useful way the problems noted in this most heterogeneous group of children.

CHAPTER
4
THE BRAIN
AND
LEARNING
DISABILITIES

Theories and vocabulary, diagnostic and remedial practices, both past and present, have reflected assumptions about the relationship between the brain and the behavior of the learning-disabled child. The historical link between brain dysfunction and the field of learning disabilities outlined in Chapter 2 makes this bias understandable. What is important is the influence of these assumptions upon diagnostic procedures currently in vogue. To understand these diagnostic procedures requires some familiarity with current ideas regarding the relationship of the brain to behavior. For this reason, a description of the brain and the theories which have sought to describe the relationship of brain dysfunction to the etiology of learning problems is included in this chapter. Several hypothetical explanations for learning disabilities can be traced to theories regarding the cerebral cortex.

Historical Link

There have been three sources of information linking the brain and learning disabilities. One has been experimental studies of lower animals (Geschwind, 1968; Dykman et al., 1970, 1971). The second has been studies of adults afflicted with war wounds or other forms of cerebral trauma, such as stroke (Strauss and Lehtinen, 1947; Luria, 1961; Schuell, Jenkins and Jiménez-Pabón, 1965). The third source has involved experimentation with epileptics undergoing brain surgery (Penfield and Rasmussen, 1950). The study of samples of animals and adults has its limitations in furthering our knowledge of the etiology of learning disabilities in children. Children are not likely to experience the state of "cathood" or "rathood," stroke or war wounds, or brain surgery. Knowledge about the relationship of the brain and learning problems is technologically limited to analogies rather than being based upon direct observation and experimentation.

Adult trauma usually affects large portions of the brain. It is thus difficult to pinpoint specific locales which might be relevant to problems of learning. Epileptics who undergo brain surgery have typically experienced longstanding severe brain damage before this radical operation is performed. The chronicity of the disease, the effects of brain surgery and electrical stimulation involved in exploring the brain may well obscure the relevant features of the brain and learning which specialists might wish to explain. In addition, the loss of a function may have different causes and effects than the lack of development of the same function (Hebb, 1949). For example, are the same places, processes and effects upon persons observed when one has lost the ability to speak and the other has never developed this skill?

Many professionals believe it is an exercise in futility to be concerned with the brain, as it may not be related to the occurrence of learning disabilities. It is often suggested that the technology of brain research has not yet advanced to the state where it can provide evidence that brain damage, dysfunction, maldevelopment or delayed development are implicated in learning-disabled children. Even when there is strong medical and neurological evidence to support the possibility that a child has some kind of neurological malfunction, the brain locale cannot be specified with any assuredness. While there has been a good deal of speculation about neurological signs in learning-disabled children, there has not been a corresponding abundance of empirical attempts to study the signs and symptoms associated with a brain-damage hypothesis of learning disabilities. It is argued that unless there is evidence that medical intervention is necessary, learning problems are the domain of the educator.

It is also argued that if a teacher has knowledge that a child with learning disabilities is suspected of having neurological involvement, the teacher will demonstrate less motivation in her efforts to remediate the educational difficulty. This argument can be reduced to concern about public relations or the political effects of knowledge. Better teaching performances might be obtained from the teacher if the teacher is uninformed or misinformed concerning the child's neurological integrity. Presumably, the good results accompanying these good intentions serve to justify the suppression of information. The concern for the manipulation of teacher motivation leads ultimately to the suggestion that teachers should be kept in a state of ignorance for the good of the brain-damaged child.

It is probably true that speculations regarding brain processes and learning disabilities have led to few successful educational programs. It is not true such speculations are worthless. Studies of the effects of assaults upon the brain have led to interesting theorizing. These in turn have produced empirical efforts bound to increase our sophistication concerning learning-disabled children. These studies have given rise to ideas about the brain and language, the brain and information processing, the role of sensory modalities and the relationship of modalities to each other as these affect the receipt, storage and use of information. As will subsequently be discussed, Dykman's fertile theory of attentional deficits of learning-disabled children, Geschwind's ideas of the manner in which brain locales and pathways can result in dyslexia, Kirk and Kirk's work based on the Osgood model of information processing and Johnson and Myklebust's typology and remediation of learning problems have been the products of these studies on cats, rats and the wounded adult.

The theoretical position which emphasizes the relationship of the brain to learning disabilities is based upon the control of human behavior by the brain. It is believed that inadequate behavior and learning might reflect inadequate brain control or functioning. Presumably, knowledge as to the discrete brain processes or locale responsible for this inadequacy should facilitate appropriate educational programming. The theoretical emphasis upon brain processes and their relationship to learning and behavior is reflected in the diagnosis of learning disabilities. Behaviors observed on various tests are used to infer the adequacy or inadequacy of various brain areas and processes. Because of this emphasis on the brain to interpret test data, some discussion of relevant structures and functions of the brain are included. Accompanying figures present schematic representations of the brain to aid understanding of the following discussion.

Anatomy of the Brain

The spinal cord and the brain are the two major components of the central nervous system. The spinal cord serves as one important center for the integration of motor activities. The brain is comprised of three major parts: the brain stem, the cerebellum and the cerebrum (cerebral cortex). The major functions of the brain stem involve the integration of several visceral functions (*e.g.,* control of heart and respiratory rates) and control of a variety of motor reflexes. The cerebellum coordinates the efferent, voluntary muscle system and plays an active role in controlling balance and coordinated muscle movements. The cerebrum plays a dominant role in the nervous system, as it is concerned with conscious functions or those behaviors which distinguish man from lower animals. Major theories related to learning disabilities have focused on the functions of the brain stem (Dykman et al., 1970) and the cerebral cortex (Geschwind, 1968).

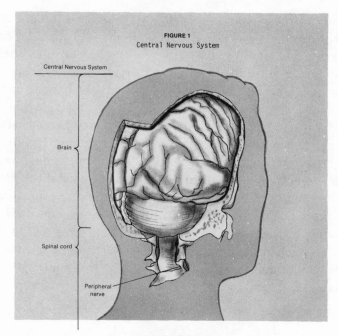

FIGURE 1
Central Nervous System

FIGURE 2
The Three Connections between
the cerebellum and the brain stem

The Brain and Learning Disabilities

Brain Stem

The brain stem is composed of four regions which have discrete functions. These are the medulla oblongata, pons, midbrain and diencephalon. The medulla, a continuation of the spinal cord, has nuclei (cell bodies) and tracts (axons) which have functions in controlling respiration and the cardiovascular system. The pons is associated with sensory input and output, flow to the face and is located at the upper limit of the medulla. The midbrain has a huge pair of tracts which carry messages down from the cerebral hemispheres and it has the sensory tracts which start in the spinal cord and go to the brain stem. The midbrain is associated with wakefulness or the conscious state of the entire brain. Some theorists attribute attentional deficits in learning-disabled children to breakdowns in the midbrain (Dykman et al., 1971). The diencephalon, the upper portion of the brain stem, is a major center for the passage and integration of sensory information. The thalamus is the largest (and most famous) part of the diencephalon.

Cerebral Cortex

The cerebral cortex is divided into right and left hemispheres which are connected by the corpus callosum. This is a large tract of fibers which connect the two sides and keep them at least reasonably well informed as to their mutual activities and interests (Mountcastle, 1962). The surface of the cerebral cortex has many convolutions, an economical spatial arrangement for cramming many cells into a relatively small area. The convolutions have been labeled as *gyri* (ridges), *sulci* (valleys) and *deep sulci* (fissures). Maps of the brain have been drawn to mirror these ridges and valleys. Some of the gyri and sulci have been linked to behavioral functions. In other cases, the functional role of the area in affecting behavior is not known.

The organization of activities in the cortex differs for various behaviors. Certain functions, such as vision and audition, are controlled by both the left and right sides of the cortex. Motor movements, such as of the arms and legs, are coordinated by both sides, but in a contralateral fashion; the left side of the brain controls the right side of the body, while the right side controls the left side of the body. There are some skills that are not represented in these fashions, but are controlled largely by one hemisphere. For example, across cultures there is a great preponderance of right-handedness and left-hemisphere dominance for language. About 93% of the adult population is right-handed and about 96% has left-hemisphere dominance for speech and language functions (Curtis et al., 1972). The right hemisphere is purportedly more in control of making complex visual discriminations and processing of nonverbal and perceptual information, such as music and mathematical symbols, than the left hemisphere (Milner, 1962).

While the dominance of the left hemisphere for language skills in adults has been well demonstrated, there is some question about the equipotentiality of both sides of the brain to develop language processing skills in children. For many years, the development of one hemisphere's dominance over the other was considered critical in a child's ultimate language and academic development. For example, Orton's (1937) work was based on the notion of the necessity for one side of the brain to achieve dominance over the other, with the accompanying hypothesis that failure to learn to speak or read reflected a lack of cortical dominance. Tests of hand, arm and eye usage were part of the clinical battery to assess brain damage or inadequate neurological maturation. For many years, parents would try to train a left-handed child to use his right hand, as it was believed harmful to the child's language development to be a "lefty." More recently, however, Lenneberg (1967) has stated that damage to the dominant left hemisphere in a child 12 years or younger will not have enduring damaging effects upon the child's ability to use language, because the right hemisphere will have the capability of compensating for the damage. At this point, we are not so concerned about right- or left-hemisphere dominance as we are in some signs of neurological integrity and maturity. Rather than being concerned as to whether the child uses his right or left

The Brain and Learning Disabilities

Superior Surface of the brain

Longitudinal Fissure

Left Hemisphere

Right Hemisphere

Frontal lobe

Precentral gyrus

Central sulcus

Postcentral gyrus

Central sulcus

Parietal lobe

Occipital lobe

FIGURE 3

Left and Right Sides of the Cerebral Contex

Adapted from: DeArmond, Fusco, and Dewey, *A Photographic Atlas Structure of the Human Brain.* New York, Oxford University Press, 1974.

hand, of more critical importance is the child's consistency or preferences for one over the other.

It should be noted that for many years it was assumed that only the cerebral cortex was involved in the learning process. While most of the foregoing discussion is focused on the role of the cerebral cortex in governing behavior, remember that other parts of the nervous system between the spinal column and the cortex are involved in learning. The brain is organized vertically as well as horizontally (Thompson, 1967).

The cerebral cortex has been divided into four major regions. These are the frontal, temporal, parietal, and occipital lobes. There are major landmarks used to set some of the boundaries for individual lobes. For instance, the lateral sulcus is the landmark to separate the frontal from the temporal lobes, while the central sulcus separates the frontal from the parietal lobe (Figure 4).

Frontal Lobe

Different areas of the frontal lobe are related to emotional control, coordination of complex motor movements and the ability to speak. The anterior section of the frontal lobe, shown in Figure 4, has many connections with other parts of the brain and the brain stem. This prefrontal region is considered involved in controlling virtually all of man's behaviors referred to as abstract thinking, mature judgment, tactfulness (Gatz, 1966) and to "maintain the integrity of personality and intellect" (Schuell et al., 1965, p. 69). Experiments on the frontal lobe of monkeys have indicated that damage to this area will result in changes in short-term memory, will reduce the rapidity with which new tasks are learned and affect extensive hyperactivity (Thompson, 1967). Knowledge about the role of the prefrontal area in humans has come also from prefrontal lobotomies for persons suffering severe chronic pain or exhibiting uncontrollable and unacceptable behaviors. In these surgical procedures, the frontal lobe fiber connections to and from other cortical and subcortical areas are disconnected (Curtis et al., 1972). The results of such treatments are personality, intellectual and emotional changes in patients, such that patients may suffer considerable impairment and become less sensitive to the possible consequences of their behavior.

The motor strip lies anterior to the central sulcus. It is organized in homunculus fashion so that one end is responsible for the control of toe movements, while the other end is related to swallowing, with the remaining motor movements organized in an orderly fashion along the strip (Curtis et al., 1972). Anterior to the motor strip is the premotor strip, which is believed responsible for an elaboration of motor movements more complex than those controlled by the motor strip. Experiments using lower animals have indicated that damage to the premotor area results in spasticity (abnormal, involuntary contractions of muscles), whereas damage to the motor strip results in flaccid paralysis (softness and weakness of muscles) (Gatz, 1966). When human beings suffer cerebral lesions in this area, the damage usually affects both the motor and premotor areas, resulting in paralysis with spasticity (Gatz, 1966). In some epileptic attacks, the person may suffer massive discharges in all parts of the motor cortex which result in tonic spasms (muscles contract in steady and uniform manner) and clonic movements (muscles contract and relax alternately).

Directly below the motor strip is Broca's area and anterior to it is the supplementary motor cortex. These are two of three cortical areas related to the production and control of speech. Broca's area is in the posterior part of the inferior frontal gyrus near the motor area which controls tongue and larynx movements (Gatz, 1966, p. 112). As mentioned earlier, Broca was the surgeon who noted the association between the loss of the ability to speak in two patients and subsequent autopsy revelations of damage to this cortical area. Brain surgery on epileptic patients (Penfield and Roberts, 1959; Penfield and Rasmussen, 1950) has corroborated Broca's observations. Damage to Broca's area, in the dominant hemisphere, results in expressive or motor aphasia: a person who has no paralysis of the tongue or other body parts connected with speaking, who knows what he wants to say, but cannot speak or who produces garbled speech (Gatz, 1966). Penfield and his associates have revealed the supplementary motor cortex also to be related to speech, but evidently excision of the supplementary motor cortex does not have the drastic and long-lasting negative effects on speech as damage to Broca's area. Aphasia, loss of the ability to speak, is more likely to result from damage to Broca's area and is more likely to be long-lasting than when damage is in the supplementary motor area.

Temporal Lobe

One particular function can be specifically and uniquely related to the temporal lobe. The primary auditory cortex is located at the "posterior and dorsal margin of the temporal lobe buried on the inner slope of the lateral fissure" (Curtis et al., 1972, p. 3). Receipt, comprehension and interpretation of sound is a specific function of this area. When a brain lesion affects the primary auditory cortex, the result is sensory aphasia, an inability to understand the meaning of spoken language. The person's ability to hear remains intact, but the ability to interpret what is heard is impaired. This is noted when the damage occurs to the dominant, usually the left, hemisphere, but the same effect is not noted when the damage occurs in the right or nondominant hemisphere. Sensory aphasia is also known as receptive aphasia and as Wernicke's aphasia, after the surgeon who first noted the difficulty certain persons had in interpreting spoken language. The deficit in comprehension of language usually has a reciprocal effect upon the person's ability to speak in a meaningful manner.

The functions of the remainder of the temporal lobe are not as well known. Curtis et al. (1972, p. 516) have summarized the results of Penfield and his colleagues' work on the temporal lobe. They report that stimulation of the temporal lobe results in auditory sensations (tinnitus—ringing tone, buzz or knock), vestibular sensations (vertigo—dizziness), alterations in perception (auditory or visual illusions or hallucinations of previous experiences), fear, hallucinations in the auditory or olfactory spheres, arrest of speech, repetitive motor movements (*e.g.*, rubbing ear), complex emotional behavior and confusion in association with

FIGURE 4
The Cerebral Cortex—Side View

Occipital lobe

Angular gyrus

Supramarginal gyrus

Cerebellum

Postcentral gyrus

Central sulcus

Precentral gyrus

Medulla

Temporal lobe

Frontal lobe

FIGURE 4

The Cerebral Contex (Side View)

Adapted from: DeArmond, Fusco, and Dewey, *A Photographic Atlas Structure of the Human Brain.* New York, Oxford University Press, 1974.

defects in memory (*e.g.,* confusion plus amnesia).

When it has been necessary to perform a bilateral temporal lobectomy, usually done to relieve severe, chronic epileptic seizures, the individual is reported to suffer impairment in the ability to form new associations and remember newly occurring events, although events which occurred in the distant past remain recallable.

Parietal Lobe

The parietal lobe is architecturally separated from the frontal lobe by the central sulcus and from the temporal lobe by the lateral fissure. The separation from the occipital lobe posteriorly does not have such well-defined landmarks. The parietal lobe is the primary receptive cortex for impulses from sensory receptors in the skin and for the higher integration of language, reading and writing.

The organization of sensory reception is such that specific areas along the postcentral gyrus receive projections from specific parts of the body. The parietal lobe functions so as to allow us to be aware of body movements, the position of the body in space and to be able to make discriminations of size, shape and texture. The specifics of these sensations are evaluated in neurological examinations and a number have been specifically linked to learning-disabled children. These include evaluation of:

a) Position sense—perception of movement and direction of movement.

b) Tactile localization—the ability to accurately localize the specific portion of the body which is being stimulated.

c) Two-point discrimination—the ability to perceive that a double stimulus with a small space of separation has touched a particular part of the body.

d) Stereognosis—the ability to distinguish and recognize objects based on feeling but not seeing them.

e) Graphesthesia—the ability to recognize which numbers

or letters have been traced on the finger, hand, face or leg.

f) Weight discrimination—the ability to discriminate among relative amounts of pressure.

g) Perception of simultaneous stimuli—the individual recognizes that both sides of the body have been simultaneously stimulated.

h) Perception of texture—the ability to perceive the patterns of things felt (Curtis et al., 1972, p. 498).

Ablation, or damage to areas in the parietal lobe, will affect these various functions. Thus, a person who suffers damage to some part of the postcentral gyrus may be able to feel pain when stuck with a pin but be unable to tell the location of the pinprick. Destruction of one side of this area of the brain may result in loss of awareness of the actions of the contralateral side of the body. Persons have been observed to forget to put on one sleeve of a shirt, evidently unaware of that side of the body.

Several problems associated with learning-disabled children, labeled minimal cerebral dysfunction, have been linked theoretically to the parietal lobe. The critical parietal areas referred to in descriptions of these syndromes are the supramarginal and angular gyri of the dominant left hemisphere. One problem is Gerstmann's syndrome. The symptoms include *dysgraphia,* an inability to write in the absence of paralysis; *dyscalculia,* a deficit in the ability to manipulate mathematical symbols; *left-right confusion,* difficulty learning directions; and *agnosia* errors in finger recognition in spite of intact sensory reception. These have been associated with *dyslexia* (serious difficulties in learning to read), and *apraxia* (difficulty in performing skilled motor movements on command), again in the absence of paralysis or losses of sensations. Two things should be noted. The first is that the syndrome is somewhat of a mirage insofar as these symptoms do not always occur together, sometimes appearing in isolation or in varying combinations (Benton, 1959). Second, these particular symptoms are problems noted in children suffering from severe rather than mild problems in reading.

Problems of body image are often presumed to be associated with learning disabilities. While definitions of body image are often not presented or are so vague as to be of little value, it is known that damage in the nondominant parietal lobe may produce a lack of awareness of the left side of the body, a lack of awareness of partial paralysis and disturbances in perception (*e.g.*, neglect of the left visual field, inability to interpret drawings or pick out objects from a complex figure) (Curtis et al., 1972).

Occipital Lobe

The occipital lobe is the cortical area responsible for vision. Specific visual skills can be matched to specific areas in the occipital lobe. When there is destruction of both sides of the occipital cortex, blindness results. Damage to discrete areas has predictable differential effects. Depending upon the site of the damage, a person might only lose peripheral vision or show blindness to only particular areas of the visual field. It is believed that damage which occurs in the visual association area, that area surrounding the primary visual cortex, may affect visual recognition and reading. The problem is that the damage is seldom limited to just these association areas and the surrounding areas might also play a role in affecting these visual deficiencies (Curtis et al., 1972).

Association Areas

The parietal, temporal and occipital lobes are primary sensory receptors for the various modalities of audition, vision, tactile and kinesthetic perception. What arrives at the cortex is just the raw data, however. These must be elaborated and analyzed in order for comprehension and subsequent appropriate responses to occur. The elaboration of the various sensations is believed to be the business of association areas which surround the primary reception zones. Communication between the modalities is the domain of the association areas. The elaboration and interpretation of the message is believed to occur in and among association areas. Thus, for the hand to know what the eye is doing requires messages passed between the appropriate parietal and occipital association areas. It has been theorized that one major difference between man and lower animals is the development of these association areas (Geschwind, 1968).

The Brain and Learning Disabilities

Relatively discrete areas of the brain have been demonstrated to be responsible for specific behaviors by man. A number of these are particularly relevant to the understanding of learning disabilities. Those systems in the brain related to speech and language production and to perceptual skills are most closely tied to certain conceptualizations of children with learning problems.

Penfield and colleagues (1950, 1959) electrically stimulated the brain cortex and identified three areas as involved in the production of speech and language. They have postulated that speech and language are the responsibility of the centrencephalic system. This is a central system which includes the three speech centers in the cortex, two in the frontal lobe and one in the temporal lobe, plus connections with the descending pathway to the spinal column. Fibers project from the cortex to the midbrain, brain stem and spinal cord and carry messages to and from each other at various levels. Damage to any of these areas in the adult has debilitating effects upon that person's ability to use speech and language. According to Lenneberg (see Fig. 5), the child's language development until 30 months of age involves his entire brain, with left-hemisphere dominance for language beginning to show towards the end of this period. Between ages 3 and 10, language functions are assumed by the left hemisphere along with polarization of other behaviors to either the left or right side. It is still possible, however, to reverse this polarization if the child experiences some trauma. That is, before ages 10 or 11, damage to the left hemisphere which results in language problems can be compensated for by the right hemisphere. It apparently is not easily accomplished, but is possible. By the mid-teens, language

FIGURE 5

Language and Brain Development

Age	Usual Language Development	Effects of Acquired, Lateralized Lesions	Physical Maturation of Central Nervous System	Lateralization of Function	Equipotentiality of Hemispheres	Explanation
Months 0 to 3	Emergence of cooing.	No effect on onset of language in half of all cases; other half has delayed onset but normal development.	About 60 to 70 per cent of developmental course accomplished.	None: symptoms and prognosis identical for either hemisphere.	Perfect equipotentiality.	Neuroanatomical and physiological prerequisites become established.
4 to 20	From babbling to words.					
21 to 36	Acquisition of language.	All language accomplishments disappear; language is reacquired with repetition of all stages.	Rate of maturation slowed down.	Hand preference emerges.	Right hemisphere can easily adopt sole responsibility for language.	Language appears to involve entire brain; little cortical specialization with regard to language though left hemisphere beginning to become dominant toward end of this period.
Years 3 to 10	Some grammatical refinement; expan-	Emergence of aphasic symptoms; all disorders recover without	Very slow completion of maturational	Cerebral dominance established between 3 to 5 years, but evi-	In cases where language is already predominantly localized	A process of physiological organization takes place in which

	sion of vocabulary.	residual language deficits (except in reading or writing). During recovery period two processes active: diminishing aphasic interference and further acquisition of language.	processes.	dence that right hemisphere may often still be involved in speech and language functions. About one quarter of early childhood aphasias due to right hemisphere lesions.	in left hemisphere and aphasia ensues with left lesion, it is possible to re-establish language presumably by reactivating language functions in right hemisphere.	functional lateralization of language to left is prominent. "Physiological redundancy" is gradually reduced and polarization of activities between right and left hemisphere is established. As long as maturational processes have not stopped, reorganization is still possible.
11 to 14	Foreign accents emerge.	Some aphasic symptoms become irreversible (particularly when acquired lesion was traumatic).	An asymptote is reached on almost all parameters. Exceptions are myelinization and EEG spectrum.	Apparently firmly established, but definitive statistics not available.	Marked signs of reduction in equipotentiality.	Language markedly lateralized and internal organization established irreversibly for life. Language-free parts of brain cannot take over except where lateralization had been blocked by pathology during childhood.
Mid-teens to senium	Acquisition of second language becomes increasingly difficult.	Symptoms present after 3 to 5 months post insult are irreversible.	None.	In about 97 per cent of the entire population language is definitely lateralized to the left.	None for language.	

SOURCE: Lenneberg, V. E. Biological Foundations of Language. New York: Wiley, 1967 is definitely localized in the left hemisphere and traumas to this area are not compensated for by the right hemisphere.

On the basis of clinical observations, children have been described as having different types of aphasia, expressive and receptive. When a child has difficulty in understanding what is said, he has a receptive language problem. Expressive problems relate to the child's ability to produce spoken language. There can be a breakdown in this speaking process at various points. The child may have an expressive problem which is related to transmitting a message. If the child has deficits in controlling motor movements associated with speaking, in the absence of any kind of paralysis or weak muscles, the child has an expressive deficit. This particular kind of expressive problem is referred to as *dysarthria* or *apraxia*. The child might have an expressive language problem which is related to the conceptualization component of language production. In this type of expressive problem, the child might have difficulty in remembering the right words, using appropriate words to express his ideas, connecting the words with proper syntax, putting words together to formulate a sentence or connecting words with their symbolic meanings.

The bases upon which we associate such behaviors in children to specific brain sites are hypothetical and are founded primarily upon sources of information largely unrelated to children. More recently, Lenneberg has provided some evidence, derived from studies of children, to support the notion that specific language deficits can be linked to particular areas in the brain. Lenneberg (1967) has reported two types of difficulty which result in dysarthria (*i.e.,* a problem of articulation). Children who have suffered damage to or experience abnormal growths in the area which immediately surrounds the thalamus often show problems of articulation. Lenneberg's findings lend support to the notion that when a child has difficulty in the acquisition of language skills some brain area may be directly involved. It also lends support to Penfield and his colleagues' inclusion of the midbrain as part of the speech system.

Still at the hypothetical level, the work of Norman Geschwind, a neurologist, is quite relevant to theories of learning disabilities. Two of Geschwind's theses are particularly salient. In one case, Geschwind links the developmental sequence of the neurological process of myelination to successive stages of psychomotor and language development. Myelination refers to the process whereby an outer sheath develops to cover and protect nerves. The nervous system is not completely developed when the infant is born and the areas of the brain which myelinate last are vulnerable to insult for a longer period. The order in which parts of the nervous system myelinate reflects the development of man's brain across centuries. The older parts of the brain from a phylogenetic view myelinate first. The areas are those concerned with sensory and motor functions and the limbic system, a system controlling experiences of pain and pleasure and survival of the organism. The sensory areas which show early myelination include the auditory, visual and somesthetic cortex, which have connections with their adjacent association areas, but not directly with each other.

The second areas to myelinate are the association areas. These areas surround the sensory areas, but allow, through long interconnecting fibers, various sensory areas to communicate with each other.

The last areas to myelinate are in the parietal lobe, the angular gyrus and a spot where the temporal, parietal and occipital lobes meet (see Figure 4). These particular areas are described by Geschwind as critical to language and, consequently, to language problems. The angular gyrus and the occipital-parietal-temporal lobe junction are presumed responsible for man's ability to make cross-modal associations, that is, to transfer information from one modality, such as vision, to another modality, such as audition. In man, unlike other animals, cross-modal associations can be made directly through the association areas without going through the more primitive limbic system. This is the anatomical basis for labeling, and Geschwind suggests that damage to this area may be one explanation for learning disabilities, particularly dyslexia. His hypothesis is that since this area myelinates last and boys mature more slowly at this stage of development than girls, the overrepresentation of boys in learning disability samples indicates that boys are more likely to have suffered some damage to this area of the brain. Boys are seen as susceptible to damage to slowly myelinating brain centers longer than girls.

Geschwind's thesis regarding the critical nature of certain areas in the parietal lobe, particularly the angular gyrus, or the association areas which connect fibers from the occipital, parietal and temporal lobes, has been expanded into an area of study referred to as cross-modal associations or cross-modal integration. This is a body of research which focuses on the means whereby messages are communicated and integrated between the various sensory modalities. Geschwind notes that man differs from monkeys in his ability to transfer information from one major sensory input system, such as the visual cortex, to another major system, such as the auditory cortex, without going through midbrain transmissions. The angular gyrus is of particular importance, because its strategic position and connecting fibers allow it to integrate information from all sensory and motor areas. Translating a thought into a motor act is likely to involve this area. One notion to explain learning disabilities is that these pathways or areas are dysfunctional. The child's inability to achieve in a variety of areas may be indicative of varying degrees of dysfunction. Damage to these pathways may affect relatively easy tasks, such as learning names, as well as complex ones, such as learning to read and write. There is some support for Geschwind's hypothesis concerning the importance of the angular gyrus in learning disabilities. Birch and Belmont (1964) studied the ability of retarded readers to make auditory, visual and tactile associations. Children with reading problems were less competent than comparison children in making these associations. While the study did contain some methodological flaws, the results are consistent with ideas regarding the functions of the angular gyrus and the hypothesis is quite provocative.

Dykman and his colleagues (1970, 1971) have developed a theory of learning disabilities in which the core problem is defined as an attentional deficit. The corresponding neurological structure implicated in this theory is the midbrain, particularly the reticular formation within the midbrain. This subcortical area is deemed responsible for maintaining a state of consciousness and awareness. A disturbance in the midbrain area affects the individual's ability to pay attention. This includes his ability to stay alert, to maintain vigilance and to focus on important stimuli in any given situation. Learning-disabled children are viewed as having an organically based deficit, localized in the midbrain, which affects their ability to maintain states of attention. The reticular activating system in the midbrain is described as follows:

The reticular formation is a diffuse network of polysynaptic fibers which begins in the spinal cord and enlarges greatly in the brain stem. Some of its fibers pass directly through the thalamus to the cortex while others go indirectly. . . . The reticular formation receives fibers from the cerebellum, the spinal cord, and the higher brain structures. The limbic structures are important in memory, emotions, and drive states. Electrical stimulation of the reticular formation alters respiration, vasomotor tone, muscle tonus, cortical neural activity, subcortical neural activity, and receptivity of certain sensory neurons. It also produces certain phasic movements similar to those seen in states of motor restlessness. These effects are mediated by fibers which descend from the cortex to the reticular formation (descending system) and by fibers which ascend from the reticular formation to the cortex (ascending system). If the reticular formation is damaged or cut off (*e.g.,* by anesthetization), sensory messages reach the cortex but there is no awareness of stimulation of perception (Dykman, Walls, Suzuki, Ackerman, and Peters, 1970, p. 777).

The hypothesis that learning-disabled children have an attentional deficit which reflects midbrain dysfunction is based upon extensive laboratory research studies of reaction time, impulsivity and the conditioning of learning-disabled children. The results have indicated that children with learning disabilities, defined as children with limited reading skills and excessive motor activity, demonstrate slower patterns in reaction times, different electroencephalographic responses (that is, different brain wave activity), and decreased physiological reactivity when compared to nondisabled children. These are behaviors which have been linked to reticular system activities. Dykman offers additional evidence to support this theory. In one case, evidence is drawn from the effects of drugs upon learning-disabled children. Stimulant drugs are believed to increase children's attentiveness, but have no effect on their performance on intelligence tests. The reticular activating system is thus indirectly implicated. More circumstantial evidence is derived from test score patterns on the Wechsler Intelligence Scale for Children. Learning-disabled children reportedly do particularly poorly on subtests which are supposed to tap attention (*e.g.,* memory for a sequence of numbers).

The signs indicating midbrain dysfunction, such as hyperactivity and poor performance on certain tests, attenuate with age. Children younger than 10 years who are experiencing learning problems are more likely to evidence these signs of "neural ineffectiveness" than children older than 10 years. This decrease in differences between adequate and inadequate learners suggests that the initial problem is one of developmental immaturity, or developmental lag, rather than permanent dysfunction. Geschwind points to cortical areas responsible for naming and for carrying information to and from cortical and subcortical areas. Dykman and colleagues have concentrated on the role of the reticular system in the midbrain in inhibiting and arousing behavior as the central explanation for the wide variety of learning problems. It is interesting to note that both theorists have drawn upon the theories and related research of Luria (1961-1966), a man whose work has been particularly concerned with the development of self-control through the use of verbal mediation. It should be noted that the discussion of verbal mediation represents an expansion of usual notions of the role of speech and language. We traditionally think of and define language in terms of communication and academic achievement. Now we are expanding upon the role of language to direct our thoughts and subsequent behaviors. Research studies which have been concerned with verbal mediation typically investigate the changes in learning which occur when children are instructed to use some kind of verbal mediation when learning or executing the task. These studies direct the child to view materials in a certain fashion and to rehearse what is viewed in order to remember it. It has been demonstrated that such rehearsal facilitates learning (Bandura, 1969; Flavell, Beach and Chinsky, 1966) and hypothesized that instruction to learning-disabled children on how to use verbal mediators will facilitate their achievement. While Bryan (1972) failed to find that rehearsal aided learning-disabled children, Palkes, Stewart and Kahana (1968) and Palkes, Stewart and Freedman (1971) did find that such instructions facilitated performance of hyperactive children. As yet, little is known concerning the training of self-control, attention or discriminations through alterations of verbal mediations, but interest in this important question is increasing. Studies of different types of mediators for learning different types of materials at varying ages and for varying types of learning problems should provide us with very useful knowledge to translate into educational practices.

The theories and research discussed thus far have been addressed to the role of the brain in causing learning disabilities and to areas of the brain which may be involved in cases of academic and behavioral difficulties. It should be noted, however, that within recent years, questions have been raised as to the value of such research in aiding the learning-disabled child. For example, Kirk and Kirk (1972) focus upon overt behavior, not brain waves, and upon psychological tests, not neurological examinations, as the most productive means toward understanding and aiding the learning-disabled child.

The position of Kirk and Kirk has had tremendous influence in shifting perspectives of learning problems from the neurologist's to the psychologist's office. But, the views of Kirk and Kirk can be construed as consonant with the ideas expressed by both Dykman and colleagues and by Geschwind. The Kirks' approach is based upon the Osgood model of communication. In essence, this model schematizes communications according to *receptive, expressive* and *organizational* processes which take place through *sensory* channels of audition and vision and are expressed through speaking and movement. These processes can occur at a *representational* level, which requires some verbal mediation, or at an *automatic* level, which involves complex motor actions but not verbal mediation.

The Illinois Test of Psycholinguistic Abilities (ITPA) has been developed to reflect these sensory, expressive and integrative processes using tests of children's auditory, visual and motor skills. The ITPA has been constructed to permit assessment of a child's skills in processing information receptively, that which is seen and heard; and the child's ability to respond expressively, either through speech, pointing, manipulation of objects and mimicry of well-known acts (*e.g.,* lighting a cigaret). The organization process is believed to occur as the child must be able to make associations between what is seen and heard and appropriate spoken and motor responses. The two levels at which communicative behavior is tested is the automatic level and the representational level. The automatic level tests highly integrative, but less voluntary types of patterns, such as the ability to repeat a sequence just heard or reproduce a pattern just seen. The representational level requires the child to use some type of mediational process to complete the task, and by this the authors refer to behaviors which "require the more complex mediating process of utilizing symbols which carry the meaning" (1972, p. 22). The test is constructed to permit the profiling of a child's performance so that his assets and deficits can be seen relative to himself and to same age peers.

The Kirk model is fundamentally based upon a psychological approach to learning disabilities, substituting educational for neurological perspectives. However, parallels between the neurological approach as developed by Geschwind or Dykman and the psycholinguistic model presented by Kirk and Kirk should be noted.

One can translate low scores on subtests of the ITPA which measure receptive and expressive language processes into indicators of Broca's or Wernicke's aphasia. Kirk and Kirk, like Geschwind, are dealing with the ability to deal receptively and expressively with information and include the need to integrate sensory information from different modalities into their respective models. Aspects of the ITPA which deal with automatic responses, such as learning a pattern or rote learning, seem very much in agreement with Dykman's descriptions of the role of the reticular activating system in controlling attention. The inclusion of symbolic mediators integrates into this schema Luria's work on verbal mediation and self-control of behavior. While very different perspectives are taken by these researchers, it appears that each model provides some means of explaining sensory-expressive processing of information plus the role of language to integrate this information.

With this introduction to the brain and a few perspectives on how the brain may influence a child's ability to learn, it is hoped that greater sensitivity will be developed to the rationales which are the basis for procedures often involved in the diagnosis of a child's academic or behavioral problems.

CHAPTER
5
INTELLIGENCE
AND
LEARNING
DISABILITIES

By definition the child with learning disabilities has intellectual capacity within the normal range. Adequate intellectual potential is a major factor used to categorize a child as learning disabled rather than mentally retarded and to separate the field of learning disabilities from the field of mental retardation. One popular definition of learning disabilities specifies a discrepancy between normal intellectual status and age- or grade-level, academic achievement (Bateman, 1964).

An intellectual standard is established for purposes of identification. Children on one side of a given measurement are said to be mentally retarded; children on the other side are said to be learning disabled. We can say that a child has a learning disability when a score on an intellectual measure is within normal range but scores on reading are 6 months below grade level at first grade or 1½ years below grade level at fourth grade. The assumption that follows a discrepancy definition is that the child with learning disabilities can function as competently as academically successful peers if the proper instructional interventions are provided. Normal achievement and adjustment are the expectation. Parents and teachers believe that the child will achieve in accordance with demonstrated potential. The implications are serious for the psychological testing staff, which makes decisions about class placement; for school administrators, who set policies and allocate resources; for parents and teachers, who set up expectancies of performance for the child and for themselves; and for the child, whose attitudes and self-concepts play an important role in setting life goals.

Given the impact our assumptions about intelligence have had on the life courses of children in this country, it would be irresponsible not to ask, "What is intelligence; what does it mean for learning disabilities and why bother anyway?"

Defining Intelligence

The nature of intelligence has plagued mankind since at least the time of Plato (Robinson and Robinson, 1965). Insofar as the answer is essentially arbitrary, definitions and explanations have varied. Definitions of intelligence have ranged from an inherited capacity to act appropriately to a manifestation of accumulated learned facts (Bayley, 1970). One theorist, Terman (1925), limited intelligence to problem-solving activities. Wechsler (1958) offered a broad definition of "the aggregate or global capacity to think rationally, to act purposefully and to deal effectively with one's environment." Whatever the theoretical definitions and their distinctions, it appears that the public believes that intelligence has two properties. First, laymen believe that intelligence is the capacity to act in all those ways necessary to lead a meaningful and acceptable life and to make all the decisions necessary for maintaining that life. Laymen also assume that intelligence remains fairly stable from early infancy to old age. McCall, Hogarty and Hurlburt (1972) nicely summarize popular conceptions of intelligence as "an unchanging characteristic that governs nearly all of the individual's mental performance at every age"

(1972, p. 728). Finally, many people believe that intelligence tests measure this capacity. These assumptions are now being challenged.

Testing Intelligence

To understand the uses and abuses of the concept of intelligence, it is necessary to take note of the history of the intelligence testing movement. The development of the first individual intelligence test was accomplished by Alfred Binet in 1905. Binet's mission, mandated by the public schools of Paris, France, was to screen children who would be likely to have difficulty in regular elementary school classrooms. Binet devised a test to serve this very practical and important function. Thus Binet undertook the development of a screening measure which might predict schoolroom performance; he did not undertake to develop a measure of adjustment, general competence, social skills or future success as a doctor, butcher or crook. Quite sensibly, many of the test items were devised to measure skills directly related to school activities; indeed some of the items were adaptations of French teachers' materials. As a result, many items on the original scale assessed verbal skills. Competencies in other arenas of life outside the classroom were not included. The mission dictated the method and these methods have had a pervasive, enduring influence upon the intelligence testing movement to this day.

Binet's test development and more current methods are far removed from any theory. Assessments of intelligence using any kind of broad definition are not made. Rather, we have several good instruments which can be used to assess present or near future academic performance or achievement. Most people, however, do not conceive of or use intelligence tests as merely another form of achievement test. Intelligence test results are presumed to transcend academic achievement assessments. But, what do such tests tell us? Do they predict behaviors? Which behaviors? Is this information about a stable phenomenon, not subject to

91

significant change? Is this information useful, and fair, for discriminating among children, be it for diagnosis, special classroom assignment, tutoring or psychotherapy? Can an analysis of parts of such a test be used to help describe difficulties and prescribe remedies for the learning-disabled child? The remainder of the chapter is addressed to these and other questions on intelligence and intelligence tests.

To assess the utility of a test a number of questions should be kept in mind. First, can the test predict later performance for most people? If not, is it useful for certain people? Second, if the test does have predictive utility, does the test have utility which increases predictions or "efficiency over the information otherwise easily and cheaply available" (Sechrest, 1967, p. 369). An evaluation of a test which is being used in an applied setting should include questions concerning the incremental, as well as predictive, validity of the test. The time, cost and inconvenience associated with administering the test need to be justified in terms of the additional knowledge yielded compared to that which is already known or easily available.

Infant Intelligence Tests

The development of infant intelligence tests has a long history. The assumption of a number of early theorists was that intelligence might be inherited, or at least it was something that was not easily influenced by environmental forces. If this were the case, it is theoretically possible to develop a measure of this capacity in the infant. If it were an unlearned capacity, early detection would allow society to maximize its responses by separating the bright from the dull—with suitable placement for both.

The initial goal was to develop a measure of intelligence appropriate for infant use that would correlate with intelligence test scores obtained on the same child some years later. Although several infant intelligence tests exist, there are three particularly well-known infant scales. These are the Bayley Scales of Infant

Development, the scales developed by the Gesell Institute and the Cattell Mental Test for Infants and Young Children. With respect to such measures, Kagan (1971) has said,

Much of the research on infant mental development has been guided by two related—and essentially unproven—hypotheses. The first posits a hypothetical entity, called intelligence, which can be measured by noting the rate of development of those response systems that are emerging at the moment. . . . There are neither adequate data nor persuasive theory to support this axiom. . . . A second assumption guiding work with infants presumes that early cognitive structures are derivatives of sensori-motor actions, a view usually attributed to Piaget. The significance of sensori-motor coordination for adaptive functions is readily acknowledged, but their necessary casual connections to cognitive development are, we believe, still open to debate (pp. 177–78).

Kagan thus directly challenges the utility of current concepts of infant intelligence and, by implication, the utility of infant tests.

Other reviewers of research on infant intelligence tests have generally concluded, with varying degrees of pessimism, that these tests as generally used are of little use in predicting later intelligence test scores. Bayley (1970) has written,

The findings of these early studies of mental growth of infants have been repeated sufficiently often so that it is now well-established that test scores earned in the first year or two have relatively little predictive validity (in contrast to tests at school age or later), although they may have high validity as measures of the children's cognitive abilities at the time. . . . The lack of stability in the first three years cannot be attributed to poor reliability of the measuring instrument (1970, p. 1174).

McCall, Hogarty and Hurlburt (1972) write,

It is something of an over-statement to say that there is "no prediction" from the infancy period to childhood IQ. There are correlations that attain statistical significance between certain ages from some tests, but the size of the relationships is not particularly impressive and certainly not adequate for clinical application (p. 729).

By and large it is safe to say that there are no genuinely valid infant intelligence tests, if this is meant to imply that some test given to an infant under two years of age will predict his scores on intelligence tests given years later. As early as 1939 Anderson failed to find correlations between scores on several scales administered at 3, 6 and 9 months of age with scores obtained by the children on the Stanford-Binet Intelligence Scale at age 5. In 1972, McCall, Hogarty and Hurlburt summarized the results of nine separate longitudinal studies and indicated that none reported consistent findings which would suggest that intelligence test scores correlated with those obtained by the same children some years later. Pease, Rosauer and Wolins (1961) administered the Gesell and Cattell scales to 100 infants at ages 3, 6, 9 and 12 months and found no correlation of the test scores with scores obtained in adjacent months. And Hindley (1960) failed to find that children's scores on the Griffiths Scale of Infant Development (another often used test) at 3, 6, 12 and 18 months were correlated across ages on any of the five scales on this test.

These are but a few of the many studies which led to the conclusion that there is a lack of predictive validity in infant intelligence tests. The interested or disbelieving reader is referred to a more complete review by Bayley (1970), Lewis (1973) and McCall et al. (1972) for further documentation. The evidence on this point has been well summarized by Lewis, who states,

Within a wide variety of standardized tests such as the Bayley and Gesell there is relatively little interage consistency in test performance during the first two years of life. Thus, children who are precocious at one age are not necessarily precocious at another. Moreover, early precociousness in the first two years seems to be unrelated to childhood performance on standard IQ tasks (1973, p. 111).

Why are infant intelligence tests such poor predictors of performance? Most of the items comprising such tests are addressed to sensory and motor skills, skills not assessed by childhood IQ tests such as the Stanford-Binet or Wechsler Intelligence Scale for Children (WISC), which primarily tap linguistic skills. Bayley has suggested that the

lack of consistency over time in mental test scores reflects a series of changes in the nature of mental processes as they progress from simple sensori-motor adjustments to increasingly complex forms of adaptations, generalizations, abstractions, and their accompanying reasoning processes (1970, p. 1177).

On the face of it, it would be surprising if simple sensori-motor abilities were correlated with vocabulary levels of older children.

Not all aspects of the infant scales fail to be predictive, however, nor is the total score useless for all children. McCall et al. (1972) report a number of studies which suggest that there is some hope for the utilization of infant scales, but that there is some need to reexamine what leads to what and for whom. In one study infants who had been administered the Gesell scale at 6, 12, 18 or 24 months were subsequently administered the Stanford-Binet at 3½, 6 or 10 years or the Wechsler scale at a later time. It was found the items which involved vocalizations best predicted later IQ scores, particularly for girls. The authors referred to other investigations suggesting this. In a study conducted in England, for example, the results were that the speech quotient on the Griffiths Infant Scale obtained from 18-month-old children was predictive of vocabulary, comprehension and general IQ scores at eight years of age, with the average correlation of .53. But these correlations were obtained only for girls. "In summary, three studies indicate that vocalization in infancy may have a special salience for females that it does not for males with respect to predicting later mental performance" (McCall et al., 1972, p. 735).

Total scores on infant intelligence tests may not be useful for predictions of later IQ scores for most children. But they may be more predictive of IQ scores obtained by children who will be subsequently labeled as subnormal (Reese and Lipsitt, 1970). One purpose of developing these scales in the first place was to detect which children might have severe dysfunctions and apparently the tests have been somewhat more successful in predicting later IQ scores in children with severe intellectual problems. The predictive validity of the test may be increased by limiting testing to children who are considered abnormal. There is danger, as McCall's review indicates, that infant scales have enough errors of prediction to preclude their use for individual diagnosis.

Sechrest (1967) has suggested that tests need to be evaluated on the basis of their power to increment knowledge over that obtained by more economical procedures. After reviewing many studies in which infant tests were compared to other sources of information, McCall et al. concluded that ". . . these results imply that parental education may be a better predictor of childhood IQ than an assessment on the child during the first two years of life" (1972, p. 733). For the average and above average infant, the parent's socioeconomic status is a better predictor than the infant intelligence measure. But when there is some suspicion of defective development, such as mental retardation or learning impairment, the infant scale may be usefully employed.

The bulk of the data leads to the inference that infant scales are not measures of intelligence, if one means scores on subsequent childhood intelligence tests. There is little to indicate that the use of these tests with very young children is justifiable with the important exception of infants who may be severely disabled. In this case, the assessment should lead to differing interventions, such as would occur if it were established that the child was hearing impaired rather than severely retarded. At the same time, concern must be voiced for children who are misdiagnosed as either pathological or normal. There is no compelling evidence to suggest that these errors are so few that we can feel comfortable in applying infant tests for individual diagnoses. We do not know that such tests increase our information above that which is obtained by ratings or observations made by parents, or pediatricians or sensitive and experienced child watchers. And if there is a slight increment in knowledge, is it worth depriving other children of the scarce and costly time of a professional psychologist or psychometrician?

The discouraging results of these infant intelligence test studies have led researchers along two empirical paths. Some are attempting to refine the psychometric approach, eliminating items that are not predictive of later scores and adding items which may be more predictive. An example of such efforts is the work of Cameron, Livson and Bayley (1967) on infant vocalization as a predictor of later intelligence test scores.

A second approach is to emphasize the study of cognitive processes, rather than the development of new and better test items (Kagan, 1971; Zigler, 1968). Determinants of attention, such as heart rate deceleration and inhibition of motor activity, become the types of behaviors studied in this approach. When the emphasis is upon cognitive processes, researchers focus on determinants of what might constitute encoding and decoding of stimulus inputs. How do infants receive information, organize it and respond to it?

With the notable exception of the severely handicapped child, it is no longer possible to assume that infant intelligence tests, loaded at the younger ages with measures of sensori-motor skills, yield useful information about subsequent IQ scores or academic success to be obtained during childhood.

Childhood Intelligence Tests

The most widely used tests of intelligence for children are the Stanford-Binet (S-B) and the Wechsler Intelligence Scale for Children (WISC). The properties and formats of these tests are described elsewhere in this text and the interested reader is referred to the detailed reviews of these and other tests by Anastasi (1961) and Freeman (1962). These reviews provide information about test construction, standardization scoring procedures and interpretation difficulties which go beyond the scope of this chapter. Professionals, however, should be concerned with issues of test standardization and interpretation.

The purpose of this chapter is to outline the problems associated with the use of the concept of intelligence. The first problem is that conceptualizations of the nature of intelligence and what intelligence tests actually measure are two very different things. Many people believe that there is a "true intelligence" or a "potential intelligence," which is an ability, relatively constant and perhaps genetically influenced, which is pervasive in determining the child's behavior in a wide variety of situations and with a wide variety of people. The search for culture fair, culture free tests of intelligence reflects the belief that there is a "potential intelligence" located under the skin which can be and should be separated from cultural influences and experimental history (Liverant, 1960).

Aside from these beliefs, what behaviors do intelligence tests predict? The scores on these measures may tell us something about people, such as the social class and attitudes of the child's parents (Bayley, 1970; Reese and Lipsitt, 1970; McClelland, 1973); but is that what is meant by the concept of intelligence? When the test of intelligence is used, it is most certainly not for the purpose of ascertaining parental educational level, parental achievement demands or other cultural influences upon test scores. But these are the variables with which intelligence test scores correlate. Two explanations of this phenomenon are possible. One is that the test is a very imperfect measure of the concept or that these cultural variables are determinants which affect this "true" or "potential" ability which resides within us.

Intelligence test scores can provide us other information about the child. They can tell us who is likely to do well in most schools and on tests designed to assess the child's academic achievement (McNemar, 1964; McClelland, 1973). ". . . the Stanford-Binet is primarily a measure of scholastic aptitude . . ." (Anastasi, 1961, p. 208). The WISC is primarily a measure of how well the child will do on the Stanford-Binet (Littell, 1960). It is extremely important to note that the Stanford-Binet, which was designed to predict academic achievement, is best at predicting this complex domain of behavior, whereas the majority of studies related to the predictive power of the WISC have been based primarily on how well the WISC predicts scores on the Stanford-Binet.

Important as it may be to predict school grades, and test-taking performance on achievement and other intelligence tests, these scores do not provide support for the implicit assumptions often made about intelligence. Scales which tap verbal skills are likely to predict how people are evaluated or graded within situations in which there is an emphasis upon the acquisition and use of verbal skills. One such notable situation is the classroom. It is important to note as well that the margin of error in predictions of academic achievement when dealing with children within the "normal" range of intelligence test scores is rather high. When children with severe retardation are excluded from studies, the power of the test to predict academic achievement diminishes.

Constancy of Intelligence

The constancy of IQ scores from infancy to childhood is relatively low. As mentioned earlier, this is not surprising, since infant tests focus on sensori-motor skills and childhood intelligence tests focus on verbal skills. If sensori-motor skills are critical in determining the development of verbal skills, we do not now know which sensori-motor skills are important for which verbal skills, nor do we know how to measure them.

Constancy of children's intelligence test scores is assessed in two ways. The most frequently employed method is to correlate scores obtained by the child at two or more distinct points in life. The correlational method indicates the degree to which a child maintains his rank relative to others also tested. If the highest to lowest scoring children are the same on two testings, the correlation between the two tests will be perfect. Correlations refer to relative rankings. The second method of assessment of IQ score constancy is examination of a child's change in scores across two testings. The interest in this case is in terms of absolute levels of scores, not relative rankings of children. An inspection of Table 1 will assist in understanding the differences between these two methods.

TABLE 1

Child	IQ Score at 6 yrs of age	IQ Score at 10 years of age
Gail	175	160
Nancy	160	110
Ara	150	109
Cara	110	108
Lynne	100	95
Donna	100	80
Justin	80	74

Danny	70	73
Peter	69	72
Sheri	65	68

Notice that the ten hypothetical children maintain the same relative rankings when tested at age 6 and age 10. The correlation between the two tests would equal 1.00. There is a perfect prediction from one test to the other and one might conclude that IQ is constant. But notice how individual scores shift across the testings. Our inferences about Nancy's school performance based upon scores obtained at age 6 would be very different from inferences drawn at age 10. The same might be said about Ara, Lynne and Donna. Moreover, confidence based upon the belief that intelligence is constant might be abused by such data. Let us now consider research results which pertain to the constancy of intelligence as a function of these two assessment methods.

Studies of the correlation of test scores obtained by children at various intervals yield high correlations, particularly if the tests are administered after the child reaches 5 years of age. For example, Bayley (1949) found that tests given to children older than 6 years were highly correlated with scores obtained at age 18. The closer in time the administration of the two tests, the higher the correlation and these correlations are likely to be .80 or more. Thus the correlation between tests administered at ages 15 and 18 was .96. Bradway, Thompson and Cravens (1958) found correlations above .55 between two administrations of the Stanford-Binet after a lapse of 25 years. Even the test scores obtained at ages 4 and 29 years were rather highly correlated. Anastasi has written, "In terms of group trends, the long-range predictive validity of a Stanford-Binet IQ, especially when obtained with school-age children, is remarkably high" (1961, p. 206). Note that this conclusion is directed toward *group trends,* relative rankings of children within their group. What we are concerned about in learning disabilities, however, is the constancy of IQ scores of individual children.

There appears to be an abundant amount of evidence to suggest that frequent and marked changes in IQ scores occur for individuals. Honzik, Macfarlane and Allen (1948) reported that more than half of their sample of children obtained changes in IQ scores greater than 15 points and 9% obtained changes exceeding 30 points. McCall (1970) reported that individuals he tested shifted, on the average, 24 points. McCall, Appelbaum and Hogarty (1973) investigated the stability of IQ scores and test profiles of 48 males and 66 females who had had at least 12 assessments made of their intellectual performance between the ages of 3 and 13. The result was that the

average individual's *range* of IQ between 2½ and 17 years was 28.5 IQ points, one of every three children displayed a progressive change of more than 30 points, and one in seven shifted more than 40 points. Rare individuals may alter their performance as much as 74 points (1973, p. 70).

Baker, Sontag and Nelson (1958) found that 62% of a sample of 50 children changed more than 15 points in their Stanford-Binet IQ scores between the ages of 3 and 10 years. It is quite clear that the individual IQ score is subject to marked shifts and that such scores are not constant.

There are a multitude of factors which contribute to the waxing and waning of IQ scores. Some moderate shifting is likely due to simple measurement error. A high or low score can be obtained by the child because he was good or bad at guessing that day or had good or poor rapport with the teacher. On retesting, a child's score is likely to be lower if it was high on the first evaluation and higher if it was particularly low on the first evaluation. Additionally, IQ score shifts have been linked to a number of personal and social characteristics of the tester. McCall, Appelbaum and Hogarty (1973) have reported that boys are more likely to show increases in IQ with age than are girls, and girls who are "relatively more favorably disposed to traditional masculine roles tend to increase in IQ more than girls who are less so" (p. 70). Low-income groups are less likely to show shifts than middle- or upper-income groups, or are likely to show decreasing scores with age. Personality characteristics of both children and parents have been associated with score shifts. Children who are independent and competitive appear to be more likely to show shifts upward. Parents who encourage children in their intellectual tasks and use moderate and rational discipline techniques are likely to have children who show upward increases in IQ scores (McCall et al., 1973).

Correlation with Test Scores

There is thus a good deal of evidence to allow one to assert that commonly used tests of intelligence do not measure what many professionals and laymen conceive as intelligence. The IQ scores show marked fluctuations at the individual level and predict but a narrow range of behavior, school achievement and achievement test scores (McClelland, 1973). The notion that IQ scores are constant and correlated with socially significant behaviors is strongly contradicted by the evidence to date. There is now an increasing tendency to redefine the results of intelligence tests as reflections of school-related abilities (Cronbach, 1960).

While IQ scores correlate reasonably well with school-related activities, it is of critical importance that learning disability specialists and other professionals dealing with children disavow the notions that we test intelligence when we employ intelligence tests and that whatever is measured is constant and predictive of performance across time.

Rather than regarding intelligence tests as measures of a single dimension (general intelligence) it is more in keeping with the evidence to interpret them as assessing culturally expected standards of academic preparedness involving a number of complexly interrelated variables (*e.g.*, implicit reaction patterns, motives, habits, expectancies, reinforcements, etc.) to account for the results (Liverant, 1960, p. 109).

This represents a changing view of intelligence tests. Today, as in the past, "scores derived from psychometric instruments were used to classify, segregate, track, advance, employ, institutionalize, and educate people" (Bersoff, 1973, p. 892). It is likely that in the future there will be an increasing emphasis upon assessments of the particular skills needed to accomplish specific goals. To better predict school achievement, more attention must be paid to the particular tasks required by the school curricula vis-à-vis the demands made by the classroom teacher, the requirements specific to the individual task and the individual differences among children in terms of these necessary skills. There will be greater attention paid to the specific demands made upon the child in light of his abilities and to the conditions which may or may not motivate the child to undertake and pursue the academic demands. As McClelland has written, "If you want to know how well a person can drive a car (the criterion), sample his ability to do so by giving him a driver's test. Do not give him a paper-and-pencil test for following directions, a general intelligence test, etc." (1973, p. 7). If you want to know whether or not a student can read, write or compute, test his reading, writing and arithmetic. If intelligence tests are to be used, they should be administered frequently to monitor whatever changes in scholastic aptitudes have taken place. Superior to the use of achievement measures would be assessments made on the basis of the material to be learned. The corollary to this is that predictions about academic success should encompass a limited time span. Short-range predictions are more likely to be accurate than long-range predictions. School achievement is related to many factors, including the reinforcements administered by the teacher, the expectancies of the child, the task's demands and the skills required to perform them. The best way to estimate a child's performance is to study him, the class and the teacher within the classroom context. "It is likely that the future rests in an increase in classroom assessments, to the benefit of everyone" (Bersoff, 1973).

Present concepts of intelligence are too narrow and not especially useful; and standardized measures of intelligence for the child above 5 years predict school achievement reasonably well, but not too well, and do very little else. "Potential," "underlying" and "true" scholastic capacity are terms which need to be better defined before we can begin to assess whether tests tap such factors.

Intelligence and Learning Disabilities

The chapter has thus far been focused upon the role of intelligence tests in capturing the essence of whatever we mean by intelligence. The IQ score is critical to the field of learning disabilities, since, by definition, we use this score to limit the population to which we channel our resources and energies. The IQ score is used to indicate "potential." A gap between the potential and performance on achievement tests is one method to define children as learning disabled. But is it true that IQ tests assess "potential," "underlying" or "true" scholastic capacity? Insofar as we have yet to define such terms as potential as other than the score on an IQ test, we are engaging in circular reasoning. Until such terms are better defined, answers cannot be forthcoming. It is not true that all "bright" children should learn in school, irrespective of the teacher, tasks, incentives employed or the motives in operation. Nor is it true that all dull children are doomed forever to low scholastic productivity irrespective of the influence of motivational and contextual factors which influence them.

Learning Disabled vs. Mental Retardation

IQ scores are critical to the learning disability specialist, as these scores are used to limit the population to whom these services are available. While IQ scores form the legal basis on which to determine provision of services, types of children and application of treatment, the question needs to be raised as to the actual adherence to this specification regarding normal intelligence as a requirement for classification as learning disabled. Ames (1968) reported that 24% of the children referred to the Gesell Institute for school learning problems had IQ scores below 90. Ames argues that complicated diagnostic interpretations of learning disabilities might be eliminated by recognition of the fact that such children do poorly in school because of low intelligence. Bryan (1972) examined the case histories of 65 children diagnosed as having learning disabilities at a prestigious hospital clinic. Virtually the same percentage of children had IQ scores below 90.

Birch and Belmont (1964) studied WISC patterns for retarded and normal readers. The retarded readers had scores below the 10th percentile on three of four reading tests. Belmont and Birch reported that the entire group of retarded readers had significantly lower IQs than normal readers. When the data were analyzed with the omission of the borderline 80–89 IQ subjects, the retarded readers were still significantly lower in IQ than normal readers. In a number of experimental studies, IQ differences between learning-disabled and control groups have been found to be significant. In each case learning-disabled children had lower IQs and in each case their performance on the experimental task was significantly poorer than that of the comparison group. In two of these studies the data were analyzed so as to control the intelligence differences among groups. In one (Dykman et al., 1971) the experimental differences between groups remained even after the intelligence differences had been eliminated; in the second (Browning, 1967) the differences between groups disappeared when intelligence was held constant between groups. Other researchers (Schwartz and Bryan, 1971) have restricted the range of intelligence from 85 to 115. Nonetheless, significant group differences resulted as learning-disabled children had lower intelligence levels than the comparison group.

It may be that a sizable percentage of children who are labeled as learning disabled could or should be diagnosed mentally retarded. A sizable minority of these children could be expected to do poorly in school on the basis of the results indicated by standardized tests of intelligence. This is not to say they do poorly in school because they have low intelligence. Insofar as we stress concern for what such a term as intelligence means, we do not intend to imply that low intelligence always causes poor academic performance. But, whatever it is that contributes to academic success that is captured by intelligence tests suggests that these mysterious abilities, motives, factors are frequently less represented in learning-disabled children than in random samples of children.

The inclusion or exclusion of below-average-IQ children from the learning disabilities category may depend upon a number of political, budgetary and humanistic considerations. It may be that labeling children who are experiencing a host of developmental problems (*e.g.,* mental retardation, emotional disturbance) as learning disabled will result in their experiencing less stigma and better educational opportunities. It may also be that inclusion of these children may retard the development of therapeutic interventions, as these, in turn, have been predicated upon the assumption of normalcy. Irrespective of these considerations in making placement and treatment decisions, the reality of the current situation is that many children labeled as learning disabled do obtain lower IQ scores than their peers. Perhaps the definition of learning disabilities or diagnostic policies should be changed. The question still remains as to whether "dullness" makes a difference. We have to consider the benefits of obtaining IQ scores and ask whether these scores really make a difference after all. It is of import, and empirically feasible, to know whether obtaining a low IQ score leads to school programs which are better suited to the skills of the students or to more biased and discouraged teachers and pupils.

Factors Other Than Intelligence

It should be recognized that intelligence tests are often employed for the purpose of diagnosis of various conditions which are remotely, if at all, related to problem solving. Wechsler (1958) and Rappaport (1946) both have suggested that diagnoses of emotional and mental states of persons might be made on the basis of the pattern of intelligence scale subtests. For instance, if the scale score on the Verbal section of the Wechsler Intelligence Scale for Children (WISC) is higher or lower than the scale score on the Performance section, or if the result on the Digit Span test is markedly different from the Vocabulary test score, inferences could be made regarding the person's mental processes and emotional status. Differences in subtest or subscale scores are thus considered indicative of psychological processes and pathology.

Psychologists have conducted a large number of research investigations to associate intelligence test profiles with psychological processes, personality traits and pathology states (Frank, 1970). The results of these research efforts have indicated that groups of subjects cannot be discriminated on the basis of profile analysis of intelligence test scores. Even were these results positive, the problem would still exist as to the utilization of test profiles for diagnostic analyses of individuals. Researchers have followed the path of the psychologists in attempting to employ test profile analyses to determine the clinical status of children. Two general orientations have characterized research in this area. In one case there has been an attempt to determine whether learning-disabled children can be discriminated from nondisabled children on the basis of discrepancies between verbal and performance scores on the WISC. In the second instance, attempts are made to determine whether a pattern of subtest scores might be uniquely associated with the learning difficulties.

Huelsman (1970) reviewed 23 studies of performance on WISC subtests by children with reading difficulties. In general, it has been found that children with reading difficulties obtain lower scores on Information, Arithmetic, Digit Span and Coding relative to other subtest scores. Huelsman, however, investigated the WISC patterns of 101 underachievers and 56 achievers (defined on the basis of not having reading problems). These groups of children could not be differentiated on the basis of the total number of subtests in which they showed marked deviation from their own general performance. Overall scatter of scores did not differentiate the achievers and nonachievers. In addition, these groups were assessed in terms of their performance on Information, Arithmetic and Coding subtests, as low scores on these three subtests have been associated by others with reading problems. In general, there were a greater number of underachievers than achievers who scored low on one or another of these subtests. But, Huelsman underlines the finding that *individ-*

ual underachievers in reading do not necessarily demonstrate this pattern of low scores on these three subtests. Indeed, only 13% of the groups had poor performance on all three subtests, and only 11% showed low performance in two of the three subtests. It was also found that large deviations in particular subtest scores from the average score obtained by a particular child did not differentiate among children. In effect, achievers appear to have about the same incidence of high and low subtest scores as underachievers. Kender (1972) reached similar conclusions after a review of the literature of WISC patterns of poor readers.

The second issue was related to the discrepancies between Verbal and Performance scale scores. Huelsman reported that 61% of the underachievers had higher Performance than Verbal scores; only 38% of the achievers demonstrated a similar discrepancy. This does provide some support for the discrepancy notion, but note that if the discrepancy scores were used as a basis of diagnosis, 39% of the underachievers and 38% of the achievers would have been misdiagnosed. Huelsman writes,

It appears advantageous at this point for research to turn away from searching for a WISC subtest pattern and to turn toward analysis of the possible significance of low subtest scores in the instructional program of individual children (1970, p. 545).

Recently, Keogh and associates have called for a closer examination of the differences in cognitive styles which may be associated with different types of learning disabilities. Keogh and Hall (1973) suggest,

It is time to begin differentiating the teaching methods in order to see the emergence of real clinical teaching, where the goal is a precise match between the cognitive style of the learner and the cognitive demands of the task. Specification of particular areas of strength and weakness through the proposed process analysis may provide some direction for individualized program planning, thus increasing the usefulness of the WISC in psychoeducational evaluation (1973, pp. 4–5).

Several investigations have been completed by Keogh and her associates to determine differences between learning-disabled and educable mentally retarded children in performance on the

WISC. Unlike other investigators we have discussed, Keogh suggests that WISC subtest scores reflect three major psychological categories. The first category, Verbal-Comprehension, is comprised of scores on the subtests Vocabulary Information and Comprehension. The second, Analytic-field approach, is comprised of subtests Object Assembly, Block Design and Picture Completion. The third category, Attention-Concentration, consists of Arithmetic, Coding and Digit Span subtests (Keogh and Hall, 1973). The performances of clinically diagnosed educable mentally retarded, learning-disabled and hyperactive–learning-disabled boys were compared on these three categories (Keogh, Wetter, McGinty and Donlon, 1973). The hyperactive–learning-disabled boys were defined as children who had been referred for evaluation on the basis of learning problems and hyperactivity. As could be predicted, the retarded children scored significantly lower on all factors than did the two learning-disabled groups. The patterns of scores are, however, of interest. The retarded children scored significantly higher on the analytic-field approach than on the other two categories. The learning-disabled children, particularly the hyperactives, scored lower on the attention factor relative to the other categories. In a follow-up study, Keogh and Hall (1973) enlarged the size of the sample and studied learning-disabled and retarded children. The same results were obtained, at least when investigating the performance of the boys. These findings appear to be stable. Groups of retarded and learning-disabled children demonstrate varying degrees of competence within certain psychological processes. At the same time, the overlap of performance of these children with members of other diagnostic groups is likely to be great, possibly sufficiently great to preclude the use of this classification scheme for the purpose of individual diagnoses. Keogh and colleagues have, nevertheless, demonstrated that learning-disabled children, *as a group,* appear to be deficient in attentional skills relative to verbal comprehension and field approach strategies. It is this deficiency that may differentiate these children from educable mentally retarded children.

There is evidence to suggest that groups of learning-disabled children might respond differently than comparison children to certain WISC subtests. It is also clear that the degree to which these WISC patterns differentiate groups is insufficient to permit basing individual diagnoses upon such test scores. Errors in classification of individual children are likely to be so frequent that diagnostic use of subtest patterns is useless, if not damaging. Even if there are refinements of samples and procedures, further studies are not likely to yield additional useful information. The rationale for this negative prophecy stems from the low reliabilities of difference scores between subtests. Chance fluctuations which affect scores are likely to have marked influence upon any particular pattern of scores "discovered" (McNemar, 1957). Until subtests have adequate reliability, there can be little hope for attempts to develop a diagnostic procedure based upon pattern analyses of subtest scores. In our opinion, the test is not sufficiently reliable to be put to such use. Clinicians may wish to continue such diagnostic procedures in light of the absence of a better replacement, but they should do it with awareness of the great likelihood that many errors will be made.

Intelligence Tests and the Schools

The use of intelligence tests within schools has been vigorously challenged. A primary reason for the attack has been the belief that intelligence tests are biased against ethnic and racial minority groups and that use of these measures deprives members of minority groups of valued opportunities in education. Insofar as ethnicity and race may be confounded or associated with socioeconomic status and lower social class members typically do more poorly on such tests relative to nonminority group persons, these charges have some credibility. Currently there are sophisticated debates concerning what criteria should be used to identify and evaluate the biases of tests (Schmidt and Hunter, 1974). There is no question that such debates will increase our knowledge and sophistication in the development of valid psychological tests. The problem is that in spite of admitted difficulties associated with intelligence tests they are among the best predictors of school performance. If this is true, we must ask if academic achievement is primarily a function of adopting those values and skills associated with middle and upper socioeconomic classes. Intelligence tests appear to be biased instruments, in the sense that they measure factors associated with success in American schools. The test may be less at fault in the propagation of biases than the criteria by which it is being evaluated. Damage generated from the use of the intelligence test does not stem from the test itself, but from educators' assumptions about the nature of intelligence.

Whether the focus of concern is the learning-disabled child and/or ethnic and racial minority group members, it is folly to imbue intelligence tests with characteristics of constancy and unmodifiability and to assume that precise categorization of children or placement in classes can be made on the basis of such tests. Intelligence test scores can be used to suggest appropriate class placement for children at the very low end of the intelligence continuum. But there are children who score in the lower end of the normal range who subsequently blossom, and high-scoring children who wither (Robinson and Robinson, 1965). Are conceptions of intelligence, diagnostic procedures, classroom schedules and teacher and parent expectancies sufficiently flexible to note and adjust to changes in the child?

We have relied too long on the intelligence test for information concerning the acquisition of information. Attention should be directed toward the classroom itself; to the demands made by the teacher, the skills necessary to meet the demands and the motives which sustain a child's endurance in what to most children is an aversive situation. By way of example, Carver (1974) has predicted the demise of standardized achievement tests and a revolution in educational measurement. Carver suggests that *psychometrics,* which emphasizes the normal curve and percentile rankings of students, will be replaced with *edumetrics,* a means of assessing the individual's gains within a specified curriculum. Evaluation in edumetrics will focus upon such questions as whether or not the student can read the curriculum materials and has learned the information the teacher has been presenting.

While this approach does not eliminate some kind of assessment of the child's ability, intuitive or standardized, it does place the emphasis upon the material to be learned and the student's demonstration that he has or has not achieved this goal. This approach is promising for learning disabilities insofar as it removes the onus of proving the child has intelligence in this or that range and allows effort and resources to be placed in what we conceive as one proper area, the means by which children can successfully complete academic assignments, and, in the event of failure, the means to provide alternate routes to learning.

CHAPTER
6
BEHAVIOR
OF THE
LEARNING
DISABLED

The most frequently mentioned characteristics of the learning-disabled child are hyperactivity and short attention span. In addition, other characteristics have been added. Common among these characteristics are behavior difficulties. The argument is not made that the learning-disabled child suffers an obvious physiological, nutritional, intellectual or emotional difficulty, but rather that he behaves inappropriately. To a considerable degree, the difficulties of the learning-disabled child are social in nature. He is judged by others to act in ways which may be dissimilar to his peers, self-defeating in their consequences or disruptive to the social organization of the family and classroom. The learning difficulties which children experience may be an outcropping of the behavior problems. Not sitting still, not paying attention, not initiating self-instructions affect the acquisition of information. Case studies of learning-disabled youngsters are replete with descriptions of untoward behavior, particularly within the testing situation, if not the classroom. Yet texts which outline intervention techniques have focused on learning tasks and procedures, not on remedies for behavior problems. Perhaps we feel more comfortable establishing programs to teach a child the difference between long and short vowels than we do in establishing a program for a child whom the teacher describes as unable or unwilling to work alone, to attend under the usual classroom conditions, to sit or stand still or to remain quiet. At the same time we recognize that if we could successfully program that child to work by himself, to be a self-starter, his learning the difference between short and long vowels would be greatly facilitated.

Behavioral Characteristics

In this chapter we shall review the data available on the behavioral characteristics of the learning-disabled child. This information is organized into two sections. The first presents descriptions of these behaviors by parents, teachers, peers, educators and clinicians. The second concerns the data relevant to the issue of hyperactivity. Hyperactivity is a central concept employed in discussions of learning disabilities and specialists should be aware of the limited amount of systematically gathered data available. There is not much research to discuss because not much research has been done.

Before reviewing some of the findings concerning the behavioral differences between the learning-disabled and the nondisabled child, some points concerning the diagnostic process itself should be made. It has long been recognized that labeling others as deviant, inadequate or emotionally ill is determined not only by the characteristics of the labeled person as evaluated and measured on certain tests, but also may be affected by the subjective characteristics or functions of the person doing the labeling (Becker, 1963). It has been noted that normal children are viewed by their mothers as experiencing many problems in growing up (Lapouse and Monk, 1964), and teachers view many children as evidencing hyperactivity without labeling them learning-disabled or pathological (Young, 1974). What factors result in the labeling of the child as learning disabled? One might assume that the critical feature is an adequate IQ score and low academic achievement, but labeling does not appear to be that simple. How can the kindergarten and first-grade child, and indeed, the pre-school child, be judged academically incompetent? The criteria for attaching a label to a child are being increasingly removed from the original definition of such problems, while other features of the child or his judge constitute, in part, the basis for labeling. There is no way to know how much "luck" plays a role in defining a child as inadequate, but it is certain that the role of the adult in responding to the child is critical. Moreover, once a child is labeled, it is likely that observers who "know" of the child's difficulties are likely to interpret a variety of behaviors as reflections of the pathological condition (Rosenhan, 1973). Thus, the diagnostic labeling of the child, whether correct or incorrect, is likely to have a profound influence upon others' judgments of the child. What might be tolerated antisocial behavior by the normal, becomes for the learning disabled, a serious reflection of the "basic difficulties" which he is experiencing. As yet we know very little concerning the characteristics of the adult and child which might interact to affect the labeling process. Perhaps we should be studying adult tolerance for children's movements, fidgetiness, talking and defiance within the classroom. What is clearly needed are studies concerning the individual differences among adults, teachers and parents in their readiness to initiate the referral process, and those characteristics of the teachers or classroom situations which might be associated with quick, slow or incorrect labeling and referral practices.

Parents' Observations

There are some limited data concerning how peers and adults view the learning-disabled child. Wender (1971) has categorized clinical data on children diagnosed as having minimal cerebral dysfunction within a developmental framework. Infants and pre-schoolers are reported by their parents to have been very active and restless. The child is likely to be described as one who walked early, and who, by virtue of getting around easily, was unintentionally destructive to household objects. Wender summarizes the parents' view of the child as reflecting an infant "King Kong," a perennial two-year-old. Parents report further crises when the child enters school. To the considerable annoyance of others both at home and in school such a child is likely to be fidgety, appearing to be incessantly in motion. Parents describe these children as obstinate, sassy, bossy, stubborn, negativistic, disobedient, difficult to discipline, resistant to adult domination and yet attempting to dominate peers. These terms reduce to the parents' perception that the child will not conform to their wishes. When the child reaches adolescence, he is described as manifesting poor impulse control, an inability to delay gratification and to persevere in tasks, and poor judgment and planning. Apparently, he is still doing what he wants.

It should be noted that the adequacy of these data remains in doubt. Little information is given as to the sampling of parents. It is not known, for example, whether or not these parents are in the process of seeking help for their youngsters. If such were the case, it is likely that they would paint a gloomy picture of the youngster's behavior, emphasizing the child's inadequacies rather than his strengths. It is not known whether the parents are referring to their youngster's present behavior or behaviors which may have occurred in the distant past. Descriptions of the behavior of the preschool infant may have required a considerable amount of retrospection concerning events several years past. This point is important, as it is generally recognized that parents' recall of long past behavior of their children is likely to contain a considerable amount of error (Yarrow, Campbell and Burton, 1970). The lack of details concerning the sampling and interviewing procedures makes a critical evaluation of the descriptive scheme forwarded by Wender impossible. Whether these descriptions reflect facts or stereotypes concerning these children remains to be seen.

Support for parts of Wender's descriptions is obtained from an excellent study by Owen, Adams, Forrest, Stolz and Fisher

(1971). These investigators interviewed the parents of educationally handicapped (California's term for learning disabilities) and
noneducationally handicapped children. Parents were selected
from these two populations approximately matched on social
class and race, age of youngster and the youngster's siblings.
Mothers describe the learning-disabled child as having less verbal ability (in effect this meant that the child did not like to listen,
was difficult to talk to and had trouble expressing himself), less
ability to control his impulses and to structure the environment
and more anxiety than his siblings or nonhandicapped children.
Unfortunately, the authors fail to provide sufficient information
as to just what constitutes ability to structure an environment or
to control impulses.

Strag (1972) asked parents of learning-disabled, mentally
retarded and normal children to complete a questionnaire in
which they rated their children on items associated with behavioral and emotional disturbances and items indicative of neurological dysfunction. The comparison of the parents' ratings of
learning-disabled and normal children revealed that these groups
were differentially rated on several variables. The learning-disabled child was characterized as showing less consideration for
others, less ability to receive affection and more clingingness than
normal children. Learning-disabled children were distinguished
from the mentally retarded by being rated as less stubborn, more
clinging, demonstrating greater jealousy and being less able to
receive affection than the mentally retarded youngster.

Putting these studies together, it would appear that parents'
perceptions of the learning-disabled child is to describe them as
clinging, yet unable to receive affection, and showing little impulse control, being rather uncontrolled in their emotional and
motoric expressions. Birch and Belmont (1964) paraphrase parents' views of these difficult problems:

. . . not a nice handicap. Such technical descriptions as catastrophic behavior,
perceptual impairment, perseveration, disinhibition, mimism, short attention
span, exogenous behavior contagion, learning disability, Strauss syndrome,
neurological impairment, and hyperactivity are translated by the outside world

as spoiled, bratty, bad-mannered, ill-behaved, badly brought up, undisciplined, obnoxious, and by the other children as queer" (p. 11).

While not all learning-disabled children can be so characterized, the fact that many can should be clearly recognized. While virtually unexplored, there seems little reason to question the assumption that the presence of a learning-disabled child may produce considerable stress and strain on the family unit. The difficulty is not simply that such children are not reading, but that they are not pleasant.

Teachers' Observations

Surprisingly few studies have been conducted concerning teachers' perceptions of the behavior of learning-disabled children. Recently, however, a number of investigations addressed to this issue have been conducted. Myklebust, Boshes, Olson and Cole (1969) found that of 49 different tests, teacher ratings of child behavior was the second best predictor as to whether the child would subsequently be diagnosed as learning disabled. Learning-disabled children were judged as being less competent in auditory comprehension (following directions, comprehending class discussions), spoken language (vocabulary, sentence length), orientation (time concepts), behavior and motor ability (general coordination), than nondisabled children. Of particular interest was the teachers' judgments concerning the behavior of the learning-disabled child. Teachers rated these children as less cooperative, less attentive, less able to organize themselves, less able to cope with new situations, less socially acceptable to others, less accepting of responsibility, less able to complete assignments and less tactful than nondisabled youngsters. In a subsequent investigation (Bryan and McGrady, 1972), teacher ratings were obtained on 183 learning-disabled and 176 control children on those items used by Myklebust and Boshes. The Bryan and McGrady results replicated the Myklebust and Boshes investigation, as all items pertaining to the behavior of the child were found to discriminate the learning-disabled from the nondisabled child. Behaviorally, then, the learning-disabled child is seen by the teacher as less desirable within the classroom than is the nondisabled child.

Keogh, Tchir and Windeguth-Behn (1974) extended our knowledge concerning such teacher attitudes by obtaining teachers' views of learning-disabled and mentally retarded children. This study indicated that teachers were quite consistent in detecting behaviors which they associated with learning disabilities and that they made distinctions between learning-disabled and mentally retarded children. A high percentage of teachers associated the following characteristics with educationally handicapped children: aggressiveness (violent, cruel, destructive—66% of the teachers); hyperactive (63%); short attention span (44%); withdrawn (44%); no sense of responsibility or self-discipline (44%); poor interpersonal relationships (41%); parental problems (34%); disruptive (talking, noisemaking, 31%); disinterested, poor attitude toward school (28%); angry, hostile (28%); poor coordination (25%); low academically (25%); anxious and nervous (22%); demands a great deal of teacher time (22%); attention seeking (19%); loner (19%) (1974).

The discriminable differences between learning-disabled and mentally retarded children from the teacher's perspective is that the teacher views the retarded child as having primary difficulty with school work, whereas the educationally handicapped child has behavior and personality difficulties. The learning-disabled child is hyperactive, has problems with his parents, has no sense of responsibility, is angry and hostile; the mentally retarded child is smiling, friendly and lovable, but unable to work with academic materials and abstractions.

Peers' Observations

So far we have seen that, by and large, learning-disabled children are viewed quite negatively by both parents and teachers. The question may also be raised as to how such children are evaluated by their peers. Bryan (1974a) has conducted two large-scale investigations designed to assess peer reactions to learning-disabled children. Children in 62 third-, fourth- and fifth-grade classrooms were administered a sociometric scale. In each classroom there was at least one learning-disabled child, so that peer reactions to 84 learning-disabled children were obtained. Since peer popularity and peer rejection are not always highly correlated—that is, a child who is not popular is not necessarily rejected (Hartup, Glazer and Charlesworth, 1967)—the sociometric test used consisted of items designed to assess a child's popularity and his rejection by others. Items to assess peer popularity included asking children to nominate three classmates whom they desire as friends, to sit next to and to invite to their birthday party. Items to assess peer rejection directed the child to name three children they would not wish as friends, to invite to their birthday party or to sit next to in the classroom. When the learning-disabled child was compared to a randomly selected classmate of the same sex and race, it was found that this child was significantly less popular and significantly more rejected by his peers than the nondisabled child. This was particularly true if the learning-disabled child was both white and a girl. School problems of white girls are associated with considerably more rejection by peers than either black or white boys or black girls. Also noteworthy is the fact that while the peers of learning-disabled children do not view them as hyperactive, they do judge them as being worried and frightened, as children who never appear to have a good time, as being sad, not being neat and clean, not very good looking and as children to whom nobody pays much attention. Peer assessments of these same children were made one year later in order to assess the degree to which the learning-disabled child's status with his peers remained stable over time (Bryan, in press). This follow-up investigation assessed the peer popularity of white learning-disabled children, mostly males. The results replicated those obtained the previous year. Once again, these learning-disabled children were more rejected and less accepted by their peers than the randomly selected comparison child.

Parent, Teacher, Peer Rejection

The data are convincing that the learning-disabled child is likely to be rejected or in conflict with parent, teacher and peers alike. As yet, we know very little concerning the basis of such rejection, but studies towards this end are now being undertaken. In one investigation, Bryan (1974c) compared the interactions of learning-disabled, potential learning-disabled and nondisabled children with children one year younger. Each child was brought to a laboratory and allowed to play a miniature bowling game. After playing the game, the child was informed that he was to teach a younger child how to play the game in such a way as to obtain high scores. In reality, the game scores were preset, but this was unknown to the participants. A younger child was then brought into the room, the experimenter left and the teaching lesson was initiated. The lesson was videotaped by a concealed camera for subsequent analysis.

There is some evidence that peer popularity and rejection are associated with children's use of social reinforcements, essentially praise and punishment (Hartup et al., 1967). The particular emphasis in the analysis of these tutorial sessions was the degree to which learning-disabled and nondisabled children employed such reinforcements. No differences were found. The adults who tested these children felt strongly that learning-disabled children did, in fact, act very differently from the nondisabled children while interacting with their peers, and insofar as these interactions were videotaped, all was not lost. To check these intuitions, randomly selected video tapes were shown to a group of education students who had no knowledge concerning which of the children were learning disabled and which were not. Unlike the investigators, then, they were "blind." Each rater viewed video tapes which were no longer than four minutes in duration and was asked to rate each child as to his physical appearance, speech and language competence, academic achievement and attractiveness to other children. It was found that education majors rated the learning-disabled child as significantly less competent in speech and language use, as having lower academic achievement and attractiveness to peers. Physical attractiveness was the only item which did not differentiate the learning-disabled from the nondisabled child! Thus, strangers to learning and reading problems, inexperienced at evaluation and in dealing with young children, could view this short tape of a dyadic interaction and differentiate the learning-disabled from nondisabled child.

While there are, no doubt, many factors which might contribute to this differing behavior by these children, one starting point is to focus upon the child's ability to accurately discriminate the various affective states in others. For this purpose Bryan (1974b) employed a test devised by Robert Rosenthal, which is known as the Kiddiepons. The test consists of a film and an audio tape. The film has forty segments which display an adult female expressing either positive or negative affects combined with dominant or submissive expressions. Examples of the situations used are: *a)* positive/dominant—an expression of motherly love; *b)* positive/submissive—expressions of gratitude; *c)* negative/dominant—nagging a child; *d)* negative/submissive—asking forgiveness. Besides varying the affects and styles of expressions, the amount of information available to the child is also varied. On some occasions the child views only the face of the actress, while on other occasions, the torso and face are viewed. The forty audio segments present the same affects, but the messages have been made uninterpretable by removal of high frequency sounds or by scrambling and resplicing the tape. The viewer-listener sees or hears emotional expressions without being able to understand any of the words spoken. The viewing child is instructed to indicate on a questionnaire which one of two statements best describes the scenario.

Taking care to ensure that the children had understood the questionnaire, Bryan found that learning-disabled children were less able to accurately describe the scenario than were nondisabled children. The learning-disabled child apparently has more difficulty in understanding subtle communications concerning affects than do nondisabled children. To what degree this ability might be tied to their interpersonal difficulties with parents, teachers and peers remains to be determined. Clearly, however, this finding provides a lead as to future possibilities concerning remediation efforts involving such children. The evidence indicates that many of the problems experienced by the learning-disabled child involve interpersonal interactions. Considerably more attention should be addressed to both the understanding and the remediation of these problems. Learning-disabled children do not only suffer only from academic failure; many carry an additional burden of social failure.

Conduct of the Learning Disabled

In addition to studies concerned with the social interactions of children, research has been conducted within school settings to determine just how the learning-disabled child conducts himself. Are such children disruptive, hyperactive, quiet, talkative, nontask-oriented, ignored, rejected, in attendance or absent during the school day? There is very little information available and the existing information is of very recent origin. Forness and Estveldt (1971) studied children in the process of being referred for evaluation for academic difficulties. Observations were made within their classrooms to determine if, in fact, their behavior distinguished them from their classmates. These investigators studied 24 boys, 6 to 11 years of age, all having intelligence scores within the normal range, over a 15-month period within a regular elementary school classroom. Observers visited the classrooms over a period of two weeks and recorded the children's behaviors while they were engaged in small group reading and math instruction. A data coding cycle was set up so that the subject's behavior was coded for the first six-second interval; then the observer coded the behavior of each of the other children in that group and started the cycle again. The behaviors recorded were interactions, attending behaviors and the responses of the teacher and peers. The results indicated that most of the time was spent in attending to the academic task at hand. More than 80% of the behaviors which occurred appeared to receive no overt response from anyone. The target subjects in the reading group attended from 22–78%, while the peers attended from 36–92%. The target children received more attention from teachers than peers and this attention was in the context of task-related help. The main difference between the target children and comparison peers was that related to attending behavior and their frequency of interaction with the teacher. It was noted that many of the nonreferred children attended to the school task less than half of the time; in fact, children who were referred were no less attentive than children who were not deemed as needing remedial help.

In the Classroom

Two classroom observation studies were conducted to observe children already classified as having learning disabilities and receiving supplementary services from a learning disability specialist (Bryan and Wheeler, 1972; Bryan, 1974d). The method used in both studies was an Interaction Process Analysis. A behavioral code is developed which includes the behaviors defined as relevant to provide an accurate picture of the occurrence of behaviors in an elementary school class. The categories of behaviors which were recorded were: task-oriented behavior, nontask-oriented behavior, social interactions and waiting. Task-oriented behavior was defined as "becoming engaged in a purposeful activity that has been prescribed for us by someone else" (Jackson, 1971, p. 84). This includes reading, library, art and miscellaneous tasks (passing out paper to the class, watering the plants). Non-task-oriented behavior was defined as nonproductive behavior and/or activities the child was not supposed to be engaged in. This included such behaviors as staring out the window, roaming around the room, pretending to be attending (flipping the pages of the book with no observable signs of reading or writing) and singing during quiet time. Social interactions were defined as verbal and/or nonverbal behaviors emitted between two or more persons. The child's approaches to the teacher and peers, their responses to him and their initiations to the child were included. Waiting was used to describe transitional periods, such as when the teacher organized the class activities for the day, when the class was changing activity or when the individual child finished his work and was waiting for further instructions.

In the first study (Bryan and Wheeler, 1972), classroom teachers nominated four boys, two of whom had been diagnosed as learning disabled and two whom the teacher considered average achievers. These children were then observed by two raters for one school day. Neither of the raters knew which of the children was learning disabled. The children were observed for periods of five minutes, with their behaviors recorded within ten-second intervals. The results were that the learning-disabled child spent less time in task-oriented and more time in nontask-oriented behaviors than did comparison children. The learning-disabled children spent an average of 57% of their time in task-oriented behaviors compared to the comparison children's average of 70%. The learning-disabled children did not interact with the teacher more than did the comparison children; indeed, neither group interacted with her significantly (only 2% of the time was spent in such interactions).

In the second study (Bryan, 1974d), five learning-disabled boys in the third grade were studied one day each month for a period of five months. Their behaviors were observed in both a classroom and a resource room situation. In this case the goal was to determine whether learning-disabled children's task-oriented behavior would vary according to the task at hand (reading vs. music), whether the frequency and type of teacher/peer interactions would vary from the regular classroom to the special education setting, and to determine whether or not there are qualitative differences in the social interactions of these children.

As in the first study, the learning-disabled children spent less time in task-oriented behaviors and more time in nontask-oriented behaviors than comparison peers. While learning-disabled children spent an average of 68% of their time in task-oriented behavior, the comparison children devoted an average of 88%. Learning-disabled children spent an average of over 30% of their time on nontask-oriented behavior, while comparison children devoted but 11% of their time to such activities. The learning-disabled child was particularly "turned off" (spent less time than did comparison children) to lessons in arithmetic, language and the arts (music, art, games). Finally, the learning-disabled children simply paid less attention to the teacher, irrespective of topic discussed, than did the comparison children.

The social interactions revealed that the learning-disabled and comparison children did not differ on the proportions of time they spent interacting with the classroom teacher (5.1% and 3.7%, respectively), or with peers (9.8% and 10.4%, respectively). There were very significant differences, however, in the patterns of interactions which the learning-disabled child had with teachers and peers. The number of times the adult responded to an initiation of contact by the child was very different for these groups. The teacher responded to 76.7% of the contacts initiated by comparison children, but only to 43.6% of the contacts initiated by the learning-disabled children. Whatever the reason for the lack of responsiveness by the teacher, the result is likely to be an increasing alienation between child and instructor. When the teacher did interact with the children, the nature of the teacher's interactions with the learning-disabled and comparison children differed. About 50% of the time that the teacher interacted with the learning-disabled child was devoted to helping him with his academic work. Only about 25% of the time the teacher interacted with the comparison child was devoted to academic matters. The teacher was more likely to interact with the comparison child for purposes of sending him on errands, eliciting his aid in organizing games, obtaining his help in helping other students and other nonacademic matters.

Classroom Relations

Also of interest was the nature of the reinforcements given these children by their teachers. While the learning-disabled children received as many positive reinforcements (statements of praise and approval) as did the nondisabled children, they also received more reproofs. The teachers appeared to be generally reluctant to respond to the learning-disabled child's attempts to initiate an interaction, did not employ more encouragement or praise for such children who might be in particular need of such encouragment, and tended to give such children more negative reinforcements!

Peer interactions were also studied. As the reader will recall, the learning-disabled child is generally rejected by his peers. Classmates describe the learning-disabled child as untidy, not one whom one would wish for a friend and one who tends to be ignored by other children within the classroom. The results of this observational study confirm at least one feature of the results of the sociometric studies. While learning-disabled and comparison children did not differ in the amount of peer interaction in which they engaged, the learning-disabled children were more likely to be ignored by peers than were comparison children when they initiated peer contact.

The comparison of attending behavior and social interactions of learning-disabled children in the special education classroom and in the regular classroom revealed that the children engaged in more task-oriented behavior in the special classroom. While in the resource room, the learning-disabled child interacted more with the teacher and received proportionally more positive and fewer negative reinforcements.

There seems to be little question that the learning-disabled child is likely to be rejected by parents, peers and teachers. If you ask either adults or peers, by and large, they will tell you so. Moreover, analysis of the classroom situation suggests that the learning-disabled child's social life is rather different from that of other children. Apparently, he is more often ignored when attempting to initiate a social interaction, is less likely to be interacted with by the teacher for matters not essentially academic, gets more negative and less positive reinforcement from teachers than his nondisabled counterpart. In short, people do act as if they dislike the learning-disabled child. Whatever distinguishes the behavior of the learning disabled from the nondisabled in peer interactions is manifested very quickly. Strangers to children can reliably detect differences between learning disabled and nondisabled children and after viewing such interactions but a few minutes (Bryan, 1974e). As indicated, there is evidence that the learning-disabled child is somewhat disabled in detecting or correctly perceiving subtly expressed affective cues by others. One major source of the disabled child's difficulty with peers and parents can be linked to this type of insensitivity. Perhaps it is their faulty language, their intrusiveness or all manner of possible combinations of such behaviors. We do not know. What we do know is that such children are not liked by others. Finally, it should be noted that most remedial efforts are devoted to the correction of the learning-disabled child's reading, writing or arithmetic failures. To our knowledge, virtually no remediation efforts are studied or recommended for the academic failure's social failures. This is perhaps justified, according to one's values and resources. However, ignorance concerning the disabled child's social difficulties is not justifiable. There is no question that they exist and that both parents and teachers should be alerted to that fact.

Organic Causes of Failure

The social and academic failure of the learning-disabled child has not been unrecognized by workers in this area and various explanations as to the etiological or causative factors have been advanced. These views reflect the medical, psychological and social systems models. While the exact site, processing and nature of the defect are controversial, there are many who view the problem as organically based. Cruickshank, Bentzen, Ratzeburg, Tannhauser (1961) suggested that

> . . . hyperactivity is . . . defined to include much much more subtle deviations in behavior, and is more specifically considered to be related to matters of short attention span, visual and auditory distractibility, and disturbances in perception leading to disassociative tendencies. . . . All of these characteristics have been observed in individuals with definitely diagnosed brain pathology (1961, p. 10).

While recognizing that many cases of hyperactivity may be more associated with emotional problems and may not demonstrate any organically significant deficits, the weight of the view is upon the degree to which these children have established cortical control of attention and perception. Johnson and Myklebust (1967) described cases of children with psychoneurological learning disorders as having "social imperception." These authors suggest that the parietal lobe of the right hemisphere of the brain is responsible for a child's inability to comprehend his social world. This brain damage is seen to affect the child's nonverbal skills, resulting in unintentionally reckless and tactless behavior.

Dykman and colleagues (1971) have developed an extensive research program to test the notion that learning disabilities are primarily a reflection of an attentional deficit and that this is the result of a breakdown in the reticular activating system of the brain. Brown (1973) also suggested that behavioral characteristics typical of learning-disabled children reflect individual differences in the maturation of brain centers responsible for the control of emotion. As such, it would appear that we are simply viewing individual differences in control for which we should have more tolerance. Brown argues that we expect differences in the rates at which children acquire motor-cognitive skills and we should extend this to expectancies concerning the child's development of self-control.

Finally, an interesting case has been made for the role of allergies in affecting children's behaviors. Franklin (1973) believes that the number of learning-disabled children who are sensitive to chemicals and additives used in drugs and foods is seriously underestimated and that many of the problems people experience are a result of this sensitivity. Somewhat supporting this position is a *Newsweek* article (1973) which reports the work of Feingold and his colleagues. Working with a group of 25 hyperkinetic children, they found that many had a history of allergies and had consumed large quantities of processed foods. A diet free of artificial flavors and coloring was reported to reduce these children's hyperactivity. These findings lack corroborative data from other systematic research, but are nonetheless intriguing.

Psychological and Social Causes of Failure

While the above-mentioned theorists have focused upon the role of organic dysfunctions in affecting the learning-disabled child's behavioral problems, others have looked toward psychological and/or social processes as possible causative factors. Friedland and Shilkret (1973) suggest that hyperactive behavior results from traumatic interactions with adults. It is argued that the child becomes hyperactive in order to avoid interpersonal relationships with adults within his environment. This explanation is not persuasive. By and large, hyperactivity itself is not the cause of social problems; rather it is how the activity is directed or its nature which turns others off (Pope, 1970). Additionally, there is little systematically gathered data suggesting that learning-disabled children avoid adults. In neither of the observational studies conducted by Bryan (Bryan and Wheeler, 1972; Bryan, 1974d) was it found that learning-disabled children attempted fewer interactions with the teacher than did nondisabled children. Avoidance conditioning does not appear to characterize the history or reflect accurately the behavior of such children. The "unsuccessful extrovert" (Wender, 1971) seems to better describe the children.

In her research involving hyperactive children, Barbara Keogh (1971) has advanced two hypotheses concerning psychological factors which may be important in understanding such children. She suggests that one view of the effect of hyperactivity is that of producing a deficit in information collection and/or processing. Hyperactivity reduces the amount of information the child can obtain under conditions where motor activity must be inhibited. You cannot run and read at the same time. The longer the period of hyperactivity, the greater the accumulation of the deficit of information. Keogh also suggested that hyperactive children may have different conceptual styles than nonhyperactive ones. Conceptual styles reflect individual differences in decision-making styles, particularly the time in which decisions are likely to be made (Kagen, 1965). Some persons take a long time to make a decision and make few errors. These individuals are said to have a reflective tempo. Other children tend to make rapid decisions and make many errors as well. These children are presumed to have an impulsive conceptual style. Hyperactive children are defined as children who exhibit extreme degrees of impulsive conceptual tempos, a reasonable hypothesis since they are often described as responding too quickly for their own good, as lacking the ability to think things through and as being unable to delay their responses.

Other investigators have suggested that situational influences play an important role in eliciting maladaptive behaviors. It is not that the brain-damaged child is maladaptive because of the damage, but rather that such children are likely to find themselves in situations in which they are continually frustrated in achieving their hopes and aspirations (McReynolds, 1966). Owen and collaborators report that children with learning disabilities experience a family life which is quite different from that experienced by their siblings and other academically successful children. Families of learning-disabled and comparison children were rated by observers on the degree of organization of family living. The scale ranged from "family activities and schedules planned to give structure to family living rather strictly adhered to" to "practically no structure; disorganized pattern of living; lack of schedules or assigned responsibilities" (1971, p. 45). The authors concluded that the "educationally handicapped children lived in a family atmosphere that tended to be less well organized and less emotionally stable than the atmosphere of the control families" (p. 46).

Peck and Stackhouse (1973) hypothesized that learning-disabled children, in this case defined as reading problems, were experiencing difficulties as a result of intrafamilial conflict. To assess this hypothesis, 15 normal and 15 reading-problem families were asked to complete a 38-item questionnaire. Twenty items on which the mother, father and son disagreed were then selected for the experimental task. The triad, operating as a unit, were asked to solve these 20 problems. Their interactions were recorded and later analyzed for the amount of time spent in solution of the problems, the percentage of time spent in silence and for categories of types of verbal interactions. A comparison of the interactions for the reading-problem son, mother and father with those of the comparison son, mother, father teams revealed that the reading-problem families spent more time completing the decision-making tasks, more time in silence and exchanged less explicit and more irrelevant information. Contrary to expectation, conflict was not more evident with the reading-problem groups, it was in fact less evident. The authors concluded that the ways in which reading-problem families interacted produced "mystification." In effect, they communicated in such a fashion as to avoid open disagreement, however legitimate, by misdefining the issues under discussion. The families appear to argue about arguing and fail to reach a decision. The results of such interactions, if frequent within the home, may well be to teach the child how not to confront an issue and how to remain stupid about things, issues and people.

There is another interpretation to these results. Perhaps there is a general language problem within the families of learning-disabled children. It is known that there is a correlation between parental academic accomplishment and children's accomplishment, for reasons of either genes, and/or example and/or tutorial efforts. Thus, Owen et al. (1971) reported that the parents of the educationally handicapped children had lower high school English grades than comparison parents. In addition, the fathers of these children had lower Wide Range Achievement Test scores than comparison fathers.

In summary, there is mounting evidence that the learning-disabled child experiences a very different social world than does the comparison child. He appears likely to be ignored, at best, and outright rejected, at worst. The controversy as to the causative factors to this social rejection is, so far, marked more by speculation than by data. Considerably more effort should be addressed to the understanding and remediation of the social failures exhibited by these children.

Hyperactivity

We have reviewed the few studies concerning other people's views of the learning-disabled child. But research into the behavior of disabled children has not been simply limited to the social status of such children. Perhaps the central characteristic associated with the learning-disabled child is that of hyperactivity. Virtually any discussions or readings about learning-disabled children indicate that a "hard sign" of such disabilities is hyperactivity. What have researchers determined about hyperactivity? Before discussing some investigations addressed to this matter, a few caveats should be issued. First, there is no doubt that some children are more active than others in some situations. Apparently, reliable diagnoses of children along the dimension of hyperactivity can be made (Keogh, 1971). But the issue is not whether some children are hyperactive (some no doubt are), but rather whether learning-disabled children or their categorical cousins, brain-damaged children, are hyperactive. That children vary on activity levels there can be no doubt. The issue is whether learning-disabled children are more active than nondisabled children. Is hyperactivity a "hard sign" indicating the presence of a learning deficit?

The fact that peers of learning-disabled children do not perceive them as more active has already been mentioned. But other attempts have been made to assess the presence and the correlates of activity in disabled children, typically brain-damaged children. Data concerning the activity level of brain-damaged children is important to the learning disability specialist insofar as the assumption of the association of hyperactivity and learning disabilities is apparently well accepted.

Motor Activity

An ingenious study of motor activity in brain-injured children was conducted by Pope (1970). The study was undertaken

133

with the realization that we have little quantification of levels of activity of children during their early school years. How can we say a child is too much or too little of something if we have no normative data?

Pope studied the activity level of two groups of children, each consisting of nineteen boys. One group consisted of children diagnosed as suffering from some form of brain injury; the other group was comprised of children with no damage. The children were between the ages of 7 and 11. So that differences between groups would not be obscured, drug treatment was suspended several days prior to the administration of the tests. Children were observed in four different situations: *a)* when they were assigned to do a simple task and *b)* a difficult task, *c)* when they were in an undirected play situation and *d)* when they were instructed to refrain from moving. The child's activity was measured by an accelerometer, a device developed by Scholman, Kaspar and Throne (1965). The accelerometer is an automatically winding calendar wrist watch modified in such a way that there is a direct drive from the pendulum to the hands of the watch. Two of these devices were used for each child, one attached to a hand, the other to a foot. In addition, activity was assessed by a behavior recorder, a keyboard device for recording direct visual observations. The experimental area was a hospital ward in which the floor area was divided into four equal zones by means of tape. Each of these four areas contained identical equipment and toys. In the undirected play situation, the child was allowed to play in the playroom. The simple task situation to which the child was exposed was the administration of the Sequin Form Board test, a test in which the child is asked to place objects into an appropriate hole within a wooden board. For the difficult task, the child was asked to complete the Sequin Form Board test while the board was at an angle. Finally, the child was asked to sit quietly without leaving his seat for a period of five minutes. All other situations lasted for a 15-minute period. Children were observed through a one-way vision mirror. The activity recorded included the movement of the child across the zones, and within zones, and such behaviors as standing, sitting and contact with available toys.

The results were somewhat dependent upon the situation in which the child was assessed, but generally indicated the following. When children were in a free play situation, brain-damaged children showed more gross motor activity and less attention to particular toys than did the control children. When a task demand, whether simple or difficult, essentially constrains movement in space, brain-damaged children are likely to show more energy expenditures within the space limits allowed. They will not leave the task to run in an open space, but will tend to show more movements and greater energy expenditures in the vicinity of the task than will control children. Finally, when instructed to inhibit motor behaviors, to sit still in a chair, the brain-damaged are less likely to demonstrate such inhibitions than are nonbrain-damaged children. It should be noted, however, that the children did persist in completing the task even though motor movements during the task situation were evident. It should also be noted that many of the brain-damaged children were less active than were the nondamaged ones. While there is some reason, then, to believe that brain-damaged children may show evidence of hyperactivity, such behavior may not be so strongly associated with brain damage or so infrequently associated with nonda-maged children as to warrant it useful in individual diagnosis. Moreover, it should be remembered that this evidence does not directly support the hypothesis that learning-disabled children will be hyperactive.

Distractibility

The question as to other behaviors which might be associated with hyperactivity has also received some attention. For example, is hyperactivity associated with stupidity, distractibility or short attention spans? A now classic study of the behavioral correlates of hyperactivity was conducted by Scholman, Kaspar and Throne (1965). These investigators conducted an extensive study of the behavior of brain-damaged children in laboratory and commonplace settings. The children were between 11 and 14 years of age, obtained IQ scores ranging from 46 to 87 and lived in a residential school or attended a day school. These investigators administered a battery of standard clinical measures, such as the Wechsler Intelligence Scale for Children and the Bender-Gestalt tests. The children's activity was measured for three days by attaching two actometers or accelerometers to each child. Distractibility of the brain-damaged child, presumably a characteristic of the learning disabled as well, was assessed by the child's performance on four laboratory tests. One, the clock test, required the child to press a lever at the appropriate instant to prevent a mechanical mouse, which was moving around the clock, from being "trapped." The second assessment device, the box test, demanded that the child indicate the shape, color or position of one of three boxes out of which a puppet popped at varying intervals. Third, a card test required the child to indicate whenever the picture of a baby appeared in a deck of 200 picture cards rapidly presented. Finally, a tone test was administered wherein the child was presented with a tape recording of various tones. The child's task was to indicate when a particular tone was presented.

This investigation was unique in several respects. First, the authors employed a multitude of measures to assess the same concept. Given imperfection of any one measure, the use of many measures lends greater confidence to any results obtained (Webb, Campbell, Schwartz and Sechrest, 1966). The assessment of activity across situations provides information concerning the generality of the findings. Questions were asked whether distractibility and hyperactivity were correlated with each other, or whether one or the other was correlated with neurological signs and psychometric test scores. Some very surprising results were obtained. First, hyperactivity and distractibility are not general traits of the child; children show marked variations in both, given changes in the situation and task. Second, these two measures do not correlate with one another. The presence of hyperactivity does not guarantee the presence of distractibility. Third, the presence of neurological signs is likely to be correlated with *hypo,* not hyper, activity. In their summary of the results, the authors indicated that:

... individual diagnostic measures employed are not sufficiently reliable to be acceptable. . . . Measures used to measure "brain damage" do not co-vary significantly and tend instead to be separable into at least two loose types of measures. . . . Only one set of behaviors correlates significantly with both the diagnostic clusters and that correlation is in the wrong direction (1965, p. 74).

One response to the negative findings of this study is to conclude that brain damage, hyperactivity, distractibility as syndromes or even as problems are figments of someone's imagination. Many professionals did turn their backs on the business of syndromes and brain damage as such. But let us reexamine the data. Each of these behaviors, hyperactivity and distractibility, were measured using different techniques. Each should be further evaluated as separate constructs, both complex and multidimensional. In the case of the distractibility measures, the child had to respond quickly and had to respond verbally or motorically. Not only was the child's ability to attend to a puppet or mouse being evaluated, but also his ability to organize himself motorically in order to respond by pressing a lever, pointing to a card or naming colors and shapes. Distractibility as assessed in this study would appear to be more related to the ability to call up words quickly, the ability to respond to a visual or auditory stimulus with a motor response and the ability to sequentially order these responses. In retrospect, it appears unreasonable to assume that such diverse behaviors and abilities would be correlated. It is now unforgivable that professionals, in this day and age, continue to talk about brain-damaged and/or learning-disabled children possessing personality characteristics as global as distractibility or hyperactivity.

Types of Hyperactivity

To date we have used the word hyperactivity to represent some unitary dimension residing in the person rather than being affected by both the person and the situation. The use and overuse of the term have made it imperative to take a much closer look at the meaning of the term. Several specialists have suggested that children might be usefully categorized into various types of hyperactive behavior. For example, Denckla (1973) has suggested three types of hyperactive behavior and has hypothesized, apparently on the basis of clinical observations, that various types of hyperactivity might respond differentially to various drugs. Denckla suggests that there are three different types of hyperactivity, only one of which will respond favorably to drug intervention. One type is characterized by the child demonstrating anxious, aggressive, destructive, unpredictable and impulsive behavior, a kind of demonic emotionality. A second type of hyperactivity is that in which the child is placid, sweet, socially gauche, flits about aimlessly while accomplishing little and is motorically clumsy. Neither of these types of children, according to Denckla, will respond well to drugs employed to alter their hyperactive behaviors. The third type of child is described as "on the go," very verbal and talkative, a happy child who fails to act his age, and a fidgety one who "thinks out loud" (p. 446). This type of child is described as responding well to the drug Ritalin.

Solomons (1971) has suggested that it would be heuristic to devise a classification scheme where finer differentiation is made with regard to hyperactivity. He suggests four categories. A child might show *hypokinesis,* a chronic low level of energy expenditure. Or he might demonstrate *fidgetiness,* constantly moving parts of the body while not locomoting in space. The third category is termed *overactivity.* The child does not stay in place the usual length of time. Finally, the category *hyperkinetic impulsive* is suggested to describe the impulsive, distractible, irritable and hyperexcitable child. Solomons' categories reflect a one dimensional scale ranging from low to high activity as he defines them. The scale may or may not be useful for the researcher or practitioner. Solomons, like Denckla, relates categories to the efficacy of types of drug intervention. He suggests that the hyperkinetic impulsive type of child may show behavioral improvement when treated by an amphetamine, while the fidgety type is more responsive to a tranquilizer.

A word of caution is in order. Clinical observations, apparently the data base for both Denckla and Solomons, are often fruitful generators of useful hypotheses to be tested, but they are notoriously poor sources of data. The observations of Denckla and Solomons need and certainly deserve further investigations. For example, neither investigator has presented evidence pertaining to the reliability of judgments when their particular classification systems are employed. Even with training, will people agree as to whether a particular child is overactive or fidgety, or flits about aimlessly but is not destructive? Indeed, the question remains as to whether any type of hyperactivity is independent of any other type of hyperactivity. Are destructive hyperactive children verbal children as well? Maybe yes, maybe no. This is an empirical matter and before any typology of hyperactivity can be accepted, independence of the types from one another needs to be demonstrated. Warnings aside, both Denckla and Solomons have made an important point, buttressed by research. It is time to refine the global concept of hyperactivity and to focus upon the specific behaviors which lead audiences to infer the presence of hyperactivity. Once this is done, then the relationships between such acts can be determined, and the concepts of hyperactivity will begin to take on additional meaning and utility.

✔ Characteristics of Hyperactivity

The focus of this discussion on hyperactivity has been whether brain-damaged children and, by inference, learning-disabled children demonstrate hyperactivity, and whether hyperactivity in such children is associated with other behaviors. There is yet another question which pertains to the characteristics of hyperactive children. When you have hyperactive children, what else do you have? Two frequently mentioned characteristics associated with hyperactivity are difficulty in learning abstract concepts and rigidity in thinking. One method of assessing rigidity is evaluating the child's ability to switch from one form of behavior under one reward condition to another form of behavior in order to obtain further rewards. Freibergs and Douglas (1969) undertook to investigate the validity of these two assumptions. These investigators conducted a laboratory study of the performance of hyperactive and nonhyperactive children on two types of concept problems under a variety of reinforcement conditions. There were 65 hyperactive children, as defined by psychiatrists in concurrence with parents and school authorities, and 99 children who were judged not to be hyperactive. Children in both groups ranged in age from 6 to 11, were not under drug or psychiatric treatment and demonstrated comparable performance within the normal range on the vocabulary subtest of the Wechsler Intelligence Test for Children.

The child was seated before a screen on which two pictures could be projected. The child was asked to select one of the two pictures and to indicate selection by pressing one of two levers. If the choice was correct, he would obtain a marble as a reward. There were four concept problems, each represented by a set of 150 pairs of stimuli. Each time a stimulus pair was presented, one stimulus would reflect the correct concept. There were two concepts involving objects, birds and flowers. Additionally, there were two sets on the concept "2," one cued by black figures of different geometric shapes, the other by different colored dots. Each child was given four sessions and was tested until he either could make ten consecutive correct responses or until he had a maximum of 300 trials per concept. The number of trials the child took to reach the standard of ten correct consecutive choices served as a measure of his ability to learn abstract concepts. Following this learning procedure, the basis upon which the child received the reward was reversed. Rather than being rewarded for selecting a bird from a pair of stimuli, he would be rewarded for selecting the stimulus other than a bird. The number of trials which the child took to reach the standard in the new learning situation served as an index of his rigidity. The investigators also studied the effects of different schedules of reward. Some children were rewarded every time they made a correct response, others only part of the time they made such choices (the partial reinforcement group, PR), and others every time they made a correct choice but only after a delay of eight seconds.

In terms of the learning of the concepts, the results presented by Freibergs and Douglas indicated that the hyperactive and normal children learned at different rates only under conditions of partial reinforcement. That is, when rewards were given after every trial, even after a delay of time, both the hyperactive and the normal children learned at the same rate. When the children only occasionally received rewards for their correct choices, normal children were able to learn more rapidly than were hyperactive children. In fact, while normal children slowly improved under conditions of occasional reinforcement, the hyperactive children showed decreases in their performance over trials under such reward conditions, results which essentially paralleled those reported by Palkes, Stewart and Kahana (1968) and Palkes, Stewart and Freedman (1971).

The authors explored possible explanations for this finding. They pointed out that an explanation of differences in memory fails to explain the group difference. Under delayed reinforcement the subjects had to wait twice as long, eight seconds compared to four, for the next stimulus to appear. Had memory been a critical factor, the performance of the hyperactive children should have been inferior, but such was not the case. The group differences were related to the reinforcement conditions. Freibergs and Douglas hypothesized that hyperactive children have a higher than average sensitivity to the frustration effects of nonreward and thus abandon attempts to solve the problems sooner.

It should be noted that when groups were matched on the basis of their original learning, there were no differences between the hyperactive and nonhyperactive child in assessments of rigidity. There was no support from this experiment for assumptions underlying the hyperactive child's difficulty in learning abstract concepts or his rigidity of thinking processes. It appears that the hyperactive child will show difficulties in learning under conditions where reinforcements for correct responses are occasional rather than continuous. A reasonable hypothesis offered by the authors is that the hyperactive child's difficulty in learning reflects motivational rather than intellectual difficulties. A reasonable implication of these results is that reinforcement may well serve to keep the child's attention to the task rather than to the irrelevant features of the situation. Perhaps teachers should be particularly sensitive to reward correct responses from the hyperactive child on every occasion, a condition not necessary for the learning of the nonhyperactive child.

In summary, it appears clear that the learning-disabled child is confronted with a social world in which he is disliked, at worst, or ignored, at best, by his peers, classroom teachers and even, perhaps, his parents. Moreover, there is evidence to suggest that he has difficulty in understanding subtle messages concerning adults' affective states, a lack which might well be expected to lead to social rejection. It is increasingly obvious that it is a grave error to assume that the social world of the learning-disabled child is either benign or comparable to that of the nondisabled one. The data pertaining to the social rejection of the learning-disabled child appear to have important implications for the contemporary style of providing remediation while allowing the child to remain in regular classrooms (*i.e.*, mainstreaming). While the mainstreaming approach might ultimately be more desirable than segregated classrooms, the possibility that the learning-disabled child will be rejected by peers and teachers alike should not be overlooked.

In spite of the emphasis of the concept of hyperactivity as a "hard sign" of learning disabilities, it is becoming increasingly clear that hyperactivity may or may not be associated with brain damage, brain damage may or may not be associated with learning disabilities and hyperactivity may or may not be associated with learning problems. Children who are hyperactive are not hyperactive all the time, or in all situations or under all motivational conditions. In fact, we do not have a good definition of hyperactivity and there are many behaviors which are called hyperactive which may or may not be indicative of anything else. The characteristics which have, through folklore, become associated with hyperactivity, such as rigidity or concrete thinking, have not been found to be so when systematically studied.

Finally, evidence concerning such situational variables as teacher tolerance, task difficulty and social reinforcement is sparse. Yet, to understand the behavior of the learning-disabled child, these situational variables must be explored and their impact upon behavior detailed.

CHAPTER
7
INFORMATION
PROCESSING

The most important new theoretical concept is that of a human being as a sampler of the information around him. . . . We are born into a world of constantly fluctuating stimulation. We sample from this flux, we do not experience it totally. We formulate ideas about our sampled "bits." We construct expectations and concepts. We test these concepts in various ways, and often revise them on the basis of our tests. . . . (Farnham-Diggory, 1972, p. xxxi).

Emphasis upon how children process information in their attempt to know the world about them has been the heart and soul of the field of learning disabilities. Theories, assessment techniques and remediation programs have often been addressed to the role of children's perceptions and memory in academic performance. Assessments are made concerning the differential effectiveness the child might exhibit in processing or understanding visual or auditory signals, and remediation attempts are directed toward improving the child's ability to process information in the deficit sensory channel. Lying behind these efforts is the implicit belief that the learning-disabled child is particularly deficient in the reception, coding or retrieval of information presented to him in a particular sensory channel.

The behavior of concern in information processing consists of all sorts of things. Attention, perception, labeling of perceptions, storage of perceptions and the connection and integration of information perceived in different modalities all fall under the general topic of information processing. Virtually all cognitive activities from sensation to language are included.

There are certain assumptions frequently made concerning information processing. One is that there is a developmental sequence in the acquisition of skills used for processing information presented through various channels. For instance, it has been assumed that children learn in one modality (auditory or visual) *before* they learn to integrate information presented in both modalities. A second assumption is that the crux of the learning-disabled child's difficulty is a breakdown in information processing and that the more specific the identification of that breakdown, the more useful the analysis. Care is taken to diagnose the degree to which memory problems reflect a deficiency in remembering information presented auditorily (auditory memory) or visually (visual memory). A third assumption is that effective treatment can be initiated when an information processing deficiency has been specified. These assumptions have underestimated the complexity of information processing.

The remainder of this chapter will be devoted to a discussion of auditory, visual and cross-modal integration. Information will be presented concerning the developmental sequence, assessment techniques and general research data in each of these areas.

Auditory Processing

The detection of the signal is the first step in making sense out of what is heard. Although signal detection occurs prior to information processing, it is important for the learning disability specialist to be sensitive to problems of acuity. The lack of awareness by diagnositicians concerning the distinction between acuity and comprehension have produced misdiagnoses which have caused no small amount of pain to all concerned. Acuity problems are easily misinterpreted as problems associated with the processing of auditory information. As a result deaf children have been misdiagnosed and treated as mentally retarded, emotionally disturbed or aphasic (DiCarlo, 1960; Reichstein and Rosenstein, 1964).

Hearing acuity is assessed by an audiometer, an instrument which permits assessment of the capacity to hear different sound frequencies (pitch) at different decibel (loudness) levels under different sound conditions (pure tones, words). A screening assessment of children's hearing is typically performed within the schools at periodic intervals. Most people are acquainted with "flat" hearing losses in which the child can hear various pitches if they are presented loudly enough. Thus, they can hear both high frequency sounds, such as *s, f* and *t,* and low frequency sounds, such as *m, n* and *b,* when these sounds are presented loudly. But there are other kinds of hearing losses in which the child or adult can hear some sounds but not others. In "nonflat" hearing deficits, the child may respond appropriately when some sounds are quite soft and not respond to sounds that are quite loud. For example, a child may not hear the *s, f* and *t* presented reasonably loudly, but will hear the low frequency sounds.

When teachers and parents are unaware of a problem of hearing acuity, the child is likely to be misunderstood, because his responses in school and home settings appear erratic and unpredictable. Consider, for example, the child trying to do phonics and spelling when he cannot hear the difference between *f* and *s.* The child who hears part of the message may signal his confusion by constantly asking for a repeat of the message, withdrawing, responding incorrectly or waiting until he can observe his classmates and imitate them as best he can.

It is not difficult to detect a severely hearing-impaired child or to recognize that if a hearing problem is suspected, the child should be referred for a hearing test. But it is considerably more difficult to distinguish between a hard of hearing and a learning-disabled youngster. A hearing test may well resolve the issue of whether the child is hearing impaired or not, provided that he does not have a fluctuating hearing loss because of recurring infections or seasonally based allergies. But a hearing test may not resolve the issue when the child cannot or will not respond to the test itself. What is one to make of a child who fails to

respond when he hears (or does not hear) a bleep from the audiometer? Suppose the child has a severe language problem and is
not easily understood. Thus, a difficult differential diagnosis is
that of discriminating an aphasic from a hard of hearing child.
Goldstein, Landau and Kleffner (1960) examined 183 children
who were diagnosed as aphasic or deaf. They reported that there
were few etiological categories which helped distinguish these
two groups of children. Of the children labeled aphasic, 32% did
not exhibit neurological abnormalities, and about 40% of both
the aphasic and deaf children had abnormal electroencephalo-
grams. Moreover, it should be noted that the presence of a hearing loss does not preclude an aphasia in a child. Merklein and
Briskey (1962) assessed the hearing of children with aphasia and
found that many such children did suffer from a high-frequency
(high pitch) hearing loss. The conscientious teacher should be
sensitive to the fact that hearing problems often cause school
related problems.

Auditory Perception

Auditory perception has been defined as:

A system specialized for dealing with temporally (serially organized) stimulus
patterns. To the extent that verbal symbolic system is linked to the auditory
sensory modality, it must be characterized as a sequential processing system.
. . . [The] verbal system is also sequentially organized as a symbolic system by
virtue of its syntactical nature; the grammar of a language involves a temporal
ordering of its elements. All language has a form which requires us to string out
ideas even though their objects rest one within the other. . . . There is flexibility
in the sequential ordering but . . . the information conveyed depends on what
came before and what is yet to come in the sequence. . . . (Paivio, 1971, p. 33).

Learning in the classroom, or in any situation which involves
responding to sounds, requires the child to be able to sort the
auditory signal into meaningful units, order these units temporally, remember them and respond appropriately. Classroom activities, particularly responding to teacher instructions, require
the child to listen to what the teacher says, produce the appropriate response, and to do so easily, quickly and automatically

(Rosner, 1973). The child must perceive the message, select the salient details and produce a response. The complexity of the process depends upon the meaningfulness of the verbal units being used, as well as the length of the message and the task demanded of the child. It is one thing for a child to be directed to get his coat and quite another for him to process a long series of instructions, presented in complex sentences, which demand a serial performance. The child who does not process this type of information quickly and as well as his peers finds himself expending an inordinate amount of time and energy trying to make sense out of what is heard and the implications of this message for what he is to do. At the perceptual level auditory information processing demands that the child attend, receive, discriminate and remember the signals as long as the task requires. The ability to do this is measured by the appropriateness of the verbal or motoric responses. One approach to understanding children's auditory information processing is to consider the tests developed for assessment of problem children and the resulting intervention programs. Perceiving sounds is measured by the child's ability to assign appropriate meanings to the sounds presented, memory span for sounds, ability to discriminate differences and similarities across sounds, skill in sequencing a string of sounds and comprehension of others' speech. All of these behaviors have been the targets of diagnosticians.

Assumptions Concerning Auditory Processing

There are at least three important assumptions concerning these behaviors which should be noted. The first is that each of these behaviors is thought to represent or to be part of the auditory processing system. This suggests that if one of these behaviors is measured, generalizations concerning other behaviors within the auditory processing system can be made. For example, if the child shows a deficiency in memory span, the assumption can be made that he will be likely to show less adequate responses in discriminating sounds, sequencing sounds, comprehending others or assigning appropriate meanings to the auditory inputs. The second assumption is that these defects are associated with and indeed contribute substantially to inadequate school performance. The third assumption is that remediation is facilitated by training the child on tasks which include only stimuli and responses within the auditory modality. It is thought that to train a child to learn a list of words, he should hear the words and be required to speak the words. Both the input and output are within one modality. This is believed preferable to having the child see the words and then speak them where the input modality differs from the output modality (Johnson and Myklebust, 1967).

Children with learning disabilities have been noted to have difficulties on some of these tasks, but the reliability of the second assumption has not been fully established. For instance, auditory discrimination of sounds is commonly assessed by having the child indicate whether two words sound the same or different (Wepman, 1958). Some children will perform poorly on this task, and presumably such children are thought to have deficiencies in their auditory processing (not just their ability to discriminate sounds). Wood (1971) found, however, that while discrimination of sounds was correlated with the child's age and his verbal intelligence, it was not correlated with the child's committing speech distortions, substitutions or omissions. Wood then raises some question as to whether these various measures actually do assess a single process or whether these behaviors are diverse and relatively uncorrelated with one another. A question is raised then about the first assumption. But if these measures do not correlate with one another, how good is one measure in predicting school achievement? While it is clearly an empirically answerable question, as it stands now, assumption two rests more on faith than fact.

The third assumption, that remediation efforts involving deficits in auditory processing are best treated by focusing upon inputs and outputs which involve auditory activity, has also been challenged. Brooks (1958) found that the use of a verbal response system to facilitate short-term memory of sounds interfered with the child's acquisition of the material. It was found that a child's learning of sounds was assisted by having him commit a response based upon visual inputs (*i.e.,* having him point). The implication is that learning is facilitated if the child can use different information channels to receive and respond. This really should not be very surprising, since memory is intimately tied to the child's ability to make meaningful associations to the stimulus. However these associations are made, whether through visual or auditory cues or responses, meaningful associations should improve memory (Underwood, 1964). Although much progress has been made toward understanding auditory processing, how responses are associated, if indeed they are, and how the learning-disabled child might be helped to better master his social and academic skills through modality training, have yet to be completely determined.

Irrespective of the adequacy of current conceptions about the auditory processing system, it is important for parents and teachers alike to have some notions concerning the appropriate development of the processing of auditorily presented stimuli. The developmental sequence involved has been outlined by Zigmond and Cicci (1968). The authors indicated that the area of the brain considered critical in at least one aspect of auditory processing of information, Broca's area, matures later than brain areas which control other kinds of motor movements. Not until the infant is 17 months old does Broca's area reach the anatomical differentiation observed to exist in other motor centers by 11 months of age. According to Zigmond and Cicci, the infant can discriminate the sounds around him by five to six months of age. At this time the infant can distinguish familiar and unfamiliar sounds and can localize sounds outside his visual field. By 8 months of age the infant responds to "no-no," can imitate speech sounds and the intonations of another's voice. By 12 months the child can stop an activity upon hearing "no" (should he so decide) and can follow simple commands. By 15 to 17 months the child can respond to "give me that" when the request is accompanied by a gesture and can point to body parts such as the nose, eyes and hair.

A rapid increase in the ability of the child to comprehend language follows. These are integrated with expressive language development as the child learns to appropriately say and combine strings of words. By two years of age a child can select objects which others name. By age 2½, the child can identify objects by their use, and by age 3, the child recognizes the names of colors, adjectives like *big* and *little,* and can follow simple commands which use prepositions. A child, by age 2, can reproduce 2 digits; by 3 years, 3 digits; by 4, 4 digits. Memory for short sentences appears about age 4. These are simple yardsticks to assess whether or not auditory information processing and receptive language development are progressing at expected developmental rates.

Testing Auditory Perception

There are a variety of means by which to assess auditory perception. At the preschool age, informal observations can be made of the child's responses to sound making toys, responses to auditory signals from different areas of the room and by noting whether the child associates a sound with an event *(e.g.,* the ringing of a telephone with the object telephone). Can the child discriminate familiar voices, does he respond to simple commands, such as "give me," or "show me"? Learning disability specialists and the classroom teacher can also make informal assessments. For example, to assess the child's auditory discrimination (skill in distinguishing sounds), the teacher may ask the child to repeat words and take note of his inaccuracies in pronunciation (Stephens, 1970). If the child incorrectly pronounces the word, then it is possible that the sounds are not being correctly discriminated. Of course, the error may also be due to a hearing acuity problem, or a problem in the child's simply getting his tongue to mind his brain. At least the teacher should be alerted to the presence of a problem which should be more systematically assessed. Teachers can also informally assess auditory memory, both of immediate and delayed recall. Immediate recall can be assessed by having the child repeat a series of numbers or words immediately after hearing them. Delayed recall, obviously important to academic achievement, might be assessed by having the child hear a short story on which his recall is later tested (Stephens, 1970). Obviously, all of these informal methods, and indeed most of the standardized ones which will be discussed, are quite imperfect. Children's reproductions can be affected by many things, notably familiarity with or interest in the material being presented. But like the story of the gambler who played on the rigged roulette wheel because it was the only wheel in town, the learning disability specialist, like other professionals, must often use far from perfect methods in an attempt to understand the child.

Standardized tests of intelligence, achievement and specific diagnostic techniques tap the various components of auditory information processing. Items on the Cattell Infant Intelligence Scale (Cattell, 1947), the Wechsler Intelligence Scale for Children (Wechsler, 1949) and the Stanford-Binet Intelligence Test (Terman and Merrill, 1960) assess the child's ability to comprehend and express auditorily received material. Many assessments are indirect insofar as they measure language rather than simple responses to auditory signals. But any test which requires a child to respond verbally is, after all, tapping auditory processes. By way of example, items on the Binet from the two- to five-year-old levels ask the child to identify objects by name, by use and identify pictures of objects by use. Evaluation is based on the ability to follow directions, to use words in combination and the rote memory for increasingly lengthy spans of numbers.

In addition to informal techniques and intelligence tests, there are a variety of standardized tests designed specifically for the assessment of a child's auditory information processing. There are essentially three areas of auditory processing which have been of interest to learning disability specialists: auditory reception, auditory discrimination, and auditory memory.

Auditory reception tasks assess the degree to which children understand what is told them. Do they comprehend verbal messages? Initial assessment should have established that the child is neither retarded nor hearing impaired; yet many children do not comprehend relatively simple verbal inputs. Thus, in administering the Illinois Test of Psycholinguistic Ability (ITPA), the

151

examiner reads a short statement to the child and the child is required to respond "yes" or "no" to the sense of the statement (Kirk, McCarthy and Kirk 1968). On another subtest the child is required to fill in the final word to complete a short verbal statement given him.

Auditory discrimination refers to the child's ability to recognize whether symbols heard are alike or different. The most well-known test for such an ability is the Wepman Test of Auditory Discrimination (1958). In this test, the child indicates whether two words sound the same or different. In a laboratory setting, a child may be asked to indicate the similarity of tones (Dykman et al., 1971).

Auditory memory is measured by the child's ability to repeat verbally a series of words or numbers immediately after the examiner. The Digit Span subtest on the Weschler Intelligence Scale for Children (WISC) requires the child to repeat a series of numbers orally presented to him. This is presumed to assess his auditory memory. The ITPA and the Stanford-Binet Intelligence Test also include such tasks. The Detroit Test of Learning Aptitude (Baker and Leland, 1935) has subtests in which the child is asked to repeat words and sentences, and to follow verbally presented orders by the tester. These tests are measures of immediate, short-term memory in which the child is asked to repeat words or digits immediately after hearing them. His adequacy in doing this is related to the number of units, the rate with which the verbal units are presented, the meaningfulness of these units and the child's attentiveness during the task.

We have, for purposes of illustration, mentioned some standardized tests which have been designed to assess these particular forms of auditory information processing. It would be remiss, however, not to point out that simply designing a task to measure an event is not the same as measuring it. The tests referred to may or may not have validity in detecting auditory processing and may or may not be applicable to particular groups of children. The ITPA, for example, appears to have reasonably good reliabilities among the subtests and may also differentiate deficits in the auditory and visual areas. However, its use with children other than middle-class whites is likely to be unwise, since few such children were included in the original standardization. Information as to what to expect in the performance of the black or Spanish-speaking child is relatively absent. Moreover, the original form of the test has been shown to be influenced by examiner characteristics, so it is likely that a child's scores on the tests will not only reflect some ability on his part but the nature of the examiner as well (Chase, 1972; Carroll, 1972).

The Digit Span subtest of the Wechsler Intelligence Scale for Children is also reported to have rather low reliabilities, and for the 10½ and 13½ year old child it has the lowest reliabilities of all subtests (Wechsler, 1949). Thus, individual diagnosis of auditory memory by this subtest alone is not warranted.

As is evident, neither informal nor formal methods of assessing a child's auditory information processing tell us much about process. These methods are not "pure tests" but may be contaminated by the child's school learning, his skill in reproducing sounds which may reflect not auditory processing but his ability to talk, or by other activities he may be involved in between the time the inputs are made and the reproductions required. The tests may tell us about stable differences between children which may affect their classroom performance, whatever the source of the differences. To better understand the processing of auditory information, laboratory experiments are an important source of information. The results of some of these experiments will now be reviewed.

There are many ways to study auditory processing within the laboratory. Studies have typically employed one of three techniques in attempts to understand this process. One technique used to study the developmental sequence of processing complex auditory stimuli is to present some auditory stimulus (words, tones, or numbers) masked by background noise (Impellizzeri, 1967). This procedure is particularly relevant to learning disabilities, because it is believed that learning-disabled children may be unusually distracted by environmental noise. This method is concerned with the child's ability to focus upon the relevant auditory signals and to exclude attention to masking sounds.

A second method involves lengthening the time intervals between parts of words and thereby disrupting the hearing of a chain of sounds as a word. Instead of words, the child hears isolated sounds. His task is to put the sounds together. This method is an analogue to phonics learning. The learning-disabled child, with an auditory processing problem, may have more difficulty in integrating these sounds into a meaningful unit than will the nonlearning-disabled child.

The third method employed is to present two words which are very similar in sound and require the child to make a discrimination between them. This method is an auditory discrimination task.

Several studies have outlined the development of auditory processing. Impellizzeri studied five- to eight-year-old boys and girls who were free of any apparent abnormalities. Words which were partially erased were presented to these children. Sometimes these partially erased words were presented closely in time, sometimes not. Subjects were asked to indicate the words presented, initially by repeating the word heard, later to both repeat the word and point to a picture which identified the word. Impellizzeri found that older children were more likely to give the correct response than younger ones.

In another study, Maccoby and Konrad (1966) employed a dichotic listening procedure in which normal kindergarten, second- and fourth-grade children heard on some occasions two voices presented to both ears or, on other occasions, each voice presented to a different ear. Subjects were to repeat the word spoken by one voice. These investigators found that correct responses were more frequent for the older than younger child and that for both the young and the old children, the dichotic listening condition was easier than when both voices were presented to both ears. Children did show the effects of practice, improving in their performance as their opportunity to perform increased. In addition, children show fewer errors when presented multisyllable words than single syllable ones. Children become more familiar with words as they age and are consequently better able to process auditory inputs as a function of this familiarity.

Age effects may be different for children of one social class than for children of another. Peisach (1965) asked first- and fifth-graders from both lower- and middle-class families to produce words which had been deleted from speech samples of teachers and children also of varying social class backgrounds. Her results indicate the complexities involved in auditory information processing. Differences in the performances of children from varying social classes became evident to the fifth graders, but not to the first graders. Hence, with increasing age, social class differences become more significant. Fifth-grade girls performed better on this task than did fifth-grade boys if both boys and girls were from the lower class. Of interest was the general finding that race of the child made little difference in performance. Black and white children, matched for social class, showed no difference in their performances.

It is not surprising that age and social class are associated with adequacy in children's auditory information processing. Of particular interest to the learning disability specialist is the ability of the learning-disabled child to process auditory information. There have been several studies addressed to this concern.

Auditory Signals

Rourke and Czudner (1972) compared normal and brain-damaged children in their attention to auditory signals. The child's task was to press a key with the onset of a high-pitched sound and to release the key when a low-pitched sound was presented. These investigators found that young normal (6 to 9 years) and older children (10 to 13 years), brain damaged and normal, did not differ in their attentiveness to the auditory signals. Young brain-damaged children did evidence difficulty in performing these tasks. Rourke and Czudner hypothesize that the older brain-damaged child has managed to recuperate from his earlier attentional deficits.

Grassi (1970) did not find such recuperation when he assessed the performance of brain-damaged adolescents and compared them to their peers who were deemed either as normal or as evidencing behavior problems. In this study, subjects were asked to record each time an auditory signal was presented. Grassi found that normal children performed best on this task, followed by behavior-disordered children, with the brain-damaged children doing least adequately. From this study, then, evidence is forthcoming that brain-damaged children, even as late as adolescence, have relatively more difficulty in attending to auditory tasks than do nonbrain-damaged children. Factors other than brain damage influence attention as indicated by the finding that behavior-disordered children did appreciably worse than normal children.

Other sources of evidence also point to the difficulty of learning-disabled children in dealing with auditorily presented information. Dykman et al. (1971) in a series of studies, compared the performances of learning-disabled and normal children in their ability to discriminate sounds for purposes of obtaining a reward. The task required children to attend to the tones, to remember which of the tones led to a reward and which did not and to remember what to do when they heard the tones. The results reveal that brain-damaged children had greater difficulty than normal children in discriminating the tones, were less able to follow instructions and were less able to profit from practice in learning how they could receive the reward. McReynolds (1966) found that aphasic children 4 to 8 years of age were less able to discriminate sounds and showed slower improvement with practice than normal children when discrimination had to be made with sounds embedded in the context of nonsense syllables. A simple auditory perceptual problem in the aphasic was not evidenced, rather the performance deterioration was a function of the complexity of the auditory signal presented. Doehring and Rabinovitch (1969), using very different methods and samples, also arrived at a similar conclusion based upon their results.

Short-term Memory

Connors, Kramer and Guerra (1969) investigated the role of short-term memory in word synthesis in a comparison of learning-disabled and normal children. Short-term memory was measured by children's ability to remember numbers presented to them on a dichotic listening task. Auditory synthesis was assessed by the children's ability to indicate the correct word which had been presented to them in elements. While learning-disabled children performed significantly less adequately on the word synthesis task, little difference was found between the groups on the dichotic listening task. These investigators concluded that short-term memory problems are not critical to deficits in auditory processing as assessed by the word synthesis method.

A comparison was made of the ability to learn a list of words presented auditorily by tape recorder and visually by pictures on slides. Bryan (1972) found that both learning-disabled and comparison children learned the list of words with fewer trials when the stimulus was visual. But the learning-disabled children were significantly less adequate than the comparison group learning under both the auditory and the visual treatments.

There are certain results which are pervasive in these research studies even though the researchers use very different tasks, different kinds of samples, and are testing very different hypotheses. First, the learning-disabled child, however defined, does appear to have difficulty in dealing with information presented auditorily. But, by and large, it does not appear that such children find simple discriminations of sounds difficult. Rather, decreases in performance are most evidenced when the auditory information is complex, either because it is associated with masking noise, involves words rather than tones or is embedded in irrelevant stimuli. Second, a pervasive, recurring result reported across studies is the lack of improvement with practice. Learning curves which present the adequacy of performance as a function of the number of learning trials to which the child has been exposed show that the learning-disabled child learns at a slower rate than do comparison children. One implication of this finding is that the learning-disabled subject may not have a qualitatively different means of processing auditory information, but rather may simply be slower in learning from such information. The differences may not be a function of perception or discrimination of sounds, but rather the means by which he can use the information in such a way as to be able to remember it and use it appropriately. It is certainly not clear at this point how the auditory

157

signal is related to those factors which have been found to differentiate the learning-disabled from the normal child.

Remediation

Various suggestions have been offered as to the appropriate remediation techniques for children evidencing auditory difficulties. The suggestions range from offering fairly simple classroom exercises to fairly explicit and elaborate programs. All of the suggestions have one thing in common. No one knows with any degree of certainty that any of them will work, much less just what part of the program might be responsible for whatever improvements might be shown by the child. Like imperfect tests, however, imperfect treatments will have to be tried. After all, children do have difficulties that cannot wait for treatment until science becomes sophisticated regarding them. Until that time does come, the learning disability specialist and the classroom teacher will have to continue to try to help those children in need. It is hoped that the activities prescribed for improving auditory discrimination, memory, attending and sequencing will correct the child's deficit in dealing with the particular training materials and that this correction will be evidenced in other classroom activities which require the same general skills.

A variety of suggestions to help the young child attend to auditory stimuli have been offered (Johnson and Myklebust, 1967; Lerner, 1971; Zigmond and Cicci, 1968). Teachers are encouraged to allow the child to practice listening. They may have the child clap his hands upon hearing one of a number of stimulus sounds, or the child may be requested to tell how many times he heard a sound. Variations in such practice might be created by changing the complexity of the task and by requiring of the child a variety of responses to indicate his detection of the sound. Training children to discriminate one sound from another, to string sounds together, should start at the level of the child. You do not start by demanding discriminations of sounds with which he is unfamiliar. For young children exercises are suggested which try to assist the child in becoming conscious of sounds within his natural environment. Progressions are then made to exercises involving discriminations among consonants and vowels. Activities in rhyming and word games for sounds follow. Initially, the sounds to be discriminated are distinctly different; as the child progresses, finer discriminations are required.

Auditory memory exercises include placing objects in front of the child and instructing him to complete a string of commands. The child can be required to follow a series of commands which revolve around a written exercise. The commands can be taped and the child completes the exercise by following the taped instructions. Some suggest working directly on auditory memory by having the child attempt to increase the number of digits, or words, he can recall at one time. Using nursery rhymes, finger play and poems are considered useful in auditory memory (Lerner, 1971). Relating stories, facts of stories, making up stories are all believed to stimulate better auditory memory.

There is really little evidence to support the efficacy of such exercises in increasing children's academic performance. We don't know whether the exercises work, and if they work, just what their effects will be in increasing the academic performance of the learning-disabled child. It is our bias that remediation focus on teaching the child that academic related behavior in which he is deficient. For instance, if the child appears to have difficulty comprehending teacher instructions when these are presented before the entire class, activities should be devised to assist this child in comprehension of speech and language under similar circumstances. Tape recording of the teacher's voice and peer voices with background noise could be used for treatment. The focus of the exercise then is not upon improving auditory memory or sequencing or some particular skill, but rather in improving the behavior which is causing the child difficulty by using tasks and situations most similar to those surrounding the deficit. A model of this approach has been developed by Lindamood and Lindamood (1969) for remediation of reading difficulties. The program is designed to help the child understand the sounds of our language and to learn to associate sounds in sequences with patterns of syllables and words. The child is additionally taught the correspondence of oral patterns and the graphic symbol patterns (written words) which are used to represent them.

Consonants and vowels are grouped according to similarities in mouth formation and the child is taught labels to facilitate the association between the formation and the letter. Examples are "lip poppers" for *p* and *b;* "scrapers" for *k* and *g.* In a step-by-step progression the child, using colored wooden blocks, is led to make discriminations among sounds. Visual and tactile manipulation of blocks provides practice in tracking the order of sounds presented sequentially. Initially, isolated sounds in short sequences are presented; later longer strings of more complex sound combinations are tried.

To aid the child in associating letters and sounds, games like Bingo are recommended. Such games allow practice of recall of sounds and letters, left-to-right orientation, position in space, start and stop points, order and sequences, plus responses to auditory and visual cues. The child learns to read by working with exercises and games which use auditory, visual and tactile representations of sound and symbol relationships, progressing from single sounds and symbols to complex combinations. There is no focus upon training within a single modality in this program. The emphasis is upon using all the modalities in order to aid the child. A detailed outline of the program has been put into a manual which is available.

While the efficacy of this program and others has not been convincingly demonstrated, it is possible to train young mentally retarded children's listening skills. Ross and Ross (1972) trained one group of educable mentally retarded (EMR) to listen in a training program ten weeks in duration. The program consisted of the children playing games which required "extensive repetition of listening skills," with the experimenters using material and social rewards and peer modeling as aids. In addition, the experimenters paid careful attention to the timing of the verbal instructions given and the task demands made on the child. They reported that the EMR children who went through the training performed more adequately than EMR children not so trained on such tests as story comprehension, following directions, digit span and repeating sentences. A total listening test score, a combination of 10 such tests, was much greater for those EMRs who received the training than those who did not. While it is still not clear what components of the Ross and Ross training program made the difference, it is clear that differences in listening skills were found and that listening to auditory signals is a teachable skill. Noteworthy is the fact they used all modalities, along with a variety of reinforcements, in order to accomplish this.

There is really no reason to believe that deficits in attentional skills and auditory processing of information cannot be remediated. Children do learn these skills. What seems unwise, however, are those remediational efforts which limit themselves to working through and upon but one modality. Remediation efforts should employ, in our opinion, any of the child's skills in affecting the remediation of any particular problem.

Visual Information Processing

Our eyes are general purpose instruments for feeding the brain with comparatively undoctored information, while the eyes of animals possessing simple brains are more elaborate, for they filter out information which is not essential to their survival, or usable by the simple brain. It is this freedom to make new inferences from sensory data which allows us to discover and see so much more than other animals. . . . We do not perceive the world merely from the sensory information available at any given time, but rather we use this information to test hypotheses of what lies before us (R. L. Gregory cited by Farnham-Diggory, 1972, p. 411).

Visual perception, understanding a visual stimulus and perceptual-motor functions, wherein a complex and coordinated act is performed in response to a visual stimulus, have been theoretically linked to learning disabilities since the conception of the field. Integrating the early work of Werner (1948), Strauss and Lehtinen (1947), and Piaget (1954), various professionals have advocated that learning disabilities are the result of an insufficient development of visual perception and visual perceptual-motor skill, the result of which adversely affects the child's ability to achieve those cognitive skills necessary for adequate academic performance. The perceptual deficit hypothesis has been nurtured, promulgated and sold by both special educators and professionals within the field of vision. There has been widespread consensus regarding the importance of the linkage of visual inputs to motor skills and to cognitive development in affecting the child's academic skills (Cruickshank, 1972; Frostig, 1972; Barsch, 1967; Kephart, 1960; Getman, 1965). It is not surprising that assessment and intervention programs have been developed which are based on this belief.

Before discussing the available data on visual information processing as it applies to the field of learning disabilities, several points need to be made. When people refer to perception and perceptual handicaps, they usually mean visual perception and perceptual-motor inadequacies. Visual perception concerns professionals in a number of fields, such as optometrists, psychologists and educators. Perhaps because of the many professional hats thrown into the perceptual handicap ring, there is a healthy body of data as well as confusion regarding visual information processing. Finally, the same three basic assumptions made about the relevance of auditory information processing are implicitly made about visual information processing. That is, it is often assumed that a defect in one component of the visual processing system implies a deficit in another component, that such deficits are associated with poor academic performance and that remediation is facilitated by training the child on tasks which include only stimuli and responses within the visual modality.

Development of Vision

Before discussing the information concerning the role of vision in affecting learning-disabled children, a brief overview of the general development of vision will be offered. Lawson (1968) summarizes the infant's development of vision in a sequence that is a modification of Worth's and Chavasse's (1959) description.

Age	Visual Acuity	Other Visual Factors
6 weeks		Eyes more mobile. Aware of large objects in line of vision at close range.
8 weeks		Looks down, not up. Momentary fixation. Eyes coordinated fairly well. Likes bright objects.
4 months		Can hold eyes momentarily on object of attention. Recognizes familiar objects and people at near range.
6 months	20/800	Relates self to environment. Develops spatial relationships. Follows moving objects.
9 months	20/200	Inquisitive, reaches, probes. Concentrates attention.
18 months	20/100	Focusing reflex becomes active. Early appreciation of more distant objects.
2 years	20/70	Aware of details in peripheral field of vision. Fusion reflex present, but poorly organized.
3 years	20/40	Fusion reflex established but deteriorates from disuse. Proper orientation of objects in spatial relationship.
4 years	20/30	
5 years	20/25	
6 years	20/20	Fusion reflex and visual acuity.

The developmental sequence indicates that "normal" 20/20 vision is achieved at approximately 6 years of age. In addition to visual acuity, other aspects of vision are also developing. For instance, coordination of the eyes to allow depth perception is not firmly established until a child is 6 years old.

Eye and Learning Disabilities

There are three major parts in the visual processing system: the eye muscles (ocular-musculator); the eye, which among other things acts as a transducer; and the occipital lobe of the cortex, which acts as a visual processor (Chalfant and Scheffelin, 1969). Distinctions must be made between eye defects which have nothing to do with reading, eye defects which may be related to reading efficiency and reading deficits which reflect faulty cognitive management of visually presented information. The role of the vision field grew from concern for visual acuity to much more sophisticated concern for coordination of visual skills and training of such skills to improve cognitive processes.

Examination by an eye practitioner includes a check for acuity, how well a child can see from how far. For normal vision it is necessary to have 20/20 vision or better either uncorrected or corrected by refraction (with glasses) and good stereopsis (both eyes working together to produce a single image to the brain). There are two common types of visual errors, those involving refractive errors and those concerning binocular vision. A refractive error is the result of a defect in the eye lens (Lerner, 1971) and there are three such types of errors. One is called *myopia* (nearsightedness). While this problem can develop anytime from age 6 on, it is likely to show an increase in incidence around age 11 and 12 for girls and 13 to 14 for boys (Tanner, 1970). Myopia is characterized by visual images coming to a focus in front of, rather than on, the retina. This results in the child having difficulty seeing distant objects. A second refractive error is called *hyperopia* (farsightedness). Here the visual images are brought to a focus behind the retina, with the result that the child has difficulty in seeing objects which are near him. The third type of problem is called *astigmatism*. Here the lens fails to correctly transmit the light or image to the retina, with the consequence that the child sees blurred images.

Binocular vision concerns how well the two eyes coordinate in bringing together two visual inputs to produce one visual image. There are three principal processes involved, the coordination of extraocular and intraocular muscles, the fusion of the monocular images into a single perception and the individual's personal response to the visual stimulus (Park, 1969). The binocular defects which occur in children are *strabismus, inadequate fusion,* and *aniseikonia.* Strabismus occurs when one of the eyes strays from the proper direction, so that both eyes do not look at the same thing at the same time. This, believe it or not, is called a squint. Inadequate fusion is a defect in which the eyes do not accommodate to get a monocular effect. Simply put, one eye is adjusted to see at a different distance than the other. Aniseikonia is a condition in which the images of an object fixated are unequal in size or shape in the two eyes (Lerner, 1971).

There appears to be agreement that refractive defects do not contribute to reading difficulties or learning disabilities. Refractive problems are just as likely to occur in academically high achievers as in poor readers. Indeed, good readers appear to have a higher incidence of myopia than poor readers, although there does seem to be a higher incidence of hyperopia among poor than good readers (Lerner, 1971).

Severe binocular problems also seem unrelated to learning disabilities. According to Krieg and Windsor (1974), many severe binocular problems can be solved by the organism. A person with a severe binocular problem will suppress one of the retinal images and become visually monocular. When the reading deficiency is caused exclusively by a binocular deficiency, an internal adjustment to monocular vision alleviates the reading deficiency. However, it should be noted that milder binocular difficulties might be associated with reading defects. As early as 1930, Eames (Lawson, 1968) compared good and poor readers to find that children with reading problems showed less ability to maintain coordination between the two eyes over long periods. It is now believed that if a child is struggling to maintain fusion or has any kind of mild binocular difficulty his struggle will have adverse effect upon his reading skills.

Visual Defects and Reading Failure

Lawson (1968) summarized the studies which relate ophthalmological factors to reading and learning disabilities. Early work, namely Orton's, focused on the eye as it reflected the development of cerebral dominance. Many characteristics seen in dyslexic children, such as reversals of letters and mirror writing, were interpreted as symptomatic of slow cerebral development. Others focused on the abilities of good and poor readers to coordinate the movements of the eyes, irregularities in depth perception and astigmatism. By and large, early studies, such as those conducted by Witty and Kopel (Lawson, 1968), reported that fusion, muscle balance, visual acuity and refractive errors were not related to the ability to read. Ocular dominance and hand preference, and the match of these, were also investigated and also found to be unrelated to reading achievement. As late as 1963, Belmont and Birch assessed the hand-eye preference and left-right awareness of retarded readers. Left-right awareness did have some relationship to reading skills, but hand-eye preferences did not.

Other areas of concern were the speed with which the reader could recognize words and the amount of information which could be processed at one moment by the reader. The factors which influence the span of perception is the efficiency of the visual mechanism, the kind of reading material, the size of type, the language background of the reader and the ability to organize what is seen at each fixation. Lawson points out that the average reader cannot be trained to read at high speeds. In addition, he specifies studies to indicate that mirror reading and the tendency to make reversals are psychological, and that good readers may make reversals and poor readers may not. All in all, these studies do not support early interpretations of the symptomatic behaviors of children who failed to learn to read as related to eye acuity, hand-eye preferences or cerebral dominance.

Vision Training

While Lawson has challenged the notion that poor readers invariably have some visual defect, Greenspan (1972) provides an extensive summary of studies, several of which support the efficacy of optometric training programs. Perceptual and perceptual-motor training, according to Lawson, can improve visual functioning, which in turn will result in improved reading ability. It is not that all children with reading problems have visual defects, but that children with visual defects can benefit from certain visual exercises which then will improve their reading. There are a number of questions concerning the source of this improvement, however, as there are a variety of explanations that can be offered to account for it. In the studies reviewed by Greenspan, training techniques included more than one exercise. For example, they might use a combination of the following: exercises in gross motor skills, body balance, fine motor skills and hand-eye coordination, oculomotor skills, and tracking, form perception, tachistoscopic perception, auditory perceptual training, to name a few. When such exercises work, it is difficult to explain just what the child is learning which improves his visual information processing and his reading.

Other kinds of eye training, such as attempts to increase the child's reading speed, or the number of words a child sees at one glance or eye movements across the page have not met with success. In effect, when there is a shift from training the eye to receive the visual stimulus to training the child to understand what he sees, optometric training should be put aside.

There are really two difficulties associated with the evaluation of the efficacy of optometric training programs. The first is the nature of the sample. Often children are studied whose only apparent deficiency is lack of reading skills. It would be naive to assume that all poor readers have poor vision. There are many possible causal factors associated with poor reading, poor vision being only one. In using such subjects, instead of children who have known eye defects, the possibility of determining the efficacy of such programs is reduced. Second, the training programs involve a lot more than simply ocular exercises. For example, Painter's (1966) training program included gross motor and body balance activities, body image training and motor responses to visual and auditory stimuli. This program involved more than ocular training by requiring cognitive learning as well.

Because of the popularity of and confusion regarding optometric training for the learning-disabled child, a prestigious

committee of ophthalmologists, optometrists, otolaryngologists
and learning disability specialists studied the programs in use
(Helveston, 1969). The following conclusions were drawn:

1. Children with learning disabilities, be it dyslexia or reading
   underachievement, have the same incidence of ocular abnormalities (refractive and binocular) as children who are normal achievers and reading at grade level.
2. These abnormalities should be corrected.
3. Since clues in word recognition are transmitted through the
   eyes to the brain, it has become common practice to attribute
   reading difficulties to subtle ocular abnormalities presumed
   to cause faulty visual perception. . . . There is no peripheral
   eye defect which produces dyslexia and associated learning
   disabilities. Eye defects do not cause reversals of letters,
   words, or numbers.
4. Treatments which depend upon visual training (muscle exercises, ocular pursuit, glasses) or neurologic organizational
   training (laterality training, balance board, perceptual training) have no scientific support to claims of improvement of
   academic abilities.
5. Beware of such limited training. It is expensive, and may
   delay more beneficial intervention.
6. Glasses are important for the correction of ocular defects.
   Other than this they play no role in specific treatments of
   any academic problems.
7. Learning disabilities, dyslexia, reading retardation, school
   underachievement . . . are educational problems. Ophthalmologists should offer the knowledge and expertise of their
   science, in the identification of specific ocular defects, early
   recognition of problems and appropriate medical intervention.

A variety of tests have been offered to the learning disability
specialist which are purported to assess the visual perceptual
abilities of children. Tests either entirely or partially devoted to
assessing visual perception have entered the market with alarm-
ing rapidity. Tests devised to assess visual perception, including

the Illinois Test of Psycholinguistic Abilities (ITPA), the Developmental Test of Visual Perception (DTVP), Detroit Test of Learning Aptitude, the Perceptual Motor Survey and the Winterhaven Perceptual Forms Test, to name a few, have been offered to the testing specialist.

As would be expected, the hypothesis and claims of these test constructors have been questioned and put to a variety of empirical tests. Essentially, two questions have been asked. One has been whether the tests are internally consistent; that is, whether the items of the test correlate with one another in such a fashion that the test is measuring what it is supposed to. If, for example, it is found that items that are presumed to be measuring auditory information processing are highly correlated with those assessing visual information processing, one would be unlikely to conclude that the test is measuring two different types of information processing.

The second question is whether the tests have any practical utility. Can deficient children be discriminated from nondeficient ones on the basis of their scores on the tests? Can predictions of children's school performance be made on the basis of their performance on the tests?

Testing Visual Processing

The following discussion will concern itself with the research pertaining to two very popular tests of visual processing, the ITPA and the DTVP. These tests are focused upon because of the relatively large number of research projects concerned with them and because of their apparent popularity with the learning disability specialist. It should be said, however, that many research questions have not been answered and that definite statements that can be made concerning these tests are relatively few.

Studies concerned with the internal consistency of a test, that is, the degree to which the items correlate with one another in the appropriate manner, have employed a statistical technique called factor analysis. This technique attempts to determine the fewest number of concepts or "factors" which can account for the correlation among all items of the test. By and large, reviewers of the factor analytic studies of the ITPA suggest that this test does not measure nine different processes, as originally believed, but a lesser number. Meyers (1969) suggested that the test measures six and possibly seven separate abilities, at least when using an early edition of the test. With regard to the test assessing some ability which uniquely reflects visual processing, the evidence is discouraging. Uhl and Nurss (1970) found that the intercorrelations of the items could be reduced to but three or four dimensions and that there was no evidence suggesting that the visual processing tests were simply or solely measuring visual processing. Burns and Watson (1973) did find that the visual processing items did tend to correlate, but that these were also correlated with subtests presumably assessing language ability. Thus, tests which are designed to assess visual processing also tap to some degree language skills. In support of this finding were the results obtained by Huizinga (1973). He found that the Visual-Motor tests of the ITPA correlated .69 with scores on the Stanford-Binet Intelligence Scale and .56 and .54 with the verbal and performance scores, respectively, of the Wechsler Intelligence Scale for Children. Scores on these intelligence tests are markedly affected by children's verbal skills and thus the results suggest, but do not prove, that the visual processing subtests of the ITPA tap language as well as visual skills. As Carroll (1972) has written, "A casual inspection of the subtests will reinforce the conclusion that many of them, even the 'non-language' ones, measure a 'vocabulary' factor, or rather, a factor having to do with the range of cultural experiences to which the child has been exposed" (p. 442). He points out that in the Visual Association subtest "the child may be shown an item requiring him to make a distinction between a microscope and a telescope" (p. 442). Such associations involve more than simple visual processing; they also involve language skills and/or a variety of everyday experiences.

Another popular device for assessing visual processing is Frostig's Developmental Test of Visual Perception (DTVP). This test consists of five subtests which are presumed to tap five different aspects of visual perception. However, it has generally been concluded that the test measures but one perceptual ability rather than the five originally postulated (Chissom, 1972; Mann, 1972). As Mann has pointed out, "Profile analysis and specification of areas of perceptual strength and weakness are patently not feasible on the basis either of reliability or of factor analysis data" (p. 872).

In general, the internal consistency of these two popular tests of visual processing, the ITPA and the DTVP, indicate that they do not measure those separate abilities which were originally hypothesized as being assessed by the tests. This does not necessarily mean that neither test has any practical usefulness. Questions can be posed as to whether these tests do make predictions about the children's school performance, and whether test performance is changeable as a result of particular kinds of training programs.

Apparently, as yet there is relatively little information concerning the degree to which either the ITPA or the DTVP can discriminate among children regarding deficient performance or can be used to predict children's future academic performance. Carroll (1972) points out that there is no reason to assume that the test would have any validity when applied to other than white middle-class children and warns against employing it when assessing the disadvantaged child. But even for white middle-class children the evidence is mixed. Some studies suggest that the tests, as a whole, might be helpful in predicting reading difficulties, while others suggest that the test has no practical utility in this regard (Carroll, 1972). Similarly, studies of the predictive power of the DTVP yield mixed results. Chissom (1972) and Mann (1972) suggest that the weight of the evidence is that the test can yield useful predictions of children's reading in the first and second grades, but Chissom points out that the test may be of little value in aiding one to predict specific reading difficulties. On the other hand, Hammill (1972) has argued that there is no good evidence suggesting that the test has predictive value in assessing reading skills.

In summary, it does appear that the test constructor's hypothesis concerning which abilities are being measured by the test have not been substantiated empirically. Factor analytic studies of both tests suggest that the individual subtests within them are not measuring independent abilities, but rather abilities that are reflected in more than one subtest. Second, the practical usefulness of these tests in aiding testers to make difficult diagnoses has been far from established. There is a dearth of evidence to substantiate that these tests are powerful predictors of school achievement, more specifically reading levels, or that subtle differences among children are easily detected through the tests. For these reasons alone, they are useful when carefully analyzed and applied.

Visual Processing and the Learning Disabled

The surface of the visual information processing system has yet to be scratched, but there is an increasing number of experiments designed to assess differences between the learning-disabled and the nondisabled child on such functions as visual memory, attention to visual stimuli, and general rapidity in visual processing.

Lyle and Goyen (1968, 1974) and Goyen and Lyle (1971, 1973) have conducted a series of research studies addressed to the general issue of whether retarded readers perceive visual inputs as well as adequate readers. Using tachistoscopic presentations of various visual stimuli, such as geometric lines or letters of the alphabet under different rates of presentation and incentive conditions, they have compared young and old, adequate and retarded readers. They have consistently found that younger retarded readers, below 8.5 years, perform less well than older retarded and all young and old normal readers. The difference in performance in younger retarded readers was related to their relative inefficiency in noting critical details of the visual stimuli and this was related to their slowness in processing visual information relative to other children.

It is unlikely that in the academic world many children get less than a one-second exposure to the visual materials they are expected to master. In this sense, the results of the Lyle and

Goyen experiments have limited applicability. Nonetheless, it is important to note that these investigators have raised an interesting challenge to the belief that poor readers have a perceptual problem. What might be important is the time that children spend in focusing upon the visual stimulus and the amount of effort involved in discriminating the relevant features which aid in coding the material for purposes of remembering it. The results of the Lyle and Goyen experiments should also be noted for their age-related findings. Differences occur primarily for retarded readers under 8½ years of age. This suggests that younger retarded readers may be characterized by perceptual and perceptual-motor difficulties, while older children may differ with regard to their verbal or intellectual skills.

Visual Memory

There have been a number of studies addressed to possible differences in visual memory of the learning-disabled and non-disabled child. Doehring (1960) compared short-term visual memory of aphasics, deaf and normal children and reported that aphasic children performed less adequately than did the remaining two groups of children. Unfortunately, the aphasic children also had lower intelligence test scores than the remaining two groups and thus interpretation of the results is somewhat ambiguous. The role of visual memory for sequences in normal and disabled readers around 8½ years of age was studied by Guthrie and Goldberg (1972). They presumed that visual sequential memory is necessary for the comprehension of written sentences and word recognition. They tested children on the Benton Visual Retention Test, which requires the child to identify a "correct" form from several incorrect alternatives. Additionally, children were tested on a subtest of the Illinois Test of Psycholinguistic Abilities in which the child is requested to reconstruct from memory a series of geometric shapes in the proper sequence. It was found that the tests of visual sequential memory did, by and large, correlate with several measures of reading. The exception to this was that no significant correlation was found between the ITPA subtest and reading ability in children previously defined as reading disabled. The Benton Visual Retention Test showed the most significant correlations with reading skills for both normal and disabled readers. The authors suggest that the reason for the Benton test's success revolves around the additional demands placed upon the child. Both the Benton and the ITPA test visual sequencing memory, but, in addition to the sequence, the Benton requires the subject to remember both the form and the direction of the form. In effect, then, it is still not clear as to how great a role visual sequencing memory plays in determining the reading skills of the child.

Visual Sequencing

Poppen, Stark, Eisenson, Forrest and Wertheim (1969) conducted a study on the visual sequencing of aphasic children. There were nine aphasic children in the study, ages 6 to 12½, and nine normal children, ages 7 to 11½. Children were exposed to visual inputs by means of flashing lights onto keys in various sequences. The children's task was to press the keys in the right sequence at the end of the visual sequence presented to them. The delay following the presentation of the sequence and the child's key pressing was varied from 2 seconds to 27 seconds. It was found that normal children made fewer errors than aphasic children, that errors increased with an increase in the delay between the stimulus presentation and the child's responses and that the delay had a greater effect upon the aphasics than the normal children. Additionally, each child was tested on the auditory and visual memory subtests of the ITPA, the Knox Cube Tapping Test and the Auditory Vocal Sequencing with Language Test. Aphasics demonstrated inferior performance on all tests when compared to the normal children. They concluded that aphasic children have a general deficit in the ability to sequence information which underlies and causes general problems in language and learning. On the other hand, it is quite conceivable that language problems lead to sequencing problems, insofar as language deficits may well interfere or decrease the child's capacity to code and retrieve information.

Dykman, Ackerman, Clements and Peters (1971) investigated children's impulsivity in response to visual cues (certain flashing lights on a panel). In one study, 26 children with minimal cerebral dysfunction and 26 nondisabled children were investigated. The task confronting the child was to press a lever in response to particular flashing lights and to refrain from pressing the lever to other flashing lights. Children were scored as to whether they committed impulsive errors (pressing the button to the wrong visual stimulus) and as to their rapidity in making the correct response. The minimal brain-damaged children committed more impulsive errors and responded less quickly when correct than did the comparison children, particularly after practice.

Dykman et al. extended and replicated these results using learning-disabled children. In this study, learning-disabled children were divided on the basis of school and parent reports into hyperactive, normoactive or hypoactive children. The performances of these groups were compared with those of nondisabled children on a task similar to that previously used. The results were that learning-disabled children made more errors in following instructions and showed greater impulsivity in their responses. Response latency to visual signals, measured under several different conditions, was consistently longer for the learning-disabled children than the nondisabled ones. Unfortunately, the age of the nondisabled children was greater than that of the disabled ones and, therefore, these differences can be attributable to general maturational factors. Of interest is the fact that hypoactive children were slower to respond in a variety of situations than either the hyperactive or normoactive learning-disabled child.

Dykman et al. suggest that learning-disabled children cannot attend to visual signals with the same competence as normal children and that some types of learning-disabled children, such as the hypoactive child, are much slower in processing visual signals than other types, such as hyperactive ones.

Pursuing similar lines, Czudner and Rourke (1970) studied

reaction time in brain-damaged children. The purpose of the study was to assess the ability of brain-damaged children to maintain a state of readiness to respond to a visual light stimulus and to compare the reaction time of brain-damaged and normal children. The brain-damaged subjects were 15 children diagnosed as having cerebral dysfunction with a mean age of 10.7 years; comparison subjects were 15 children with a mean age of 10.5 years. All subjects were exposed to two experimental procedures. The experimental apparatus had a telegraph key and two lights, a white warning light and a red reaction time light. All subjects were exposed to two procedures: in one series of trials, the preparatory interval which occurred between the onset of the warning signal and the onset of the reaction time stimulus was the same; in the second, the preparatory intervals were varied for 2, 4, 6 or 8 seconds. The results of the study indicated that the brain-damaged children tended to perform slightly better on the regular than irregular preparatory interval trials; but the same results occurred for the normal group. As with Dykman et al., it was found that the overall performance of the brain-damaged group was inferior to that of the control group.

But the story is certainly far from complete. So far the evidence does suggest that learning-disabled children have difficulty in paying attention to visual stimuli. If the learning-disabled child cannot attend, it would seem reasonable to assume that he is being distracted. This hypothesis was tested by Browning (1967). Contrary to the hypothesis, it was the nondisabled child who was distracted by the irrelevant visual stimuli! These somewhat discrepant results are difficult to resolve. Perhaps they are due to the different methodologies employed, or the samples used or to some other source. What is suggested, though by no means proved, is that the source of inattentiveness of the learning-disabled child is not likely to be irrelevant visual stimuli.

Little in the way of general conclusions can yet be offered regarding the visual processing of learning-disabled children. It does appear that learning-disabled children are no more likely to suffer from visual acuity problems than are nondisabled children. It appears as well that learning-disabled children have problems in maintaining attention, and in determining what to pay attention to. This problem is not simply in the processing of visual stimuli, but is present in the case of processing auditory stimuli as well (Dykman et al., 1971). Aside from these few generalizations, little more can be offered regarding the differences between learning-disabled and nondisabled children in processing visual stimuli.

The lack of information concerning differences can be attributed to many factors. First, studies in visual information processing which are relevant to this field have focused upon a variety of aspects of such processing. The work has been broad in the topics addressed, but not very deep in the work on any particular topic. In addition, the performances by the child which have been used to index such processing have been many, but rarely repeated in more than one study. Thus, reaction time, errors in response and errors in following instructions have been used by particular investigators. The results from different laboratories are often not comparable. Third, many of the tests employed in studies as measures of the child's competence in visual processing have a certain intuitive validity, but not necessarily an empirical one. It remains to be determined whether such measures as the Frostig (1964) are, in fact, assessing visual processing of the child. If these measures are not valid, then the findings of any particular study employing them are open to serious question. Fourth, many of the studies of visual processing which have reported group differences between learning-disabled and nondisabled children also report differences between these children in terms of age and scores on intelligence tests (Doehring, 1960; Dykman et al., 1971; Browning, 1967). Interpretations of such results, therefore, are not obvious. Finally, tests which are made to assess the same visual processing activity have been found not to correlate with each other (Guthrie and Goldberg, 1972). This suggests that if the tests are measuring something, they are not measuring the same thing. All of these considerations suggest that the hypothesis that learning-disabled children have particular difficulties in processing visual stimuli has not yet been demonstrated.

Cross-Modal Information Processing

So far, we have discussed information processing through single modalities, the auditory and visual systems. But it is clear that information is obtained through the integration of material introduced through separate modality channels. It is reasonable to be concerned with the procedures or mechanisms through which cross-modal integration occurs. Within the field of learning disabilities, three sources gave impetus to concern with cross-modal integration. One source was the incidence of reading problems. While it was initially believed that reading was primarily associated with visual processing, a view under challenge (Hammill, 1972), more recently it has been recognized that learning and comprehending written material are also highly related to auditory stimuli. Children do not learn to read by seeing the written word, but rather by both seeing it and hearing it. The realization of the importance of auditory as well as visual processing in affecting reading achievement stimulated a hypothesis that children who have difficulty learning to read suffer a deficit in the ability to process information from two or more modalities.

A second stimulant to the study of cross-modal integration has come from studies of lower animals which suggest that animals cannot perform tasks which require cross-modal integration. These findings led to the hypothesis that the capacity for language may be a critical variable in affecting cross-modal processing (Ettlinger, 1967).

A third source has been studies involving brain-damaged humans. Studies have been conducted with individuals who have suffered trauma to the corpus collosum, a major fiber tract which connects the right and left sides of the brain. If the left-side language section of the brain is disassociated from the right side of the brain, the difficulty for the individual to verbally respond to a stimulus presented to the right hemisphere is greatly increased (Sperry, 1964; Gazzaniga, Rogen and Sperry, 1965). These results dovetail with those reported in studies involving lower animals.

Studies concerning deficit populations, such as brain-damaged or reading-disabled children, have increasingly focused upon their abilities to integrate information across or between modalities. Insofar as there is a ". . . discrepancy between the sensory input and the finished product" (Gibson and Gibson, 1962, p. 5), this approach has received a great deal of attention within the field of learning disabilities.

Integrating Information

Laboratory and developmental studies of integrative information processing have employed a variety of procedures and measures. One approach is to assess the individual's ability to make judgments as to whether complex stimuli presented to two different modalities are the same or different. For example, in a procedure devised by Birch and Belmont (1964, 1965), a subject might be presented with a complicated series of long and short sounds and be asked to match the sounds with one of several patterns of dots and dashes presented to him visually. A second method is to present to the individual information in two modalities, visual and auditory or visual and tactile, and ask the subject whether or not the stimuli are equivalent. Another method has involved various adaptations of the Broadbent (1958) dichotic listening task. In this case, subjects might be presented with information through two modalities at a very rapid speed. The subject is asked to recall the information presented. Of interest is whether the testee remembers the information in the order presented (*e.g.,* auditory, visual, auditory, visual, etc.) or whether the individual differentially recalls visual rather than auditory materials or auditory rather than visual stimuli. Presumably, such tests give the learning disability specialist information concerning the testee's ability to process and organize information from two modalities. The learning-disabled child is hypothesized to differ from the nondisabled in his organization, as inferred from his recall, of the material. Individual differences in the organization of such material are assumed to reflect neurophysiological differences.

Information Processing

Several studies have been concerned with the development of cross-modal processing. Birch and Lefford (1963) studied the development of the ability to process visual, haptic and kinesthetic information in 145 children, 5 to 11 years of age. These researchers presented a stimulus object to the child so that he could look at it, feel it with his hands without looking at it (haptic presentation) and/or trace it with a stylus (kinesthetic presentation). The child was presented with a stimulus by one means and then asked to judge whether a second stimulus was the same or different from the standard stimulus. As would be expected, the number of correct judgments increased with age of the child. Materials presented visually and then judged by feeling were easiest. Materials presented visually and tested kinesthetically, and information presented kinesthetically and tested haptically were more difficult. Schevill (1973) also found that first graders were better able to integrate cross-modal information than children in kindergarten. While it is clear that the research into the developmental aspects of cross-modal integration is hardly complete, the evidence does suggest that this ability is associated with the age of the child.

Considerable work has been conducted concerning cross-modal integration by deficit populations. Studies have been completed which have tested these processes in psychiatrically disturbed adolescents, schizophrenic children, retarded readers, brain-damaged individuals and even malnourished children (Freides, 1974). Of particular interest to learning disability specialists is the work concerning the retarded reader, both because of its direct relevance to his work and because there is a fair amount of evidence concerning these children's cross-modal integration.

An early study by Birch and Belmont (1964) seems to have had considerable influence on many of the subsequent investigations concerning cross-modal integration in retarded readers. These investigators hypothesized that integration of auditory and visual stimuli is basically what is required in the act of reading and that children unable to read might very well demonstrate a deficit in this type of task. Retarded readers in the Birch-Belmont study were 150 boys, ages 9.4 to 10.4, who had scored at the lowest 10% level on at least three of four reading tests. Normal comparison subjects were 150 boys randomly selected from boys who were not in the lowest 10% of readers. The experimental task was a multiple choice problem in which children had to indicate which tap pattern heard was identical to one of three dot patterns seen. Results were that retarded readers performed significantly more poorly than comparison subjects. The authors concluded that the inability to make such auditory-visual equivalence judgments is an underlying and major source of reading retardation.

The finding that retarded readers perform significantly more poorly than nonretarded ones on cross-modal integration tasks has been reported by a variety of other investigators (Blank and Bridger, 1966; Birch and Belmont, 1965; Muehl and Kremenak, 1966; Schevill, 1973; Senf, 1969; Senf and Freundl, 1971). Whether readers are compared with nonreaders in terms of their responses to two inputs (Birch and Belmont, 1964), their quickness in giving their responses (Freides, 1974) or their recall of information (Senf, 1969; Senf and Freundl, 1971), it does appear that good readers perform more competently than do less adequate readers.

Evaluation of Tests and Studies

Things are not that perfectly clear, however. First, it should be noted that many investigators who have studied cross-modal integration in deficit populations have generally failed to determine whether such failures of integration are problems of integration or problems within a modality, a point correctly made by Schevill (1973) and Freides (1974). For example, can one argue that a child has an integration problem of auditory and visual stimuli if, in fact, the child may have a deficiency in one modality? Before the conclusion is reached that cross-modal deficits distinguish good from poor readers, more carefully controlled research wherein intramodality competence is demonstrated must be conducted.

A second question is the degree to which cross-modal integration is uniquely associated with the learning-disabled child. Is the learning-disabled child particularly likely to have problems in cross-modal integration? Apparently, children with many various types of problems have been studied and they also suffer from cross-modal integration difficulties. It has been suggested and presumably demonstrated that the schizophrenic, the emotionally disturbed and malnourished suffer from such difficulties.

A question might also be asked whether cross-modal integration difficulties are evidenced by the child in his daily social intercourse with peers and adults. Is the learning-disabled child more likely to remember verbal or visual inputs, and will he be particularly insensitive to contradictions between these two sources of information? There have been only two studies conducted on the question and apparently no such gross or massive deficit in functioning occurs (Schwartz and Bryan, 1971).

Freides (1974) has recently published a valuable review of the research in this area. While we will go into some detail concerning his conclusion, it is clear that the phenomenon of cross-modal integration is more complex than has been heretofore assumed. Freides has recently challenged some commonly held beliefs concerning this process and has advanced some provocative hypotheses. The following points are to be credited to that author. First, the assumption that cross-modal integration of information is more difficult than intramodal processing has not been empirically supported. Second, the assumption that specific difficulty in cross-modal processing would distinguish brain-damaged and learning-disabled children from nondisabled children cannot be claimed insofar as deficit populations have been found to have as much difficulty in processing intramodal tasks as cross-modal ones. Freides further suggests two hypotheses which appear buttressed by the data. One is that the information received by the child is translated into the form required by the task at hand. The second hypothesis is that each modality has particular aptness for handling certain kinds of information. Spatial information appears to be translated into a visual code, temporal information into an auditory code.

Freides has also summarized some basic differences between

audition and vision which should be noted. Complex auditory and visual information appear to be stored in a different manner. Apparently, memory for things heard and seen show different patterns of decay. Additionally,

visual memory for words favored the early inputs of the sequence (primacy), whereas auditory memory favored the later inputs (recency); . . . retrieval of information increased with faster auditory inputs and slower visual inputs . . . (p. 307).

No doubt, knowledge will increase concerning the processing of information and cross-modality integration. As yet, however, considerable caution should be maintained when arguing the proposition that learning disability, and particularly reading deficiencies, are attributable to the child's deficit in integrating information from two or more modalities.

CHAPTER
8
LANGUAGE DISORDERS AND LEARNING DISABILITIES

The most prevalent conditions to be found among specific learning disabilities are those in which language abilities have been impaired (McGrady, 1968, p. 215).

Early theorizing concerning delayed language development was based on analogy to the brain-injured, adult aphasic. The assumption was made that similar physiological processes characterized children who never developed speech and language and adults who had had speech but lost it. The category of childhood aphasia served to separate children with deficits in language development from children with language deficits which were attributable to mental retardation, hearing impairments or emotional problems. Since the field of learning disabilities historically has been concerned with the diagnosis and treatment of brain-injured children, aphasic children have been a concern to specialists within this field.

Characteristics of language disturbances were cited in Clements' (1966) report on children with minimal brain dysfunction. These language dysfunctions included: aphasia, impaired discrimination of auditory stimuli, slow language development and frequent mild speech disorders. As language and thought are integrally connected, thinking deficits are also related to language problems. Thinking deficiencies were named as poor ability for abstract thinking and concept formation, thinking which is concrete, poor short-term memory, disorganized thinking, thinking which appears to be autistic and thought perseveration. Kirk and Kirk (1972) describe the study of learning disabilities as

a relatively new educational approach which involves handicapped children with specific disorders in perceiving, thinking, talking, reading, writing, spelling, arithmetic, and related disabilities primarily in the communication process (p. 12).

Although language disorders are firmly placed within the history and definitions of learning disabilities, language disorders have been very much underestimated and understudied. It is our bias that language disorders may be a central problem in learning-disabled children and that such disorders might be reflected in a wide variety of problems, including reading and attentional deficits. It is our belief that a number of different types of research on language development can and should be related to the field of learning disabilities. Studies of the development of syntactic and semantic competence, the relationship of language to conceptual development and the social communications of children appear to be germane to the work of learning disability specialists. Whether or not our biases are correct, the area of language development has been relatively understressed within this field. In the remaining parts of this chapter we shall discuss the assessment techniques relevant to the measurement of language and the empirical data available concerning the language skills of learning-disabled youngsters.

Language Development

There is evidence that language is learned rather than instinctive, that development proceeds in predictable stages and that this development requires an intact nervous system (Dale, 1972). It also appears that early vocalizations are not simply incorrect imitations of adult speech, but reflect the child's conceptual development (Piaget, 1954). Language production is affected by the child's ability to understand that others may have a point of view different from his own, that objects can exist without being in view and that one can employ words to refer to abstract events or phenomena. The stages at which language skills appear can be marked within a fairly restricted timetable, but the order of appearance of these skills is more predictable than the specific age. While it is also apparent that an enormous amount of language development occurs by the time a child reaches four years of age, language development continues for several years thereafter (Menyuk, 1963; Lee, 1974; Palermo and Molfese, 1972).

Because of the rapid, massive development of language, most studies of language acquisition have been conducted with children 1½ to 3 years of age. McNeill (1970) specifies three basic foci of researchers in psycholinguistics. Researchers have been concerned with phonetic development, the production of speech sounds, such as the ages at which children use *r* or *sh* in their spoken language. Another area is the emergence of the grammatical system. In this case the researcher examines the child's ability to use forms of grammar, such as negatives or interrogatives. Finally, the experiential conditions which affect language production have been studied.

Prelinguistic Period

McNeill (1970) provides an excellent review of the field of psycholinguistics. Summarizing language development benchmarks, McNeill indicates that normal children start to babble about six months of age, say their first word at 10 to 12 months, combine words at 18 to 24 months, and have a syntactic system virtually complete by 4 to 5 years of age. Initial sound production finds infants use more vowels than consonants, with the consonants emerging later. Sounds produced during the first year of life are made in the back of the mouth with a gradual shift to sounds produced in the front of the mouth. Parents' claims to the contrary, vocalizations are made by the infant before he emits true words.

The initial period of prelinguistic life seems to be fairly immune from all but severe traumas. Brain damage, physical trauma or serious health problems might affect early vocalizations. But even hearing-impaired infants exhibit the early stages of vocalization. Parents may describe them as quiet or more quiet than their siblings, but they do vocalize. Hearing-impaired infants' vocalizations tend to decrease as they age and there may be a failure to demonstrate later stages of prelinguistic development. They fail to imitate sounds (echolalia), or demonstrate jargon (speech made up of nonsense sounds with correct sounding rhythm and voice inflection).

There are some theorists, Lenneberg (1967) and Chomsky (1967), for instance, who argue that language is a biologically guaranteed skill of man. There have been, however, a number of demonstrations that prelinguistic development can be affected by environmental events. Spitz (1946) reported that the vocalizations of infants were depressed when they were placed in institutions which provided them with little human or environmental stimulation. Brackbill (1958) demonstrated that an adult's smiling and hugging in response to an infant's vocalization resulted in an increase in the infant's vocalization. Brackbill also found that cessation of the adult's contingent hugging and smiling resulted in a decrease in infant vocalizing. While prelinguistic development will occur in many types of environments, and in the face of various abnormalities, it is clear that prelinguistic development can be altered through deprivation or reinforcements.

Comprehension

While the tape recorder is the primary instrument used to study language acquisition, its usefulness is limited when examining comprehension. There are standardized tests to assess children's comprehension of language. Interest in the child's ability to understand language spoken by others was stimulated by concern for aphasics and it is intimately linked to clinical practice. In this context standardized tests which include assessments of language comprehension have been used. The REEL Scale (The Bzoch-League Receptive-Expressive Emergent Language Scale, Bzoch and League 1972) and the NSST (Northwestern Syntax Screening Test, Lee, 1970) are two well-known comprehension tests. In the REEL Scale, assessment of comprehension is achieved through parental interview; on the NSST the child is asked to indicate which of two pictures describes a statement made by the examiner. Experimentally, various forms of the missing word approach have been devised in which the child is asked to add the appropriate endings to words embedded in sentences (Berko, 1958; Lerea, 1958). While knowledge concerning language comprehension is sparse relative to language production (McNeill, 1970), there is information as to its course of development. Benchmarks of the development of comprehension during the first thirty-six months are based on the Bzoch-League REEL Scale; and from Binet and Gesell from 36 to 60 months. Sample items from each age level follow.

0 to 12 months: (Bzoch and League, 1972, p. 22)

Respond with gross reflexes to sudden loud noises.
Localize the source of sounds or voices.
Recognize and distinguish familiar sounds and voices.
Understand the general meaning of speech utterances with different rates and inflectional patterns (*e.g.,* warning, loving) . . .
Recognize and respond to some familiar words uttered in con-

nected speech (*e.g.,* names of family members) . . .

Respond appropriately to some simple commands, questions and statements in a manner that indicates some discriminate language decoding skills.

12 to 24 months: (Bzoch and League, 1972, p. 23)

Increased interest in the names of things.

Increased ability to understand some new words each week.

Interest in listening to rhymes, songs, or jingles.

Ability to identify one familiar object from among a group of several familiar objects when the object is named.

Increased ability to follow simple directions and commands.

Ability to learn new words by associating the names of smaller parts of whole known objects . . .

Remember and identify two or more familiar objects from among a group of four familiar objects when asked to do so in a single request.

Ability to learn new words by association in categories (such as foods) . . .

Understand and carry out three requests combined in a single utterance.

. . . learn new words almost daily.

. . . recognize the names of almost all common objects or pictures of such objects.

. . . understand the meaning of some complex sentences.

Increased interest in learning and listening to the meaning and reason of words and sentences.

Binet and Gesell items related to
Language Comprehension
from ages 24 to 60 months

24 to 36 months:

Understands direct vocative better (*i.e.,* "Peter kick the ball," instead of, "You kick the ball").

Likes to listen for reasons of language as well as of sound.
By listening acquires sense of descriptive power of words.
Listens to simple stories, especially liking those he's heard before.
Understands two prepositions.
Identifies at least six of the following pictures from names: dog, cup, shoe, house, flag, star, leaf, basket, book.
Understands three prepositions.
Identifies pictures from name (at least seven of the following: dog, cup, house, flag, clock, star, leaf, basket, book).

36 to 48 months:

Learns to listen and listens to learn. (Single word spoken by mother may instantaneously reorganize whole stream of activity.)
Suggestions take effect.
Memory span lengthening—recalls events of yesterday.
Beginning to distinguish between black and white.
Generalization common in comprehension—in, on, under.
Distinguishes one and many.
Listens and can be reasoned with verbally.
Listens to longer and more varied stories.
Tends to re-enact in body postures and gestures what is told in a story.
Comprehends: what do you do when hungry, thirsty, or tired.

48 to 60 months:

Can single out one word and ask its meaning whereas formerly reacted to sentence as a whole.
Genuine interchange of ideas remains limited.
Tries to use new words, can define some simple ones.
Considerable time looking at books—likes to be read to.
Understands some abstract words (connectives, colors).

Phonemic Development

Phonology refers to the study of the emergence and production of single sounds and the rules whereby sounds are combined in sequences appropriate to the language. There is a good deal of data concerning the emergence of individual sounds. This may be due to the longer history of attention given articulation problems in the field of speech pathology. Knowledge as to the rules governing the sequencing of sounds is more limited (McNeill, 1970).

Developmentally, children across cultures emit sounds of their language and other languages during the babbling stage. Sounds of other languages drop out of the babbling repertoire (Berry, 1969). By age 2 much of the child's sound production may be difficult or impossible to understand, but by age 3 about 90% of the normal child's utterances can be interpreted by the adult listener (Templin, 1957). Templin has provided useful guidelines to the developmental sequence of sound production. The expected age of acquisition is that age at which 75% of the children can be expected to produce that sound in either the initial, medial or final parts of words.

TABLE 1

Development of Sound Production

CA	*Phonemes and Phoneme-Blends*
3 years	Vowels:
	ē, i, e, a, o, u, oo, ōō, ō, ô, ȧ, ûr
	Diphthongs:
	û̄, ā, i, ou, oi
	Consonants:
	m-, -m-, -m, n-, -n-, -n, -ng-, -ng, p-, -p-, -p, t-, -t-, -t, k-, -k-, b-,
	-b-, d-, -d-, g-, -g-, f-, -f-, -f, h-, -h-, w-, -w-
	Double-consonant blends:
	-ngk
3.5	Consonants:
	-s-, -z-, -r, y-, -y-
	Double-consonant blends:
	-rk, -ks, -mp, -pt, -rm, -mr, -nr, -pr, -kr, -br, -dr, -gr, -sm
4 years	Consonants:
	-k, -b, -d, -g, s-, sh-, -sh, -v-, j-, r-, -r-, l-, -l-

191

Double-consonant blends:
pl-, pr-, tr-, tw-, kl-, kr-, kw-, bl-, br-, dr-, gl-, sk-, sm-, sn-, sp-, st-, -lp, -rt, -ft, -lt, -fr
Triple-consonant blends:
-mpt, -mps

4.5   Consonants:
-s, -sh-, ch-, -ch-, -ch
Double-consonant blends:
gr-, fr-, -lf

5 years   Consonants:
-j-
Double-consonant blends:
fl-, -rp, -lb, -rd, -rf, -rn, -shr
Triple-consonant blends:
str-, -mbr

6 years   Consonants:
-t-, th-, -th-, -th, v-, -v, -th-, -l
Double-consonant blends:
-lk, -rb, -rg, -rth, -nt, -nd, -thr, -pl, -kl, -bl, -gl, -fl, -sl
Triple-consonant blends:
skw-, -str, -rst, -ngkl, -nggl, -rj, -ntth, -rch

7 years   Consonants:
-th-, -th, z-, -z, -zh-, -zh, -j
Double-consonant blends:
thr-, shr-, sl-, sw-, -lz, -zm, -lth, -sk, -st
Triple-consonant blends:
skr-, spl-, spr-, -skr, -kst, -jd

8 years   Double-consonant blends:
-kt, -tr, -sp

SOURCE: *Certain language skills in children* by Mildred C. Templin, Child Welfare Monograph No. 26. University of Minnesota Press, Minneapolis, © Copyright 1957 by the University of Minnesota. P. 51.

Vocabulary Development

The number of words used by children and the number of words used in sentences have been traditional guides to assessing language development. Between the ages of 1½ and 4, the child acquires an impressive number of words. It has been estimated that the child's vocabulary increases from 460 to 910 words between the middle of his second year to 3 years. By 4 years, the child has a vocabulary of about 1500 words (Berry, 1969). Table 2 presents some developmental norms associated with vocabulary growth.

TABLE 2

Vocabulary Growth as a Function of Age

Age (years, months)	*Number of Words*	*Increment*
0; 8	0	
0; 10	1	1
1; 0	3	2
1; 3	19	16
1; 6	22	3
1; 9	118	96
2; 0	272	154
2; 6	446	174
3; 0	896	450
3; 6	1222	326
4; 0	1540	318
4; 6	1870	330
5; 0	2072	202
5; 6	2289	217
6; 0	2562	273

SOURCE: Adapted from Smith, M. E. An investigation of the development of the sentence and the extent of vocabulary in young children. *University of Iowa Studies in Child Welfare,* 1926, 3, No. 5.

Expressive Language Development

Counting the number of words children use does not account for the major contemporary thrust of students of language development. As a result of the efforts of Noam Chomsky and colleagues, the emphasis within the field of psycholinguistics shifted from studies of word counting to defining "deep structure," the underlying meaning of sentences. Children do not merely spout isolated words when they begin to acquire a vocabulary; their utterances of words reflect unspoken and perhaps unknown sentences. Before the child is able to use sentences, he can use a word to reflect a complex event. For example, the child who says "milk" may be crying over spilled milk or may be indicating a desire for more milk. The context in which the word is uttered is likely to influence the listener's interpretation.

The initial words used by children about 18 months old are called *holophrastic* and *telegraphic*. Holophrastic speech "refers to the possibility that the first single word utterances of young children express complex ideas" (McNeill, 1970, p. 1074). To develop holophrastic speech requires the child to be able to name things, and there is speculation that holophrastic speech is linked to action (for example, the child may get up from a chair and say "walk") and to emotional states. Telegraphic speech refers to the first multiple word combinations of the child. Like a telegram certain words are omitted; for example, "me milk."

Children's speech at this age is described as having two classes of words, *pivot* and *open* (Braine, 1963). Pivot class words are always accompanied by open class words. For instance, a pivot class word may be "my" accompanied by an open class word "mommy." Children's utterances will vary as the pivot word may precede or follow the open word, or the child may use the open word without a pivot word. The initial linguistic skills of the child are described by noting the use of telegraphic and holophrastic speech.

According to Lee (1974), the child quickly acquires the ability to use pronouns and negatives, to ask questions, to join sentences, to use infinitives, participles and gerunds and to make contextual generalizations. The progression of learning has been exemplified in Klima's study (1964) of learning negatives. Children proceed from attaching a negative ("no") to a holophrase and then positioning negative words within the sentence. This is followed by using auxiliary verbs with transformational rules. The initial sentences of the child are thus quite simple and consist of a noun and a verb; by 36 months of age children employ very complex sentences.

At the same time it appears that children develop "socially," as they also learn to make assessments of the situation and the persons who are their listeners. Shatz and Gelman (1973) completed three studies of 4-year-old children's ability to modify their communications to accommodate the age of their audience. Under varying conditions the 4-year-olds were asked to relay information to an adult and to a 2-year-old listener. Four-year-olds used speech to communicate to 2-year-olds which differed from their speech to adults. Communications to the 2-year-old contained more short, simple utterances and more attentional utterances. The younger the listener, the greater the simplication in the 4-year-old's communications.

Bzoch and League (1972) have outlined the development of spoken language during the first two years. The Bzoch and League manual for the REEL Scales of receptive and expressive language development specify the following events as occurring during the first two years of life (1972, pp. 23–24).

0 to 12 months:

. . . cry frequently with some variety in force and patterns, and to produce random reflexive vocalizations from time to time . . .
Signal developing hunger . . . by use of a specific differentiated cry or vocal pattern . . .
Communicate several states of pleasure or discomfort or pain through specific vocal signals that provide early vocalized social interaction with the mother . . .
Babble in chains of two or more syllables with increasing use of back vowels . . .
Respond to vocal stimulation by babbling and sometimes by attempting to imitate the specific sound heard . . .
. . . "talk" to objects and people in jargon patterns; . . .
. . . use some true words in interpersonal communication to satisfy wants or needs (p. 23).

12 to 24 months:

. . . express wants and needs by using some true words in combination with other vocalizations and gestures.

. . . name more objects (and pictures of objects).

Development of speaking vocabulary from 10 to 20 words.

Combine words into short, simple sentences.

More rapid development of expressive vocabulary . . .

Increased use of simple sentences consisting of four or more syllables.

Expansion of the speaking vocabulary to 100–150 words.

Increased use of two- and three-word sentences, coupled with decreased use of jargon utterances.

. . . speak regularly in sentences of two or more words, with expansion of the speaking vocabulary to more than 250 true words.

Borrowing again from Binet and Gesell, expressive language development from ages 24 months to 60 months includes the following skills:

24 to 36 months:

Often talks while he acts and acts while he talks.

300 words in vocabulary; reaches about 450 words

Names of things, persons, actions, and situations greatly predominate.

Adverbs, adjectives, prepositions in minority.

Pronouns "mine," "me," "you," and "I" coming into use in approximately that order.

In same sentence expresses intention and action. (Peter slide down.)

Jargon may have disappeared, but not sing song which often made jargon musical. Sing-song sentences.

Does not relate experiences in well-defined past tense.

Pleasure in matching words with objects.

Language is *beginning* to be used more extensively as communication for wants, needs, ideas. Simple experiences are verbal.

Tries to use words in telling his physical needs or answering simple questions, but does not carry on conversation.

Carries on "conversation" with self and dolls.

Asks names of things, "what's this?", "what's that?"
Sentence length of two words on the average.
Names 3–5 objects.
Refers to self by name.
Identifies many pictures by name.
Sentence length of 3 words on the average.
Repeats 4 syllables (2 words).

36 to 48 months:

Vocabulary of nearly 1000 words. Averages 900; reaches about 1500 words

Words become instruments for designating percepts, concepts, ideas, relationships.

Indulges in soliloquy and dramatic play in order to match his words and phrases and syntax. Combines acting and talking. Suits action to word and word to action in his monologue.

Asks questions to which he already knows the answers.

Uses language easily to tell a story or relay an idea to someone else.

Plurals, past tense, personal pronouns, prepositions such as "on."

Refers to self as "I."

Knows last name, sex, name of street on which he lives, and a few rhymes.

Speech may be infantile, but usually understood even by those outside the family.

Sentence length average of 3 to 4 words; reaches average of 4 to 5 words

Long sentences—compound and complex.

Nonpresent situations dealt with verbally.

Generalizations common in talking.

Complete sentences are used.

Number concept barely goes beyond "one," "two," and "many."

Can count to 4 or more by rote.

Powers of generalization and of abstraction are present.

Speaks of imaginary conditions: "suppose that" and "I hope."

Speech is forthright, not likely to carry on long conversations.

Plays with words.

Verbal rather than verbose (associative thinking).

May have imaginary playmate, but communicating is sketchy rather than organized and dramatic play does not long sustain a role.

Can tell lengthy story mixing fact and fiction.

Can carry on lengthy conversation with adults and children, though may make grammatical errors and misuse words.

Aggressiveness may appear in words as well as actions; calls names and brags.

Talks about everything, social rapport and to attract attention.

Questions at a peak, not always interested in explanations but more interested in how answers fit own thought.

Speech quite understandable, although some traces of infantile speech may remain.

48 to 60 months:

Vocabulary of 1900 words; reaches about 2200 words

Sentence length averages 4–5 words.

Can count 10 objects. Can tell his age.

Can carry a plot in a story and repeat a long sequence accurately.

Talks without infantile articulation.

Answers to questions more succinct and to the point.

Questions for information, not merely social intercourse or practice in speaking.

Defines in terms of use. ("A horse is to ride.")

Language essentially complete in structure and form.

Uses all types of sentences, including complex sentences with hypothetical and conditional clauses.

Uses conjunctions more freely, but generally frequency of parts of speech same as at four years.

Less literal and concrete than formerly.

Dramatic play full of practical dialogue and commentary which has to do with everyday functions (kitchen, grocery store, etc.). Good deal of talk with these. Function is to clear ideas and relationships through words rather than indulge in make-believe.

Distinguishes left and right hand in self, but not others.
Lacks power of explicit reasoning.
Names primary colors.

Physical Interference with Development

Lenneberg (1967) has described the effects of brain damage which is not congenital or genetically caused upon language and speech development. His hypothesis is that during language development, the effects of brain damage will be more debilitating as the child ages. The impact of physical assaults upon the brain is thought to have different effects upon language development depending upon the age of the child and the severity of the damage sustained. According to Lenneberg, the child who suffers a lesion will experience delayed but normal development of language if the child is younger than about twenty months of age at the time of the trauma. This recuperation is attributed to the equipotentiality of the cerebral hemispheres at this age, which allows the nondamaged areas of the brain to assume the functions of the damaged sections. At this time, symptoms and prognosis are the same irrespective of the side of the brain which suffers damage. The delay in language development is thought to reflect the delay of the nondamaged areas in assuming the functions of those parts suffering the lesion.

During the 21- to 36-month period of the child's development, brain damage to the language areas of the brain (left hemisphere areas) will produce greater debilitation. This period of development is the major one in which the child develops language and a lesion at this time necessitates repetition of previous language learning. According to Lenneberg, however, spontaneous recuperation of the language deficits produced will be evidenced.

Children who suffer damage between the ages of 3 to 10 will demonstrate aphasic symptoms similar to those exhibited by brain-damaged adults, but spontaneous recuperation is still possible. Interestingly and importantly for the learning disability specialist, Lenneberg has hypothesized that children suffering such damage during this period of their lives may demonstrate reading and writing handicaps.

If the lesion occurs during the 11 to 14 year period, the child will exhibit aphasic symptoms, and some of these symptoms may persist as residual deficits. By this time, lateralization of brain functioning has occurred and the nondominant hemisphere can no longer take over as it did during younger age periods. The child now retains problems which resemble those of the adult who suffers brain damage, such as expressive and receptive language deficits.

A final point needs to be made concerning language deficits, physical assaults and childhood aphasia. It is entirely reasonable to assume that some children who suffer brain damage also suffer aphasia. But we agree with Birch (1964) when he argues that there is a difference between the fact of brain damage and the concept of brain damage. Apparently, Birch's well-taken point is that diagnosticians will illogically argue that because a child has a language deficit, he must be brain damaged. Such is not logically nor empirically the case. Because brain-damaged children may have trouble talking, or more correctly, in employing language, does not mean that all children who have language problems suffer from brain damage.

Nonphysiological Interference with Development

Children, even without physical evidence of brain damage, may well show delayed language development. What is the nature of the delay? Do such children simply resemble younger children, or is their speech production different in quality as well as quantity from their peers? What are the implications of delayed language development?

Menyuk (1969) studied the linguistic competence of language-delayed children between 3 and 6 years of age and compared their performances with children not suffering such delay. In the study, children's speech was obtained in response to a projective test, conversation with an adult and a peer and by having the child repeat a list of grammatical and nongrammatical sentences. Menyuk reports that at no age level did the syntactic structures of the language-delayed children match those employed by the normal children. The second finding was that the language-delayed children resembled each other in the linguistic structures employed, irrespective of their age. The 3-, 4- and 5-year-old language-delayed children used similar syntactic structures in their verbal productions. There were two major findings: language-delayed children were similar to each other across the age range of 3 to 6, and were different in their expressive language from nondelayed children irrespective of their age. The normal child was found to be more sophisticated and competent in using grammatical structures. The characteristics of the language-delayed child included: using sentences which seem to be "reflections of a basic 'unmarked' grammar" (p. 130); articles were omitted; the verb phrase was almost never expanded; incorrect usage of words was frequent and grammatical rules were ignored *(e.g.,* "My like guns" p. 134); the simple transformational structures produced were generated by the operation of conjoining elements *(e.g.,* "I want milk" and "I want cookies" rather than "I want some milk and cookies"); and failure to produce correct negatives and questions. In addition, some of these children failed to speak at all and others spoke with correct syntax but with such poor articulation that they were unintelligible. In the linguistically deviant children, there seemed to be, in general, a static state of nondevelopment between the ages of 3 and 6 years in the production of sentences. When asked to repeat sentences, the language-deviant children repeated sentences omitting phrases or using the final part of the sentence. The difference between the normal and deviant children was that the errors made by normal children reflected their efforts to correct ungrammatical sentences, but the linguistically deviant modifications reflected nongrammatical modifications of transformations. While sentence length and the ability to repeat sentences was not related for the normal children, it was highly related for the deviant children. The 3-year-old literally repeats the last word or part of the sentence. The language-delayed 5-year-old could repeat a sentence better than a 3-year-old, but was still limited in his ability to understand and repeat the sentence. Menyuk hypothesizes that the performance of the language-delayed child reflects poor auditory memory and suggests that such a deficit will have profound effects upon the child's subsequent ability to expand the rules in his grammar, and observe more contextual constraints (i.e., be sensitive to the grouping of words to convey particular meaning). When a young child cannot remember more than two or three morphemes (the smallest meaningful unit within a sentence), he is at a considerable disadvantage in developing his language through his everyday experiences. The degree to which such a child can form hypotheses about sentence production, or understand and generate sentences will be sorely limited. Table 3 presents some examples of the sentences produced by normal and language-delayed children.

TABLE 3

Sentences by Normal and Language-Delayed Children

Normal-speaking 3,0	Deviant-speaking 3,0
Do you see it over there?	Which mine?
I want the fire engine to talk.	I go wash hands.
He's going up the ladder.	He's go there.
There's a fire and here's the ladder.	My like gun.
The monster's not coming.	Not take mine.
He isn't coming.	This is not buttoned.

SOURCE: Menyuk, P. Sentences Children Use. Research Monograph No. 52. Cambridge, Mass: The M.I.T. Press, 1969.

Lee (1974) also has described many of the language acquisition difficulties of children with language delays. The following is a summary of the Lee studies.

Whereas normal speaking children learn to use complicated linguistic structures by age 4 years, language delayed children have great difficulty in the acquisition of a variety of such structures. For instance, children learn to use pronouns very early, but language delayed children have an inordinately difficult time learning pronouns. The use of negatives is apparently easily achieved by normal speaking children. They learn to use no, and, then add not; but language delayed children cling to the use of "no" or just add "no" to the end of sentences. Children learn to ask two kinds of questions, yes-no and "why" questions. Yes-no asks for confirmation of something as right or wrong and "why" questions ask for information. But children with delayed language seldom ask "why" questions and they have difficulty learning to make the interrogative reversal *(e.g.,* "What that is"). The absence of the use of questions reflects both linguistic and conceptual shortcomings. To use questions the child has to understand yes and no, and have the concepts of time and causality. Normal children learn to join sentences using conjunctions, an early appearing conjunction is "and." But language delayed children may just put words in a series and omit the conjunction or they may use an inappropriate one. The language delayed child is similarly delayed and inconsistent in his acquisition of infinitives, gerunds and participles.

Language and Learning Disabilities

Children who have been labeled as learning disabled have been described as demonstrating inadequate language development.

Research and Observations

Owen , Adams, Forrest, Stolz, and Fisher (1971) interviewed parents of such children, their siblings and nonrelated peers. The parents reported that the learning-disabled child, in comparison with siblings and other children, had less adequate verbal skills as well as other difficulties. The fathers perceived the *main* difference between the learning-disabled and comparison children to be verbal ability. In this monograph, the investigators divided the learning-disabled children into categories which were associated with various problems. Children were divided into five groups, those who had a history of organic or physical abnormality, those who had high WISC performance scores relative to their verbal scores, those who had relatively low IQ scores, those who had relatively high IQ scores and those who demonstrated some emotional difficulties. Children designated within the first three categories appeared to demonstrate language deficits. Children who had some history of medical difficulties appeared to have receptive and expressive language problems and difficulty in reproducing auditory stimuli. Children with high performance scores relative to their verbal scores (fifteen IQ points or higher was the criterion for inclusion) appeared to have problems of articulation in which they made distortions ("mushy" sounds such as *shss* for *s* sounds), substitutions and omissions of sounds. The errors seemed to be related to difficulty in sequentializing auditory stimuli (*e.g., aminal* for *animal*). Also of interest was that the mothers and siblings also evidenced language problems.

The children categorized as belonging to the relatively low IQ score group (IQ scores between 90 to 99 on the Wechsler Intelligence Scale for Children) showed both problems of articulation and in expressive and receptive language. Mothers described these children as having difficulty listening in school, being difficult to talk to and as having a history of limited sound production. Siblings and parents of these children did not exhibit language problems.

Children of the remaining two groups, that is, those with relatively high IQ scores (scores ranging between 117 and 154), and those with some emotional problems, did not appear to have language problems.

Two important suggestions or hypotheses can be derived from the results of the Owen et al. study. First, language problems might well be extensive in that population of children called learning disabled. The second point is that many learning disabled children may have and are currently suffering from delayed language development. These are important suggestions, but a few cautionary notes about this study should be added. Whether the particular groups of learning-disabled children as categorized by the investigators have particular speech problems really remains to be seen. The post hoc partitioning of subjects and the resultant findings often yield chance results, or results which will not be found if the study is conducted again. Second, the evidence pertaining to delayed language development is based upon the recollections of the children's parents about the early behavior of their child. Whether these reflections actually are descriptive of those children's behavior or are distorted by more contemporary experiences of the child and mother cannot be determined. Nonetheless, this study does provide some evidence that language problems, perhaps from delayed language development, are extensive among the learning-disabled population.

Two recent studies have examined syntax used by the learning disabled child. Bartel, Grill and Bartel (1973) studied normal and learning-disabled children's language using the technique of free association. Changes in linguistic development are noted through the analysis of children's associations to stimulus words. Thus, children move from using syntactic associations, where the response to a stimulus word is based upon a description or function of that word (*e.g.,* apple . . . eat; apple . . . red) to paradigmatic associations, where a response to the stimulus word is to indicate the class in which the stimulus word belongs (*e.g.,* apple . . . fruit). While the investigators found that younger children were less likely to give advanced associations than older children, no differences were found between the learning-disabled and the nondisabled children. The authors suggest that the learning-disabled children performed as well as the nondisabled ones because of the nature of the task. The response required of the child was immediate; it required no memory, no extended attention and no sequencing of information. These disappointing results seem similar to many others in which differences between groups are not found when the task employed is simple and does not make demands on attention, memory or sequencing skills.

Group differences were found, however, in a study conducted by Wiig, Semel and Crouse (1973). These investigators studied four groups of children using the Berko (1958) test of morphology. This test assesses the child's use of grammatical forms. For example, the child is asked, "This is a tor, now here is another one. There are two _____." Four groups of children were tested. Ten 3- and 4-year-old children were designated as high-risk children on the basis of neurological involvements. A second group of 10 children of approximately the same age served as the control group. These children showed no signs of neurological impairment. A third group of 10 children were of school age (8 to 10 years) and were drawn from a population of learning disabled children who presumably had no speech or language disorders. Finally, a fourth group of 10 subjects of approximately the same age as the learning-disabled group, and who were academically competent, served as the control for the third group.

When comparing the young children, the high-risk and their control group, it was found that the normal children were much better than the high-risk group, particularly on sentences involving the progressive tense, the third person singular and the past tense of verbs. Likewise, when comparing the learning-disabled with their control children, the learning-disabled children performed much less competently. Unlike their peers, the learning-disabled children could not form plural forms of possessives, or form the progressive tense, a transformation that the 3- and 4-year-old normals could accomplish.

The fascinating aspect of the study was that close inspection revealed that high-risk and learning-disabled children who apparently had adequate language development did not. These results again suggest that linguistic development, and the conceptual development that corresponds with it, may well be delayed for the learning-disabled child.

Fry, Johnson and Muehl (1970) compared the oral language of second graders who had been classified as above or below average readers on the basis of their total word knowledge, word recognition and reading subtest scores on the Metropolitan Achievement Test, Primary I Battery. Oral language samples were obtained by having the child tell a story in response to 20 picture stimuli. Analysis was made of the children's communication units, grammatically independent clauses with any of its modifiers. A variety of variables were analyzed, including the types of linguistic patterns used, the number and length of communication units and incomplete communication units. Three major differences discriminated the good from the poor readers.

One was the size of the speaking vocabulary and fluency. The good readers appear to have larger speaking vocabularies and were also more fluent. A second difference was the type of linguistic patterns used by the above- and below-average readers. It was found that below-average readers were more likely to use subordination in the subject position, whereas above-average readers used more subordination in the predicate position. The below-average group made greater use of a category of "movable expression (phrase or subordinate clause) of purpose, cause, or condition. . . . 'The mother didn't have anything because she wasn't hungry' . . ." (p. 127), whereas more of the above-average readers were likely to use the subject-predicate (clause) satellite of the verb. . . . 'Before they wrote a story they had to stand up and pledge' . . ." (p. 129). The authors then hypothesize that subordination itself may not distinguish groups of good and poor readers, but the position of the subordination may reflect linguistic development. The third difference between groups was the finding that the below-average readers used the "existence" type of sentence more than the above-average readers. An existence type of sentence refers to introducing a sentence by "there" followed by a form of the verb to be (*e.g.,* "There's a dog"). The authors hypothesize that the below average readers employ more existence type sentences than the above average readers because they are less skilled in organizing, integrating and telling a coherent story. These children appear to be likely to enumerate picture content, whereas the better readers were more likely to create a meaningful story.

The evidence, such as it is, generally supports the hypothesis that children with learning disabilities can be distinguished from nondisabled ones on factors related to language development. But there is more to language development than simply the acquisition of generative grammar. Children must not only develop the use of phonemes, morphemes and syntax, but must also know when to use them in everyday discourse. As the child develops, there is an increasing number of situations which demand of him not simply primitive motor responses, but linguistic ones (Flavell, Beach and Chinsky, 1966).

Mediation

Mediation, what goes on within the organism after seeing a stimulus and before making a response, has been long thought to be critical in facilitating the child's learning, be it of a motor, a conceptual or an interpersonal skill (Flavell, Beach and Chinsky, 1966). While the various forms that such mediation might take are often disputed, many theorists agree that one important form of mediation is language (Osgood, 1957; Osgood, Suci and Tannenbaum, 1957; Vygotsky, 1962; Luria, 1966; Bandura, 1969; Kohlberg, 1969). If, and how, the child uses language in his problem-solving activity is deemed particularly critical in the development of the child.

There is evidence that as the child ages, he will rely increasingly upon his self-generative language in order to encode and deal with problems. For example, Flavell, Beach and Chinsky (1966) noted that the spontaneous verbalizations by the child increased with age. Miller, Shelton and Flavell (1969) found that children began to employ self-instructions by age 3½ and by age 5 children's self-instructions were as facilitating as those generated by the researchers.

It is also clear that all children do not generate an adequate set of instructions or rehearse the instructions given them by the experimenter. Many children do not appear to mediate the problem at hand. This lack of mediation might be due to a vocabulary lack, a production deficiency, or the child may have the words but fail to use them in the problem-solving capacity, a mediation deficiency. An important question, then, is the degree to which children might be trained toward greater mediational efforts.

There is now evidence to suggest that children can be trained to use covert self-instructions in approaching learning tasks and that such training will facilitate their performance on these tasks. Of particular relevance to the learning disability specialist are two studies of verbal mediation which employed hyperactive children (Palkes, Stewart and Kahana, 1968; Palkes, Stewart, and Freedman, 1971). Children, ages 7 to 13, were defined as hyperactive on the basis of receiving psychiatric treatment for that symptom. Those children who had received directions to orally instruct themselves to think before they act, to listen, to stop before they responded, performed significantly better on the Porteus Maze tasks than children who had not received directions or written instructions.

Bandura, Grusec and Menlove (1966) tested 6- to 8-year-old children in their imitation of a model they had observed. One group of children was instructed to verbalize all the actions of the model as they observed the scene. A second group was given no instructions relevant to verbalizations, while the third group was instructed to verbalize material which would interfere with their verbal codings of the model's behavior. As expected, children who verbalized the actions of the model showed more imitation than those who passively observed, and those who passively observed showed greater imitation of the model than those who were told to verbalize competing material.

The utility of directions to produce self-instructions has also been demonstrated with training adults. For example, Meichenbaum (1971) was able to reduce adult females' fears of snakes by having them observe a model who verbalized intentions and techniques while herself approaching and handling a snake. Those who observed a vocal model subsequently showed less fear of the snake than those women who viewed a nonvocal model.

It is clear that much remains to be determined about the effectiveness of instructions to self-instruct. Sometimes such instructions are simply ineffective (Bryan, 1972), sometimes they may simply interfere with learning the adequate performance of a skill (Bandura, Grusec and Menlove, 1966; Miller, Shelton, and Flavell, 1969). While we do not know all of the parameters affecting the power of self-instructions, certainly there are enough data to suggest that they may play an important role in problem-solving activities of children and may well play an important future role in the remediation of some forms of learning disabilities.

Social Relations

Compared to data concerning other effects there really is little information available concerning the language production of learning-disabled children and the social repercussions of their defects. The paucity of information necessarily makes the following highly speculative. It is our belief, however, that language problems are crucial for the disabled child and that such problems may generate a variety of interpersonal difficulties for the child which have been well documented (Bryan, 1974a; Keogh et al., 1974; Owen et al., 1971).

Entwisle (in press) has argued forcibly for the importance of rather subtle language factors in affecting the social and academic life of the child. As she correctly notes, children not only acquire basic grammar and language skills, but they also learn how to use various styles of language, what to say when and to whom. She refers to this knowledge as "sociolinguistic competence." This competence requires learning a large number of variations in style and timing. The child is expected to learn to use different phonology, grammar, vocabulary, pitch and loudness when speaking in various situations and to various parties, and when expressing various attitudes or feelings. This competence is attributed to familial interactions, primarily in the form of modeling the family's own style of language deployment. For example, if the family relies on physical forms of punishment rather than verbal control of behavior, the child may well enter the classroom quite ill-equipped to respond to the typical verbal control techniques of the teacher. Similarly, it has been well demonstrated that children do imitate the language habits of the adults around them (Adams and Hamm, 1971; Bandura and Kupers, 1964). If the models are poor, the child's performance is destined to be similarly inadequate. Whatever the cause of such incompetence, evidence has been presented indicating that the learning-disabled child does not exhibit the same degree of linguistic competence that his nondisabled peers do. But even if the incompetencies are of such a nature as to produce sociolinguistic incompetence, a fact yet to be demonstrated, will he be at a disadvantage within the classroom, and if so, what is the nature of the disadvantage?

There is considerable evidence that teachers' expectancies of children's performances are relevant to the eventual performance of the child (Rosenthal and Jacobsen, 1968; Seaver, 1973). Is there evidence that language factors will affect these expectancies or, more importantly, the behavior of the teacher towards the child? Rist (1970) has provided some provocative, if not altogether persuasive, observations directly relevant to this point. This investigator conducted a longitudinal study of black children who entered kindergarten and whose teacher was black. He observed the class at the beginning of the term and found that within a few days the children had been more or less divided into three groups. The groups were differentiated on the basis of how far they sat from the teacher. Interestingly, the teacher's behavior towards the children was rather predictable on the basis of these stable seating arrangements. Thus, the children who sat closest to the teacher were more likely to be allowed to help her. They were asked to perform such activities as leading the pledge and running errands. Moreover, the closest students engaged in more verbal interactions with the teacher than did children of the remaining groups. What distinguished the groups of children besides their seating arrangements was whether they spoke to the teacher using standard English or black dialect. The children closest to the teacher spoke most frequently in standard English, the children furthest removed from her spoke black dialect. Interestingly, the children's spatial arrangements continued to reflect those of the kindergarten years when they entered the first and then the second grades.

This study is not conclusive, since the results might simply reflect the biases or idiosyncrasies of a single teacher. Yet, this may not be the case, and if this teacher represents many teachers, future teachers should be very sensitive to their own treatment of children with language styles differing from their own. Moreover, the learning disability specialist will be confronted with children who have not only subtle language deficits, but obviously different language styles as well. The speech and language of learning-disabled children are readily discernible from nondisabled children of the same age, sex and socioeconomic status. In the chapter on behavior the authors cite a study which is worth repeating for this discussion(Bryan 1974e). College students who had no previous interactions with or knowledge about the children they viewed on video tape were asked to rate them on a variety of characteristics. Some of the children were learning disabled, some were not. All were videotaped during an interaction they had with a younger peer involving their giving instructions to the younger child on bowling. These students rated the adequacy of the language of the learning-disabled child significantly less than that of the nondisabled ones. This discrimination was possible after viewing the interaction of the children no longer than four minutes!

The position is taken that many of the academic and behavioral characteristics associated with learning disabilities in many children may reflect language disorders. Admittedly, language may be one factor of many, or language problems may reflect other problems. But there is good reason to believe that language disorders have been much underestimated in explanations of learning problems. First, learning disability is often a synonym for reading failure, and both reading failure and learning disabilities have been linked to low scores on measures of verbal intelligence (Birch and Belmont, 1965). In addition, many of the studies of other factors, such as auditory or visual information processing find that the discriminating variable between the learning-disabled and comparison child are verbal rather than nonverbal or perceptual stimuli (McGrady and Olson, 1970).

One hypothesis is that many of the behavioral characteristics associated with the learning-disabled child reflect language disorders, albeit perhaps subtle ones. Hyperactivity or short attention span may well reflect a language disability and thus may be a symptom rather than a cause of deficit learning by the child. The child who has difficulty in attaining early levels of comprehension or the syntax and semantic rules of language, may miss a great deal of information which is expected to occur in the natural course of development. Commands may not be heeded, readings understood or sociolinguistic competence obtained. An evil cycle may thus be set into motion, wherein the child's conceptual development shows particular lags and the expectancies and affective responses of adults toward the child further deprive him of the remediational training so needed, which further contributes to his conceptual incompetence. When this occurs, a cumulative deficit may result. Language is intimately linked to conceptual development, hence, any decrease in language skills would reciprocally affect conceptual development adversely.

When a child fails to respond as expected to parents, it seems reasonable that parents will become irritated, upset and/or confused and have difficulty socializing, understanding and controlling this child. In addition, a child whose behavior is seen as erratic, unpredictable and uncontrollable, who has difficulty in understanding or expressing himself, will not elicit positive feelings or high expectations from others. Not only will parents feel less affection, but lower expectations are also associated with differential treatments—all to the disadvantage of the child.

Given the lacuna of data, the authors can be justly accused of making a mountain out of a molehill. But, whether the molehill will generate a mountain does need exploration, and it is our hope that considerably greater attention be paid not only to the language development of the learning-disabled child but to the social consequences of these inadequacies upon the everyday life of these children.

CHAPTER
9
READING
AND
MATHEMATICS

Reading is a perceptual process, a response, a developmental task, an interest, a means to learn and a means of communication (Dechant, 1964). In the United States, reading instruction dates back more than 200 years, with the method and materials used reflecting contemporary religious and educational beliefs and cultural needs. The technological nature of our society and the public's concern for equal opportunities for its citizens has led to an increasing interest in the reading achievement of citizens. The public's concern regarding reading achievement has generated a wealth of data about reading and the techniques appropriate for its development. Insofar as the failure to learn to read is frequently defined as a learning disability, information about reading becomes important to specialists in the field.

Dyslexia

Historically, reading failure was linked to adult aphasia and was called dyslexia, a medical term which connotes defective reading associated with a neurophysiological disorder. Dyslexia is a syndrome in which a child has unusual and persistent difficulty in learning the components of words and sentences, in integrating segments into words and sentences and in learning other kinds of representational systems, such as telling time, directions and seasons. Often the child has a history of delayed language development, sometimes a history of soft neurological signs. Invariably, the child has concomitant problems in writing and spelling. The characteristics of dyslexics seemed to form a syndrome which Gerstmann (1940) described as consisting of problems in reading, space-form disability, left-to-right disorientation, dyscalculia (defect in math), dysgraphia (difficulty in writing) and finger agnosia (inability to meaningfully interpret stimuli, gathered by the fingers).

Clinicians have reported various characteristics of the dyslexic child and these descriptions have gained a certain degree of acceptance within the field. Many of these characteristics appear, on closer study, not to be evidenced by these children, but nonetheless are still in vogue. Be that as it may, the composite picture of the child experiencing reading problems, according to clinical lore, is that he has perceptual, linguistic, motor and social skills less mature or in some respects deviant from his peers. Clinicians report that by age 9 or 10 the language and speech of dyslexic children seem adequate and aberrant behavior (mainly hyperactivity) has diminished. Reading, writing and spelling problems are marked by persistence in errors, which while common for young children, is not for older ones. Such problems as making reversals, omissions or substitutions while reading, spelling and writing are evident. Specifically, the dyslexic child is believed particularly likely to commit errors of spatial direction and sequential ordering. Directional confusion in reading refers to prolonged difficulty in differentiating similar looking letters (b-d, p-q). Difficulty in sequencing appears when the child reverses the position of letters and numbers (was-saw, 14-41). Oral reading is marked by slow, word by word reading. Arithmetic and spelling performance will mirror the problems in deciphering the reading code (Edgington and Blackmon, 1962). These particular difficulties have frequently been attributed to presumed difficulty in the child's visual perception.

It has also been noted that the dyslexic child is often confused about words relating to time and direction. For example, confusions include *up* for *down, go* for *stop, now* for *later* and *first* for *last.* It should also be noted that it is believed that dyslexic children mirror their reading problems in their speech, and apparently have or did have a history of problems of auditory discrimination (Owen et al., 1971). Thus, dyslexics, who may or may not have accompanying articulation errors, may show peculiar grammatical constructions, wherein prefixes and suffixes are confused and distorted.

Since there are so many children committing so many errors of reading with so many people studying them, it is hardly surprising that a variety of proposals as to how such children should be subcategorized have been made. Rabinovitch and Ingram (1962) have proposed dividing reading retardation into three major diagnostic categories: *a)* primary reading retardation, *b)* brain injury with resultant reading retardation and *c)* secondary reading retardation. The primary reading retardation group evidences a number of symptoms. These include difficulties in both visual and auditory information processing (cannot translate letters and letter combinations into meaningful concepts, cannot translate sounds into letter symbols), left-right directional confusion with or without mixed laterality, broader language deficits (difficulties in name finding, imprecise articulation and primitive syntax), a specific concept symbolization deficiency in orientation and body image problems. The primary reading retardation case is presumed to be neurologically based, often familial in origin and related to parietal lobe dysfunction. The brain injury with resultant reading retardation group is similar to adult aphasics and has a history of some kind of brain injury, such as birth trauma, encephalitis or head injury. The secondary reading retardation group has the normal potential to read but fails to do so as a result of environmentally induced problems (*e.g.*, poor schooling) or emotional-motivational problems (*e.g.*, negativism, depression, anxiety, psychosis).

Boder (1971) suggests three categories of dyslexics. Group 1 is the *dysphonetic dyslexic.* In this group the child has a limited sight vocabulary in which he can easily read only a small number of words. When this child encounters a word he does not know, he is at a loss as to how to decipher it. He may try to guess, using the first or last letters of words, but essentially he has no phonics or word analysis skills. For this child, reading from context is easier than reading single words because his speaking vocabulary is sufficiently large to allow him to employ clues embedded in the context to infer the puzzling word.

The second category proposed by Boder is *dyseidetic dyslexic.* This child has difficulty remembering the appearance of letters or words. Apparently, such a child has difficulty recognizing the whole word and infers the letter or word from analysis of the component parts. Unlike children categorized as dysphonic dyslexic, these children read analytically by sounding out familiar and unfamiliar combinations of letters. The child can read phonetically a list of unknown words. This child may spell poorly, as he is likely to spell phonetically.

The third group is *mixed dysphonetic-dyseidetic dyslexic.* Boder refers to these children as "hard core" dyslexics. This child has neither the visual nor the auditory means to decipher the written word and may remain a nonreader unless he receives intensive help. Even then, remediation is slow and painful. The urge on the part of the child to withdraw from trying to read is quite understandable.

Common to all three types of dyslexics is difficulty in spelling. Boder indicates that normal readers can spell correctly to dictation about 70 to 100% of the words in their sight vocabulary. Dyslexic children in the dysphonetic and mixed groups usually spell no more than 40% of the words in their sight vocabulary.

Several theorists have suggested that children with reading problems can be divided into two groups, visual and auditory or visual and verbal dyslexia (Lyle, 1969; Kinsbourne, 1973; Bateman, 1969).

Johnson and Myklebust (1967) divide reading retardation into two major categories, visual and auditory dyslexia. Visual dyslexics have visual discrimination difficulties and confuse letters or words which appear similar. These children make discriminations about visual configurations which are accurate, but these are made slowly. Many of the children appear to make spatial and orientation errors by reversing and inverting letters. Visual memory shortcomings are presumed to affect the child's ability to follow and remember sequences of symbols.

The auditory dyslexic has difficulty making the association between the visual presentation and sounds heard, as well as discriminating sounds, particularly short vowels. For such children, thinking of rhymes or listening for parts of words and making associations to other words are very difficult tasks. Separating words into components or reuniting segments into wholes are very difficult for these children. There are problems in remembering auditory symbols and stringing them into sequences. As a result words may be mispronounced or distorted.

We have reviewed some of the important taxonomies proposed for viewing the dyslexic child. But noteworthy is the fact that children can be categorized in an infinite number of ways. In evaluating taxonomies, it is important to note that good ones differ from poor ones on one basis and that is that members grouped together should bear important similarities with one another and important differences from others not within their group. Whether a proposed taxonomy does in fact accomplish this is an empirical matter, not solved by armchair speculations. The verbal-visual taxonomies do appear to have some empirical support; that is, children do appear to respond in one or another of these fashions (Lyle, 1969). Whether the remaining proposals for such categorizations will be useful will be determined by future researchers. As of now, these proposals reflect hypotheses, not empirically validated groupings.

As the field of learning disabilities has expanded, reading problems have become a major focus of its practitioners. The magnitude of the reading difficulty necessary for a child to be defined and labeled as learning disabled or dyslexic has been reduced. More and more children with fewer and fewer problems have fallen onto the professional turf of the learning disability specialist. The child need not exhibit all, any or some of the associated characteristics of dyslexia to be considered a severe reading problem. Using a standardized reading test to define reading disabilities, a lag of six months in first and second grades and a year thereafter is sufficient to warrant an evaluation and intervention program.

Etiology of Dyslexia

Many theories have attempted to account for failure to learn to read in the absence of mental retardation and environmental deprivation. The majority of explanations have been nested within the medical model. Reading problems have been associated with genetics by Hermann (1959) and Critchley (1964); and with events before, during and after birth by Kawi and Pasamanick (1959) and Ernhart, Graham and Eichman, (1963). Geschwind (1968), Dykman, Ackerman, Clements and Peters (1971) and Wender (1971) offer the explanation of minimal cerebral dysfunction, although they differ in opinion as to the specific dysfunction. These theoretical stances have generated three major hypotheses to explain reading retardation. Reading retardation has been viewed as a result of perceptual deficits, inadequate sensory integration and specific deficiencies in verbal intelligence.

Perceptual Deficit Hypothesis

The most popular explanation for reading failure has been that children have difficulty in the perception (discrimination, memory, translation) of visual symbols. This emanated from Orton's (1937) observations of reading retardates who reversed letters in reading and writing. Proponents of this hypothesis focus upon directional confusion (Hermann, 1959), difficulties in figure-ground perception (Strauss and Lehtinen, 1947; Bender,

1938), deficits in visual analysis and synthesis (Birch and Belmont, 1964), perceptual motor problems (Kephart, 1960; Frostig, 1964; Cruickshank, Bentzen, Ratzeburg and Tannhauser, 1961) and disturbances in optical control (Getman, 1965). Using the same behaviors, others have interpreted reading disabilities as reflections of deficits in attention, organization of visual arrays, verbal labeling and verbal rehearsal (Lyle, 1969; Lyle and Goyen, 1968; Vellutino, 1974; Hutson, 1974).

To determine which factors might be related to reading retardation, Lyle (1969) did a factor analytic study of 54 retarded and 54 adequate readers, 6 to 12 years old. A battery of tests was administered to each child. Included were tests of reversals in oral reading and spelling, writing reversals (from dictation), the WISC, Graham and Kendall memory for designs, spelling and arithmetic tests along with data concerning perceptual skills, lateral dominance and hand-eye dominance. Lyle found that there were two distinct factors, unrelated to each other, associated with reading retardation. One set of related items consisted of tasks in which there was a strong perceptual component. Letter and sequence reversals in reading and writing, and to a lesser degree memory designs, were intercorrelated and associated with reading retardation. The second factor consisted of items which required verbal skills. These included spelling, arithmetic, arithmetic information and coding subtests of the WISC. The verbal factor was also related to reading achievement. Lyle did not find reading disability related to mixed laterality, crossed hand-eye dominance or the Gerstmann syndrome. Reading-disabled children below 8 years were particularly likely to demonstrate difficulties on the perceptual tasks. Among the older adequate and inadequate readers, perceptual disturbances were less discriminating.

Lyle found that not only did the younger deficit readers demonstrate inadequate performance on perceptual skills, but that they also had a history of delayed language acquisition. Lyle concluded that there are two major kinds of reading retardation. One is nonverbal and related to perceptual skills; the second is verbal. The perceptual factor appears to be more characteristic of younger retarded readers, the verbal factor more characteristic of older retarded readers.

Programmatic research to investigate the perceptual skills involved in reading has been undertaken by Lyle and Goyen (1968), Goyen and Lyle (1971 a,b; 1973) and Vellutino and associates (Vellutino, Pruzek, Steger and Meshoulan, 1973; Vellutino, Steger and Kandel, 1972). Lyle and Goyen (1968) investigated visual recognition of 40 second- and third-graders, 20 of whom had reading deficits, defined by reading at least nine months below grade level. Through the use of a tachistoscope, children were presented with letters of the alphabet commonly confused by deficit readers, with 15 lines simpler in form than letters and 15 two-dimensional line drawings which represented the contours of four-letter words. The child viewed one figure and then had to indicate which one he had seen from a multiple choice response card. Children's responses were obtained under three conditions: immediately following the tachistoscopic presentation, after a short delay and with three consecutively presented stimuli. In the latter condition, children were required to indicate the order of presentation. To prohibit verbal labeling or rehearsal and kinesthetic rehearsal, the children had to clasp their hands and recite multiplication tables aloud before the presentation and while waiting for the response card. Children were tested on several occasions.

The results were that the retarded readers performed significantly more poorly on all the tests than did the adequate readers, although the magnitude of differences was related to the age of the children. While retarded readers committed more of all kinds of errors, it was the young retarded readers who erred the most. Lyle and Goyen interpreted these results to indicate that young retarded readers do have a perceptual deficit.

Lyle and Goyen (1974) compared the performance of 21 retarded and 21 nonretarded readers, 6 and 7 years old, on speed of processing information, perceptual discrimination and short-term memory. Reading retardation was defined as at least 9 months below age level for 6-year-olds and at least one year below age level for 7-year-olds. Children briefly viewed tachistoscopic presentations of 30 pairs of rectangular shapes; one half were the same, the remaining different from each other. Some children viewed both items of the pair simultaneously, thus short-term memory was not involved. Other children viewed each item of the pair separated by a two-second delay. A third group viewed the items separated by a seven-second delay. The results replicated earlier studies (Lyle and Goyen, 1968; Goyen and Lyle, 1971 a,b), indicating that retarded readers experience difficulty in visual recognition tasks which require rapid information processing. When stimuli are presented rapidly, retarded readers have more difficulty than adequate readers in subsequently recognizing these stimuli. It should be noted, however, that retarded readers performed as well as adequate readers when judgments had to be made on identical pairs. Differences between adequate and inadequate readers resulted when the items of the pair were different; retarded readers were more likely to judge the items as equivalent. It appears that poor readers either have difficulty in making perceptual discriminations or they have a verbal bias which leads them to report stimuli as equivalent.

There was no evidence that retarded readers have deficits in short-term memory. Additionally, there were no effects found for the administration of rewards for competent performance (Goyen and Lyle, 1971 a,b).

Learning to read has been compared to mastery of a paired-associate learning task. In studies of paired-associate learning, subjects must learn to combine two stimuli so that upon presentation of one the person can recall the second. In reading, the child must learn to associate two stimuli, visual symbols with their respective sounds. To study the relationship of visual recognition memory to children's performance on a paired-associate task, Samuels and Anderson (1973) divided children into two groups, those with good and those with poor visual recognition memory. The children were then presented with two paired-associate learning tasks, one presumed to be easy and the second difficult. The child's intelligence test scores, visual recognition memory and performance on the easy paired-associate task were unrelated. Performance of the hard paired-associate task was related to visual recognition memory and to vocabulary and total reading scores on the California Achievement test.

The evidence for perceptual problems underlying reading deficiencies is quite mixed. Vellutino and colleagues (Vellutino, Steger, DeSetto and Phillips, in press; Vellutino, Harding, Phillips, and Steger, in press; Vellutino, Pruzek, Steger, Meshoulan, 1973; Vellutino, Steger and Kandel, 1972) have failed to find, in spite of considerable effort, that the reading-impaired child suffers from perceptual deficits. Perhaps failure to find perceptual differences between adequate and inadequate readers reflects methodological flaws, inadequate sample definitions or a variety of other factors. Nonetheless, the consistent findings of Vellutino and colleagues that reading-disabled children do not differ from adequate readers on perceptual discriminations raises serious questions as to the adequacy of the perceptual deficit hypothesis.

Vellutino and colleagues argue against the perceptual deficit hypothesis of reading dysfunction. In place of the perceptual deficit hypothesis, they suggest reading difficulties are the result of the child's failure to label perceptual experiences and that the child's cognitive operations are faulty.

At first blush, the results of the Vellutino and the Lyle and Goyen studies appear to be contradictory. Lyle and Goyen find evidence that perceptual deficits may be characteristic of young deficit readers but not older retarded readers. The Vellutino et al. studies often employed children somewhat older than the children in the Lyle and Goyen studies. Second, the differences in presentations in the studies may affect children's ability to employ mnemonic devices. Lyle and Goyen used rapid tachistoscopic presentations and in one case (1968) prohibited the children from employing their mnemonic devices by requiring them to clasp their hands and recite multiplication tables. In the Vellutino et al. studies the children might have been able to use their own cueing systems. These methodological differences might serve to mask perceptual differences in deficit and adequate readers.

The role played by visual perception has been an elusive and perhaps exaggerated one. The results of several studies indicate that auditory, rather than visual, perception may be particularly important in facilitating reading. Kinsbourne (1973) administered a battery of tests of auditory and visual processing and associative learning. The visual tests measured the child's ability to discriminate forms; the auditory test required the child to repeat a pair of speech sounds, repeat three phoneme series and indicate whether two words sounded the same or different. The associative part of the battery included having the child learn a nonsense word which was to be associated with a shape.

The test was administered to several hundred first-grade children, and then readministered to them in their classrooms at varying times during the next two years. These items were correlated with the children's scores on the Metropolitan Reading and Arithmetic tests. Kinsbourne found that the factor which discriminated good from poor readers was the increase in the performance on the *auditory* tests from the first to the second testing session. Neither performance nor improvement on the visual tests were predictive of reading achievement.

Rosner (1973) produced results very similar to those of Kinsbourne. First- and second-grade children were administered a visual analysis test, which required the child to copy designs, and an auditory analysis test, in which the child is asked to listen to a meaningful word and then repeat it with a sound omitted. Scores on these tests were related to scores on the Stanford Achievement Tests. It was found that the auditory analysis test was related to word reading, paragraph meaning, spelling and word study skills. There was not a significant relationship between the visual analysis test and reading scores, although the visual analysis test did correlate with arithmetic scores. Similar difficulties with auditory rather than visual stimuli by dyslexic children have been reported by Estes and Huizinga (1974) and Zigmond (1966).

On the basis of the evidence, it would seem that the role of visual perceptual dysfunctions in producing reading retardation has probably been overestimated. There is evidence that such dysfunctions may characterize the young child, but even that evidence is mixed. Language, attention, auditory processes all come to bear upon the acquisition of reading, and any failures in such acquisition may reflect these processes. Indeed, there is evidence of the role of auditory processes in affecting reading performance and no doubt future work in the area of reading will further delineate their role.

Deficits in Cross-modal Information Processing

A second popular explanation for reading failure is the difficulty in integrating auditory and visual information. Several researchers have found that reading-disabled youngsters are less competent than adequate readers in making associations between auditory and visual stimuli. This area was first initiated by the studies of Birch and Belmont (1964), Blank and Bridger (1966) and Blank, Weider and Bridger (1968). Senf and Freundl (1971) and Vande Voort and Senf (1973) have offered evidence that disabled readers were less able than adequate readers on a variety of tasks which required associating visual and verbal stimuli.

As has been pointed out in the chapter on Information Processing, many studies concerned with cross-modal integration have failed to control for intrasensory processing or for the verbal demands placed upon the child. The same general comment can be made regarding such studies which employ the dyslexic child as subject. Studies which determine that one group of children is worse than another on either visual or auditory processing cannot infer that one group has a problem in cross-modal integration, because the difficulty might be attributable to failure in intrasensory processing. Zigmond (1966) found that 9- to 12-year-old dyslexic boys performed significantly worse than nondyslexic ones on various auditory tests and in paired-associate tasks, which, presumably, required cross-modal integration of inputs, although groups were comparable in the visual tasks. The failure of the dyslexic child to perform adequately on the paired-associate task might be due to *a)* auditory processing difficulties or *b)* cross-modal integration problems.

Cross-modal integration is likely to be facilitated by the linguistic development of the child. The child who can connect, through labels, the visual and auditory signals is probably more likely to make an adequate response than one who does not or cannot apply such labels. Insofar as the linguistic development of the learning-disabled child is likely to be different and less adequate than that of nondisabled children, differences in cross-modal integration among dyslexic children may reflect a linguistic deficit rather than a sensory processing difference. Indeed, in one study which attempted to remove the verbal components involved in most tests of intra- and intersensory processing, no differences between the dyslexic and nondyslexic children were found (Vellutino, Steger, and Pruzek, 1973).

Recently, there has been some tendency to move away from concepts involving intra- and intersensory auditory and visual processing towards conceptualizing stimuli as either involving spatial or temporal features (Freides, 1974; Blank and Bridger, 1966). Freides has argued that separating stimuli according to their spatial and temporal nature may be more efficacious than focusing upon whether the stimuli have a visual or auditory component. He suggests that the visual system is best suited for processing stimuli with spatial features, while the auditory system is best able to process stimuli with temporal features. He suggests that with age these features of the auditory and visual systems become even more specialized and thus there is a diminution rather than an integration of the modalities. Future learning disability specialists should be sensitive to the spatial-temporal, rather than the auditory-visual, features of the tasks confronting children.

Verbal Deficits

A third explanation for reading retardation is that poor readers have a deficit in verbal skills. There is both direct and indirect evidence to support this view. Indirect evidence stems from the studies of information processing and of the developmental histories of retarded readers. In the information processing studies, there are invariably group differences in favor of normal readers when the experimental task requires the child to process auditorily presented linguistic information, and rarely are there group differences when the task is strictly one of visual recognition demanding no linguistic skills. Studies which investigate the developmental histories of retarded readers report a very high incidence of linguistic developmental difficulties and delays in the acquisition of language.

On the basis of the evidence, it appears reasonable to assume that reading reflects a two-step process. In the beginning, reading may be highly dependent upon certain perceptual skills, such as discriminations among phonemes and graphemes. After adequate discriminations are learned, competent reading may require more advanced conceptual skills. The question remains whether we are talking about two groups of children with reading deficits: one group who have perceptual problems but who may be academically successful when they learn the discriminations, and a second group who are successful initially but experience school difficulties because of verbal deficits. The data suggest that there is one group of children, a group who demonstrates a history of difficulty with reading, or decoding processes, even at a young age (Owen et al., 1971).

Whether or not reading acquisition is a two-step process which the reading-disabled child cannot master, there is evidence to support the hypothesis that reading retardation is associated with language difficulties. Hutson (1974) has provided a summary of this evidence. She points out that language is a central factor in auditory and visual perception of complex stimuli, including words; that verbal mediation serves as an important facilitator in dealing with such stimuli; that disabled readers are generally found to have lower verbal intelligence scores than competent readers and that studies of language skill differences among good and poor readers find differences in the areas of phonemics, semantics and syntax, always to the detriment of the poor readers. Hutson concludes:

Although the ability to read, as a multifaceted phenomenon, is potentially subject to interference from several sources, a principal dimension along which good and poor readers differ is language skill. These differences are not always apparent at the lower levels of difficulty, but become evident in tasks of sufficient complexity to tap differences in the use of language, awareness of language, and in knowledge of more advanced language patterns (p. 4).

227

The verbal problems of children destined to have reading difficulties are evidenced at the onset of these difficulties. Indeed, the frequency of children with both early verbal and reading problems led Rabinovitch and Ingram (1962) to propose a subcategory to the classification of dyslexia, primary reading retardation. Owen et al. (1971), as the reader may recall, also found that reading difficulties were associated with early problems with language development. Likewise, DeHirsh, Jansky and Langford (1966) developed a battery of tests, many of which contained items tapping language skills, in order to predict which child might have reading difficulties. The test, given to kindergarten children, did have some success in prediction, although the test yielded many false negatives and positives. DeHirsch and his colleagues felt that the reading, writing and spelling difficulties of the school failures they tested reflect a comprehensive verbal-symbolic disturbance.

The evidence pertaining to the correlation of verbal or language problems with reading difficulties is not limited to studies of the young child. The relationship holds for older children as well. Blank, Weider and Bridger (1968) found that reading retarded and nonretarded first-grade children differed in their performances on tasks which required verbal coding, with retarded readers performing less adequately than nonretarded ones. Vellutino (1974) summarizes research conducted on differences in phonemic analysis by good and poor readers. Generally, it is found that normal readers are linguistically more sophisticated, as they have greater verbal fluency and better syntax than poor readers. When defective and adequate readers read aloud, the defective readers commit more errors by repeating nonsense words as "real" words, and when they err in reading "real" words, they err by distorting the vowels, particularly those in the middle or final positions of the words. Vogel (1974) compared good and poor readers, ages 7 and 8, on their performances on a variety of tests which were administered orally and often required spoken responses from the child. Again, it was found that poor readers were less adequate than good readers in their language skills. To make matters worse, there is evidence to suggest that language handicaps of the poor reader will slow his learning of meaningful sentences. Weinstein and Rabinovitch (1971) divided fourth-graders into two groups, good and poor readers. The children were then given a paired-associate task and a task in which they had to repeat four sentences, two structured and two unstructured. The structured sentences were constructed by inserting a word in certain positions in a sentence. The unstructured sentences consisted of random insertions of this word into the sentence. The groups did not differ in their learning of the paired-associate test. They were able to learn the correct verbal response to the stimulus word. The groups differed, however, in their learning of the sentences. Good readers learned structured sentences faster than poor readers, and good readers learned the structured sentences faster than the unstructured sentences. Poor readers learned the structured and unstructered sentences with the same degree of difficulty. The results suggested that for adequate readers, good syntax either facilitated the learning or bad syntax disrupted it. For the poor reader, syntax apparently failed to make any difference in their learning; they learned as if they were unaware of it. To compound the problem, Freidlander and de Lara (1973) found that children with relatively poor language skills were more likely to prefer distorted and relatively unintelligible speech than children with good linguistic skills, and children with poor language skills may be less likely to attend to meaningful language inputs.

The evidence concerning perceptual deficits and cross-modal integration as important processes in the production of reading difficulties has, at best, received rather equivocal empirical support. The data on verbal deficits and reading problems is much stronger. There is evidence that children who have difficulty learning to read have language deficits, and this relationship has been found in studies using a wide variety of language measures and relatively mildly handicapped youngsters. These findings may have important implications for efforts at early detection of learning problems. We know that language development undergoes tremendous growth during the preschool years, but it is also becoming apparent that language development continues well into the elementary school years (Palermo and Molfese, 1972). Such development has been linked to school achievement.

In detecting or predicting learning disability during the preschool years, that is, in predicting reading achievement, it is very likely that attention should be withdrawn from the study of simple perceptual and motor skills and be directed instead towards a finer analysis of the child's language abilities.

Reading retardation has been studied from the perspectives of deficits in perception, sensory information integration and verbal abilities. It is clear that problems in learning to read are multifaceted, as studies have demonstrated differences between retarded and adequate readers in various reading skills, using children of varying ages and severity of reading inadequacy and varying techniques of measurement.

The samples of children used to study reading retardation have ranged from 5 to 11 years of age and, not surprisingly, the results found are somewhat dependent upon the age of the sample used. It appears that young children who have reading difficulties may have perceptual ones as well, particularly if the perceptual tasks involve auditory stimuli. Whether their faulty performance is due to a perceptual or linguistic problem remains to be seen. The younger child may do more poorly on tests which presume to tap more purely visual perceptual processes, but the evidence is mixed.

When differences are found between good and poor readers at an early age, they are differences of amount, not type. The patterns of errors made by retarded and adequate young readers has been found to be the same, except that poor readers make more errors than adequate ones (Lyle and Goyen, 1974; Kinsbourne, 1973). Apparently, it is not until the child is well into his primary school years that patterns of errors distinguish the good from poor reader. The limited amount of information available suggests that good readers make more errors than poor ones when the stimuli used are somewhat familiar (Vellutino et al., in press; Willows, 1974). It is likely that good readers allow intrusions of errors because of the overlearning of words which appear similar to the stimuli. Poor readers have weaker habits for omitting these erroneous but similar words and thus intrusion errors are not likely to occur.

One of three major hypotheses advanced concerning reading

deficiencies, that which suggests the presence of verbal deficits, has received considerable empirical support. Whether the researcher looks to phonemic analysis, syntax, comprehension or the use of verbal labels in learning a task, the retarded reader has a more difficult time than the adequate reader. There is little support for the perceptual deficit hypothesis, although this conclusion is somewhat dependent upon the definition of perception. There are certain perceptual tasks which discriminate good and poor young readers, but there are many which do not. It is difficult in light of these mixed results to believe that as a group poor readers have a gross visual or visual-motor defect when these inadequacies are only occasionally found and are dependent upon the methodology involved. While the hypothesis might be intuitively compelling, the evidence is not.

Teaching Reading

How shall we teach children to read? No single approach in 27 years of research on teaching reading has overcome or eliminated reading disabilities in children at the first-grade level (Lohnes, 1973).

Studies of teaching methods find a quagmire of unrelated theories, methods and poor research designs. Chall (1970) summarizes research from 1910 to 1965 and Diederich (1973) from 1960 to 1970. Chall points out that in many studies the authors fail to indicate how children were divided into experimental and control groups, how much time was given to reading treatments, how teachers were selected, whether the teachers, in fact, taught the method they were assigned to teach and, finally, failed to specify the contents of the teaching program. Diederich points out that there is more research on reading than on any other subject taught in school, more than 1,000 studies each year. In spite of this, there are *no* important facts about methods of teaching reading which are incontestably known.

Moreover, the research on teacher characteristics associated with good reading programs has likewise failed to yield many results. The results lead to the conclusions that teacher training may well be unrelated to teacher effectiveness and that bright, friendly people are better at teaching reading than dull, disagreeable ones (Diederich, 1973).

While the data pertaining to the best method of teaching reading has yielded little fruit, there is a good deal of evidence to suggest that most children do learn to read and they do so under a variety of teaching techniques. For instance, Graeme and Harris (1970) used dictionary skills to teach word recognition to retarded readers, Hollingsworth (1970) taught reading by having children read aloud and in unison with the teacher (impress method), and Humphrey used a game approach in increasing children's reading skills. There is no doubt that reading can be taught and that disabled readers can be helped (Balow, 1965).

Phonics vs. Whole-word Method

While the particular method which is best for teaching reading is still unknown, we can say with some assuredness that programs which include phonics instruction appear to yield better results than programs which employ whole-word methods (Diederich, 1973). A classic study of reading methods was conducted by Bliesmer and Yarborough (1965). Ten reading programs were compared at the first-grade level. Five of the programs used phonics, emphasizing letter-sound relationships and pronunciation rules to synthesize whole words. Five programs used the analytic approach, emphasizing teaching many whole words recognized on sight. Later the children learned to analyze the sounds in the words. The assignment of teaching method to classroom was attained by having principals draw lots. Teachers were then randomly assigned to method, but no inexperienced teachers were included. Intensive training and supervision throughout the year was given to help the teachers. The amount of reading time each day was specified to be no more than 45 minutes. First-graders were randomly assigned to rooms and given the Metropolitan Reading Readiness and California Test of Mental Maturity at the start and the Stanford Achievement tests at the end of the treatment. The Stanford tests included measures of word reading, paragraph meaning, vocabulary, spelling and word study skills. The achievement of children in the five phonic groups was compared to that of the five groups of children who received a whole-word method technique. Of the 125 comparisons made, the skill level of the phonically trained children exceeded that of those who received the whole-word method in 93 instances. In no case did the whole-word method show itself to be superior to the phonics technique.

Similar conclusions were reached by Gurren and Hughes (1965) after a review of competent research studies comparing children who had intensive phonics instruction with those who did not. All the studies yielded results which favored the phonetic approach to the whole-word method. The phonics approach has also been urged by Bateman (1969).

Teaching Dyslexics

Aside from the emphasis on phonics, other teaching techniques suitable for aiding the dyslexic child have been offered. Bryant (1965) has suggested some important principles that should be borne in mind when dealing with reading-disabled children. The first principle is based upon the observation that dyslexic children have difficulty in retaining the detailed image of a word. They may recognize a word on one line and fail to recognize it on the next. Details of word configurations need to be explicated frequently. Writing and tracing the word might be useful insofar as such activities require the child to attend to the details of the word. In light of this suggestion, it should be noted that Johnson and Myklebust (1967) indicate a variety of exercises that might facilitate the child's skill in discriminating differences between the shapes of letters and words.

The second principle offered by Bryant is based upon the rather well documented evidence that dyslexic children have difficulty in learning the connection between graphemes and phonemes. Bryant suggests teaching these associations one or a few at a time until they are well learned. He further argues that the teacher should use words rather than isolated sounds or sylla-bles.

A third suggestion by Bryant is that the child should not be allowed to practice incorrect responses. The incorrect response which is learned will interfere with subsequent performance. A fourth suggestion pertains to teaching discriminations. When the child cannot discriminate letters or sounds which are similar, Bryant recommends teaching one until it is well learned before introducing learning trials on the second element. The fifth suggestion is that there should be frequent reviews of the child's reading skills. Improvements may be short-lived and teachers should be alerted to the possibilities of worsening performances by the child and the need for follow-up remediation.

Information Coding

Studies of the verbal coding deficits of dyslexic children point to other helpful remediation techniques. The results of the studies lead to the inference that the efficacy of many teaching efforts involving dyslexic children might be enhanced if instruc-tions on how to code and organize information are included. Strategies for dealing and coding the information essential to reading may be critical in aiding the dyslexic child to read. Both the clinical observations of Frostig (1972) and the experimental results of Palkes, Stewart and Kahana (1968) and Palkes, Stewart and Freedman (1971) suggest that the performance of children can be effectively altered by the use of verbal instructions as to how to proceed in learning and by teaching the child to explicate his course of action for himself.

The data to date suggest that teaching the child verbal or other coding strategies for learning may well help him learn to read. But dyslexic children are a heterogeneous lot. The large individual differences among this group called dyslexic would suggest that children will not respond equally to particular strategies and that the future will bring further refinements of classification and treatment of reading-disabled children. The now popular area of study called ATI (aptitude by treatment interaction) reflects efforts in this direction. Different coding stategies may be necessary for different children. For example, Levin (1973) and Levin, Divine-Hawkins, Kerst and Guttman (1974) have provided some evidence regarding the interaction of individual differences and the efficacy of various encoding techniques. Levin found that visual imagery instructions (*e.g.,* think of a picture which might flow from the text) did not aid children who were reading more than one year below grade level. Visual imagery instructions did help children who were not this deficient.

In a second study, Levin et al. (1974) found that children who could learn words best by viewing their pictorial representations would also demonstrate better learning on a reading comprehension task when given instructions to use visual imagery than when they were given instructions to read the words. The children who did poorly on learning words from pictures did not benefit from the imagery instructions. These authors concluded that there is a large group of children for whom the instructional strategy concerning encoding will make a large difference. These authors have made a significant contribution in initiating studies which will aid in identifying those individual characteristics and instructional variables which should be joined in aiding children's reading competence.

Dyscalculia

Mathematics is a specialized and abbreviated language, a highly technical jargon. Mathematical constructions are only symbols which have meanings in terms of relationships. Numbers have no substance and mathematical data are arbitrary sounds or marks called symbols. "Behind these symbols lie the boldest, purest, coolest abstractions mankind has ever made"

(Langer, 1957, p. 21). *Dyscalculia* is the term used to describe difficulty in mastering mathematical concepts and/or computations. Like dyslexia, the difficulty has been linked to a breakdown in the functioning or development of the central nervous system.

In general, it is thought that children who have difficulty in learning to read do not have comparable difficulties learning mathematics, and conversely, children having difficulty learning mathematics will not necessarily have problems with reading (Johnson and Myklebust, 1967; Kosc, 1974). There have been attempts made to develop a taxonomy of learning disability syndromes in which dyscalculia represented a syndrome distinct from dyslexia. There is evidence that performance on different kinds of readiness measures differentially predict children's subsequent performance on reading and mathematics tests (Rosner, 1973). At the same time, however, there may well be an overlap of skills necessary for obtaining competence in both reading and mathematics so that it is unlikely that these problems are entirely independent. Our understanding of dyscalculia is greatly complicated by the interrelationship of the comprehension of mathematics with other language or symbolic systems (Piaget, 1952; Dienes, 1963).

Chalfant and Scheffelin (1969) summarize the basic skills needed by the child to successfully undergo the various stages of mathematics learning. One essential characteristic is intelligence, or those skills tapped by intelligence tests. General intelligence accounts for the major variance in mathematics learning. A second major factor appears to be spatial ability, "ability to comprehend the nature of elements within a visual stimulus pattern" (p. 121). The child must know up and down, right and left, that four objects are four objects, whether in a row, column or pile, or indicated by the symbol 4. A third factor associated with mathematics learning is the child's verbal ability, which may be another way of saying his intelligence. Mathematics is a form of language and any language development deficit may affect the learning of mathematical symbols and operations. The child needs to be able to label and use words related to magnitude, conservation, time and numbers. A fourth skill is the child's approach to problem solving. The method by which the child compares and organizes the data prior to the solution of the problem, be it presented in verbal, arithmetical or spatial forms, will critically affect the product given by the child. Finally, Chalfant and Scheffelin suggest neurophysiological processes may impede the acquisition of mathematical operations.

As we have so often seen in relation to other problems labeled learning disabilities, considerable attention has been paid to the role of neurophysiological deficits in producing dyscalculia. Here, as elsewhere, theory by analogy was attempted. If brain-damaged adults have problems with mathematics, then children with problems with mathematics might be brain damaged.

Clinical Observations of Adults

Most of the research on dyscalculia stems from clinical studies of adults who have suffered brain trauma. In 1919, Henschen observed that number blindness (*i.e.,* a failure to recognize a number) could occur without word blindness and vice-versa. Henschen defined calculation as a mental process which requires a series of thinking tasks, so that dyscalculia could result from lesions in the occipital, parietal, frontal and temporal lobes of the cortex (Chalfant and Scheffelin, 1969). In his work with brain-damaged adults, Goldstein (1948) also noted the presence of dyscalculia, apparently with sufficient frequency to propose subcategories of this problem. And, for many years, it was erroneously believed that dyscalculia was one part of the Gerstmann syndrome, a syndrome associated with known brain damage (Benton, 1959). The historical linkage between dyscalculia and brain damage has been a relatively long one.

Given this history, it is not surprising that there have been attempts to link dyscalculia empirically to brain damage in adults, apparently with some success. One type of dyscalculia suggested is parietal dyscalculia. According to Luria (1966), adults suffering from parietal lobe trauma and dyscalculia would exhibit the following problems: incorrect alignment of one row of figures under another, inability to memorize numbers, particularly those with more than one digit, inability to arrange numbers in the order of their magnitude, inability to count backwards, inability to enumerate odd or even numbers in a series. The person may also have difficulty manipulating operational symbols, (*e.g.,* plus, minus), as they may be unable to comprehend the symbol and/or execute the reading and/or writing of figures.

A somewhat different parietal dyscalculia has been described by Luria (1966) and Goldstein (1948). Insofar as traumatic involvement with both the parietal and occipital lobes is presumed, Goldstein employed the term *visual agnosia.* Individuals so afflicted have been characterized as having a loss of spatial organization and visual discrimination and as being unable to copy or reproduce the direction of a symbol or the entirety of a geometric design. Paradoxically, these individuals are said to understand the concept of number, the nature of groups or methods of calculation. It is believed that the closer the lesion to the occipital lobe, the more visual in nature the problems. Thus, the patient may have particular problems in understanding the directionality of symbols. For example, the patient might have great difficulty in understanding carats, signs indicating more than or less than.

When lesions occur in other sections of the brain, other forms of dyscalculia may occur. When the lesion occurs in the frontal or frontal temporal regions of the cortex, there is associated disintegration of skilled movements and complex intellectual operations. Calculations may be slow and the repertoire of strategies might be greatly diminished. Addition may be carried out, but slowly and by counting the series one element at a time. The most simple multiplication must be relearned, often without accompanying insight as to the correctness of the answer, much less alternative strategies for arriving at that answer. The operations of computation require laborious effort (Chalfant and Scheffelin, 1969).

More recently, there has been an emphasis upon the functions of the left and right sides of the brain as they may affect dyscalculia (Cohn, 1961; McFie, Piercy and Zangwill, 1950; Curry, 1966). It has been increasingly realized that it is too simplistic to assume that one side or the other of the brain would have great control over the production of dyscalculia. Curry (1966), after summarizing the literature relevant to this issue, indicates that verbal functions are mediated in the left hemisphere, nonverbal functions in the right hemisphere. To the extent that nonverbal functions are facilitated by verbal skills, the left hemisphere has an important role in coping with nonverbal stimuli. The right hemisphere is dominant in the process, but probably only slightly so.

These works with adults served to provide both important information concerning dyscalculia and brain damage in adults and to form the underpinning of analogies to the child with deficits in mathematical competence.

Observations of Children

The same general concerns dictating the observations of adults with dyscalculia guided that of children with similar difficulties. Problems with mathematics were considered to reflect brain dysfunctions which differed in nature from those involved in disrupting verbal development. It was presumed that dyscalculia reflected disturbances in the nondominant hemisphere of the brain, while dyslexia was an outcropping of trauma to the left hemisphere of the brain (Johnson and Myklebust, 1967).

Children with dyscalculia have been variously described. Kalaski (1967) describes such children as having difficulties with spatial relationships. For example, they may have trouble learning the concepts of up and down, right and left. They are described as having difficulty understanding size relationships, and if this is so, they will have trouble mastering number concepts. Motor disinhibition is also said to characterize such children, and impulsivity, which interferes with their ability to manipulate objects in the environment and consequently to master basic concepts of mathematics. Left-right confusions are said to be evident in such children as well as habits of perseveration (an inability to shift psychological sets). Finally, Kalaski indicates that dyscalculic children will have language difficulties which prevent adequate mastery of mathematics. Johnson and Myklebust (1967) have described the dyscalculic child as having difficulty learning to count meaningfully, master cardinal and ordinal systems, perform arithmetic operations and visualize clusters of objects as groups. They also suggest that such children find it difficult to associate auditory and visual symbols, to understand the conservation of quantity, to remember sequences of arithmetic steps and to choose principles for problem-solving activities, to name but a few. At the same time, these children are described as having good auditory and verbal abilities.

Kosc (1974) has presented an extended taxonomy of dyscalculia in which he suggests the following terms be adopted.

1. *Verbal dyscalculia:* Wherein the child has difficulty understanding mathematics when presented orally or under conditions in which a verbal response is required.
2. *Practognostic dyscalculia:* Wherein the child is unable to adequately manipulate objects, symbolic or otherwise, for purposes of arithmetic.
3. *Lexical dyscalculia:* This condition refers to problems in reading mathematical symbols (*e.g.,* numbers, operation signs).
4. *Graphical dyscalculia:* This refers to a difficulty in writing mathematical symbols.
5. *Ideognostical dyscalculia:* A problem in which the child has difficulties in understanding mathematical ideas and relationships, and in doing mental calculations.
6. *Operational dyscalculia:* In this condition, the child is said to have difficulty in carrying out operations. Thus the child may add rather than subtract, divide rather than multiply.

It is distressing to report that the amount of systematically gathered information on childhood dyscalculia is appallingly small. The characteristics enumerated in this section have been based upon clinical observation and rarely demonstrated by a more rigorous method. Indeed, even the data presented by Kosc were such as to suggest that distinct types of dyscalculia were not found. Moreover, the frequency of problems experienced by dyscalculic children, whether in spatial orientation, time sense, or what have you, have rarely been compared to those of the non-disabled child. Aside from clinical observations, we are quite in the dark about the nature of dyscalculia.

CHAPTER
10
DIAGNOSIS
AND
EDUCATIONAL
ASSESSMENT

The terms *learning disabilities, minimal cerebral dysfunction,* and *educationally handicapped* are generic terms for a very wide variety of children's learning problems. Children who were the original inspirations for the development of the field of learning disabilities evidenced quite severe problems. These extreme cases of brain damage, language pathology and hyperactivity provided the stimuli which elicited theories and therapies from diagnosticians in various disciplines. The efforts of the various diagnosticians—medical, educational and psychological—were subsequently extended to an ever widening group of children who had one thing in common, some problem in development, learning or behavior. Many types of diagnostic evaluations became a part of the multidisciplinary approach to learning disabilities, as the problems evidenced by such children cut across several child care areas. The rationales, methods and materials used by these various professionals will be discussed in this chapter.

Purpose of Diagnosis

There are three primary rationales or functions of diagnosis as it is practiced. Diagnosis may serve scientific, therapeutic or moral functions. In a scientific enterprise, it is important that events, objects or persons be categorized within specified dimensions so as to stimulate further knowledge. Thus, children may be diagnosed as schizophrenic, autistic or normal for the purpose of studying one or more of each group. The goal is to increase our knowledge about persons who share the defining characteristics. In a therapeutic enterprise, a diagnosis may be directed toward categorizing a person as a member of a larger population in order to better understand the individual and situational constraints. The goal in this case is to provide appropriate therapeutic intervention. Finally, and unfortunately, diagnosis may be a case of name calling, in which the professional serves to propagandize the desirability or undesirability of particular behaviors. Often the propoganda follows establishment lines, but uses a language of technical jargon rather than religious rhetoric (London, 1964). A neutral example of the latter point, from the standpoint of this text, is the recent debates among psychiatrists and between psychiatrists and representatives of the Gay Lib movement as to whether homosexuality reflects mental illness.

Each of these rationales for diagnosis is relevant and important. Science has progressed through the taxonomies which have been developed in various mental health fields; people have benefited from diagnostic links with therapies and education; and perhaps, with the decline of the theologian, a new spokesman for morality is needed within our culture. At issue is the particular hat, scientific, therapeutic or moralistic, the professional diagnostician chooses to wear. While the public may be confused about the differences among these enterprises, the evaluator cannot afford such confusion. It is of critical importance that the professional learning disability expert make discriminations among these functions in his own diagnostic evaluations.

The criteria used to judge the adequacy of a diagnosis will

vary according to the function the diagnosis serves. A diagnosis within the scientific framework whose purpose is the advancement of knowledge must meet contemporary standards set for good science. The method used and the resulting evidence determine the evaluation of such diagnoses. The evaluation of diagnostic procedures within the therapeutic domain rests with the degree to which the diagnosis specified treatment which reduces the behaviors of concern or increases the child's happiness, or competence or whatever is at issue. Like the scientific enterprise, however, empirical evidence is required before an evaluation of the evaluation can be claimed. Perhaps the moral enterprise is reducible to political or persuasive criteria. If the diagnostic proclamations inhibit bad (pathological) behavior or facilitate good (normal, adjusted) behavior in large segments of the population, diagnosis may be adequately serving its purpose.

Diagnostic Models

Diagnostic models used in the field of learning disabilities differ in rather radical ways. The old and new models are related to the different hypotheses regarding childhood pathology which were discussed in Chapter Two. A diagnostic evaluation in the context of the medical disease model focuses upon the assessment of abilities and/or attributes of the "patient" in a search for the etiology of symptoms. Amelioration of symptoms is to occur through the elimination of their causes. The presumption is that unless one understands the source of difficulty, which resides within the patient rather than in the environment, one cannot make an accurate diagnosis or appropriate prescriptions for treatment. In the psychometric or statistical model, there is somewhat less concern for etiology, but the search is on through the use of standardized tests for those skills and inadequacies which are the cause of the child's problems. The position in which knowledge is demanded of the stimulus (etiology) which elicits the response (symptom) before implementation of remedial efforts has been vigorously attacked by Skinner and his followers (Skinner, 1971). Whether or not this model is logically coherent, it is a prominent model subscribed to by many clinicians throughout the country.

The social systems model is radically different from the medical disease model. Perhaps the increasing popularity of this approach is a backlash against the shortcomings of the medical disease and psychometric approaches to childhood pathology. In this context, the position taken seems to be that all, or at least most, problems children experience reflect the imperception, incompetence or limitations of significant persons in their environment. Diagnosis and treatment are directed toward evaluation and changes in the environment, not in the assessment of the child. Proponents of this approach have been active in attempts to attenuate the degree to which children are labeled as defective or isolated into separate school programs by virtue of labels. This is supported by the observation that children who share the same label and even the same problem are, in fact, quite heterogeneous. The labels and associated segregated programs serve to generate and sustain stereotypes which are not, in fact, descriptive and certainly not helpful for such children. But if one does not look at the cognitive and personality characteristics of the child, what does one look for? The social systems model certainly does bring our attention to the possible difficulties which may be related to the biases of diagnosticians, the aspirations of parents, the incompetencies of some teachers and the hazards to individual welfare faced when dealing with bureaucracies. But the focus of attention is on the manipulation of large units or samples, not on intervention and assistance for individual children.

A behavioristic approach is easily incorporated into this model, particularly that segment of behaviorism which uses operant conditioning as a diagnostic and intervention approach. A child's aberrant behaviors are viewed as controlled by the reinforcement or reward strategies of individuals in the child's environment. The diagnosis of learning disabilities would be the evaluation of teachers', parents' and peers' responses to the behaviors of the child. For instance, is the child rewarded for poor performance? Is there a lack of reward for competent or desirable behaviors? Or is the child ignored for both?

Whichever model proves to be the most heuristic, it is important to realize that definitions of what is normal (good) or abnormal (bad) behavior vary from place to place, from person to person and from time to time. Definitions of children's behavior as deviant, maladaptive, inappropriate and incompetent are as much reflections of the world around the child as they are reflections of the child himself (Becker, 1963).

Another important point to remember when thinking about children defined by someone as abnormal is that everybody has problems, a point frequently forgotten by mental health workers. According to parents, many children who are never seen in any diagnostic setting have many difficulties in growing up. Behaviors, traits, habits and circumstances currently thought to be uniquely associated with some form of pathology have been found in children never defined as abnormal in any way. A classic study conducted by Lapouse and Monk (1964) reported that more than 50% of mothers of normal (*e.g.,* nonclinic) children rated their children as overactive or as having seven or more problems! Problems were more numerous in children 6 to 8 years of age, and declined during the ages 9 through 12. Not surprisingly, boys were the problem, not girls. Evidently, parental management of boys presents greater difficulties than girls; hence, the greater frequency of reported problems.

A third point to consider in diagnostics is the discrimination which should be made between problems which are transient and problems which are likely to be chronic or produce other, more severe, difficulties for the child. It is obvious that a child with hearing and vision defects will not be suffering from a transient developmental difficulty, whereas the child who experiences a school phobia may well require minimal intervention on the part of professionals. We do not wish to overdramatize or overgeneralize problems which may frequently occur in many children and will soon be eliminated through unknown social, parental or developmental forces. As long as professional skills are in greater demand than supply, limited resources must be judiciously applied. When other social forces can act as therapists, by all means let them do the work.

Finally, it should be remembered that definitions of problems are intimately tied to developmental levels. Once a learning-disabled child drops out of school, becomes a marginal graduate or leads a routine existence of work and family rearing, he may no longer be defined as abnormal. He may remain illiterate, but he may no longer be of concern to school officials. Chronic difficulties are those which require continuous institutional or professional resources. The learning-disabled child may escape the definition of deviance by virtue of aging. While the individual may be sad, angry or peculiar, the ability to work and/or love assists him in avoiding the scrutiny of the professional diagnostician.

To summarize, definitions of normalcy, pathology and disabilities are culture bound. Significant persons must view the attributes of a child as negative and wanting in order to bring the child to the attention of specialists in intervention. As a result of great concern within our culture for academic achievement, numerous diagnostic approaches have flourished, outstripping our skills in evaluation of the empirical worth of any of these approaches. It must be remembered that many of the behaviors defined as problems in children are normal variants of development and often represent parental and teacher intolerance of these behaviors or their sophistication regarding current theories pertaining to these problems. Diagnosis must not be simply the evaluation of a child, but an evaluation of the labelers as well (Becker, 1963).

Multidisciplinary Team Approach

The following discussion outlines those procedures typically employed in a multidisciplinary approach to children evidencing academic difficulties. These procedures are employed by professionals in varying disciplines in their attempts to contribute to a delineation of the best therapeutic program for the child. The very heterogeneity of children with learning problems, across diagnostic categories and within any one category, has resulted in the inclusion of diagnosticians with varying perspectives. In some cases the multidisciplinary team approach is to administer a wide range of medical, psychological and educational measures to the child. In other cases the team is comprised primarily of the classroom teacher, learning disability teacher and school psychologist, whose approach is to use the evaluations made within the school. In the case of the wider use of professionals, the team approach using medical as well as psychological and educational evaluations, the goal is to determine the primary causes of the problem. The team is responsible for determining which of the diagnostic categories best describes the child's problem and which type of educational program is best suited for this child. Once a child has been assigned to the learning disability category —that is, mental retardation, emotional problems and hearing and vision impairments are presumed to be ruled out or of secondary importance—the diagnostic evaluation becomes focused upon the exact nature of the learning problem. Tests administered are shifted from those concerned with personality functioning or intellectual assessment to tests of specific skills believed to be related to academic achievement. Some of these tests have become an accepted part of the learning disabilities specialist's arsenal.

The professional members of the diagnostic team typically include the psychologist, pediatrician, neurologist, electroencephalographer, social worker, teacher and, sometimes, speech therapist and audiologist.

One major determinant of which of these professionals become involved is the age of the child. If problems are noted in the infant or during the preschool years, the parents are likely to seek advice in a medical setting, whereas if the problem is not so severe or does not evidence itself before the child enters school, the child may be assessed through the procedures established by the school district, in a hospital clinic or by a private practitioner. Analysis reveals that different professionals are qualified to do overlapping jobs. The social worker and the psychologist consider a case history an important source of information. The educational specialist and the psychologist are trained to administer educational and diagnostic tests. A pediatric neurologist, pediatrician or family physician may administer a medical examination. Which professional becomes involved may be a function of who notices the problem, where (*e.g.,* parents or teacher) and the availability of resources within the school or community.

Referral: The First Step

Phase one of the diagnostic process is the referral. Who makes referrals? Why? When? Where do people go? What is the diagnostic significance of the referral system? We know very little about the referral process in learning disabilities. The information so far available stems primarily from studies of the labeling of minority group members as mentally retarded by the school system (Mercer, 1973). Studies of this issue have sensitized workers in the social services to the influence of socioeconomics, religion, race and educational status of the persons who do the referring upon the referral process. It is possible that the outcome of a child's case may be significantly affected by the who as well as the why of the referral.

Referrals can be initiated directly or indirectly by anyone who comes into contact with the child. Parents, teachers, school nurses, social workers or the courts may initiate a referral. Referrals are made when the person who makes the referral becomes upset by the behavior of the child, or is pressured by someone else who has become concerned about that child. Families have traditionally sought the advice of the family doctor, while schools usually have prescribed procedures to be followed for making referrals.

The age of the child may or may not be a critical factor in the referral process. When the child is very disturbed (*e.g.,* a child who has developed no expressive language by four years), it is more likely that help will be sought in the preschool period. The timing of referral once the child is in school does not preclude the possibility that the child has evidenced developmental difficulties in the preschool period (Owen et al., 1971).

The socioeconomic level of the family and the degree to which this is similar or dissimilar to that of others in the local school district affect the referral process. It has been documented in the mental retardation literature that more affluent families are more likely to use the available institutional services to obtain desired help (Farber, 1968). At the same time, teachers are more likely to brand children of different socioeconomic status and races as candidates for the referral process.

By and large, the more affluent families are more likely to seek and demand services for their children than families of less wealth (Rowitz, 1973). Moreover, the socioeconomic status of the family is likely to influence the diagnostic label as well. Children from poor families are more likely to be labeled mentally retarded than children with the same intellectual levels from more affluent backgrounds (Mercer, 1973).

It seems likely that the facilities necessary to render services to learning-disabled children are more likely to be available and exploited by children of the more affluent than those of the lower socioeconomic levels. Judging from the availability and distribution of resources within the field of mental retardation (Mercer, 1968), it is likely that resources for diagnosis and program development in learning disabilities are likewise more available to affluent than nonaffluent school districts.

In addition, it may be more likely that when children of the poor are seen for diagnosis their problems will be construed as the result of cultural disadvantage and not specific learning disabilities, even though the definition of learning disabilities specifically excludes problems whose etiology may reflect cultural definitions. In the absence of careful individual evaluations, it may be tempting to attribute the failures of the poor to cultural deprivation and the failure of the wealthy to specific learning deficits. The concentration of efforts of learning disabilities specialists upon the children of the affluent is in the process of changing as professionals become more aware of and sensitive to specific learning disabilities, outside of the influence of cultural differences; just as attention is being carefully given to distinctions between mental retardation and the consequences of poverty (McCandless, 1964). Such biases in the distribution of resources and within the referral system should be considered by the individual teacher, learning disabilities specialist or diagnostician when dealing with the individual problem child.

The Psychological Evaluation

The purpose of conducting a psychological evaluation is to assess the child's emotional and intellectual status. Three primary processes contribute to the information needed by the diagnostician to make this assessment. These include: *a) observation* of the individual in the clinic setting; *b)* the administration of *standardized tests,* such as the Stanford-Binet test of intelligence and the Rorschach Ink-Blot test; and, *c)* the obtaining of *case history* material. On the basis of the information gleaned from these three procedures, the psychologist usually specifies the diagnostic category to which a child belongs, makes recommendations for treatment and sometimes offers some predictive statements about expectations for future performance. It should be noted that different processes are used to obtain the same information. While we will describe as separate the procedures used in a diagnostic evaluation, the information obtained from these processes overlaps. The parents, for example, are asked questions about early development of the child's use of language. In a manner appropriate for the child's age, an assessment of language is also made by the diagnostician in the observation and in the standardized test phases of evaluation.

Observation

The psychological literature has a good deal of documentation on the difficulties associated with drawing inferences on the basis of the observation of behavior. Recording statements of persons in a Gallup-type opinion poll, observing the intellectual level of a rat or the behavior of psychiatric patients is fraught with procedural problems (Rosenthal, 1966; Hyman, 1954; Goffman, 1961; Rosenhan, 1973). The probability of biases in clinical observations is quite great. The attitudes and expectancies of the observer may well influence what he views and what he bothers to record, in memory or on paper. A number of personal characteristics of the child, irrelevant from the theoretical standpoint of learning disabilities, may well influence the observer's judgments of the child. For example, when adults observe two children guilty of identical misbehavior, the prettier of the two children will be less condemned (Dion, 1972).

There are several methods by which observer error can be reduced. First, it is helpful to observe and record the behaviors of the child, rather than the inferences observers make on the basis of what has been observed. The psychologist who reports that a child is preschizophrenic without specifying the behaviors of the child which stimulated this diagnosis and the situation in which these behaviors occurred does no one a service and may do great disservice. The observer must know upon which behaviors to focus and this requires a good theory behind the recording process. It requires that a great deal of time be devoted to the collection of observations in order to obtain a reasonably large sample of the child's daily activity. But, it is time to recognize that the administration of a standardized test no longer comprises adequate diagnostic information; indeed results of a Rorschach are no longer even useful information. Diagnosis is a demanding task which requires a great expenditure of time and thought.

Observations of the child should be conducted in a variety of settings, as different situations may well provoke different kinds of behaviors. Children who are experiencing learning problems should be seen not only within the office of the psychologist, but in the classroom or home setting as well. Observational information may be collected in an informal or formal manner. For example, one might note how the child moves. Is his gait awkward? How does the child respond to sounds, to whom does the child speak and does he initiate interpersonal contacts or does he merely respond when spoken to?

Observations in the clinical and school settings extend

beyond the collection of information on the child's responses to the clinician, teacher, parents or peers. As persons are confronted with tasks to perform, their behaviors change as the tasks vary in personal difficulty. The behavior and language of the child as he attempts to do frustrating work can be highly indicative of the type and extent of the problem he is experiencing. Beginners in diagnostics and student teachers often become concerned when they see a child who appears to be fatigued. But fatigue can be an important indicator of task difficulty level for that child. Most children can outlast a clinician, even the young college student, in endurance. Fatigue, yawning, restlessness, fidgetiness are diagnostic cues of stress, frustration and boredom. Change the activity to one that is fun and these cues may disappear. The information the diagnostician obtains from observations of the child vis-à-vis language, speech and willingness to communicate, changes in affect, responses to failure and success are all integrated into the interpretation of diagnostic test performance.

Observations should be made of four areas of child functioning: physical appearance, movement, attention and interpersonal relationships. Wender (1971) described a small fraction of children with minimal cerebral dysfunction as part of a pediatric subgroup, the funny-looking kid ("FLK") syndrome. These are children who have a higher incidence than would be predicted of physiognomic abnormalities of a type also associated with schizophrenia and mental retardation. These abnormalities are "anomalies of the epicanthus (a fold of skin in the eye) and ears; high arched palate; short incurving fifth finger; single palmar crease; abnormally long third toe; syndactylism of the toes; strabismus, and, perhaps, abnormally shaped skulls" (p. 29). Physicians are trained to make such observations, but as teachers and diagnosticians we can be alerted to characteristics about a child which make us feel this child is "different."

Perhaps more critical, insofar as a larger group of learning-disabled children may be involved, is the question of physical appearance in terms of standards of beauty. There is a relationship between physical attractiveness and social popularity (Lindzey and Byrne, 1968) and children who are unattractive may be more likely to be viewed as learning disabled than their more attractive counterparts. We must ask ourselves to what extent the child's appearance affects our responses and judgments.

Observations should be made of the way the child moves. Learning-disabled children have been described as clumsy and awkward. This has been related to perceptual-motor difficulties. The child who spills paint or trips over everyone's feet is likely to be having difficulties making appropriate judgments of spatial relationships. He is also likely to be very irritating to adults, who tire of mopping up after spills. The observer should note whether the awkward movements are related to gross motor movements. Is the child clumsy when he has to move his whole body or does the problem seem more specific to manipulation of small motor movements? Watch the child as he walks (runs) down the hall, climbs steps and participates in gym activities. Observe the child as he tries to get his gym shoes tied or sharpen a pencil. Observations of the child's skills in manipulating common utensils and his ability to perform common motor movements have implications for remedial intervention.

Children with learning disabilities are notorious for not paying attention to school-related tasks (Bryan and Wheeler 1972; Bryan, 1974d), and the Dykman et al. (1971) hypothesis regarding these children is based upon a theory of an organically based attentional deficit syndrome. It may be that inattention changes as children age. In kindergarten the child's inattention is associated with inappropriate, aggressive types of behaviors—at least according to teachers (Keogh and Tchir, 1974). If the child with learning disabilities is contained within the regular elementary classroom, rather than segregated into special self-contained classes, it may be because he learns to "pass" in the absence of learning to pay attention. He learns to look like he is paying attention by flipping the pages of his book, fussing with materials on his desk, attending to one book and then the workbook and back to the first book. He is not inattentive in the same way as a kindergartener who refuses to be quiet during nap time, but he is still inattentive. Teachers complain that learning-disabled children work only when they are on a one-to-one basis with the teacher. They are inattentive much of the remainder of the time. The observer should note the amount of time the child is and is

not attentive, what he does when inattentive, if there is a difference in the activities to which he is more or less attentive, and
under what conditions he is able to attend. As with the observation of motor skills, there are both diagnostic and remedial implications for this type of information.

Observations are made of the kinds and amounts of interactions the child has with teachers, peers and, if possible, parents.
It has been reported that children with learning disabilities are
rated as less socially desirable than comparison peers (Bryan,
1974a). Studies to determine what types of interactions learning-
disabled children have with teachers, peers and parents suggest
that these relationships are different from those held by comparison peers. Parents report feeling less affection for learning-disabled children than for siblings (Owen et al., 1971) and Bryan
(1974) reported that learning-disabled children are ignored significantly more often than academically successful children by
both teachers and peers. What behaviors are to be observed
which may account for these findings? Wender has described
these children as "unsuccessful extroverts." Children with learning disabilities, in general, do not appear to be withdrawn, neu-
rotic children. They do try to interact with others, but their attempts seem to go astray. The goal of the observations of the
child's interpersonal behaviors would be to determine the degree
to which the child does interact with others, and the adequacy or
inadequacy of these interactions. Is this the child who makes
insulting remarks, who responds inappropriately to situations in
the classroom, who fails to pay attention to instructions and then
vociferously interrupts to demand he be told what to do? Again,
such information has implications for therapeutic intervention,
although we do not have programs specifically designed to alter
such inappropriate social responses.

Is it possible to link specific behaviors with specific diagnoses
just on the basis of observational data? Yes, but imperfectly.
Children who are mentally retarded do not respond in the same
ways as emotionally disturbed or deaf children. The deaf child
will probably not respond to spoken commands if he has his back
to you and is playing with a toy. He is likely to respond eventu-

ally to your presence, as deaf children have been noted to have a habit of frequently checking their environment visually even when engrossed in some activity (Myklebust, 1954), and the hearing-impaired respond when another person enters their visual fields. The emotionally disturbed child may avert eye contact and not respond when you are in his field of vision, while the brain-damaged child, usually the hyperactive type, responds erratically. Children with learning disabilities have been observed to have poor, slow, immature language development, to be hyperactive, to display aggressive behavior in preschool and early school years and poor attention for academic activities in the following school years. Distinctions as to which category may be the most appropriate diagnostic category for a particular child can be obtained by observing the child in the clinic, classroom and home. The majority of characteristics associated with the learning disabilities label and those best obtained from observation appear to be behavioral (Clements, 1966).

Case History

A major step toward understanding the child's learning problem is an intensive interview with the parents of the child. Vital information regarding the nature of the problem, its history and the effects it is having upon the child and his family is obtained by discussing the problem with the family. A successful intervention program for a learning problem in many cases requires the understanding, support and cooperation of the child's family.

The questions posed in taking a case history may vary among diagnostic models. The information determined to be important in a model concerned with the etiology of the problem as the basis for developing an intervention program is different from the information gathered by use of a model exclusively concerned with changing the child's behavior. These data focus more intently on current actions and skills of that child. In the medical disease model, clinicians are concerned about the etiology of the problem. Case history taking in the behavioristic approach either assumes the other questions about etiology were asked by someone else or the problem's solution does not depend upon such information.

Specification of etiology is very much a shot in the dark. The assignment of children to discrete categories of problems on the basis of the case history and/or the entire evaluative process currently is impossible. Nonetheless, that does not mean we should stop trying to improve upon the state of knowledge concerning etiological sources of problems, nor does it mean that we should turn our backs on the variety of problems children and families experience outside the four walls of the classroom. While we place great emphasis in the remediation chapter of this text upon specification of discrete academic problems and the solution thereof through behavior modification programs, we do not find this obviates the need to know more about the problems this child may be experiencing elsewhere. The existence of a spelling problem may test out as related to a deficit in short-term memory or inability to make associations between sounds and symbols, and this can be academically programmed. But, to stop at this point prohibits learning that this type of deficit, as measured by test performance, may reflect inability to attend to a wide variety of tasks, from teacher directions to television. It does not provide clues that the child is really more interested in playing cops and robbers, hates his mother or little brother and wants to get even with an intrusive family or a family which has branded him a dope, or that he has hypoglycemia, which affects his energy levels for any sustained activity.

Children have histories. And children's families have histories. Many of the academic failures or maladaptive behaviors manifested may be related to the family circle and family problems.

Initially, the case history requires obtaining basic information about the child and his family. Birth dates, ages, employment status, religious affiliation, church attendance and the existence of such problems in other family members is specified. The family's religious background is noted because there are some rare diseases which appear more frequently in some religious groups than others. Autism and Tay-Sachs disease are more often reported in Jewish families than in families of other religious backgrounds (Rimland, 1964). Religious affiliation is also correlated with attitudes about mental and emotional problems and is specifically related to attitudes toward handicapped children (Gurin, Veroff, and Feld, 1960; Farber, 1968). Farber, for instance, has reported that devout Catholic families were more accepting of a mentally retarded child, as their faith provided them an explanation for the occurrence of this problem. This is not to suggest that Catholic parents are more loving or devoted to their children than other families, but that religious beliefs may provide a supportive cushion when things go wrong.

Information concerning the occupational status of the family may be useful in gauging the family's attitudes toward their problem child. Presumably, the upward bound or upper-class family will experience more distress in the presence of a handicapped child than families less affluent or less ambitious (Farber, 1968). Perhaps the less affluent or more poorly educated families contend with so many other difficulties that it is difficult for them to invest much energy in this particular problem. Perhaps they begin with different expectancies for the futures of their children and are not so engaged with their aspirations for themselves or their children. Perhaps we have not accurately tapped the consternation they experience. In any case, differences have been reported for the responses to handicapped children by families of differing socioeconomic levels.

The effects of a learning-disabled child upon the family unit has not, as yet, been systematically studied. Dunn (1973) summarized the findings of the effects which a retarded child has upon the family. Those effects which may apply to learning-disabled children's families relate to increased conflict within the family, the degree to which the family participates in community activities, a restrictive effect upon an older sister or extra freedom for older brothers and siblings more concerned with the state of human beings and society.

Information is sought regarding the educational histories of family members. One major theory of the cause of one learning disability, dyslexia, is that it is genetically linked. Bakwin (1973) recently reported a study of reading disabilities in twins which corroborated Hallgren's contention that reading disabilities are inherited and familially linked. A high degree of concordance of reading disabilities was found by Bakwin, who reported that 84% of monozygotic twins compared to 29% of dizygotic twins shared reading problems. He concludes that reading disabilities which cannot be attributed to cultural difference or disadvantages are principally genetic.

Whether or not reading problems are genetically linked, another study also reported a higher incidence of school problems in the parents of educationally handicapped children compared to academically successful children (Owen et al., 1971). This study also reported a higher incidence of related academic problems in siblings of educationally handicapped children. It may be that the parents are less competent at communicating pre-academic skills to these children, with a subsequent disadvantage in their performance upon reaching school. While this hypothesis is speculative, the need for the information is an important factor in considering intervention. For instance, does the family need specific instruction on how to help this child organize his school work?

Parents' chief complaint or major concern regarding the child provides some insight as to when the problem was noticed and by whom. The severity of the problem may be indicated by the age at which parents became concerned about the child. The earlier the problem was noted, the more severe it was and, perhaps, the more it distressed the family members. The course of action followed by the family upon discovery of the problem should be noted, at the very least for the purpose of avoiding duplications among professional workers.

Case history information should include information about the pre- peri- and postnatal periods as experienced by the infant and by the mother. One factor related to developmental problems appears to be the age of the mother at the time of the child's birth and the existence of other siblings. There is some evidence to suggest that births which occur late in a woman's life, particularly late first births, are more likely to be associated with subsequent difficulties in the child. Of particular concern are conditions associated with birth trauma and brain damage. Rubella (German measles) in a pregnant woman is well known to be associated with blindness, cardiac disorders, mental deficiency and deafness. Rh incompatibility is likewise associated with brain damage (Kawi and Pasamanick, 1959).

The condition of the child at birth and immediately thereafter has been demonstrated to be significant for later development. Knobloch and Pasamanick (1959) reported that such conditions as prematurity, low birth weight, toxicity in the mother or accidents during birth could all result in "sublethal clinical neuropsychiatric syndromes." Graham, Matarazzo and Caldwell (1956) studied 346 infants and found that the 81 children who had suffered either anoxia, mechanical birth injury or infection demonstrated a lower threshold for pain, poorer vision, greater irritability and more muscle tension than children not so affected during birth. Of great importance are the results of a follow-up study of these children three years later. Children who had experienced anoxic states were not inferior on perceptual motor tasks, but showed neurological signs, behavioral problems of hyperactivity and inferiority to comparison children on all the tests of conceptual functioning. The children who had been born prematurely did not show neurological signs, but were inferior on concept formation tasks. It was thus suggested that differential competencies in learning and performance could be directly related to events which occurred during birth (Graham, Ernhart, Thurston and Craft, 1962).

To summarize, many conditions can cause developmental problems. These include abnormalities of gestation, metabolic disorders, virus infections of the mother and newborn, blood-type incompatibility and poisoning of the fetus due to lead, carbon monoxide, drugs and other substances ingested by the mother (Dunn, 1973, p. 77). According to Dunn, there has been a shift in thinking recently regarding the importance of events at birth in causing brain damage. It is now believed that the abnormal events at birth may be the result of a problem which may have arisen any time during the gestation period which then led to a difficult, problem birth.

Information is sought regarding the medical history and

medical status of the child. In the days before the development of penicillin and other drugs, many childhood diseases had debilitating effects. Mumps, measles and several other such childhood diseases are no longer viewed with the same degree of seriousness. However, the diagnostician is still concerned with any medical problems the child may have had or is still having. Illness which prohibits the child from attending school for long periods or at critical periods (*e.g.*, when prereading skills are taught) might well have deleterious effects upon the child's academic performance.

We would like to suggest that the diagnostician heed complaints from the child or parents regarding physical symptoms. For instance, when a child complains of feeling tired, is losing weight or falls asleep earlier than would be expected, it is incumbent upon the parents to seek an extensive medical evaluation. All too often parents are told by diagnosticians, medical and psychological, that the child's problem is emotional. Do not fall into this trap. Do not settle for a routine thermometer-in-the-mouth examination. It is very important that the child be given a thorough physical evaluation.

The next area covered pertains to the developmental history of the child. At what age was the child able to sit, walk or speak his first words? When did the child become toilet trained or wash his face? The child's physical maturation provides a general idea of the integrity of the nervous system. The age at which infants perform a number of rhythmic automatic activities has been studied, with the finding that children later diagnosed as handicapped achieved these milestones later than normal infants. A group of 200 normal infants from age 1 month to 12 months were compared with retarded and cerebral palsied infants on hand sucking, foot kicking, lip biting, body rocking, toe sucking and tooth grinding (Kravitz and Boehm, 1973). The age of onset for these activities ranged from 2.7 to 10.6 months for normal infants, while for cerebral palsied and Mongoloid infants these appeared later than 12 months. It is noteworthy that many or all of these behaviors are often considered abnormal; yet great numbers of normal children can be expected to manifest them. It is not the occurrence of the behavior which is associated with severe difficulties, but the age at which such behaviors appear. Children who have severe problems are likely to manifest such behaviors later than the normal child. One could say that the normal child shows his abnormalities earlier than the abnormal child. Or, maybe abnormal means doing things later and for longer.

Detailed and complete normative data can be collected in a way which yields a quantifiable assessment of the child. The ages at which children usually accomplish developmental milestones have been gathered and arranged statistically to permit comparison with peers much in the way any standardized test is arranged. One such scale is the Vineland Social Maturity Scale developed by Edgar Doll (1953). This scale has items arranged in six-month intervals from birth to 18–21 years. The items are developed to tap maturation in five areas considered critical and all-inclusive in child development. The items are scored so that a social quotient somewhat like an intelligence quotient can be obtained for comparisons of the child's social development to that of his peers. The scale can also be "double scored" so that a child suffering a particular handicap does not lose credit for the items which tap the skills precluded by that particular handicap. A child who cannot walk unaided is scored in two ways. One way subtracts for things he cannot do; the second credits the child for items specifically related to ambulation. As such the child can be compared with peers, can be evaluated intraindividually comparing one area of development with another and can be scored so as to not penalize him for his handicap. Differential diagnosis of young children is particularly aided by such a method. For instance, the mentally retarded child is predicted to be slower in social maturity in the five developmental areas, whereas the hearing-impaired child is expected to be comparable to peers except for those items related to communication (Myklebust, 1954).

Language development is a critical source of information for differentiating one type of handicapped child from another. The age of speech and language development and the use of language in social relationships are perhaps among the best indicators of whether a child is hearing impaired, mentally retarded, emotionally disturbed, brain damaged, or immature. Each diagnostic category presents varying patterns of speech and language development, although it must be admitted that this is more true of hearing impairment than the categories of mental retardation, brain damage and emotional disturbance. Questions are asked about the child's awareness of sound as an infant. Was this a quiet baby? Did he make sounds when he was alone as if to entertain himself? Did he make babbling sounds and then use jargon, an imitation of speech in the absence of real words? When did the child seem to comprehend the meaning of what people said to him? Did he enjoy having stories read to him, or listening to the television? At what age did the child use his first word? When did the child start to connect words? The parent is questioned as to the degree to which the child uses age-appropriate vocabulary and sentences to communicate and the child's ability to relate a story or experience in a logical, coherent manner. Can the child remember events and relate them? Can the child remember instructions given to him? Does the child have difficulty expressing himself or does he seem to have difficulty finding the words he needs to express himself?

Clinical guidelines to making discriminations among categories of handicap, such as mental retardation, emotional disturbance, hearing impairment and aphasia in young children who fail to develop language were delineated in a classic study by Myklebust (1954). He described the language differences among these groups in the following way. The child who is born with a severe hearing impairment will be deficit in all phases and stages of language acquisition. Parents will report that deaf infants typically do make sounds and babble until they are about 9 or 10 months of age. There is some quantitative difference in sound making between these and nonhearing-impaired infants even at this time, as the former are described as quiet. The expressive output of the infant will mirror what he hears, so the tonal quality of the hearing-impaired child's utterances will be qualitatively different as well. As the infant ages, sounds will be excessively loud or soft, and unlike normal infants sounds will not be used for play or imitation. The hearing-impaired child will use gestures and facial expressions for communication.

The critical period for language development in the emotionally disturbed, schizophrenic child is between 18 and 24 months. According to Kanner (1944), this child develops no speech, no jargon, no characteristic tonal quality, no gesture, no use of sounds for pleasure. The child lacks affective facial expression and gesture. The autistic child has been described by Rimland as different from birth; autistic children are reported to demonstrate an early use of language, but appear to fail to associate sounds or words with meaning. Their words are described as uncommunicative, high pitched and echolalic. Rimland has hypothesized that infantile autism is biologically caused and is the result of damage to the reticular activating system in the midbrain.

The aphasic child may have difficulty comprehending spoken language, be unable to recall words and to put words together to form a sentence. Menyuk (1964) has suggested that the language problem is not simply one of slower development, but a lack of complexity in sentence structure. The utterances of aphasic children are simpler and shorter in construction. Like the hearing-impaired child, the aphasic may use gestures and pantomime to communicate. But the aphasic child is not expected to have sounds which are qualitatively different as is the hearing-impaired child.

The child whose aphasia is related to a lack of understanding of language is easily mistaken for a deaf child, because he responds inconsistently to sounds. The difference seems to be that when the sound gets loud enough the deaf child will respond appropriately. But the aphasic child may respond to very soft sounds and not to loud sounds.

The language of the mentally retarded child develops at a rate commensurate with his mental age. This usually means a slower attainment of the developmental milestones, such as the age at which the child speaks his first word or uses a string of words to form a sentence. The degree of retardation is reflected in the attainment of language skills.

There are certain similarities in the language deficits reported by parents for children who are mentally retarded, emotionally disturbed, brain damaged and hearing impaired. Relative to the nonimpaired same age child, these children may have a less complex language, a reduced output of language, shorter sentence construction and an inability to control the behavior of themselves and others by using language.

There is consensus, by no means sufficiently validated, that deficits in language development are a shared characteristic among children with learning disabilities (Task Force II, 1969). This is not limited to children with severe problems brought for evaluation in the preschool years, but is descriptive of school-aged children with learning disabilities. One study which contributes significantly to this question represents an attempt to divide children with learning disabilities into distinct types (Owen et al., 1971). While there were five diagnostic categories proposed, speech and language problems were noted in three of the five categories, while the remaining two were more heavily weighted with emotional problems.

Educational History

The child's educational history is the next area of inquiry. Did the child attend nursery school, at what age, for how long? How well did the child adjust to school? If there were any problems, what was the nature of the difficulty? If the child is of school age, the parent is asked to describe the child's academic progress in various school subjects and his adjustment to teachers and peers. Which subjects do the parents perceive to be the child's best and worst? Has the child been given special tutoring in the school or on a private basis? What kind of information about the child have teachers, principals or other members of the school staff relayed? Do the parents believe the child has obtained a good education or do they define the school program and personnel as the source of, or contributing to, the problem?

Information available on problem behaviors of normal children (Lapouse and Monk, 1964) indicated that children in the early school years are more problematic than children at other ages. An educational history which indicates the child was a problem in nursery school, even though the child is not being evaluated until several years later, provides some evidence as to whether the problem is one that has been bothering the family for a long time or is highly specific to the time of evaluation. There is evidence to suggest that children ultimately diagnosed as learning disabled show signs of difficulty as young children (Owen et al., 1971). More evidence on this subject should become available with the growing emphasis on preschool education for learning-disabled children.

The diagnostician attempts to obtain a picture of the child as a member of the family. Parents are asked to describe the child's activities at home and his relationships with other members of the family. If there are siblings, the parents can often report on this child by comparing him with siblings. Questions are asked to determine whether this child has any responsibilities at home. Does he have chores to do? Can he take care of his own needs, handle the utensils in the kitchen or shed, manage an allowance, shop for himself or his family?

Do the parents believe the child shows age-appropriate "common sense"? At the preschool level, does the child recognize dangerous situations, such as inedible substances or heavy traffic? During the school years, parents complain of such problems as lighting fires and theft. The point is to determine whether the child has some notions about the consequences of his acts, in line with expectations for his age. Does the child recognize right and wrong at the real and rhetorical levels? Rhetorical encompasses the ability to verbalize what is wrong and right, irrespective of accompanying acts, and to say the right thing at the right time. Information is sought as to the appropriateness of the child's affective responses to others and as to whether the child seems to be emotionally stable. Does the child have a sense of humor, and does this seem to be appropriate?

Does the child have any special hobbies or interests? How would the parents describe the child's motor activities? Is the child able to engage in those motor skills, such as bicycle riding or baseball, which are typical for his age group? How well does the child perform such activities as skating, swimming or football? How well coordinated is the child at activities which require fine motor movements? Is this the child who could never have a stamp collection because he could not manipulate the stamps well enough?

The purpose of these questions is to determine what problems the family is experiencing with this child, what limitations learning problems are placing upon the child outside of school activities. This type of information provides diagnostic information as to the nature of the child's problem, the needs of the child for intervention and the needs of the family for assistance in managing these problems.

If the child is enrolled in any type of school program, an interview should be conducted with the teacher and any school personnel who work with this child. The classroom teacher has the best view of the child in terms of a concentrated time period, the comparison group of peers and the absence of vested motives in viewing the child in any particular way. Data would suggest that teachers ratings may be the single best diagnostic tool (McCarthy and Paraskevopoulos, 1969; Bryan and McGrady, 1972). In most instances, teachers are delighted to have an opportunity to discuss a child, especially when they have been troubled by a child's social behavior and/or lack of academic progress. Teachers provide information about the academic performance of the child, but they also provide accurate pictures of the child's ability to organize himself to do a task, the relationships he has with other children and his attitudes toward school. The information provided by the classroom teacher and the continuing cooperation of that teacher are critical components of the diagnostic and intervention process.

Interview

The interview is a powerful technique for obtaining important information from a parent and teacher. It is most important for the interviewer to be aware of the potential biases which can influence the answers given by the respondent. Persons being interviewed are very sensitive to the responses, verbal and nonverbal, of the interviewer, particularly if there are social class differences between them (Hyman, 1954). If a simple smile, nod, grunt or groan is given consistently to a particular word or theme, it is likely to increase the frequency of the respondent's answer. It is clear that the expectations of the interviewer as to how the respondent will answer a particular question are likely to influence in subtle ways the answer to the question, generally in the direction of confirming the expectation (Hyman, 1954; Rosenthal, 1966). The attitudes of the interviewer regarding the topic under discussion are also likely to influence the respondent, again subtly, to respond in a way which indicates agreement with the attitudes of the interviewer. The interviewer then may tend to elicit, by apparently subtle and undramatic actions, statements which tend to confirm either expectations of the respondent and/or the interviewer's attitudes towards the topic under consideration.

Aside from these unwanted sources of influence, the interviewer is likely to go astray in yet another way. Unless very careful recordings of the respondent's answers are made, the degree to which the interviewer's recall of the information will be flawed will be truly amazing! Lapses of only a few hours between the hearing and the recording of an interview will produce massive amounts of failures of both omission and commission in subsequent reports (Hyman, 1954).

Interviewer errors aside, what are the sources of bias likely to be introduced by the interviewee? In general, the longer the time span the interviewee is asked to recall, the less reliable the recall (Hyman, 1954). A parent may quite accurately recall how he disciplined his child the day before the interview, but his opinions of how he managed his child several years earlier are likely to be rather distorted. In a most important study, Yarrow, Campbell and Burton (1970) found that parents' recall of past child-rearing events was such as to view the early period as a happier and easier time than it in fact was and to reshape their recall to conform to their perceptions of the present personality of the child. Distortions are more likely to be introduced in the discussion of personally important events than in statements concerning facts not so ego-related (Hyman, 1954). For example, people are more likely to make themselves appear more socially acceptable in reporting how they treat their children than in reporting the place of employment, their age or their income. Generally, in the case history material the interviewer is dealing extensively with material that is particularly likely to be distorted by the respondent in the direction of making that respondent or spouse or offspring, more "acceptable" to the interviewer.

There is also some evidence to suggest that social class and race differences between the interviewer and respondent may affect the nature of the responses obtained. Apparently, lower-social-class respondents are more likely to acquiesce to the expectations of a middle-class interviewer than are middle-class respondents. Moreover, black persons may be more reluctant to admit to socially undesirable behaviors to white interviewers than are white respondents (Hyman, 1954). It behooves learning disability specialists to be sensitive in their dealings with members of other races or classes to the possible biases such differences may produce.

From the above discussion, it is clear that the interview is far from flawless as a technique for gathering information. Indeed, it was its flaws which gave rise to standardized testing methods (which have other flaws). All biases can never be eliminated; some imperfections of the interview will inevitably remain. It is possible, however, to employ techniques which might reduce some of the distortions arising from the interview material. Perhaps one of the simplest methods for gaining greater veracity from the interview is to make immediate recordings of what is being or has been said. Memories, be they of the interviewer or interviewee, are not to be highly trusted. Second, when asking the respondent to report on behaviors which might reflect negatively upon him, cast the question in euphemisms. One does not need to ask a mother whether she neglects a child when she can be asked if she feels too busy to give the child the time that she would wish to devote to him. Introduce such questions with an "everybody does it" theme. Provide the respondent with a sense that his "sinning" is not unique, that it is a problem most people experience.

Case histories should be recorded, as much as possible, in a descriptive manner, specifying examples from which inferences are based. Diagnosticians should transcend the labels used by the parents. Obtain and record the behaviors committed by the child which lead the parent to the inference drawn. The description that the child is lazy or disorganized gives us little information. That the child cannot tie his shoes, fails to respond to requests or commands and stays in his room daydreaming is of considerably greater interest. Alternative interpretations of information can be made when an interviewer has time to reflect upon what people have told him. Descriptive data, in addition to some educated guesses, provide the information needed to construct such alternative explanations.

Finally, the interviewer should not just record negative examples of behavior. As Goffman (1961) and Rosenhan (1973) have pointed out, the mental helpers are likely to either focus on only negative or socially undesirable behaviors of the patient or are likely to construe the most everyday type of behavior as reflecting pathology. We suspect the same bias may result when viewing any child defined by someone, particularly an expert, as a problem child. It is important to determine the strengths as well as the problems of any child, because the strengths of the child may well affect the interpretations given the particular problems. In one of the author's experiences, a mother of a third-grade girl was so concerned about her child's shyness in the classroom that with the school's support she sought private psychological help. The mother had allowed the child to see a private practitioner for a brief period. The psychological diagnosis given this young girl was preschizophrenic and the withdrawal behavior in the classroom was interpreted as a sign of autistic tendencies. At the start of the school year, this author was asked to diagnose the girl and to treat her, if necessary. Upon discussions with the child's new classroom teachers and her social worker, it was discovered that the girl was a straight A student throughout her school career and that her shyness was probably more related to some transitory interpersonal stresses within the classroom than to a preschizophrenic condition. The straight A record certainly did not speak of autistic daydreaming within the classroom. The author advised the parents not to seek further help and suggested to the teachers that this child would likely be much better socially adjusted during the upcoming school year. After several months, the social worker involved with this case called the author to congratulate him on his very effective therapy. Apparently, she had the mistaken impression that I was the child's therapist and was seeing this girl on a regular basis. She informed me that the girl had made considerable improvement.

Because of the fallibilities of the interview, the diagnostician must also rely upon other procedures in the diagnosis of children. Sometimes particular tests, such as intelligence tests, become virtually the only tool employed in making a diagnosis. Other problems require other tests. Tests have their flaws, but through their use in coordination with data obtained through other methods with their unique flaws, some truths may emerge. The following sections will describe some of the techniques and tests employed to diagnose processes assumed to be relevant to the learning-disabled child. Before doing so, however, the diagnostic procedures employed by the neurologist will be described.

Neurological Evaluation

The role of medical and neurological evaluations in diagnosis and placement of learning-disabled children was investigated as part of Task Force II (Rogan and Lukens, 1969). Questionnaire data collected from 236 school districts revealed that 64% of the districts required a medical assessment of the child's neurological status, although only 12% reported that the results of the evaluation had to indicate neurological dysfunction for placement of a child in a special program. The diagnostic validity of "soft" (or ambiguous) neurological signs was accepted by 45% of the responding districts. More than 50% of the children presently enrolled in special programs were indicated to have medically established diagnoses of neurological dysfunction. This figure may, of course, be an underestimate of the true number of such children enrolled in these special programs insofar as many districts do not require a medical examination.

The rationale for referral to a neurological specialist is to establish or rule out the presence of specific disorders of the nervous system and to establish developmental attainment of neurological integrities (Clements, 1966). The classic neurological evaluation is based upon knowledge of neurological diseases present in adults. This type of examination has been found to be inadequate in cases of children with learning problems. Thus, different methods of evaluation and different criteria for establishing the presence or absence of signs of abnormal neurological functioning have developed for children. The procedures and findings are reported here.

An examination of a child's neurological status is like the psychological evaluation in that it is not based on one type of measure. The data are gathered from a number of sources, the case history, observation and examination. Often measures are included which are more psychological than neurological. The neurologist seeks to synthesize information gathered on the central and peripheral nervous systems, intellectual processes and the behaviors of the child with information collected from the child's developmental history.

The neurological examination outlined here has been adapted from those described by Vuckovich (1968, pp. 16–38) and Rabe (Task Force II, 1969, pp. 69–70). Rabe defines the standard neurological evaluation to include measures of *Cranial Nerves* I–XII; *Motor System* tone and strength; *Sensation* vibration, position and touch; *Cerebellar* testing; and *Reflexes* stretch and cutaneous. The procedures have been outlined by Rabe as:

Observation of the general appearance and behavior of the child and the means by which a child attempts tasks.

Double simultaneous stimulation of the peripheral visual field: The examiner moves fingers in the child's peripheral visual areas.

a) Eye movements—By 5 years a child should be able to follow a moving object with his eyes. A child is considered to have an abnormal response if he persists in moving his head and not using just his eyes to follow the object.

b) Nystagmus is a "rhythmic oscillation of the eyeballs, characterized by a slow drifting from a central gaze toward the periphery and then a sudden snap back to a central gaze position. Both eyes usually move together; it is a conjugate movement and is usually repeated many times" (Curtis, Jacobson and Marcus 1972, p. 318). Optokinetic nystagmus (OK nystagmus) is the normal response of this type of eye movement which occurs when a person is asked to follow a moving object. The absence of this eye movement or persistent asymmetry in the rate of this movement define an abnormal response.

Facial apraxia: An inability to move facial muscles voluntarily in the absence of paralysis or weakness. The child is asked to blow out his cheeks, both cheeks at the same time, one cheek and then the other, and then to suck in both cheeks (make a "fish face"). An abnormal response is indicated when a child older than 9 years is unable to do these movements upon command.

Hearing: While an extensive hearing test may be conducted by an audiologist, the neurologist routinely checks out hearing using a tuning fork or toys which have been calibrated to different sounds and intensities. In an infant the examiner watches for reflexive responses to calibrated noisemakers.

Hearing testing of a young child is difficult, as this requires the child's cooperation. The examiner observes the child's reactions when noises of different intensities are produced near him, but out of the range of his vision. The tuning fork, watch tick, coin click and direct whispered or spoken voice tests are gross indications of hearing acuity. If there is a question about the hearing status, the child needs further evaluation using a pure tone audiometer.

Two tests can be conducted with older children who can respond verbally to the examiner. The Rinne test (Curtis et al. 1972, p. 327) is done by holding a vibrating tuning fork against the mastoid bone. The child must indicate when the fork is no longer felt. The tuning fork is immediately placed beside the pinna. A person with normal hearing would hear the tuning fork. The Rinne test is positive when the person hears better through air conduction than through bone conduction. If the person fails to hear either placement of the tuning fork, a sensory-neural hearing loss is indicated. An abnormal Rinne test, which indicates that bone conduction is greater than air conduction, may be indicative of a problem in the middle ear or the external auditory canal. Infections in the middle ear are quite common and may interfere with hearing.

The Weber test is also used by the neurologist. In this case the stem of a vibrating tuning fork is placed on the midline of the forehead just above the glabella (between the eyebrows). The result is "Weber negative" if sound is heard as in midline and "Weber right" or "Weber left," respectively, if it is referred to the right or left ear (*Dorland's Illustrated Medical Dictionary*, 1965).

Pronunciation: By age 3 to 4 children are expected to be able to pronounce sounds produced by lip movements (labial sounds such as *p* and *b*), by the tongue (lingual sounds such as *t* and *d*) and guttural sounds such as *k* and *g*. If the child is unable to make these sounds an apraxia is suspected.

Simultanagnosia: While the person has his eyes closed, the examiner touches him with his finger on the left-hand, right hand-left face, left hand-right face. By 5 to 6 years, the child makes no more than one error of identification out of 12 stimuli.

Performance of repetitive motions:

a) Serial apposition of thumb and fingers (touching each of the fingers on one hand with the thumb of that hand in a sequence); alternating pronation and supination of the hands (turning the palms downward and then upward); and repetitive heel-shin tapping (touching the shin of one foot with the heel of the other). By 5 years of age a child should be able to perform these acts with smooth rhythm. An abnormal response is described as a slow and arrhythmical performance.

b) Clumsiness, tremor and ataxia (inability to coordinate voluntary movements) can be evaluated by having the child put marbles in a cylinder. By 3 years a child can do this task smoothly and rapidly.

c) Synkinesiae is observed when a child mirrors a movement with one limb which is being done with the other limb on tests of repetitive motions. Up until about 9 years of age synkinesiae, or some motor overflow, will be seen in the limb. Beyond this age level, motor overflow is defined as abnormal.

Posture and gait: The examiner observes the child's posture when he is sitting, lying down, walking, walking on his toes and on his heels. Walking is evaluated in terms of symmetrical movements of the involved body parts. Minimal hemiparesis is suspected if asymmetry of walking movements is noted. Toe walking for a minute or so will bring out sagging of one heel, while heel walking will bring out weaknesses of feet and associated movements. Clumsiness and assorted irregular arm and shoulder movements are abnormal after 5 years of age.

Visual motor skills: The child is asked to draw a series of geometric shapes. Developmental milestones for these shapes are:

scribble	18 to 24 months
circle	24 to 36 months
cross, vertical and horizontal straight lines	36 months
square with rounded corners	3½ to 4 years
square	5 years
triangle	5 to 6 years
diamond	7 to 8 years

Conception of spatial relationships: The child is shown how three-dimensional forms of a square, circle and triangle can be placed in corresponding places traced on heavy papers. By 21 to 28 months of age children can stack all figures on one paper following one demonstration; by 24 to 30 months can place any form on any figure; and by 30 to 36 months place all the forms on the appropriate papers.

The child is also tested on ability to place a French curve appropriately on three positions outlined on paper. In this test the child is given instructions verbally with no demonstration. Normal performance is defined as one correct out of three trials by 48 to 52 months and three correct out of three trials by 54 to 60 months.

Right-left orientation: By 7 to 8 years a child is expected to be able to name the left and right eye, ear, hand and foot.

Auditory and visual word association and language usage: The child is asked to name pictures of common objects such as dog, cat and star. By 18 months a child is expected to name or point to one picture; by 24 months name 3 or point to 5; by 30 months name 5, point to 7; by 36 months name 8; by 40 months name 10.

Finger agnosia:

a) In-between test—following a demonstration, the child is asked to close his eyes and the examiner touches the fingertips of two fingers of one hand simultaneously. The child is to name how many fingers are in between the two which were just touched. It has been found that 50% of children can do this with no errors by age 4 and 95% can perform this by 7½ years.

b) Two-point test—following a demonstration the child closes his eyes and the examiner touches two points simultaneously on one finger or two fingers of one hand. The child must indicate whether one or two fingers have been touched.

Reading ability: The Rabe outline indicates that reading ability is roughly assessed by use of the Gray Oral Reading or Gates Primary Reading test. The child is to be referred for psychological evaluation if the reading score is greater than one year below grade level.

Vuckovich (1968) outlined procedures which are applicable for neurological evaluation of children older than 5 years. Up through age 15 the evaluation includes an assessment of:

a) Mental state—alertness, normal shyness, cooperativeness, attention, hyperactivity, lack of shyness or crying.

b) Language development—comprehension, expression, dyslexia, dysgraphia.

c) Visual-motor functions—performance on a Bender-Gestalt and Draw a Person tests.

d) Judgment of right and left.

e) Finger agnosia.

f) Motor functions—There are not many tests which are appropriate after the child is 5 years old. The Heath Rail Walking Test is quite common and can be used to assess the child's balance. The child's gait, ability to walk on his toes and arm swing while walking can be indicative of problems. Muscle tone, consistency and laterality are noted. The child is asked to throw and kick a ball to establish which is the dominant hand and leg. A dynamometer is used to establish the strength of one hand relative to the other.

g) Head-size and motility of facial musculature.

h) Reflexes—Abnormal signs are defined by Vuckovich as abnormal localizing signs, failure to obtain an expected response, asymmetrical responses, persistence of an initially normal response, emergence of certain signs significant to particular infections or disease states and failure of development, which is one of the most common forms of neurological abnormality.

On the basis of extensive clinical experience, it is Vuckovich's opinion that many neurological "soft signs" are of questionable significance. There are, nonetheless, certain observations which he believes occur too frequently to be the result of chance. The kinds of characteristic problems which seem to recur with greater than expected frequency in children with learning disabilities are disturbed sleep patterns and feeding problems. These children are reportedly hyperactive and distractible and apparently develop language later than would be expected. The children are reported by kindergarten teachers to be having greater problems than other children in visual-motor tasks, such as coloring and drawing in spite of appearing to be intellectually competent. Poor speech production is noted, although the child's vocabulary may be adequate. Polysyllabic words are difficult for these children to pronounce, and there is difficulty pronouncing consonants, or difficulty comprehending or responding appropriately to auditory requests. By first grade, these children have greater difficulty than others in learning to read, write and do arithmetic, while behavior continues to be a problem. The complaints received from teachers is that they are hyperactive, unable to restrain aggressive behavior and show poor adaptation in general.

A neurological evaluation has been a standard part of a multidisciplinary approach to diagnosis. Before discussing the research results of the utility of this examination in aiding discriminations of learning-disabled from other types of children, a description of another technique often included in the multidisciplinary approach is given.

The Electroencephalogram

Until recently, one part of a multidisciplinary diagnostic evaluation was the electroencephalographic (EEG) recording of a child's brain waves. A thorough diagnostic involved the question of whether or not the child had normal brain functioning and this was to be determined, in part, by measures obtained with an EEG. The current consensus is that the EEG should be limited to individual cases in which there is some suggestive evidence that the EEG pattern would indicate abnormal functioning and this type of abnormality could and should be considered for drug therapy. While the EEG is no longer considered a routine part of an evaluation, there are individual cases in which it is a desirable and appropriate procedure. Teachers should be alert to when such a referral is indicated. For this reason, and to dispel the hocus pocus often associated with the brain, this section will describe some of the procedures used and the research related to learning disabilities.

An EEG is obtained by using an internationally agreed upon system for placement of electrodes on the human scalp. Recordings are made of the signals picked up from these electrodes. The signal is detected, carried to the recording machine and displayed on a strip of recording paper traveling at a known rate, or on an oscilloscope, magnetic tape or computer.

The electrode is a small metal plate, covered with a salt paste on one side, sealed to the scalp and connected to the recording machine with a wire. Only the activity under the electrode should be detected (Gibbs, 1941). The normal EEG is a statistical concept based on empirical correlations with physiological and structurally normal nervous systems in presumably normal subjects (Glaser, 1963).

EEG records are interpreted on the basis of the organization and development of background rhythm (alpha activity), rhythmic and transient activities. Electroencephalographers have developed scaling systems which describe the quality of the various activities recorded. The scale usually describes the record as ranging from poor to excellent. For instance, alpha activity can be rated as poor, fair, moderate or well on development and organization (rhythmicity) (Hughes, 1971). The range of frequencies includes alpha, beta, mu, lambda, vertex, theta and delta waves. The occurrence of these frequencies varies with age and with the part of the brain to which the electrode is attached. Electroencephalographers examine the record for differences among and within individuals. The finding of an abnormal occurrence will be described in terms of where the abnormality is observed in relation to the placement of the electrodes.

EEGs are taken under different conditions and an evaluation is made of the record for each condition. In one part of the EEG the patient is awake. During this time the examination usually includes brain wave activity during hyperventilation. Hyperventilation requires the person to breathe deeply and regularly at a rate of about twenty breaths per minute for two to five minutes. There is a great deal of individual variation in the effects of such a procedure and the effects disappear within half a minute of the cessation of overbreathing. EEGs are also taken during photic stimulation. The subject is exposed to flashes of light at about 15-second intervals with the eyelids closed and then opened. The responses are described as: no driving (the response fails to occur), poor, good and excellent (Hughes, 1971). Responses to photic stimulation may vary considerably, as they are affected by blood sugar level, mental activity, fatigue and the subject's responsiveness to stimulation (Kiloh and Osselton, 1961).

EEGs are also obtained while the patient sleeps. Changes occur in the EEG pattern as the child becomes drowsy and falls into a deep sleep. Certain changes in the EEG pattern during sleep have been associated with epilepsy.

Abnormal responses are defined by the presence and absence of certain waves in certain places, by the symmetry among the two sides of the brain and by the presence of slower and faster than expected electrical activity.

Classic work was conducted into the developmental sequences of patterns in EEGs in young children by Gibbs and Gibbs (1941). Briefly, EEGs of newborns are found to be marked by irregular, slow waves. Each week the slow waves become faster, but not until the fourth year is there a steady frequency wave in the occipital part of the brain. When a child reaches 9 years of age, the occipital records resemble an adult's; by 14 years adultlike recordings from all electrode leads can be obtained. But it is not until about 19 years that all normal adults show adult types of records (Gibbs and Gibbs, 1941, p. 38).

Research on Brain Functioning

The historical link between brain functions and learning disabilities has led to a variety of investigations. The question is not whether brain-damaged children have learning problems, but to what degree children suffering from academic failure might be experiencing either brain damage or some neurological immaturity. As the reader will note, the characteristic research design is to compare the performances, be they on intelligence tests, reaction time measures, or on the drawing of pictures, of children already known to have a learning difficulty with those actions of children not so diagnosed. At least four rather recent investigations have provided some support to the neurology-learning disability relationship.

Dykman, Ackerman, Clements and Peters (1971) have reported the results of their study of 82 learning-disabled and 34 normal 8- to 12-year-old boys. While a variety of tests were administered, of concern here are the results pertaining to the neurological examination. They assessed each child on 41 classical signs of neurological impairment. Of these 41 items, the learning-disabled child showed greater difficulty than the normal on 24 items. Using an additional 39 "paraclassical signs," the learning disabled showed less adequacy on 21 such items. While the reliability of the discrimination of any particular sign must be established in the future, their data do provide rather strong evidence for the hypothesis of neurological involvement in learning-disabled children. Of some note was the fact that the younger the child, the better the discrimination between the learning-disabled and normal child. The authors suggest then that the learning-disabled child is likely to be suffering from a developmental lag, which might be better detected at even younger ages.

The relationship of neurological examination and intellectual status was examined by Bortner, Hertzig and Birch (1972). The learning-disabled sample was 198 8- to 12-year-old children who were labeled by the school district as learning disabled and who had had positive neurological test results prior to their placement in special education classes. A control group of 36 children was included. The psychologist and neurologist on the research team were "blind" (unknowing) as to the diagnosis and status of the individual subjects. The neurological examination was that described earlier in the text (Rabe, 1969), with special attention given to the extent of distractibility, impulsivity and meddlesomeness (*i.e.*, hyperactivity). There were two categories of abnormality; one was the presence of classically defined hard signs and the second was the presence of soft signs. This included language and speech problems, clumsiness, motor overflow, difficulty in imitation of motor movements, unresponsiveness to double simultaneous tactile stimulation and inadequate graphesthetic and stereognostic responsiveness.

Results were that the learning-disabled group had significantly more signs of neurological impairment than did the control group. Twenty-one percent of the learning-disabled sample demonstrated the presence of hard signs (*e.g.*, abnormal reflexes), and 65 percent had two or more soft signs. None of the children from the control sample had any hard signs and only 5 percent had more than one soft sign. This difference is really not surprising, since the original diagnosis was based upon the presence of such signs. At least these signs showed some reliability. Perhaps of more interest was the relationship between such signs and intelligence test scores. The greater the number of soft neurological signs, the lower the intelligence test score. No soft sign was a better predictor of intelligence than another and with but one exception there was no intelligence test pattern of scores associated more with the brain-damaged than the control children. The exception was that children with one or no soft signs who were diagnosed as learning disabled were more likely to have performance IQ scores higher than their verbal IQ scores. Insofar as many comparisons between groups on the various subtests were made, it is quite possible that this last finding may have resulted from chance. Until this finding is replicated, it is best to consider it a suggestive rather than a definitive finding.

Another conclusion supportive of the neurological differences in learning-disabled children is derived from a study by Hunter, Johnson and Keefe (1972). These investigators assessed the autonomic response patterns of 20 male nonreaders and 20 control children 8 to 11 years old. The reasoning of the authors was that if dyslexia is biological, physiological measures might discriminate between readers and nonreaders. The nonreading children had been referred for remedial reading and were tested as being more than two years retarded in reading, while the comparison children were more than one year above grade level in reading. The experimental procedures involved measurement of skin conductance potential, skin resistance level, finger, pulse and heart rate during a habituation series, a reaction time series and an auditory threshold series. The habituation series presented 15 auditory stimuli of 10-second duration while the child was in a semi-darkened room resting in a semi-supine position on a contour bed. The reaction time series presented the child with five successive 75 decibel tones of 10 seconds' duration. The child was to press a button, placed in his preferred hand, when he heard a tone. The auditory threshold required the child to press the button when he heard a sound and was essentially a control condition to ensure that the children did not have hearing loss. The results indicated the children were not experiencing hearing impairments. On the reaction time series the control subjects responded consistently faster across the five trials. While both groups showed habituation, the controls displayed greater anticipatory responses in heart rate than the reading-disability group. The latter group also showed they had lower basal skin conductance levels over the test trials. In line with this, the reading-disabled child demonstrated a longer reaction time responding to the auditory signal, than did the comparison children.

These data are in agreement with the Dykman et al. (1970) data which suggest that learning-disabled children have slower reaction times, slower learning, slower assimilation of information, shorter attention spans and decreased physiological activity.

In effect, they do not appear to have the arousal support necessary for sustained attention.

Further evidence suggesting the presence of neurological deficit or lag in the learning-disabled children stems from a study by Owen, Adams, Forrest, Stolz and Fisher (1971). In this investigation, a neurological examination was administered to 76 educationally handicapped, 76 of their siblings, 76 academically successful children and 36 of their siblings, of elementary and junior high school age. The neurological examination included the classical examination described earlier and assessments of the children's ability to imitate previously tapped patterns and to make visual right and left discriminations. In the latter test, "children were asked to perform tasks with their right or left hand, or to identify the examiner's right hand as he faced the child" (p. 29). Medical histories were also obtained. Several sources of data failed to differentiate the educationally handicapped from the control groups and these included: measure of hand, foot and eye preference, overflow movements, arm extension, walking on the balance beam, prenatal, neonatal or postnatal complications, premature births and birth weight differences. The medical histories, apparently derived from both hospital records and verbal reports from the mother, indicated that the mothers of educationally disabled children had more difficulty than mothers of the academically successful, with their infants being more irritable, having colic reactions, showing decreased sound production during prelingual development and demonstrating temper tantrums. The neurological evaluation revealed significant differences, with the educationally handicapped sample performing less adequately than either their siblings or academically successful children on imitation of tapped patterns, right-left discrimination, double simultaneous touch and fast alternating finger and hand movements. Additionally, the educationally handicapped children demonstrated a greater frequency of speech and language problems than either their siblings or the academically successful.

The authors conclude that organic damage is not a major causative problem in learning disabilities, since there were but three children who demonstrated hard neurological signs. At the same time, however, there were many soft signs of neurological differences or immaturities in the handicapped group and to a somewhat lesser extent in their siblings. It should be noted that whatever interpretation is given to the weight of organic brain damage or maturational lag in accounting for the behavior of the educationally handicapped, it is true that the specific signs found by one investigator are not found by others. There were a number of differences between this study and others which gave greater evidence for the presence of neurological differences between learning-disabled and nonlearning-disabled children. One is that the children in the study conducted by Owen et al. were considerably older than those in the earlier mentioned studies. There is evidence that neurological facts are age specific and that some neurological signs decrease in incidence as the child ages (Ackerman et al., 1971). Since Owen et al. employed children at a more advanced age than the previous studies, it might be expected that some neurological signs would not be demonstrated.

A second difference in the Owen et al. studies and those previously cited, is that Owen et al. employed children from the classrooms, while the remaining investigators employed clinic cases. It is not unlikely that children brought to a clinic, rather than managed within the classroom, may be more handicapped.

Whatever the sources of the differences in results across these studies, the absence of the usual indicators used by clinicians to point to an association between neurological factors and learning deficits led Owen et al. to reject this hypothesis. While hard signs did not discriminate groups, they did find evidence of neurological difficulties through the presence of many soft signs. Speech and language deficits and problems in the reproduction of both auditorily and visually presented tasks did discriminate the groups.

Many questions have been raised concerning the utility of the neurological examination for understanding the learning-disabled child. Clearly it is important for school officials to detect children suffering from brain damage. But given the absence of malfunction, does the neurological examination render useful information to the learning disability specialist? While the research evidence does suggest that learning-disabled children may be suffering from some neurological deficit or lag, the evidence is not at all convincing. First, research efforts have typically compared children on very many behaviors. Of the many behaviors tested, only a few will discriminate the learning disabled from the academically successful. If enough comparisons between groups are made, then some will be statistically significant by chance. Whatever signs do discriminate, results need replication in future studies, and very few such signs have been replicated. Second, as is typically done in other areas of research, the handicapped groups are those already diagnosed. That is, known learning-disabled children are compared with academically successful ones. Thus, it is likely that the handicapped groups will consist of extreme cases, children who were easy to diagnose in the first place. Third, the neurological examination is often conducted by a neurologist who is not trained to look for the kinds of information helpful in diagnosing learning disabilities (Lerner, 1971; Vuckovich, 1968). They are more likely to focus upon the signs indicative of brain damage in adults or radical syndromes in children, not those signs correlated with the presence of a learning disability. But even if appropriate soft signs are detected, the locale of the damage cannot be specified, the nature of the problem is unknown and there is no way to suggest a remedy for it anyway! This does not mean to say that research addressed to this issue should be discontinued. To the contrary, much more information concerning the relationship between brain and learning is needed. As yet, however, the nature of the evidence is not such as to make the neurological examination a particularly useful tool in the armamentarium of the learning disability diagnostician or teacher.

The future role of the neurologist has been explicated by Denckla (1973), a neurologist whose clinical practice and research efforts have been concerned with learning-disabled children. Denckla reports that information about the "minimal cerebral dysfunction" problem has become so widespread that many pediatricians are now competent to diagnose and prescribe medical intervention. The role of the neurologist should now shift to integrate the accumulated evidence on child development with that from adults with soft signs of brain damage in order to develop a system from which to infer the probable existence of brain damage with behavioral and learning problems. But Denckla is not stopping with inferences. The goal is to develop "neurometrics," a norm-referenced approach to neurological evaluations which are currently subjective, rather than statistically derived. Once the usual tasks included in a neurological evaluation have been standardized on normal children, much greater precision can be obtained in correlating observed deficiencies with brain functioning. The neurologist is to learn to do a "task analysis" in which the age of the child, the quality of the performance and knowledge of brain functioning are integrated.

Standardized Tests

The remainder of this chapter presents brief summaries and descriptions of a number of widely employed assessment devices, and all the minutiae necessarily associated with such presentations will be offered. This material is included to provide some familiarity with these tests and a useful reference source for the future.

Before discussing particular tests, several considerations which affect the utility of any measure, be it an observer's ratings, standardized tests or interviews, should be mentioned. There are three primary considerations. First is the question as to whether the test is reliable. That is, does the test measure something in such a fashion as to produce consistency in the scores obtained? For example, are the scores of one person who takes the test more than once approximately the same? If the scores vary across instances of testing, the measure is deemed to be unreliable. Irrespective of whether the cause of the variation rests in item ambiguity, confusions as to how to take the test, transient states in the test taker or other random factors, a test which yields disparate scores across testing occasions cannot be measuring anything useful. Any particular score is meaningless if there is no stability to the score obtained. Thus, an unreliable test cannot be a valid one; that is, it cannot be measuring what it is presumed to be measuring.

The second question pertains to the validity of the instrument. Even though the test is a reliable one, it may or may not be a valid one. The test may be measuring what the constructor of the test hoped it would, but it is entirely possible that it is reliably measuring another and unrelated dimension of the person. There are a variety of ways to assess the validity of a measure. For instance, one might compare the performance of people presumed to be high on the trait or skill presumed to be assessed by the test with those presumed to be low on that skill or trait. It is important, however, for the reader to remember that a test does not necessarily measure what its constructors hope and often claim it measures; tests are not valid simply because someone says so. The claim of validity must be supported by systematically derived data, not simply personal biases. In the field of assessment, the number of tests and the pretensions of many outstrip the evidence which is available concerning their validity.

The third consideration is that a test may be reliable and valid yet fail to be clinically useful. One must consider the degree to which test scores will result in a diagnostician making errors. How many persons will be false positives, judged as possessing a skill level or personality trait which in reality they do not possess? How many will be false negatives, judged as not possessing the skill or trait when in fact they do? If there are many false judgments, the utility of the test is decreased. Since many of these points are made in other sections of this book, they will not be belabored here. It is critical that the reader bear in mind that the merits of any particular test are in doubt without consideration of these factors.

The tests included here are not presented because their reliability, validity and usefulness have been clearly established. Their inclusion should not be construed as an endorsement. There is no doubt that some could and should be praised on the basis of the factors we have outlined as important. No doubt some should be eliminated from the professional's test armamentarium. Unfortunately, not enough is known about many to make strong recommendations in either direction. These tests are presented simply because they are frequently used, deservedly or not, and persons concerned with learning disabilities should be familiar with, if not accepting of, them.

Assessment devices have been devised for many purposes and many children. The particular technique selected to assess a child will depend upon the reason for the evaluation, the age of the child, the professional time available and the educational background and biases of the diagnostician. Following are examples of tests used to screen preschool, kindergarten and school-aged children, tests used in individual studies of children and group achievement batteries.

Preschool and Kindergarten Screening Scales

In the past few years concern has grown for the detection of potential learning problems in preschool and kindergarten children. Preschool and kindergarten screening tests for potential learning disabilities are predicated upon the assumption that detection and intervention at this time will prevent failure in the elementary school years. To detect and intervene requires a definition of potential failure. The assumption in this case is that failure in adequate development of certain skills or behaviors at age 3 predicts failure in school-related skills at age 8. Discrepancies in growth of critical areas, particularly language and perceptual skills, are believed to be predictive of future educational difficulties. If a child is slow for his age in the development of vocabulary and syntax at age 3, he will be retarded in vocabulary and syntax development at ages 5, 7 and later. Because of this, the child will be handicapped in the acquisition of academic skills dependent upon such knowledge. Detection of inadequacies in preschoolers is thus based upon the assumptions that a child's development proceeds in a regular and predictable fashion and that delays in defined developmental areas are linked critically to skills needed as a child progresses through the school system.

Another assumption underlying the early detection movement is that intervention provided children experiencing developmental delays will alleviate and eliminate later problems. If problems are dealt with early, the child is not expected to require special services later. These assumptions have been based in large part upon longitudinal studies of high-risk infants in which traumas related to birth were linked to conceptual and behavioral problems three years later, to post hoc analyses of parental descriptions of the developmental histories of learning-disabled children and to studies of language development in normal and language-deviant children.

The early detection–early treatment movement is not without dangers. Developers and users of testing techniques designed for young children need to be well aware of the limitations regarding the assumptions and difficulties inherent in predicting academic performance on the basis of presumably related behaviors. As the review of infant intelligence tests in Chapter 5 indicates, there are many practical difficulties involved in the development of adequate measures. Hazards aside, many tests are being developed. Before they become used, further information concerning reliability and validity must be established.

A very serious issue in constructing techniques to detect potential learning disabilities is defining the potential learning disability. We have longstanding and continuing difficulties in defining what a learning disability is in children who are already failing in school. How, then, can we define what has not yet occurred? We need to ask how many children will be falsely labeled as disabled and how many will go undetected. In which developmental areas need a child be retarded, and how far behind need the child be, for us to say with assuredness that the child needs help? What proportion of problems would spontaneously improve with a little help from Mother Nature? We must weigh the benefits to be derived from detection against the dangers inherent in labeling children as inadequate.

Finally, there is the critical issue of providing programs for children who are labeled as potentially disabled. Assuming that we manage to define potential learning problems, what effective techniques are available for remedial programs? We do not yet know which techniques will be effective, nor whether we can prevent later school problems. In a number of instances test constructors have provided remedial programs based upon the test.

Because the test constructor recommends a test-based remedial program is no guarantee of the program's effectiveness. While the tests currently being used may ultimately be found to have limited utility for defining individual children or developing intervention techniques, their use will further our knowledge as to the adequacy of the techniques and the nature of the developing child. They are thus worth our consideration.

The *Early Detection Inventory* (McGahan and McGahan, 1967) has been designed to assess preschoolers and children in ungraded primary classes. It is not a test, but a means to organize data derived from a variety of sources: parent, dentist, speech therapist, audiologist, and "test administrator." The child is assessed in the areas of school readiness, motor performance and social-emotional adjustment. Ratings in each area on a 1 to 3 scale are presumed to help in predicting whether or not a child will need help upon entering school. The lower the rating, the more extensive the subsequent need for help may be (McCarthy, 1972).

There are many shortcomings in the scoring procedure used, but the manual provides the information needed to set up a screening procedure and a preschool evaluation clinic. This procedure involves the setting up of stations in which the children move from professional to professional. Many children can be screened by varying professionals in an economic use of time. While we do not know whether this particular inventory captures a child's readiness for school or the need for special help, it does provide a means to organize a comprehensive case study of many children.

The *Gesell Developmental Tests* (Ilg and Ames, 1965) are based upon extensive data derived from observations of children and interviews with parents conducted at the Gesell Institute. The data base is large. Norms are available for children ages four weeks to 72 months for motor development, adaptive behavior, language and personal social skills. The test is useful in detecting very deviant children; but it is questionable as to whether it will be useful in detecting learning-disabled youngsters (see chapter on intelligence), although some believe it may be usable (Borstelmann, 1972). It is important to note that there has been extensive research on the scales and the user can determine the usefulness and constraints in its employment. Parenthetically, the manual presents the authors' educational viewpoint that children be placed in school on the basis of developmental age rather than chronological age or IQ. Their cautionary philosophy is worth noting in a time of haste to label and place preschoolers in educational programs.

A quick screening device for children 3 to 5 years of age was developed by a Title III program in *Early Childhood Development* (Holliday, 1972). There are no norms, reliability or validity data; the purpose was simply to identify children having problems and to refer these children for more intensive study. The areas screened include vision and hearing, speech and language, social-emotional status, cognition, gross and fine motor movement and perception.

Vision testing requires the child to place a hand in the same direction as a letter seen on the letter chart. Audition screening requires the child upon hearing a sound presented on the audiometer to respond by dropping blocks or clothes pins into a basket or by putting pegs into a pegboard. Socio-emotional status is informally judged by observing the child's response to peers.

The speech and language survey presents the child with the following items. The child is asked to tell a story about a picture shown to him, to tell what individual items are in the picture and to point to the picture named. The child is also asked to follow instructions, such as repeating numbers and acting out short instructions (*e.g.,* stand up, clap your hands, point to your shoes).

Cognition items require the child to remember and relate items put in a box by the examiner, to relate whether pictures seen are the same or different, to learn paired-associates and to classify objects.

Gross motor screening assesses the child's ability to walk backwards, forwards and sideways on a balance beam, jump on each foot and on both feet, hop on alternating feet in a rhythmic pattern, locate body parts and label them, imitate unilateral, bilateral and contralateral movements, step over and sideways to pass a yardstick, draw a circle, connect X's in a lateral position and draw parallel lines connecting two ×'s in a vertical position.

Fine motor-perceptual screening has the child replace puzzle pieces by shape and color, imitate block designs and replicate object assembly of examiner (*e.g.,* one apple . . . five birds).

Without information concerning the reliability and validity of these tests, no judgments can be made as to its usefulness in aiding the learning disability specialist, or any specialists for that matter.

The Screening of School-aged Children

The *Predictive Index* (deHirsch, Jansky, and Langford, 1966). The catalyst for much of the development of tests for preschool and kindergarten children was the study in which deHirsch, Jansky and Langford attempted to predict which kindergarteners might fail reading, writing or spelling as assessed at the end of second grade. A large battery of tests was administered to a group of kindergarten children. Those tests which predicted best the children experiencing academic difficulties in second grade now comprise the Predictive Index. Trimble (1970) expanded upon the Predictive Index so that practitioners could score the items and specified the number of tests the child should fail to indicate the need for intervention. Trimble also developed an intervention program based upon the child's performance on the Predictive Index.

The Predictive Index includes the following tests:

1. Pencil Use: Ability to hold and manipulate a pencil correctly.
2. Wepman Auditory Discrimination Test (described in Chapter 7).
3. Categories: The child must provide category name for three stimulus items (*e.g.,* red-green-blue, apple-hamburger-ice cream).
4. Gates Word Matching Subtest: The child is shown four words and must draw a line between the two which are correct.

5. Bender Visual-motor Gestalt test (described in Chapter 7).
6. Horst Reversals Test: The child must circle items the same as a stimulus item (*e.g.,* to to ot ot to ot to).
7. Number of words used in a story: Child is asked to tell the story of the Three Bears. Scoring is based upon the number of words, relevant details and ability to get across the point of the story.
8. Word Recognition I, II, and III: At the beginning of the session the child is taught to read two words, "boy" and "train," and told to copy them from a model. At the end of the testing session, the child is asked to pick from a pack of cards presented successively the words "boy" and "train" and to pick the same words when the pack of cards are all exposed on the table, and then to write as much of the two words from memory as he could recall. The child is scored 3 points for the word if spelled correctly, 2 if there are two letters of the word, 1 for one letter and 0 for no letters on "boy" and 2 for 3 or 4 letters of "train" or 1 for 1 or 2 letters.

As yet, we know of little direct evidence pertaining to this instrument. Trimble (1970), on the basis of a study of 266 children, concluded that this test might be a useful screening device for predicting reading problems of children completing the first grade.

Elementary School Screening Scales

The *Devereux Elementary School Behavior Rating Scale* (Spivack and Swift, 1967). In this device, the teacher is instructed to compare the child being rated to his peers with regard to classroom behavior problems. The child is rated on 47 scoring items related to one another in 11 categories. The categories and examples of the items within them include:

1. Classroom disturbance: Has to be reprimanded or controlled because of behavior in class.

2. Impatience: Starts working before getting directions straight.
3. Disrepect-Defiance: Breaks classroom rules.
4. External Blame: Says teacher does not help him enough.
5. Achievement Anxiety: Outwardly nervous when test given.
6. External Reliance: Looks to see how others are doing something before he does it.
7. Comprehension: Gets the point of what he reads or hears in class.
8. Inattentive-Withdrawn: Quickly loses attention when teacher explains something to him.
9. Irrelevant-Responsiveness: Tells stories which are exaggerated and untruthful.
10. Creative Initiative: Brings things to class that relate to current topic.
11. Needs Closeness to Teacher: Seeks out teacher before or after class to talk about school or personal matters.

This scale taps many of the behaviors attributed to learning disabilities although extremes in such behaviors are supposed to be more indicative of emotional than learning problems. While there may be differences in the extremes of behaviors which result in differential labeling, many of these problems are characteristic of learning-disabled children, and the profiling of them along with comparison to peers can give the teacher or learning disability specialist one means to organize information about the child's classroom behavior.

The *Pupil Rating Scale* (Myklebust, 1971). Another screening technique which attempts to tap behaviors presumably more related to learning disabilities than emotional problems is the Pupil Rating Scale. This scale was developed as part of a large study which attempted to determine the medical and psychological correlates of learning disabilities. While the intensive study of the children included medical, neurological, EEG and complete psychometric batteries, the Pupil Rating Scale was found to be a promising measure for detecting children subsequently labeled learning disabled. Using this instrument, the teacher rates each child on a five-point scale on five categories of behavior. These categories include:

1. Auditory Comprehension and Listening: Ability to follow direction, comprehension of class discussions, ability to retain information heard and comprehension of word meanings.
2. Spoken Language: Ability to speak in complete sentences using accurate sentence structure, vocabulary ability, ability to recall words, ability to tell stories and relate experiences and ability to formulate ideas from isolated facts.
3. Orientation: Promptness, spatial orientation, judgment of relationships and learning directions.
4. Behavior: Cooperation, attention, ability to organize, ability to cope with new situations and tactfulness.
5. Motor: general coordination, balance and ability to manipulate utensils.

Bryan and McGrady (1972) studied the factor structure and screening utility of the Pupil Behavior Rating Scale. An analysis of teacher ratings of 183 boys who had learning disabilities and 176 adequate achievers indicated that teachers consistently rate the problem learners lower on each area of the scale. While such scales no doubt have validity and reliability in detecting learning problems, the issue remains as to what behaviors of children elicit teachers' judgments.

The *Screening Tests for Identifying Children with Specific Language Disability* (Slingerland, 1964). This instrument is based upon the hypothesis that deficits in information processing result in learning difficulties, particularly in those areas of learning which require language. It is one of the few tests designed to assess information processing skills in groups of children for screening and diagnostic purposes. There are three levels of the test, one for each of the following grade levels: mid-grade one to mid-grade two, mid-grade two to mid-grade three, mid-grade three to mid-grade four. There are eight subtests at each level which assess various means of visual and auditory processing in the context of schoollike activities. For instance, the visual tests require the child to copy a paragraph from a distance and at a near point, to remember a stimulus presented in a multiple choice and to reproduce the answer in writing. The auditory tests require the

295

child to repeat words and a short story dictated to him, and to indicate sounds heard at the beginning and end of words.

The adequacy of this test is unknown insofar as insufficient information on validity, reliability and standardization samples is available (Deno, 1972). It should be noted also that the test lacks sufficient measures of language usage and comprehension, critical skills for adequate academic performance.

Diagnostic Tests and the School-aged Child

Up to this point the focus of this chapter has been upon screening techniques for the detection of potential and present learning problems. In the remainder of this section we shall describe some of the tests used to assess intelligence, specific diagnostic tests and achievement tests. There are many more and better tests available for the assessment of older children, no doubt as a result of the generally higher reliability or stability of older children's performance on tests.

Intelligence tests have had a long and generally useful role in education. They were devised to aid in school placement decisions and have been heavily utilized since their inception. Here we will discuss some of the instruments designed to assess intelligence, but the reader is referred to a more detailed discussion of the concept of intelligence and the utility of these tests in Chapter 5.

The *Wechsler Intelligence Scale for Children* (Wechsler, 1946). The Wechsler Intelligence Scale for Children (WISC) is widely used for the assessment of intelligence in children ages 5 to 15. (There is also a form available for testing adults, the Wechsler Adult Intelligence Scale (WAIS), and one for children ages 4 to 6, the Wechsler Preschool and Primary Scale of Intelligence (WPPSI).) The scale consists of 12 subtests, two of which are optional. Five of these form the basis for the Verbal Intelligence score and five comprise a Performance Intelligence score; the two groups combined provide a Full Scale IQ.

Most of the verbal tests correlate with each other to a higher degree than with tests on the performance scale and vice-versa. The tests labeled verbal and performance differ in the skills they measure, but both tap factors which cut across the delineation of categories.

The IQ score obtained is a *deviation* IQ. It indicates the amount by which a person deviates from the average performance of individuals of his own age group. The 100 IQ is set to equal the average score for each age. The highest one percent of individuals at any age level will have IQs over 135 and the lowest one percent will have IQs of 65 or below. Fifty percent of children will have IQs from 90 to 110 at each age level. The various subtests which constitute the Verbal Scale of the test, along with example items, include:

Social
1. General Information: From what animal do we get milk?
2. Comprehension: What is the thing to do if you cut your finger?
3. Arithmetic: The child is presented with arithmetic problems.
4. Similarities: The child is asked to explain in what manner various items are alike, for example, a peach and a plum.
5. Vocabulary: Definitions of common words are required of the child.
short-Term
6. Digit Span (optional): Children are required to repeat after the examiner sets of digits as presented and in reverse sequence.

It should be noted that the Arithmetic and the Digit Span subtests show the least correlation with verbal IQ scores, and other studies have suggested that these tests may be tapping mathematical rather than purely verbal skills (Freides, 1974). Also noteworthy is that the Digit Span subtest is the only assessment of immediate or short-term memory in the WISC and is often employed as a test of such a function. However, this subtest is not a highly reliable one and should not be used to draw general inferences about an individual's memory.

The various subtests which constitute the Performance Scale of the WISC, along with example items, include:

1. Picture Completion: The child is shown drawings and is to indicate which part of the drawing is missing (*e.g.*, a missing nose from a drawing of a face).
2. Picture Arrangement: The child is presented an array of pictures which, when arranged correctly, will yield a meaningful story (*e.g.*, arranging pictures to depict a burglary).
3. Block Design: The child is presented with a set of red and white blocks which are to be arranged to match a pattern demonstrated in a picture.
4. Object Assembly: The child is presented with a jig saw puzzle which must be arranged to yield a meaningful product (*e.g.*, arranging the pieces to produce a correct picture of a face).
5. Coding: There are two coding tests, one appropriate for children 5 to 7 years, the second for children 8 to 15 years. The younger version pictures symbols—a star, circle and other shapes. Inside the symbol is another symbol, a vertical line, horizontal line, circle and so on. Below this presentation are five lines of symbols which have not been filled in. The child is shown how to match shapes to the symbols. The version for the older child is essentially the same, but the visual stimulus is a set of boxes divided in two, a geometric symbol is in the bottom half and a number, 1 to 9, is in the top half. The child must put the appropriate symbol in the boxes below which have the numbers in them.
6. Mazes (optional): The child does a series of mazes which increase in difficulty.

Patterns of subtest scores have often been used for clinical assessments, following Wechsler's (1958) suggestions. The authors of this book believe such a use is unwarranted. The subtests are not reliable and empirical justifications for this practice are not available.

Other investigators have suggested that WISC subtest scores be combined in other than the Verbal-Performance Scales to better describe certain types of learning problems. Keogh, Wetter, McGinty and Donlon (1973) subdivide the WISC into a three factor test in which a factor of Verbal-Comprehension is comprised of Information, Vocabulary and Comprehension; Analytic-Field-Approach of Object Assembly, Block Design, and Picture Completion; and Attention-Concentration of Arithmetic, Digit Span and Coding. A comparison of learning and behavior problems, hyperactive learning-disabled and mentally retarded boys on these three WISC factors revealed that both learning-disabled groups in contrast to the mentally retarded were adequate on the Verbal and Analytic factors and lowest on the Attention-Concentration factor. This suggests that low subtest scores on this combination of subtests may typify learning-disabled children.

Studies of WISC scores in disabled readers have led Bannatyne (1968) and Rugel (1974) to suggest that the Verbal and Performance Scales of the WISC be reclassified as Spatial, Conceptual and Sequential (Rugel, 1974) or Spatial, Verbal Conceptualizing, Sequencing and Acquired Knowledge. This is recommended because the traditional split of verbal/performance appears to be invalid; tests classified as performance, arithmetic for instance, require verbal comprehension and a verbal response from the child. Bannatyne (1974, p. 273) regroups the subtests in this way:

Spatial Ability: Picture Completion, Block Design, Object Assembly.
Verbal Comprehension Ability: Comprehension, Similarities, Vocabulary.
Sequencing Ability: Digit Span, Arithmetic, Coding.
Acquired Knowledge: Information, Arithmetic, Vocabulary.

Studying the test scores of 22 disabled readers, Rugel reported that the disabled readers perform best on the Spatial category, second best on the Conceptual category and poorest on the Sequential category.

Subtest scores have also been utilized to plan remediation programs (Ferinden, 1969, 1970). Children low in a particular area are given exercises which are believed to reflect the same skill. There is great similarity between the item and the remedial technique suggested, so this may be helpful. Since there has been no empirical study of such implementation of test results, one cannot say whether or not this is an advisable practice.

The *Stanford-Binet Intelligence Scale* (Terman and Merrill, 1960). The Stanford-Binet is an individually administered test of intelligence appropriate for children ages 2 to 18. It is widely used, and is probably the preferred test of intelligence for children ages 2 to 6. The analyses of the Stanford-Binet made by Anastasi (1961) and Freemen (1962) are adapted here.

Years 2–5: At this age level the subtests involve manipulation of objects (placement of pieces in a simple formboard block building . . .), recognition of body parts, the recognition of objects referred to by name and by function. Rote memory, the use of words in combination, verbal comprehension and word knowledge are also assessed.

Years 6–12: The child is tested for form perception, visual motor skills, rote memory, word knowledge, number concepts and arithmetical reasoning.

Years 13–Superior Adult III: At this level, visual analysis and imagery, visual motor skills, rote memory for digits, words and sentences, work knowledge, problem solving are assessed.

Memory, spatial orientation, numerical concepts and language skills are tapped at scattered age levels using increasingly difficult items. For example, tests of memory may require the child to recall objects or the content of passages, numerical tests start with simple counting and proceed to complex reasoning problems.

This test is heavily weighted with verbal abilities. Anastasi (1961) reports correlations between scores on the vocabulary test and the mental age based on the entire test as ranging from .71 to .83 for children 8 through 14 years. She further indicates that this test is more reliable for older than for younger children and for lower than for higher IQ scores. The Stanford-Binet test is quite useful in predicting future school achievement. Being heavily weighted to tap verbal skills, it is not surprising that the test can yield useful prediction in activities which weight such skills. As Anastasi points out, the test is an achievement test.

The *Peabody Picture Vocabulary Test* (Dunn, 1959). The Peabody Picture Vocabulary Test (PPVT) is an individually or group administered test of verbal intelligence. The test was designed for use with handicapped children who might have unusual difficulties responding verbally to test items. Thus, the test is designed for children suffering from mental retardation and cerebral palsy, or who have speech problems, are brain damaged or emotionally disturbed. The test contains 150 test plates, each with four pictures. (See page 302) The examiner says one word and the child must point to the correct picture. The test is appropriate for children ages 2½ through 18 years and provides scores in the form of deviation IQs, mental age and percentiles. It is popular because it is quick, easy to administer and score and can be given by untrained persons. While it does correlate in the 70s to 80s with the WISC and the Stanford-Binet, there is some concern for what the test actually measures (Lyman, 1965) and this concern is increased if nonprofessional persons use the information to make judgments, predictions and pronouncements about children. The user is cautioned against using scores on this test as a substitute for standardized intelligence tests, as it samples a restricted range of human behavior. Instead, it is recommended as a measure of verbal comprehension of single words.

The *Goodenough-Harris Drawing Test* (Harris, 1963). This test, previously referred to as the Draw a Person Test (Goodenough, 1926), is a quick and reliable measure of intelligence for children 3.3 years to 13 years of age (Harris, 1963). The child is instructed to make a drawing of a man as best he can. An 8½ × 11 sheet of white paper is used and the child must complete the drawing using a pencil. The test is not timed.

The child is scored one point for each detail of the human body which is represented and additional points for the correctness of the proportions of the body. Norms and scoring procedure are also available for drawings of the self and a woman.

The child's score, like the IQ, is expressed with an average of 100 and a standard deviation of 15. The child's score is standardized by age and sex groups. The IQ from the DAP is not identical with the IQ derived from an individual intelligence test, although the correlation is quite high. The score on the Goode-

Examples from Peabody Picture Vocabulary Test

SOURCE: Dunn, L. M. *Peabody Picture Vocabulary Test*. Minneapolis, Minn.: American Guidance Service, 1959.

nough-Harris, as an indicator of intelligence, is quite reliable between the ages of 5 and 10 years.

This test can be subclassified as an assessment of visual-motor skills and compared to other visual-motor and visual-perceptual tests which require the child to remember, reconstruct, compare and discriminate visual stimuli. One further note: While the test is often employed by clinical psychologists and other specialists as a device for making inferences concerning the child's personality dynamics and content, there is reason to doubt the validity of such procedures. The test yields a good quick assessment of intelligence scores obtained on other measures, but it is unlikely that it can be used as a personality assessment device.

Specific Diagnostic Tests

Diagnostic tests are designed to measure performance on tasks which are believed to be essential to academic achievement. While general measures of intelligence define children according to some classification scheme, the purpose of diagnostic tests is to specify educational or remedial programs (Kirk and Kirk, 1972). By assessing presumed impediments to later achievement, the diagnostician can map out the specifics of an intervention program. The test which has had the greatest influence in diagnosing learning disabilities is the *Illinois Test of Psycholinguistic Abilities.* The development of this tool has had an enormous influence upon conceptualization, diagnosis and treatment of learning-disabled children.

The *Illinois Test of Psycholinguistic Abilities* (Kirk,McCarthy and Kirk, 1968). The ITPA attempts to assess three dimensions of communication skills: the channels of communication, levels of organization and psycholinguistic processes. Channels of communication refers to the sensory modality which is being used for the reception or comprehension of the stimulus and which is being employed for expression. In this case, the modalities being evaluated at the receptive level are audition and vision; the modes of expression include speech and gesture. The two *levels* of language organization are the *automatic-sequential*, activities which require retention and expression of automatic chains, and the *representational*, communication which requires meaning attached to symbols. The automatic-sequential level involves memory and imitation of spoken utterances, whereas the representational level indicates thought processes operating behind the signal.

Psycholinguistic processes refers to the acquisition and use of all the learned abilities necessary for language usage. Three main abilities are presumed to be assessed. Decoding refers to abilities necessary to obtain meaning from auditorily and visually presented material (*e.g.*, receptive language, comprehension of what is seen and heard). Association, which denotes manipulation of linguistic symbols internally, is a central process elicited by decoding, which elicits, in turn, encoding (*e.g.*, thought). Encoding is all the abilities which are required for expressive language.

There are 12 subtests in the 1968 revision of the ITPA. The test is appropriate for use with children ages 2.4 to 10.3. The test is standardized so that a number of scores can be obtained. A psycholinguistic composite age, which is a composite of the combined subtests, can be computed. Like mental age, it is an overall index of psycholinguistic abilities. A psycholinguistic age is available for each of the subtests. Scaled scores are used to plot a profile of psycholinguistic ages, which permits a direct comparison of the child's performance from one subtest to another. Tests at the representational level of language organization and examples of items follow:

1. Auditory Reception: The child is presented with a short question to which he must respond "yes" or "no." An example of such an item is, "Do scouts signal?"
2. Visual Reception: The child is presented with a stimulus picture which is then removed from his visual field. The child must then identify the same item from a set of four pictures. The hooker is that the correct choice is semantically, but not visually, identical. Examples are a baby cup and a coffee cup, a saddle shoe and a tennis shoe.

3. Auditory Association: The child's ability to relate concepts orally is presumed to be measured on this test. The test is similar to a sentence completion exercise, in which the items are presented and answered orally. An example is the item, "A kitty says meow, a doggie says _____?"

4. Visual Association: The child's ability to relate concepts presented visually is assessed. The stimulus input is visual, the response is verbal. The child is presented with a single stimulus picture surrounded by four optional pictures, one of which must be associated with the stimulus. The child is asked to indicate which of the four goes with the stimulus picture. Examples include man's hat with man, pocketknife, hammer or watch; high heel shoes with woman, man, girl or boy.

5. Expression, Verbal: This subtest refers to the child's ability to express himself verbally. The child is presented with a series of common objects (*e.g.*, a ball, a block, an envelope) and asked to describe and tell about the object.

6. Expression, Manual: Here the child's skill in communicating nonverbally is measured. The child is shown an object, then a series of pictures of objects and is asked to show, through gestures, how such objects are employed. Examples of the objects used in the subtest are a guitar and a clarinet.

In addition to those subtests designed to assess representational processes, there are those which purportedly measure language organization at the automatic-sequential level. Below are these subtests and examples of items within them are listed.

1. Automatic, grammatic closure: These items are designed to measure the child's use of grammatical forms and rules which are acquired in other than formal classroom contexts (*i.e.*, automatically acquired). In this subtest, the child is presented with a picture, the examiner starts a sentence and the child is to complete it with the appropriate form of the stimulus word. For instance, the examiner says, "Here is a dog; here are two _____. This horse is not big, this horse is big, this horse is even _____. These children all fell down,

he hurt himself, she hurt herself, they all hurt _____."

2. Automatic, visual closure: This subtest is employed to assess the child's recognition of objects when only a part of the object is visible. The stimulus picture is given to the child and he is then required to discover that stimulus in the remaining parts of the picture. Thus, he may be presented with a shoe as the stimulus and then be asked to discover shoes depicted in a picture of a cluttered room where the shoes are only partially displayed.

3. Sequential, auditory memory: The child is asked to repeat a series of digits given him orally by the examiner.

4. Sequential, visual memory: Here the child is asked to reproduce a sequence of nonmeaningful forms from memory. The child is shown a set of geometric designs, the stimuli are then removed from his visual field and the child must then duplicate the demonstrated series.

Two supplementary tests were added to the 1968 revision of the ITPA. These were the Auditory Closure test and the Sound Blending subtest. In the Auditory Closure test, the child is asked to recognize a word when only part of the word is orally presented to him. In the Sound Blending subtest, the child is required to synthesize sounds into a meaningful word.

An extensive review of the ITPA by Carroll (1972) reveals the following insights. A review of factor analytic studies suggests that the test taps three or four (not nine) factors. These include vocabulary, immediate memory span and auditory processing. Differences in these factors have been found for middle-upper- and lower-class children. The standardization sample used to construct the test scores were average middle-class children; thus, care must be taken in applying the test to children who are from different socioeconomic and cultural backgrounds and to children who have severe handicaps. Auditory handicaps, for instance, might reflect differences in ability to understand different dialects, not intellectual defects or defects in information processing. While the reliability of the test is apparently good, there is high variance among subtest scores among the average children for whom the test was intended.

A serious question is raised regarding the use of ITPA test scores to program intervention. This is particularly serious, because the practice has become so widespread and popular. There are, however, no studies showing that remedial programs chosen on the basis of ITPA test subscores are effective. Finally, Carroll raises some questions regarding the utility of the ITPA to discriminate between good and poor readers; the data are inconclusive in this regard. The ITPA thus has fairly good reliability with a fairly stable profile of scores. There are some questions about the validity of the test, and the standardization sample is middle-class, thus limiting the generalization and interpretation of test scores to other groups of children. For middle-class children, it is a widely used test of verbal comprehension and general information, immediate memory, visual and auditory perception and one kind of expressive verbal fluency (Carroll, 1972).

The *Detroit Tests of Learning Aptitudes* (Baker and Leland, 1935). This test was designed to assess auditory and visual information processing and is a battery of 19 tests applicable to individuals from age 4 to adulthood. The examiner selects those subtests suitable to the age of the person being tested; from 9 to 13 subtests are usually recommended for the different age groups. It appears to be the only diagnostic test available for children over 10 years of age. Like the ITPA, it has specific subtests to measure auditory and visual processing of information. It has, in addition, tests of social adjustment and orientation. The test was constructed in the 1930s and the standardization is not up to more modern standards, nor are many of the pictures used as stimuli contemporary ones. The test results must be interpreted with a grain of salt.

Here are examples of subtests appropriate for children above age 10.

Verbal Absurdities (9 years and older): Consists of 20 questions in which the child must indicate what is foolish about a situation described by the examiner. An example is, "If I am in a hurry, I get a horse because automobiles are too slow."

Verbal Opposites (9 years and older): This subtest requires the child to respond with the opposite of a stimulus word spoken

by the examiner. Examples are: boy . . . cooked . . . raw
. . . victory . . . ecstasy.

Speed and Precision (3 to 14 years and older): The child must put
an X in each of a large number of circles presented on one
page. A check is made at the point a child has reached at the
end of each minute.

Auditory Attention Span for Unrelated Words (3 to 14 years and
older): The examiner says a sequence of words and the child
responds by imitating the sequence. The child is scored for
each word he recalls correctly. Examples: cat . . . ice; fish
. . . clock . . . heart . . . sun . . . box . . . frog; ear . . . boat
. . . key . . . pig . . . south . . . knob . . . ink . . . rope.

Social Perception (3 to 12 years): The child is asked what to do
in a variety of situations. Example: What is the thing to do
if . . . Someone wants you to throw stones at the windows of
another person's house? . . . You have some partly worn out
clothes which you do not need? . . . You have to sit next to
someone you do not like at a party?

Visual Attention Span for Objects (3 to 14 years and older): On
this subtest, the child is shown a card with pictures on it and
must recall from memory the items on the card.

Spatial and Time Orientation (3 to 12 years): There is a series of
12 questions such as: Are you taller than I am? . . . Can you
touch the moon? . . . What season is it now?

Free Association (3 to 14 years and older): The child is asked to
say all the words he can think of, any words at all. Time limits
are suggested for various age levels.

Memory for Designs (3 to 14 years and older): This test has three
parts. In the first, the child is asked to copy a design; the
second part requires the child to finish from memory a partially complete geometric figure, while in the third part the
child is asked to reproduce from memory the total geometric
figure.

Auditory Attention Span for Related Syllables (2 to 14 years and
older): Sentences of increasing length are presented to the
child. The child is credited with the parts of the sentence he
repeats correctly. Examples are: My doll has pretty hair.
Green leaves come on the trees in early spring. Each four years

voting takes place which results in many men being placed in office for . . .

Social Adjustment (3 to 14 years and older): Child answers questions such as, "What is a jail? . . ." "What is a school nurse? . . ."

Visual Attention Span for Letters (3 to 14 years and older): The child is shown a sheet with letters on it. The child must indicate which letters he has just seen.

Visual Discrimination and Sequencing (9 to 14 years and older): The child is shown a picture of a disarranged figure, the parts of which have been numbered. On a separate sheet of paper the child must indicate where the pieces should go by placing the number in the appropriate place. There are 10 pictures and the child is scored for correctly placed pieces.

Oral Directions (9 to 14 years and older): The child is to follow a series of instructions. Examples are: Put a one in the circle and a cross in the square box. See the three circles: put a number two in the first circle, a cross in the second circle and draw a line under the third circle. Cross out the even number in a square, the odd number in the second triangle, the number in the third circle, the biggest number that is in a square and the number in a circle below twelve.

Likenesses and Differences (9 to 14 years or older): The child is to specify in what ways things are alike and different. Examples are: morning/afternoon; telescope/microscope; mentia/dementia.

An Example of a Design from The Bender Visual Motor Gestalt Test

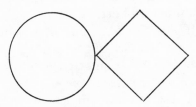

SOURCE: Bender, L. "A Visual Motor Gestalt Test and Its Clinical Use." *American Orthopsychiatry Assoc. Res. Monograph,* 1938, No. 3.

The *Bender Visual Motor Gestalt Test* (Bender, 1938). A rather popular test with a variety of professionals is the Bender Visual Motor Gestalt Test, or more commonly, the Bender Gestalt. This test is used for a variety of purposes, which range from personality assessment to measuring the presence of brain damage. The test consists of nine simple designs, one of which is shown on page 309, which are presented one at a time to the respondent. His task is to copy the design shown to him. The test performance is evaluated in terms of the adequacy of the copy. For example, rotations of the figures are noted, as well as general failures to connect components of the design. The test was originally designed to assess brain damage in adults, but now is also commonly used in clinical assessments of children.

Koppitz (1964) has provided scoring procedures and normative information for the use of this test with children between the ages of 5 and 11. Norms for evaluating the child's test performance are based upon 1104 children from public schools located in rural, urban and suburban settings in the Midwest and East. While this sample size is, at first blush, large, it should be remembered that for some age categories, such as the 10 to 10½ and 10½ to 11 years, the number of children used in developing the norms was quite small, 27 and 31 respectively. Koppitz presents data pertaining to the correlation of children's scores on the test with performances on the WISC, Readiness and Achievement Tests, teacher judgments, reading and arithmetic performances and various states of psychopathology. In general, the test appears to correlate with about everything. In spite of the author's recommendations, however, the data she presents regarding the use of the test to assess emotional problems are of such a nature as to preclude this use of the test. The number of false positives and negatives is too great to rely on the test for such purposes. Koppitz has provided a valuable empirical start in conducting and reporting the results of the studies on reliability and validity.

The *Developmental Test of Visual Motor Integration* (Beery and Buktenica, 1967). This test is quite similar to the Bender Gestalt insofar as the child is required to copy geometric shapes. In this test, however, the geometric shapes are varied in difficulty and

An Example of an Item from the Developmental Test of Visual Motor Integration

Form 7	Form 8	Form 9
Form 7	Form 8	Form 9

SOURCE: Beery, K. E. and Buktenica, N. A., *Developmental Test of Visual Motor Integration.* Chicago, Ill.: Follett Educational Corp., 1967.

are suitable for children from ages 2 to almost 16. The score obtained from the test is a developmental quotient, which is similar to a mental age and is expressed in years and months. The Beery consists of 24 geometric forms presented in a test booklet with a space underneath each form in which to copy the form. For each form the manual presents scoring criteria to determine if the child's reproduction passes or fails. Techniques for determining specific areas of difficulty in the visual-motor spectrum are also provided. A shorter test booklet with just the first fifteen forms is available for testing children ages 2 to 8. According to Chissom (1972), there are a number of advantages to this test which may make it preferable to the Bender Gestalt. The format of the test is likely to yield greater reliability in scoring. Moreover, there is some data suggesting that the test might be useful in predicting first-grade reading achievement.

The *Frostig Developmental Tests of Visual Perception* (1961). Like the ITPA, this test has been used for diagnosis of specific visual information processing problems and has been accompanied by specific remedial programs to alleviate the deficit skill. The test is appropriate for children ages 3 to 8, but it has been used with older children evidencing difficulty in visual perception. The areas tested include: eye-motor coordination, figure-ground, consistency of shape, position in space, and spatial relationships. The score is standardized to yield a Perceptual Age Equivalent. The median score is 100, upper and lower quartiles 110 and 90. The test is designed for use as a screening device with younger children of nursery school, kindergarten and first-grade ages, or as a clinical tool with older children manifesting learning problems. The test can be administered to children individually or in groups. The subtests and some example items are:

1. Eye-motor Coordination: The child is required to draw a line between two specified boundaries.

2. Figure-Ground: The child is shown figures which overlap, in one case a rectangle and triangle. The child must outline the "box" only.

3. Constancy of Shape: The child's task is to recognize various shapes (circles, squares, rectangles, ellipses and parallelograms) when they appear in a variety of sizes, shadings, textures and positions in space, and outline the shape specified by the examiner.

4. Position in Space: The child must make discriminations among reversals and rotated drawings. This is similar to reading readiness tests. The child is presented with a series and must find which of the items is different or the same as a stimulus item.

5. Spatial Relationships: The child sees a dot pattern on one side of the page and must reproduce it by drawing appropriate connecting lines between dots on the other side.

Chissom (1972) has provided a review of the research relevant to this test which leads to the following observations. Studies find that the administration and procedures for scoring the test are clear. The test-retest reliability is good when the test is used for first- and second-graders. There does appear to be some rela-tionship between scores on this test and reading achievement, but this should not be interpreted to mean that the test is useful in diagnosing *specific* reading difficulties.

It should be noted that the children on whom the test was developed did not include minority culture children and thus should not be employed with them. Additionally, studies have indicated that the test does not measure five distinct factors of perception, as implied in the format of five subtests, but rather performance on all subtests are related to each other. Thus, ap-parently one visual motor function, rather than five, is being assessed, at least when the test is applied to young children.

The *Purdue Perceptual-Motor Survey* (Roach and Kephart, 1966). This is an informal survey appropriate for testing perceptual-motor development of children in grades 2 through 4. The child receives oral instructions on what to do while performing each of the tests. The activities evaluated are laterality, directionality and skills of perceptual-motor matching. The activities include the walking board or balance beam, jumping and hopping, identifica-tion of body parts, imitation of movement, ability to move through an obstacle course, movements of arms and legs (angels in the snow), stepping stones, chalkboard drawing, ocular pursuit and visual achievement forms (copying geometric shapes). All of the items of the Purdue Perceptual-Motor Survey are arranged from easiest to hardest.

The teacher scores the child's performance informally, rating it as 1 if the child cannot perform the task, 2 if the child hesitates or is markedly inaccurate, 3 if the child shows slight hesitancy and slight inaccuracy and 4 if the performance is adequate. As with the Frostig test, the results on this survey are said to be related to various forms of remediation.

Jamison (1972) has provided a critical review of the test. She questions whether the subtests can be reliably scored on the basis of instructions in the manual. In addition, she argues that the items are not appropriately grouped to measure various abilities and that the conditions for the testing of the child are not suffi-ciently detailed to allow standardized testing procedures. In con-clusion, she writes, "It is recommended that the PPMS not be used" (p. 875). Another reviewer, Landis (1972), while commending the test for its theoretical basis, does suggest that basic information concerning the scoring of the test is lacking so as to make its use by all but the very experienced impossible.

Tests of Auditory Skills and Language

The *Auditory Discrimination Test* (Wepman, 1958). This instrument is designed to assess the ability of children 5 to 8 years of age to discriminate between sounds by indicating whether pairs of words sound the same or different. The test consists of 40 word pairs which are read aloud to the child. Test norms have been established. The child must be able to understand the concept of same/different or same/not the same. Examples of the words are:

gear—bear	led—lad	rub—rug
fret—threat	bar—bar	cart—tart

The child's score is based upon the number of errors he commits on items which are the same and on those which are different. The number of X responses (responses to word pairs which are different) which are considered diagnostically significant at various ages are:

5 year olds . . . greater than six errors
6 year olds . . . greater than five errors
7 year olds . . . greater than four errors
8 year olds . . . greater than three errors

The test is very easy to administer and takes but a few minutes. The user is cautioned to be sensitive to cultural differences, as children from a non–English-speaking background may pronounce and discriminate sounds tapped in this test in a different manner than would English-speaking children. The test reliability appears to be good. It is quickly administered and easy to score (DiCarlo, 1965) and does assess one skill without confounding performance with other skills. The technique is a limited assessment of auditory discrimination insofar as it measures auditory discrimination, on one single type of task.

The *Northwestern Syntax Screening Test* (Lee, 1970). This is a screening instrument to identify children, ages 3.0 to 7.11, who are delayed in the use of syntactical forms. Receptive and expressive use of grammatical features, such as prepositions, personal pronouns, nouns, negatives, plurals and possessives are tested at a receptive and expressive level.

To test the child's comprehension of spoken stimuli (*i.e.,* receptive functions), the child is presented with a page containing four pictures; two are decoys and two are to be identified on the basis of a grammatical contrast spoken by the examiner. For instance, the examiner would say, "This is the Mother's cat," and "This is a mother cat." The child is to point to the pictures named as the examiner repeats the sentences. To assess the child's language output (*i.e.,* expressive functions), the child is presented with two pictures on a page which are labeled by the examiner, but which are not pointed to. The examiner then asks the child to identify the appropriate picture by talking about it. Information is available indicating receptive and expressive age norms at 90th, 75th, 50th, 25th and 19th percentiles for each 6-month age group.

Several features of the test should be noted. First, it is designed to assess but one language area, syntax. No attempt is made to measure phonology (speech sounds) or semantics (vocabulary). While this is a narrow focus, it is perhaps ultimately to the administrator's advantage to assess adequately one function rather than to try to assess many functions, but to do so inadequately. Second, as has been typically the case, the sample upon which the norms have been developed is small. Thus, for the age groups 3 to 3½ only 13 children were tested; for the ages 5 to 5½, 14 children were employed; for the ages 7½ to 8, only 16 served as the normative sample. Moreover, the children used in the development of the norms were drawn from middle-class homes. The representativeness of the sample and the adequacy of the norms presented are open to serious question.

The *Utah Test of Language Development* (Mecham, Jex and Jones, 1967). In addition to the assessment of the child's comprehension of grammatical forms and production of speech sounds, it is important to note how adequately the child speaks. Mecham et al. have developed a simple test of language development for children ranging from 1 to 15 years of age. Additionally, Mecham et al. (1967) have provided a means to evaluate the child's performance by grouping items into grammatical classifications. The child's score on the test can be transformed into a language-age equivalent. The test consists of 51 items in which the child is asked to repeat digits and sentences, to name the days of the week and to perform certain motor tasks. The authors suggest that this instrument is of particular value in assessing brain-damaged children.

Butler (1972), in reviewing the test, indicates some of its rather severe limitations. First, the sample upon which the test was developed consisted of but 273 white children residing in Utah. Only 30 of these children serve as the normative population for the 12½ to 14½ year old population. Clearly, and particularly for the upper age ranges, the small number of children used precludes much confidence in the norms for this age group. Additionally, norms are based upon white children and thus should not be employed for assessing children of minority groups. Second, the number of items within the age ranges tapped are often few in number. At age 7, four items tap language skills, while there are 20 items for children ages 1 to 3. Insofar as the reliability of a score is associated with the number of items used to compute the score, the reliability of the test is likely to be greater at some ages than at others. Finally, there is little evidence concerning the validity of the test. What the test score predicts is as yet unknown. Butler suggests that the test

... is particularly useful at the preschool level due to the preponderance of items at this level and the absence of time limits. If an examiner is interested in a language screening device and keeps in mind the small normative population and its geographical bias, he may wish to use the ... (test) (p. 1367).

The *Developmental Sentence Scoring* (Lee, 1970, 1974). Lee has proposed a method for measuring syntactic language development in children's spontaneous speech. In this method the child's mastery of syntactic rules is assessed by his use of them verbally. The examiner is instructed to spend one hour in conversation with the child. Using any stimulus materials to facilitate conversation, the child's language is tape recorded. The examiner then selects 50 complete sentences to score. Sentences must have a noun and verb, be different from one another, be intelligible and nonecholalic. Eight linguistic features are scored: indefinite pronoun or noun modifiers, personal pronouns, main verbs, secondary verbs, negatives, conjunctions, interrogative reversals and who-questions. The child is awarded points for use of these parts of language plus an additional point if the sentence is grammatically correct. Percentiles are provided for 6-month age groups between the ages of 3.0 and 6.11 years so that the individual child can be compared to his peer group. This is clearly a time-consuming test, which should be applied for children experiencing real deficits in language development. Analysis of those parts of language with which the child is experiencing difficulty can be helpful in developing a remedial language program.

This test has been shown to have an adequate reliability, particularly for the older children assessed, and does appear to have validity in measuring the linguistic development of the child. At least this is so when employed with white children from middle-class homes, those children most approximating the sample used in the development of the test (Lee, 1974).

Diagnostic and Achievement Tests

The *Wide Range Achievement Test*, Revised Edition (Jastic and Jastic, 1965). This test provides scores in three subtests: reading, spelling and arithmetic for children divided into two age levels, 5–11 and over 12 years. The reading subtest assesses the child's ability to recognize and name letters and read words, while the spelling subtest incorporates items which have the child copy geometric shapes, write his name and spell in written form words dictated orally by the examiner. The arithmetic subtest involves counting, naming and solving addition and subtraction problems orally at the younger age level and solving written computation problems of addition, subtraction, multiplication and division at the older level.

The test's authors claim that it is useful to diagnose reading, spelling and arithmetic disabilities, to assign children to instructional groups, to compare school achievement with other characteristics of the person (namely intelligence and personality traits) and to study the degree of loss of skills which might result from brain damage or other physical disabilities. Some have suggested that the test might be appropriate as a quick estimate of an individual's general level of ability and educational background (Thorndike, 1972). However, the test has been severely criticized by Merwin (1972). The sample upon which the norms for the test are based is not sufficiently described so that a child's score can be meaningfully compared to other children of his age and social status. Merwin also raises questions concerning the adequacy of the reliability and validity data presented by the test constructors.

The *Gates-McKillop Reading Diagnostic Tests* (Gates and McKillop, 1962). These tests consist of a variety of techniques designed to discover the deficiencies in reading of children 7 to 12 years of age. The particular value of this set of tests is that it guides the examiner's interpretation of the errors made by the child in oral reading and instructs on how to compare these errors with the child's performance on other subtests. The tests lack clear or usable scores, but provide clinical advice on interpretation of reading problems (Della-Piana, 1965). There is no measure of reading comprehension, but the subtests and the manual's instructions make this a popular instrument for both informal and formal assessments of reading difficulties.

Below are listed some of the tests and some examples of the items used within them.

1. Oral Reading: Grade and age norms are available for this subtest, which consists of seven paragraphs increasing in difficulty. The child is instructed to read aloud until making a specified number of errors. An example of a test paragraph is: "After the rat got into his hole, he began to peek at the dog. This drove the dog nearly mad. He said: 'I like raw meat to eat. If you do not stop, I will eat you.' Then he left the rat alone."

2. Words—Flash Presentation: Here the examiner quickly presents and removes words. The child's task is to say the word. Such words as "so, perhaps, affectionate," are used as stimuli.

3. Words—Untimed Presentation: On this task, the child reads the words aloud at his own speed. Examples of the words used are: "so, king, window, irregular."

4. Phrases—Flash Presentation: Various phrases are rapidly presented and the child's task is to repeat the phrases. An example phrase is: "Go to the store."

5. Recognizing and Blending Common Word Parts: The child is to say aloud 23 nonsense words. When he errs, he is shown the sound parts and encouraged to blend the parts. An example is: tright . . . tr . . . ight . . . tright.

6. Giving Letter Sounds: Here the child tells sounds associated with letters.

Other tests are included in the battery but will not be presented here. The reader is referred to Gates and McKillop (1962) for further details.

Unfortunately, the test manual fails to provide information concerning the number and type of children tested as the basis for establishing normative or usual performances. As such information is lacking, the usefulness of the test as a precise measure is highly questionable. It may be useful clinically, as suggested by Bryant (1965), but comparison of performances of children with those of unknown origin can be quite misleading as well.

The *Peabody Individual Achievement Test* (Dunn and Markwardt, 1970). This test is designed to survey achievement in mathematics, reading recognition, reading comprehension, spelling and general information. The test is applicable to individuals from the preschool years to adulthood. Scores can be converted to grade and age equivalents, percentile ranks and standard scores. The advantage of this test is that it requires no written work by the test taker. The child can respond by pointing or speaking; it is quickly administered and easily scored.

The test was standardized on close to 3,000 children in kindergarten through twelfth grade with urban, suburban and rural children represented. The test-retest reliability of the subtests is good, although the total score is more reliable than the subtest scores. Validity has been established by correlation with the Peabody Picture Vocabulary Test. As such, the validity and test-retest reliability do not seem as strong as on other achievement tests (French, 1972). The test manual is well written, as it provides the reader with cautionary statements about use of this test. French recommends that the PIAT be used as a test which a trained paraprofessional could administer, that it could be used as a screening device to obtain a rough estimate of educational level and indications of where more intensive testing might be needed.

The *Metropolitan Achievement Tests* (Durost, 1961). This is a series of tests designed to measure achievement in content areas in school curricula. Of particular relevance to the learning disability specialist are the various reading tests. Three scores are yielded at the primary level: word knowledge, word discrimination and reading. Two scores are obtained for children at the upper levels, grades 7 through 9: word knowledge and reading. The word knowledge test consists of asking the child to identify the functions, consequences associated with or the synonyms for the stimulus word or picture from one of several alternatives. The reading test is a comprehension test. The word discrimination task requires the child to select from a list of words that word which was dictated to him by the examiner.

According to the review by Robinson (1965), the subtests show good reliability and various measures of validity have been obtained. Standardization of the test was exceptional insofar as the number of children used to develop norms numbered over

100,000. Directions for administration and interpretation are clear. Robinson concludes that this reading test is

one of the best survey tests of reading achievement on the market today for the elementary grades. It has been carefully planned, carefully tested, and well produced. It serves its purpose as a rough measure of reading achievement for comparative purposes and as a tool of identification upon which further evaluation may be based (p. 797).

The *Vineland Social Maturity Scale* (Doll, 1947). This scale represents one of the few that are designed to assess the development of social and personal competence in the conduct of everyday activities by individuals from infancy to 30 years of age. The learning disability specialist might well employ this scale as a means to determine the degree to which the child of concern demonstrated behavioral problems and incompetencies around the home. The scale is designed to tap, through 117 items, eight areas of function: general self-help, self-help in eating, self-help in dressing, self-direction, occupation, communication, locomotion and socialization. Unlike other tests, scores yielded are not based upon the child's response to some stimulus items, but rather are based upon data obtained by the interviewer from the child, parents, friends, or whoever might be knowledgeable concerning the individual's performance. The scale directs the examiner to conduct a guided interview. The subtests and sample items follow.

1. Self-help General: Cares for self at toilet (ages 4 to 5); tells time to the quarter hour (ages 7 to 8).
2. Self-help Eating: Eats with fork (ages 2 to 3); uses table knife for cutting (ages 7 to 8).
3. Self-help Dressing: Washes hands unaided (ages 3 to 4); goes to bed unassisted (ages 6 to 7).
4. Self-direction: Makes minor purchase (ages 9 to 10).
5. Occupation: Helps at little household tasks (ages 3 to 4); uses tools or utensils (ages 8 to 9).
6. Communication: Relates experience (ages 2 to 3); uses pencil for writing (ages 6 to 7).
7. Locomotion: Walks downstairs one step per tread (ages 3 to

4); goes to school unattended (ages 5 to 6).
8. Socialization: Plays cooperatively at kindergarten level (ages 3 to 4); disavows literal Santa Claus (ages 7 to 8).

The child's performance is scored so that a comparison can be made of his performance in each of the eight areas and a total score has been constructed to provide a Social Quotient. Normative information is based upon a sample of 620 subjects, composed of ten normal persons of each sex to age 30. Additional normative data have been gathered.

Several reviewers have suggested that the items are sufficiently vaguely worded and the examiners sufficiently free to impose their unique interpretations of the responses given, so that the reliability of the test might be much lower than necessary (Teagarden, 1953; Rothney, 1949; Kinder, 1938). In spite of this possibility, the test has been judged useful in aiding the examiner to make discriminations among the mentally defective and in the evaluation of the physically handicapped (Cruickshank, 1953; Loutt, 1949). There appear to be no data to indicate the utility of this test in aiding predictions about the learning-disabled child, so the test appears to be of limited validity. It would seem to these authors that many of the distinctions that are required in dealing with the learning-disabled child are sufficiently subtle that this test would not be sensitive in helping the examiner.

CHAPTER
11
REMEDIATION

History of Individualized Instruction

Remediation techniques developed in the field of learning disabilities have been based upon the belief that children differ greatly in how they learn and the rate at which they learn. Such techniques assume that children vary considerably in their styles of learning, their abilities to master skills and their motivations. These assumptions led to the individual tailoring of particular techniques to particular children to facilitate learning. Implicit is the faith or hope that professionals know enough about children and teaching techniques that such tailoring will produce an effective fit. This goal is very persuasive; after all, who could deny that the goal of greater efficiency is a worthwhile one? But the emphasis upon individualized instruction is a relatively recent one. Perhaps because we have become more sophisticated about how people vary, or because of the complex demands of the society upon its servants, educational institutions are increasingly attempting to match child and teaching method.

It was not long ago that a fixed curriculum for all students was the modus operandi. Children who failed the course of learning within a highly restricted offering of course content dropped from the system and had the choice of becoming farmers, businessmen, servants and crooks. With time, however, the skills necessary to be a farmer, businessman and perhaps a crook, increased until the public realized it was more expedient to maintain potential dropouts within the school system. School systems then devised curriculum materials more suitable to students who were heterogeneous in their talents and abilities than heretofore meaningfully acknowledged.

The psychological testing boom, a product of the World War I national emergency, produced the apparatus which enabled an increasingly complex assessment and perspective of the individual and his presumed potential. The development of intelligence and specialized aptitude tests, particularly those administered to groups, served as precursors of the present concern with individualized assessment and instruction. If adults and children evidenced wide ranges of differences in mechanical, mathematical or clerical aptitudes, then greater precision in educational matching of child and curriculum might result in closer alignment of potential and achievement. Thus, the testing movement became the vehicle and rationale for sorting "bright" from "dull" students for placement into "slow" and "accelerated" classrooms. The road to sorting, then as now, has not been a smooth one. Intelligence tests and, for adults, aptitude tests, are not powerful predictors of achievement in skill areas. While they may be among the best predictors, the competition is not very keen.

One assumption of the early users of such tests was that achievement tests could be helpful in predicting the rate of learning on tasks presumed to require the same array of skills. If a child showed achievement in mastering arithmetic, it was expected he would excel in algebra. As early as 1946, however, Woodrow challenged this position. A consideration of twenty years of research in this area led Woodrow to conclude that the rate of learning is inconsistent from one task to another. If this is the case, an achievement test score might be useful in predicting the child's performance on a particular task but useless and perhaps misleading in predicting the same child's score on a variety of related tasks. We know little about what such tests assess, what is demanded of the child in terms of successful mastery of any particular content area or the interactions of those unknown skills with the task demands. As yet, there is little justification for identifying mental test scores with the ability to learn (Cronbach, 1971).

The attempts to study learning processes within the field of educational research were and are based upon two schools of thought (Walberg, 1971). Since both are reflected within the efforts of learning disability experts, Walberg's definitions are included here. One is the experimental approach, springing from the traditions of experimental psychology with its origins in the work of Wundt and Pavlov. This approach focuses upon how conditions and processes of instruction can be employed to optimize learning. The focus is upon the immediate stimulus, with the hope of determining those processes which will increase the learning of most, or "average," children. The tendency is to ignore how children differ and to concentrate upon the discovery of processes likely to maximize the learning experiences of many children. The essence of the procedure is to randomly assign some children to one form of instruction, a second group to a variant form of instruction and then to assess the differences between these two groups of children on a common test criterion.

The second approach used was, and is, correlational and has its origins in the work of Galton and Spearman. The focus in this case is upon individual differences and their interrelationships (Walberg, 1971). The question posed in this approach is how children might differ among themselves and how these differences might be related to yet other differences. Are all slender children athletic? Are all chubby children good natured? Is the child with eyeglasses smarter? Is the child who cannot learn to read, write, or compute arithmetic problems really more motorically active than the child who can master these skills?

We do not have a great deal of research involving remediation techniques with learning-disabled children. But what we do have can be divided into these two frameworks. Examples of the experimental approach would be those studies which investigate the efficacy of different remedial approaches or studies of the effects of distractions, such as music, upon learning and performance. The second approach can be seen in efforts to establish how learning-disabled children differ from nonlearning-disabled children and efforts to group and educate children in accordance

325

with test profiles. The greatest bulk of research work appears to have been conducted within the framework of determining individual differences, in particular how the learning disabled differ from normal counterparts and how such differences might be related to one another.

The greatest impetus within special education in the study of individual differences apparently was derived from the work of Strauss (Cruickshank and Holloran, 1973). Strauss made a major contribution to special education, and ultimately to the development of the field of learning disabilities, by examining individual differences in brain-injured mentally retarded children. While the assessment of individual differences in intellectual skills had been achieved initially by Binet in his development of the intelligence test, it was Strauss who took the next step by further defining differences within a group of specified handicapped children. It was not sufficient to say that children were bright or dull, but rather, he argued that clinicians should look further at how children who were dull differed among themselves. Descriptions of the child thus underwent further refinements, permitting the growth of a taxonomy of individual differences among children. Strauss did not develop a taxonomy for naught, but went ahead to further define procedures of instruction for children based upon the individual differences he carefully observed.

The next major step in developing approaches to individualizing instruction came during World War II. Educational technology as we know it today in programmed instruction and the techniques of behavior modification stemmed from the war efforts of Glaser, Lumsdaine and Skinner, among others, who, because of the task assigned to them or because of simple boredom, generated important and significant contributions. Glaser and Lumsdaine were assigned the difficult task of developing effective and rapid methods of teaching complex motor tasks to men. Skinner was apparently assigned very little to do and thus spent his time developing a technique to teach very complex motor behaviors to pigeons (Skinner, 1960). The common element among these men was their focus upon task rather than person analysis. More than their predecessors, these contributors carefully analyzed the necessary movements and skills necessary to learn to perform a complex task. Skinner did not consider the ability of the individual pigeon, but analyzed the task at hand and trained these movements into the bird. The primary focus was upon the analysis of the job to be accomplished by the pupil, be it person or pigeon, and how to best teach him to perform this task.

Concurrently, Grace Fernald (1943) was training illiterate adults to become competent in reading to be permitted into the armed forces. It was observed that these adults had other skills which could allow them to be useful during this time of national crisis, and Fernald set about helping them to become useful citizens. Like Glaser, Lumsdaine and Skinner, Fernald addressed herself to the analysis of the task. She argued that individual differences, at least within the wide range of talents called "normal," were irrelevant to the acquisition of basic school subjects: reading, writing and arithmetic. To be an effective teacher, one must understand the requirements made by the task, or, one could adopt the Fernald technique to teaching basic subjects, as discussed below in the section *The Multisensory Approach*. This technique and the school at which Fernald taught adults and educationally handicapped children are still in use today.

Since World War II, efforts in regular elementary education and separate special education have gradually moved toward greater considerations of individual differences in learning and an increased emphasis upon task analysis. As the technology developed, tasks have been analyzed into their discrete elements and materials for evaluation of skills necessary for the tasks and their remediation of deficits have become available. Thus, more subtle individual differences can be reliably determined. While mentally retarded children could be reliably labeled for grouping into three major categories, different educational treatments had to await task analysis and the related educational materials to better educate the individual deficit child. In terms of children subsequently labeled learning disabled, a giant step had been taken, carrying the educator beyond the narrow perspective of viewing learning-disabled children as simply being unintelligent, insane, or apathetic toward viewing the learning-handicapped child as having a particular difficulty on a particular task with a solution available in a particular technique.

Such was the background for the development of much of the faith, hope, and goals of the learning disability specialist today. Yet, hard questions must be asked, not about faith, good intentions or bright hopes, but about our knowledge concerning the efficacy of educational techniques. At this point we can ask the following questions. Which variables affect learning? Which variables affect the learning-disabled child and are these different from those affecting the academically successful child? Which remedial programs used in the field of learning disabilities have been studied in a systematic way which permits evaluation of the effectiveness of the approach? Which methods should learning disability specialists incorporate into their teaching in order to more effectively serve the learning-disabled child?

Factors Affecting School Learning

There are three major all-inclusive components which can be construed as affecting school learning. These include the student's aptitudes or intelligence, general intelligence and specific skills, be they derived from genes, experiences, or both; methods of instruction; and the classroom environment (teacher warmth, organization, reinforcement properties, classroom size, school philosophy and architecture, peer relationships and what have you . . .). According to one prominent investigator's review of research on school learning, the single most important variable affecting school achievement is the child's intelligence. The least important is the method of instruction, the factor to which educators, and particularly learning disability specialists, have addressed the greatest portion of energies. To quote Walberg (1971), methods of instruction have been found to "typically make little differences in learning" (p. 18). This is not to say that children do not learn, but rather, that the particular method which is used to teach children makes little difference; many methods seem equally effective in helping children to learn. In spite of all the technological innovations surrounding instructional methods, the teacher's belief system and the child's intelligence still account for the bulk of the learning which occurs. Apparently, the same conclusion was reached by Stephens (1970) as he reviewed many years of research on teaching methods. Stephens apparently concluded that what we think should make a difference makes very little difference. This is not to say that some instructional techniques are not better than others, at least for some people some of the time and in some environments. As yet, however, no one can claim with much assurance that any particular method is more efficient than another method for most children, or that a particular method will work with a particular child some of the time in most environments. In sum, there is much to be learned about learning and much to be humble about.

Within the field of learning disabilities, data suggesting that intelligence contributes 40–60% of the variance in school achievement, and that instructional methods account for very little, are very discouraging if also enlightening. The major thrust of the remediation of the deficits in learning-disabled children has been in the attempts to develop instructional techniques better suited to such children. Yet, according to Walberg's (1971) summary of the factors influencing learning in the regular elementary classroom, it is just this factor which seems to be the most elusive in terms of development and the least potent in terms of effects. This is not to say that continued efforts should not be made to develop more refined instructional methods, but rather that to have a more effective impact on remediation of problems, it may be necessary to direct efforts to the study of other variables, such as teacher actions, rather than limiting the path of our efforts to development of ever more instructional materials.

As it now stands the important correlates and perhaps determinants of learning, intelligence and classroom atmosphere are either relatively set before the intervention is initiated or are of such a nature as to be relatively outside the influence of the learning disability teacher. The learning disability specialist cannot systematically or wittingly alter by much the child's intelligence. Nor is it likely that the elementary school teacher has the time or inclination to undergo an extensive diagnosis of her performance, be it by means of classroom observations or tests. It is likely, though by no means certain, that if alterations could be effected on these variables, in the direction and with the magnitude desired, the learning-disabled child would benefit. As yet, such changes are technically impossible in the case of intelligence and practically difficult to achieve in the case of classroom atmosphere. Ironically, those factors which appear to be most facilitative of learning, and thus most helpful to remediation of learning deficits, are those which also appear to be the least accessible to manipulation and control by the learning disability teacher.

Thus far we have discussed the lack of evidence indicating that one instructional method is superior to another when employed in regular classrooms. The question must then be raised as to whether the specialized instructional methods developed for use with learning-disabled children are more effective than those developed within the mainstream of elementary education. As far as can be determined, there are no systematically gathered data which would provide such an answer. Efforts have been concentrated on delivering services to these children. The generation and proliferation of instructional techniques have far outstripped the generation of data relevant to the question of the value and efficacy of these methods. Few data have been made available in which the appropriate comparisons have been made with the appropriate comparison groups included. We have seen the development over the past twenty-five years of certain ideas about what types of programs will facilitate learning in disabled children and the production of methods and materials to implement these ideas. The question to be asked is whether we suffer the same problem in learning disabilities which Stephens (1970) raised about regular elementary education. Do those things we now commonly believe promote learning in disabled children actually make any difference at all? The next question would be, what shall we do to try to improve the status of knowledge and remedial efforts in this field?

Remediation Techniques

Perceptual-Motor Training

Among the better-known types of remedial programs in learning disabilities are those which involve training of perceptual-motor skills. The preponderance of studies concerning program effectiveness have been addressed to the impact of various perceptual-motor training programs upon the subsequent acquisition of skills believed necessary to academic achievement. Outstanding in this tradition is the work of Kephart (1963) and Frostig and Horne (1964). The programs developed by these professionals are based upon the assumption that visual perception is a primary skill in the acquisition of reading skills and that perceptual-motor training will facilitate both perceptual-motor skills and reading competence. According to Kephart, the processing of visual information is critically dependent upon the child's previous experiences in the development of motor skills. "Behavior develops out of muscular activity, and so called higher forms of behavior are dependent upon lower forms of behavior, thus making even these higher activities dependent upon the basic structure of the muscular activity upon which they are built" (Kephart, 1971, p. 79). The remediation program is based upon observations and ratings of the child's perceptual motor skills. Five areas of perceptual motor skills are assessed: balance and posture (ratings of the child's walking and jumping); body image and differentiation (identification of body parts); perceptual-motor match (such as rhythmic writing on a chalkboard); ocular control (essentially visual tracking of a moving object) and form perception (the child is requested to copy geometric forms). If a child is rated as developmentally retarded in any of these areas, he then receives exercises specific to that area. It is believed that such exercises serve to increase the child's motor competencies and his reading, writing and arithmetic achievement as well.

Frostig, less concerned with gross motor abilities than Kephart, focuses upon the visual-perceptual skills of the child. Again, it is suggested that such skills are necessary precursors of academic achievement and that deficits in such activities have generalized effects on retarding their acquisition. Remedial efforts in the Frostig program are based primarily upon the child's performance on a test she developed, the Developmental Test of Visual Perception (Frostig and Horne, 1964). The test is purported to assess five aspects of visual motor functioning: eye-motor coordination; figure-ground capability; form constancy; position in space and the ability to assess spatial relationships. The child is asked to do such tasks as draw a straight line between two parallel lines (eye-hand coordination), discover hidden figures within a picture (figure-ground skills), or recognize and trace a square or circle (form constancy). If the child performs poorly relative to peers, on any one of the five areas, there are work sheets available which have content parallel to that tested. The assumption is made that such exercises will increase the child's ability to acquire academic skills.

Assumptions and exercises notwithstanding, what are the available research data concerning the impact of perceptual-motor training upon the academic performance of children?

Several investigators have reported results which suggest that such training can be corrective with respect to reading. Thus Kephart (1960) and Frostig and Horne (1964) reported that children exposed to some form of perceptual-motor training excelled, relative to children who did not receive this training, in their reading achievement. However, most investigators have had less success in producing these significant differences. Falik (1969) provided a perceptual-motor training program for kindergarten children and did not find differences in reading readiness or in reading achievement two years later between children who did and did not receive this training. Similarly, Sullivan (1972) studied 113 elementary, junior and senior high school students and found no evidence to support the contention that perceptual-motor training increased the reading performance of children.

Hammill (1972) reviewed 25 intervention studies. He concluded that it is not at all apparent that visual perception, as currently defined, can even be trained! While the data might be disheartening to the proponents of such training programs, one might find solace in the reports of other investigators that visual perception may not even be related to the acquisition of academic skills. Cohen (1969) was unable to demonstrate a correlation between perceptual-motor abilities and reading achievement. Goodman and Wiederholt (1972) studied the correlations between visual perception, readiness at kindergarten, first-grade achievement and intelligence to reading performance 14 months later. Only first-grade achievement was an adequate predictor of reading performance. Perhaps the most widely known study of the correlates of reading and initial school performance was that of deHirsch, Jansky and Langford (1966). On only one of 37 tests, the Bender Gestalt, was the correlation between test score and reading achievement at second grade higher than .35.

As of now, there is little evidence to support the faith that the perceptual-motor abilities of the child, at least within the broad range of talents measured in learning-disabled children, are critical to the development of traditional academic skills. And, even if such evidence did exist, there is no evidence to demonstrate that the training programs based upon these theoretical assumptions are of a nature to affect school performance. The implementation of these programs is based on tenuous theory and great faith in their efficacy. Facts and faiths aside, any intervention program should be assessed in terms of the cost of the program and the deprivations which might be experienced by the child as a consequence of being involved in this program. It was this issue which can be evaluated by looking at the Rosen study (1966). In this case, children in 12 classrooms received perceptual-motor training for a period of 29 days in an adaptation of the program outlined by Frostig. Reading achievement of these children was subsequently compared to that of children in 13 classrooms who were not given a Frostig type perceptual-motor training experience. These control classes had spent equivalent periods of time on reading instruction, in this instance listening to and talking about stories. The results might have been predicted. Children who received perceptual-motor training improved on perceptual-motor skills, while children who had activities more closely related to reading gained most in reading.

It is probably quite fair to say that perceptual-motor training programs help some children sometimes. Unfortunately, it is not likely that the current state of knowledge is such as to permit prediction of which child at which time. The use of these training programs may serve an important function as a welcome novelty for the child and teacher, providing for both a time out from orthodox methods of reading, writing and arithmetic instruction. As such they can be justified on this basis alone. At the same time, it does seem apparent that the utilization of these programs cannot be justified on the basis of their impact on progress in the acquisition of traditional academic skills. Whatever value such training programs may provide, be it in producing novelty, creating a more pleasant day for the participating child, more intellectual stimulation for the teacher or some sort of technology which serves to reassure the learning disability expert of his expertise, these programs do not have any apparent value in facilitation of school achievement in participating children.

Physical Fitness

One of the characteristics often associated with the learning-disabled child is awkwardness or clumsiness (Clements, 1966). Observations have been made that such children trip more, fall more, stumble more, spill more and generally have a difficult time maneuvering body and objects in space (Lewis, Strauss and Lehtinen, 1960). Why this occurs, if indeed it does, is a moot point. Perhaps stumbling, slipping and spilling reflect minor brain damage, perhaps a lack of attention, perhaps poor and limited experiences in motor activities. Whatever the reason for this description of learning-disabled children, at least one well-known albeit controversial, program has been developed to treat these symptoms. Doman and Delecato developed the "Institutes for the Achievement of Human Potential" (Delecato, 1963, 1966), a neurologically based program in which diagnosis and training are directly related to the authors' conceptualizations of the dynamics of the brain, brain structure and motor skills. Diagnosis and remediation reflect the idea that learning problems are directly related to a failure on the part of the child to have sequentially experienced and developed certain movements. When these motor activities are not sufficiently experienced or developed in the proper order, the brain is unable to develop properly. It is assumed that the brain can and will develop if certain motor activities and child-rearing practices are put into effect.

Diagnosis is based on an evaluation of the child's handedness, eyedness, footedness, creeping and walking patterns and body positions while sleeping. Insofar as learning difficulties are reflections of neurological disorganization reflected by performance on these activities, the remediation program requires that the child retrace the sequence the brain needs to follow to develop. Appropriate motor activities then become the vehicle for the development of more effective brain organization. For a particular child, therapy might include creeping and crawling exercises, changes in body position while sleeping, walking exercises, eating with both hands without utensils and facilitation of a variety of primitive body movements.

Virtually every aspect of the Doman and Delecato approach has been criticized, from their theories about the structure, development and dynamics of the brain to the research statistics cited to support these theories (Gearheart, 1973).

Stereotypes aside, what evidence exists regarding the effectiveness of the Doman and Delecato training procedures? Few studies have been addressed to this method and those which have been conducted focused primarily upon mentally retarded rather than learning-disabled children. Kershner, reported by Masland (1969), investigated the impact of this approach upon mentally retarded children, ages 8 to 18. A highly complicated program was administered which involved training movements, exercises in creeping and crawling, alterations of resting and sleeping posture and the use of eye patches to establish consistency of cerebral dominance. The control group was exposed to games and activities solely designed to "give reason for the teacher to direct individual and group praise and encouragement" (Masland, 1969, p. 82). It was reported that the treated group became more efficient creepers and crawlers and showed some gains in their intelligence test scores as measured by the Peabody Picture Vocabulary Test. Unfortunately, insufficient data were presented to evaluate whether these gains, be they in creeping or in intelligence levels, were statistically significant. Insofar as the experimental group had lower intelligence test scores than the control group on the pretest, any differential increment, even if significant, might reflect a regression to the mean. The results of this study must be taken as suggestive, at best, rather than as definitive.

O'Donnell and Eisenson (1969) studied the effects of the Delecato training program upon reading achievement and visual-motor integration. Second-, third- and fourth-grade children were selected on the basis of low scores on a reading achievement test and the presence of visual-motor integration difficulties as defined by performance on the Harris Test of Lateral Dominance. These children were randomly assigned to one of three treatment conditions. One group had exercises in cross pattern creeping and walking, visual pursuit and filtered reading tasks. The second group received the visual pursuit task, filtered reading and selected physical education activities. The third group was a control group which received selected physical education activities. There were no significant differences found between these three groups on retesting for reading achievement and visual-motor integration.

Other studies cited by Masland (1969) were not directly related to the Doman and Delecato approach, but are of related interest. Corder (1966) studied the effects of a physical education program on the intellectual and physical development of mentally retarded children. The program lasted for three weeks. During this time, one group of boys engaged in physical education training; a second group served as observers of the first; a third group remained in the classroom. The results indicated that the children who received the physical education program improved in physical and intellectual prowess. The hooker in this finding, however, is that the observers also demonstrated intellectual benefits. This suggests that the motor training itself was not the critical variable producing the desired changes. Finally, Masland (1969) reported a study conducted by Solomon and Pangle which resulted in the conclusion that physical education training may improve physical fitness, but not intelligence or self-concepts.

Like perceptual-motor training, the physical fitness approach has not been shown to facilitate those cognitive processes correlated with or necessary for academic achievement. The studies which have sought to link these variables have often been flawed by poor methodology (Gruber, 1969). Perhaps with better research methods such effects will be found. Gruber believes that because of a correlation between intelligence and complex play activity the play activity stimulates the growth of intellectual skills. We take a more pessimistic view. It seems more likely that the causal linkage, if there is any, in the correlation between intelligence and play activity is that intelligent children learn more readily a variety of skills, and this includes complex play activity. While athletic skills, muscle size, speed or sex appeal may be enhanced through physical education programs, it seems unlikely that reading, writing, or arithmetic proficiency will be similarly affected. Whatever values these programs have, they do not appear to include the facilitation of academic skills.

Multisensory Approach

The underlying assumption in the multisensory approach is that learning can be facilitated and maximized if the relevant information is presented through many sensory modalities (Fernald, 1943; Gillingham and Stillman, 1960). The therapeutic emphasis is upon the stimulus presentation, not upon the motor activities demanded of the child. Those motor activities which are included in the training procedures are directly related to the academic task at hand and not to any presumed precursors of these skills.

The method of Grace Fernald is discussed as one example of a multisensory approach. In the Fernald approach the child's acquisition of reading, writing and arithmetic is considered facilitated by visual, auditory and kinesthetic cues becoming conditioned to one another. To aid him in the acquisition of each word, the child follows a series of steps to learn that word. He is requested to trace and then copy the presented word while pronouncing it aloud. The child writes the word in the absence of the stimulus word. The child thus receives visual, auditory, tactile and kinesthetic cues to guide him in learning each word.

In a similar vein, Gillingham and Stillman employ multiple sensory inputs to the child in the training program they developed. There are significant differences between the Fernald and Gillingham and Stillman approaches. Fernald presents whole words to be learned and cursive writing is taught from the beginning of the program. Gillingham and Stillman use a highly structured phonics approach in which isolated phonemes are initially taught. Nonetheless, the two methods revolve around the differential use of sensory modalities to enhance the likelihood of learning.

The Gillingham and Stillman approach presents the child with a card which has a letter written on it. The child is taught the name and sound of the letter in conjunction with the presentation of the stimulus card. The visual symbol is removed and the child is taught to associate the sound of the letter with the name of it. A series of steps follow in which the child traces, copies, writes from memory and writes without looking at the card. The child learns to recognize and reproduce each phoneme using these visual-auditory-kinesthetic steps, referred to as the "language triangle" by its authors.

Fernald and Gillingham and Stillman have enjoyed fine reputations within special education. It is somewhat surprising that there has been a dearth of research activity related to a comparison of the use of the multiple sensory input approach with other methods. The only reference which can be brought to bear on this topic is but tangentially related. Travers (1964) reviewed the effects of multimedia presentation on learning and reported that there was no support for the position that multisensory presentation of information is a more effective teaching method than unimodal presentations.

It is clear that these teachers and intervention programs enjoy great respect among fellow teachers and clinicians. Unfortunately, the source of their success is still in doubt. One cannot yet determine whether their success was related to the use of multisensory inputs, the individual attention, warmth, skill or some other personality characteristic of the teacher, the selective sampling of children who were most likely to respond to these particular methods or some other accidental or conscious variable. The source of success remains an enigma.

Language-based Programs

The previously outlined remediation programs focus upon visual and perceptual training as a therapeutic approach to correcting reading deficits. Other professionals have recommended a remedial approach which emphasizes language training. One of the best-known language-based programs is that developed by Doris Johnson and Helmer Myklebust (1967). Myklebust's extensive experience with deaf and aphasic children resulted in his development of a paradigm based upon the relationship of the brain to human functioning, particularly to language-related activities. In this paradigm the brain is viewed as being organized into semiautonomous systems which allow parts of the brain to work independently or together depending upon the task to be accomplished. In addition, the brain is viewed as having the left side responsible for verbal types of material, while the right side of the brain is responsible for nonverbal types of information. Differential performance on tasks can be used to make inferences about the presence or absence of brain damage and the possible location of such damage.

Myklebust also postulated five levels of learning. The lowest level involves the ability to receive sensations. The second level is perception, the ability to recognize and differentiate between sensory inputs received. Imagery, the third level, refers to the capacity to remember or recall a sensation. The fourth level is symbolization, the ability to verbally label sensations, perceptions and images. Conceptualization, the highest level of learning, involves making abstractions and categorizations of material. Each level of the learning hierarchy requires the development and integrity of the preceding levels.

Diagnosis and remediation are based upon a task analysis of

the semiautonomous systems of the brain, the right and left or verbal and nonverbal nature of the material, the level of learning involved and the child's skills or deficits in each of these areas. To devise a remedial program requires the teacher to do a task analysis in which the material to be learned and the child are evaluated in terms of the intra- and intersensory natures implicit in the tasks and present or deficit in the child. For example, a child might be asked to discriminate whether two sounds are alike or whether two pictures are alike. This typifies an intrasensory task. If a child is to specify whether a sound he hears is the same as a picture he sees, intersensory functioning is being assessed. The verbal or nonverbal nature of the material is also considered. The child's recognition of environmental sounds or of geometric patterns as alike become part of the diagnostic appraisal, and if need be, part of the remedial program. Attention is directed to the modes of response required by the task. A distinction is made between the child's ability to receive the information or comprehend at the steps of learning and his ability to express the information he has received. A child may have little or no difficulty in comprehending the information presented, but great difficulty in expressing that information. A problem at the comprehension level is seen as having more serious implications for learning, as it reciprocally affects expression. A problem at the expressive level may be circumvented by utilization of a more intact type of expressive mode for that child. A number of types of responses are encouraged to see if a child totally incapable of demonstrating learning in one modality may be able to succeed quite well with another means of expression. Thus, a child unable to pass a dictated spelling test by writing responses may be able to pass the test if allowed to respond by orally spelling the words, or if the test is presented in a multiple-choice format (Johnson, 1967).

Remedial efforts are based upon these diagnostic evaluations of the child's intact and deficit modes of comprehension and expression. In this teaching method it is advocated that children be taught new material through their intact modalities. If the child learns well visually, present unfamiliar material in a visual format. If he learns well auditorily, then he should be allowed to learn unfamiliar tasks by listening. If a child has difficulty in writing, let him take tests auditorily or tape record written assignments. In addition, the child is given specific exercises to remediate the deficit areas. While he may not be able to take written exams initially, the goal of the remedial program is to assist him with this problem so that the child ultimately can function using the deficit areas.

A number of language-based programs have been developed to facilitate language development in preschool-aged children, normal and handicapped. An example of this type of program is that which was developed by Tina Bangs (1968). The goal of this program is to increase the language skills and conceptual abilities of children ages 3 to 6. The activities are designed to facilitate the acquisition and use of language. For instance, to develop comprehension of language, Bangs recommends a variety of exercises. The child is exposed to activities which involve recognizing objects by their names and functions, categorizing objects, serial directions and spatial orientation. To facilitate the development of expressive language, the child is asked to name, describe or dramatize objects, scenes and themes. This program provides a rather complete prekindergarten program with a particular emphasis upon language-related activities.

The more widely known language-based programs, such as those developed by Johnson and Myklebust (1967) and Bangs (1968), have not received empirical attention. It is not clear why this is so. The efficiency or efficacy of these techniques remains unknown. Whether they work is not known. If they work, it is not known why. If they work and if they work better than some other approach is also not known. It appears that Myklebust's research efforts have been devoted to testing hypotheses about brain functioning and correlates of brain damage. Johnson's research has also not been addressed to problems of training children. Bangs came to this field as a speech therapist and her program appears to be service rather than research oriented. It is possible that these programs are being placed within clinical settings which traditionally emphasize trying to help children with problems rather than concern for the effectiveness of such help. Like many critically important human problems, there is the difficulty of convincing others that some children should be denied the presumed assistance of a remedial program in order to evaluate the effectiveness of such a program. Even though we do not know just how worthwhile such remedial programs are, we are loath to develop a group of untreated children with whom to compare the treated group. While provocative hypotheses can be advanced concerning the remedial programs, little systematically gathered data can be brought to bear upon the efficacy of these programs.

Although there have been no tests of the effectiveness of a particular remedial training program or of the efficiency of one program compared to another, there has been some research regarding the skills which might facilitate language competency in young children, particularly as related to the acquisition of reading. Two separate perspectives have dominated this research. One has been the application of theories or ideas concerning the relationship of sensory modality functions to the acquisition of reading; the second is based upon a behavior modification approach.

An outgrowth of all the concern about the parts of the brain and learning has been an interest in the relationship between sensory competence and instructional technique. Theorists have hypothesized that differential reading treatments should be accorded to individual children based on profiles of sensory functioning. It was assumed that if a child were diagnosed as having visual rather than auditory strengths, or was a visual learner, he should be trained to read using a visual approach. If a child were assessed an "auditory learner," he should receive an auditory approach to reading; (Johnson and Myklebust, 1967; Bateman, 1969; Smith, 1971). In this approach, there is general agreement that children strong in learning by the visual modality be given an analytic or whole-word introduction to reading, whereas children who are strong in learning auditorily be given a phonics reading program. There is evidence directly related to this hypothesis.

Bliesmer and Yarborough (1965) compared ten beginning reading programs used in the first grade. Five of the programs were based on phonetic presentation, while five were presented by the whole-word approach. Reading achievement was evaluated by performance on five subtests from the Stanford Achievement Test. The results suggested the overwhelming efficiency of the phonetic method. If there were individual differences among the children in terms of their being either auditory or visual learners, these differences were not so great as to make any difference. Another attempt failed to find any significant association between the specific teaching method used and the presumed aptitude for this method (Harris, 1965).

Bateman (1970) studied the efficacy of dividing children into auditory and visual types for the purpose of receiving phonetic or whole-word reading methods of instruction. Eight kindergarten classes were included in the study. Four of the classes were divided so that two received a phonetic approach and two received a whole-word approach to beginning reading instruction. Children from the remaining four classrooms were divided into auditory or visual types on the basis of their scores on the auditory and visual memory subtests from the Illinois Test of Psycholinguistic Abilities. If the child's auditory score exceeded the visual score by more than 9 months, the child was labeled "auditory"; if the difference between the auditory and visual scores was less than 9 months, the child was labeled "visual." The children defined as "auditory" types received the Lippincott beginning reading program, while the "visual" types received the Scott Foresman series. At the end of the first grade a reading score was obtained from scores on the Gates Primary Word Recognition and Paragraph Reading Tests and a spelling score was obtained from a list of 12 words and 6 nonsense words.

The results were that the auditory method proved to be significantly superior to the visual method. The auditorily trained group had scores on the reading achievement and spelling tests which were significantly higher than those of the children trained by the visual method. The children labeled as "auditory" types performed significantly better than children who had been labeled as "visual" types. Of 16 good readers, 14 had had the auditory approach; of 18 poor readers, 16 were visual types and 12 had had the visual approach. The visual types who fared well were children who had IQs considerably above the average for this group, while the auditory types who were poor readers were below the average IQ for the group. It should be noted that the IQs among these children ranged from 121.6 to 126.0 and that the "poor reader" in this context was a first-grader scoring at a 2.9 grade level.

There are a number of problems in interpreting these data. The high IQs of the group in general make generalizations to other populations tenuous. In addition, the definition of poor reading in a child reading above grade level is also questionable. On the other hand, it is equally defensible to say that this study represents a good demonstration for the use of a structured phonics approach to beginning reading as superior to a visual method, especially because the results were not confounded by subjects having had low intelligence or differences among groups in intelligence; nor was it confounded by low socioeconomic status of subjects. Since the study did not suffer from effects of these other variables which are known to affect reading acquisition, we believe it makes a fairly strong statement in favor of phonetic approaches to reading, irrespective of subject types.

Carolyn Smith (1971) also investigated the efficacy of matching subject type to reading approach, but using a different sample of children. As in the Bateman study, the focus was upon the relationship of reading method and reading achievement with auditory and visual modality preferences in children. In this case children were divided into auditory and visual types by averaging their test scores on the Illinois Test of Psycholinguistic Abilities. The auditory score was an average of results on the subtests Auditory Reception, Auditory Association, Grammatic Closure and Sequential Memory. The visual score was an average of results on the subtests Visual Reception, Visual Association, and Visual Sequential Memory. Children with discrepancies greater than 12 months between their auditory and visual scores were labeled according to their higher score. There were a small number of children who fit this definition of auditory types; thus five children with 10- or 11-month discrepancies were included in the auditory group. The control group was comprised of children with auditory-visual differences of less than 1 month. There were 72 children divided so that 8 received each treatment.

The treatments were such that each group of children was taught by the same teacher for two years using one of three reading programs. The programs included: *a)* The Initial Teaching Alphabet (ITA) *Early-to-Read Series* followed by the Lippincott series; *b)* the *Words in Color* (WIC) Program (Gattegno, 1963) followed by the Lippincott series; and *c)* the Supplemental Conventional Reading Program (SCRP), which included the *Reading for Meaning Series* (McKee, Harrison, McCowan and Lehr, 1963) and supplemented by *Reading with Phonics* (Hay and Wingo, 1960).

At the end of first and second grades the Metropolitan Achievement Test was administered. There were no significant differences between the auditory, visual and control groups on the Metropolitan Achievement Test scores. With respect to individual treatments, the means were ranked. For the ITA treatment highest performers were the visual types, then control and auditory. For the WIC program, the means were auditory highest, then visual and control. For the SCRP program, the means were visual highest, then control and auditory. There was no significant interaction between type of program and type of child.

These results are contradictory to the results of the Bateman study, which indicated that auditory types with auditory methods learn to read more effectively than visual types receiving visual methods. But, there were differences in IQ, socioeconomic status and definitions of auditory and visual types in these two studies. Smith suggests that the percentages of children who can be labeled as auditory or visual learners seems to vary with IQ and/or socioeconomic status and that age and race may also play a role.

Bruinincks (1970) investigated the relationship of auditory and visual competence in the child and the effectiveness of teaching through one or the other modality. In this case subjects were selected from a sample of disadvantaged boys. One group was identified as having auditory strengths and visual deficits, while the second group was to have auditory weakness and visual strengths. Each child was taught 30 words he did not know. Fifteen of the words were taught using a phonetic method and fifteen using a whole-word approach. The results failed to confirm the notion that learning can be made more effective by matching the auditory and visual strengths of the child to an auditory or visual method of instruction.

Finally, Sabatino and Streissguth (1972) tested the hypothesis that training children who demonstrated visual strength relative to auditory deficits on a visual training program would result in their making greater gains than children with visual deficits and auditory strengths who also received this training on a number of tests: the Bender Visual Motor Gestalt, the Wide Range Achievement, the Gates-McGinitie Reading Comprehension and the Word Form Configuration. In a rather well-controlled study, these two types of children were either exposed or not exposed to a visual training technique. The results failed to support the hypothesis that "visiles" (children with visual strengths) benefited more from perceptual training than "audiles" (children with auditory strengths).

The link between sensory modality skills and learning to read has not been established. It is clearly advantageous to analyze the subskills and processes required in the act of reading so that deficits can be understood and programs devised to help a child. But it is not apparent that the correct skills or that the analysis of the task of reading have been adequately identified or defined. As of now, we cannot help but agree with Bateman's position that "all evidence supports the currently unpopular notion that reading can and should be taught as a formation of a series of rote, nonmeaningful, conditioned bonds between visual stimuli (letters) and vocal responses (sounds) . . . reading should be viewed as a rote, nonmeaningful process (1964, p. 291). Individual differences in auditory or visual processing seem to make very little difference in the acquisition of reading.

A second approach to assisting the acquisition of language skills and reading has been based upon operant conditioning. According to this perspective, behavior can be influenced through the use of reinforcements or rewards which are administered contingent upon the occurrence of a desired behavior. The technology surrounding operant conditioning is fairly sophisticated in terms of the timing and amount of the rewards which will result in optimum gains, but the underlying assumption is simple.

Children will learn to do whatever leads them to get what they want.

A number of remedial programs have been developed which combine behavior modification with a program of instruction based upon linguistic analyses of language production or reading. Gray, Baker and Stancyk (1969) developed a program for remedial reading instruction; Gray and Fygetakis (1968) applied this approach to dysphasic children (children unable to speak), and Fygetakis and Ingram (1973) reported a case study of a 5-year-old dysphasic child. This method is described in some detail because it incorporates a number of practices which may be critical to the improvement of educational approaches for children with learning disabilities. This record permits the teacher to make adjustments immediately and continuously in the rate of introduction of new material, the speed with which the child learns, the appropriateness of the level of task difficulty and the evaluation of a program over time. This approach can be easily adapted to a wide variety of learning problems, from behavior disturbances to difficulties in written language. This is the approach being promoted in "prescriptive teaching," but it provides a more exact description of the steps to be followed in evaluating the results of the learning sessions.

Gray, Baker and Stancyk (1969) based their approach on the Bond and Dykstra (1967) summary of reading research. Bond and Dykstra indicated that *a)* the best single predictor of first-grade reading achievement is the ability to recognize the letters of the alphabet; *b)* there is no methodological advantage for any single approach; *c)* class size, teacher experience and teacher efficiency do not correlate significantly with pupil success and *d)* the emphasis should be placed upon the learning situations and procedures rather than upon methods and materials. As a result of these findings, Gray, Baker and Stancyk base their reading program upon conditioning or learning principles. In this case the assumptions made are that *a)* reading is responsive to laws of learning; *b)* decoding is antecedent to comprehension and should be taught first; *c)* success should be abundant and result in immediate rewards and *d)* characteristics such as visual perception,

IQ, sequencing ability, etc., do not affect reading acquisition unless a very severe deficit exists (1969, p. 256).

The remedial reading training procedure, Performance Determined Instruction, or PDI, was developed. Children need to know the alphabet and most sound-symbol relationships to be put into this program. Children who have not mastered the alphabet are first provided with an alternate training procedure. Once the child is placed on the PDI, the following program is used. Two children receive bi-weekly 30-minute training programs. The first fifteen minutes involve training in word attack skills which requires the child to read the words on a list. The words are presented in a sequential way based upon their phonetic complexity and length. The teacher's job is to keep track of the correct and reinforced and error responses on a tally sheet. The teacher dispenses poker-chip tokens when the child reads the word correctly. When the child makes a mistake, it becomes the second child's turn to read. An error response results in the child not getting a poker chip and losing his turn to perform. The second fifteen minutes are devoted to reading contextual material. Each child is started just below his grade level in a graded reading series. One child reads and obtains a token for each correctly read sentence. An error results in losing his turn to the second child and not obtaining a token for that sentence. Again the teacher keeps track of correct responses, errors made and the transferring of turns from one to the other child. When a child responds correctly for 3 minutes, he is stopped and given a bonus token. The second child is then given an opportunity to perform. At the end of the 30 minute session the tokens can be exchanged for M&M candies, five tokens to one piece of candy.

The authors emphasize that the teacher activity is more critical than the materials employed. The material is selected to follow a sequential order in which the complexity is increased in a meaningful manner. The materials used in the instance reported here included word lists from Bloomfield and Flesch and graded reading material from Harper and Row, Harr and Wagner, Sullivan and Heath companies for reading comprehension. Materials for contextual reading can be selected to suit the mood and interests of the child because this program does not specify that there need be any relationship at all between the word lists and the contextual reading materials.

The program is arranged so that the child performs with correct responses 92% of the time. This was chosen as ideal because children who fail in reading require a great deal of success, but less than 92% correct results in less adequate reading performance, while greater than 92% correct performance results in boredom without any appreciable increase in reading skills. They also manipulate the amount of reinforcement administered when the child responds correctly. The child received either continuous reinforcement, one token to one correct response, or partial reinforcement, one token for each series of five successive correct responses, or one token for each 10 successive correct responses, or one token for each series of 15 successive words per token and 3 word lists per difficulty level. Each page of the word lists contained five word lists of eighteen words apiece. The amount of work at each level of difficulty and the rate of reinforcement were manipulated by the instructor. The child was always started at continuous reinforcement, one correct response resulted in a token, and with five word lists. After three instructional sessions, the child was shifted to receiving three word lists per difficulty level and reinforcement for fifteen successive correct responses.

The authors reported that the system was tested on nine 9-year-old boys enrolled in the Monterey Institute for Speech and Hearing for remedial reading problems. After twelve hours on the PDI, the boys improved one year on the Gray Oral Reading Passage. This approach thus appears to be quite effective, at least with respect to quickly improving the decoding skills of remedial readers. At this time, comprehension skills had not been tested.

The behavior modifiers have taken a radical approach relative to the views of more orthodox theorists. They abstain from preoccupations with the perceptual, auditory, visual and/or brain process of the learning-disabled child. Instead, the diagnosis of the child is focused upon what the child likes, what he will work for and ultimately what he will learn for. Their radicalness takes another turn when they ignore the materials to be used beyond a simple placement of the child on some graded series and when they ignore the traditional role of the teacher to instruct the child. The focus is upon careful documentation of the effects of individualized instruction upon the individual child. Careful observations are made and impact is assessed. The role of the teacher then shifts to becoming a data collector. Irrespective of whether the success of this approach is due to this careful documentation, or to these techniques being superior to those produced under differing perspectives of disability, it appears that this approach has yielded the most fruitful remedial techniques, if not the most elaborate diagnostic ones.

Miscellaneous

Thus far, the discussion of remedial techniques has been addressed to specific theories and well-defined remedial programs based upon these theories. Evidence about the effectiveness of these programs has been sparse and the results often disappointing. But perhaps we should not be surprised. As indicated earlier, Walberg (1971) did suggest that specific instructional techniques do not seem to be particularly powerful in affecting the child's academic progress. Other variables related to dimensions of classroom activity have more impact upon the child's learning success. Based upon information derived from research efforts in other fields as well as efforts in learning disabilities, it appears to us that many ideas about remediating learning disabilities may reflect more "fancy" than "fact." The remaining section of this chapter will be devoted to some speculations relevant to these "facts" and "fancies" as they relate to current practices.

The bases of our personal bias should be first explicated. We believe that many of the problems faced by learning-disabled children are not at all academic, but rather are of a social nature. There are many children who have difficulty learning in school who are not labeled learning disabled although they meet the legal definitions set up by their respective school districts. We suggest that the label learning disabled does not depend entirely upon the ability to experience academic success, but is equally, if not more, related to social behaviors. It is not simply a learning disability which marks this child (as noted by the Clements, 1966, list of characteristics); it is the inability to perform, plus additional behavioral characteristics (negative in nature) which result in this label being applied. It should be noted that the limitation of remedial techniques as noted in the literature may be related to the fact that these techniques ignore the behaviors of the child which resulted in his being labeled in the first place and concentrate all efforts on remediating the learning problems. Only the behavior modification approach included an accounting of the child's responses and this may be the secret of success of such an approach. At any rate, the remainder of this chapter will consider the topic of learning.

One prevalent view of children with learning disabilities is that they often have memory deficiencies. It is a common belief that individuals vary in their capacity to retain information, some people believing that they have a "terrible," memory while others claim some affiliation with elephants, who are noted for "exceptional" memories. Memory deficits are indexed by a person's performance on subtests of the Wechsler Intelligence Scale for Children, such as Digit Span or Coding, and by Auditory and Visual Sequential Memory tests on the Illinois Test of Psycholinguistic Ability. Remedial programs to improve memory are then based upon these test scores when a child performs poorly. There are several sources of difficulty with the assumption that children have memory deficits and that remedial programs can alleviate and improve such problems. First, Digit Span and Coding subtests on the WISC are not related to memory on other tasks, at least not yet. The statistical and empirical difficulties inherent in this procedure have been well documented (McNemar, 1957). A second point is that such tests are not simply a matter of memory, as memory is related to learning and in these tests the degree of learning is not controlled. For a child to repeat five digits, frontward and backward, requires that he learn the list, not just that he remember the list. A large body of research in verbal learning has consistently failed to demonstrate any individual differences in memory. Individual differences are evident in terms of the original learning of the material, not in their recall (Underwood, 1945). This is the source for different scores on memory tests—not memory! If the material to be learned is the same for any two people, their recall of that material will be the same. If efforts to improve the initial stage of learning are not provided, all of the efforts to improve memory are a waste of time and will never yield the desired results. When children score poorly on tests of memory, we should address ourselves to the child's technique of learning new material and an improved approach for that child in his ability to make such acquisitions.

Another assumption frequently made about the learning-disabled child is that he is distractible. Remedial programs have been designed to decrease this distractibility, with some demanding that teachers wear only plain black dresses with no jewelry and that the classroom be similarly stark. Perhaps every child who causes trouble within the schools is labeled distractible. This has been the case with the brain-injured child (Browning, 1967). Obviously, if a child is distractible when he is supposed to be working on academic materials, his performance will suffer. There have been a number of studies conducted relevant to the belief that distractibility in children will affect their performance on learning. Browning (1967) tested brain-injured and nonbrain-injured children on a discrimination learning task. During the learning trials, the child was to note the contingency between the discrimination of a triangle, from a circle or square, and the receipt of a candy reward. Some children from each group were to perform this task with multicolored lights flashing to distract them. Other children from the brain-damaged and nonbrain-damaged groups were not presented with this visual distraction. There were no differences in learning between the brain-injured and nonbrain-injured children under conditions of visual distraction. The results indicated that distraction is no more devastating to the performance of brain-injured children than it is for nonbrain-injured children.

A second study addressed to the effects of distraction upon learning in learning-disabled children was completed by Vernetti and Jacobs (1972). In this, the distraction was noise and the task was the completion of math problems in the classroom. Fifty-three children, 11 girls and 42 boys enrolled in a self-contained learning disabilities classroom, were instructed to complete pages of math problems. During this time they were exposed to regular background noise or to taped music. When the child completed the page, the teacher recorded the time to completion. Each child was tested eight times under each condition (noisy and not noisy). There were no differences reported in the performance of learning-disabled children under the noisy and not noisy conditions.

Contradictory results were reported by Hartman and Richards (1969). In this study it was hypothesized that a very quiet and sensory isolated room (no visual or auditory distractions) would enhance the ability of brain-damaged children with severe reading difficulties to learn the association between labels and pictures. Half of the subjects were presented the learning task in the ordinary classroom. The remaining children were placed in a very nondistracting environment. Children learned more within the sensory isolated condition than those who remained in the classroom. Unfortunately, the results of this study are subject to an alternative explanation. Subjects in the sensory isolated room were presented the stimulus materials through a rather elaborate apparatus, while those in the classroom had to make do with a Language Master presentation. The differential learning of children in these two environments may be related to the presentation of the material and not to the potentially distracting or nondistracting environment.

As yet, there is little support for the idea that children with learning disabilities are more distractible than other academically successful children or that eliminating sources of distractibility will enhance the results of an educational program.

It is commonly believed that children who are slower to achieve need more time, be it to apply their learning strategies to the task at hand or to assimilate the lessons proposed by the teacher. Within learning disabilities, we realize, "more" is not enough and the "more" must also be different. To express this we reject the notion of "tutoring," which is associated with simply providing "more" without taking into account how the presentation should differ from that under which the child has already failed. The term "clinical teaching" was substituted. Nonetheless, it is believed that an increased time allotment for instruction is going to raise the performance of slow students (those with less than average aptitudes) to a given criterion level, while fast students will finish the same material more quickly. There is, however, little research from classroom settings to support the idea that time is curative. There appears to be little relation between the amount of time spent in instruction and the achievement level reached by the student, given at least some exposure to the material (Walberg, 1971). In this case we have only anecdotal data to make inferences about how the time factor might affect learning-disabled children. One child with a delayed speech and language history, on drugs to control potential epileptic attacks, with very slow motor responses and questionable ability to use language in any abstract sense, was reading above grade level. The teacher complained that the child spent most of the day daydreaming and engaging in "nervous mannerisms," like playing with paper clips and shreds of paper. It is suggested that time in itself was not relevant to the academic performance of this clearly handicapped girl. Once she had the idea it stuck with her and the usual exercises in which children engage to overlearn school material may not have any more effect for successful learners than it was having for this child, who was not engaging in these repetitive tasks.

What are the factors which might affect learning? In a discussion of programmed instruction, Gagne and Paradise (1961) suggest the following variables: (1) the skills the learner has when he starts; (2) the skills he has specific to the task at hand; (3) the task to be acquired; (4) the general level of intelligence of the student. Insofar as little seems to be known about the interactions of variables associated with numbers 1, 2 and 3, these recommendations provide but a framework and starting point for attacking any learning task.

There appears to be consensus that the differences in rates of learning cannot be altered by having the child repeat a task or simply spend more time on the task. To determine the ideal amount of time a child spends on an activity, the desired repetition of responses and amount of reinforcements which will facilitate learning, it is suggested that a learning curve be drawn for the child. A recent study of learning curves in retarded readers was reported by Camp (1973). In this study, forty-two retarded readers were accepted for a remedial reading program. The materials used included the SRA Reading Laboratories, 1a, 1b, and 1c. The children received one to five tutoring sessions per week using the Staats Motivation Activation Reading Technique (SMART). Each half-hour reading lesson included the introduction of new vocabulary, paragraph reading, total story reading and answering comprehension questions. Token rewards were given which could be exchanged for money. The lesson was not complete until the child had one unprompted complete trial with each word on the new vocabulary list and one trial with each paragraph in which all the words were read correctly without prompting. Children were then exposed to the next level of difficulty. The tutor's job was to keep track of each response given on the lesson. The words on which the child made one or more errors during the lesson were used to make up the vocabulary test given at the end of each block of 20 lessons. The data used to plot the learning curve came from the daily records made by the tutor of the daily lessons and the vocabulary review tests. The daily record required the tutor to count the total number of errors produced on the vocabulary and paragraph reading parts of the lesson. Acquisition curves could then be plotted by listing the cumulative scores against the cumulative total number of lessons completed and total number of words presented. The ratio of total errors to total words presented became the measure of learning rate.

The author had presupposed that retarded readers would have more heterogeneous learning curves. But, indeed, the retarded readers' scores resulted in the same curves which are seen in nonretarded or normal readers on a variety of learning tasks. This is marked by a general pattern of initial acceleration followed by a gradual slackening of the rate of learning.

Camp suggested that this type of learning curve can be used by the teacher to regulate the flow of information presented to the child. The curve can be used to measure whether the child's learning acquisition is increased by repetition of materials or by more trials with different material. Differing curves should be used to differentiate ways of presenting material in terms of length of word lists or paragraphs and repetitiveness. In essence, Camp tried to do this. Children with error rates above 20% repeated a set of lessons. Children who had shown normally shaped curves showed decreased error rates with repetition. The children who did not demonstrate this change either had a curve with continuous acceleration or a high error rate with minimal deceleration late in the set of lessons. Camp concluded that "individual differences in learning rate may account for a large share of individual differences in reading achievement, even among a group of severely retarded readers" (1973, p. 71).

The above studies suggest that children with learning disabilities have the same general learning curves as academically successful peers. Little has yet been said about those factors which might affect learning and/or performance. Theories of learning, as studied by psychologists, are controversial in terms of their details. Some believe that children can learn simply by observation of adults and peers (Bandura, 1969; Aronfreed, 1969). Others argue that learning is linked to reinforcements, either in the child's history or in the situation at hand (Gewirtz, 1969). There is some consensus that children will perform, if not learn, because there is the possibility they will receive some material or social reward (Bandura, 1969). Whatever the "truth" of these conflicting theories, remedial techniques have taken segments of these varying positions to facilitate learning-disabled children's performance. These individual studies do not present a cookbook of procedures designed to increase the child's capacity to read, write and compute, but they do suggest some ideas as to the processes which might be followed and explored to facilitate the acquisition of such skills. The remainder of this chapter will be devoted to a discussion of those theories and research efforts which appear to have important implications for classroom and special education teachers.

Behavior Modification

Boredom has led people to drink, to sex and to busy work. It led B. F. Skinner to some of the most profound and influential studies in modern psychology (Skinner, 1960). Skinner (1971) argued that behavior is controlled through the appropriate use of reinforcements. By giving a child a reward of candy, praise or hugs and kisses, the behavior of the child which immediately preceded the reward will be very likely to recur. Skinner and colleagues developed extensive knowledge as to how such rewards might be utilized in optimal ways. These rewards came to include all the old tricks teachers have been using for centuries: stars, displays of classroom work and verbal praise.

Skinner's refinement of knowledge about human behavior can be divided into four areas. First, he and his students were not content to simply administer a pellet to the pigeon or an M&M to the child. They went much further and specified how many pellets or M&Ms need to be given, when they should be given and how often they need to be given to effect the desired behavior. The contribution of specification of the conditions under which reinforcements should be administered to obtain particular goals cannot be underestimated.

Second, a very empirical orientation was brought to education. It became necessary to note the change in a child's behavior which resulted from the actions of clinicians, teachers and parents. Third, their work involved a denial of much of the popular psychological rhetoric concerning the child. The motto might be: focus not upon nonobservable motives, thought and needs; let concepts of the id, ego and superego die of disuse. Think not in the abstract terms proposed by psychodynamic theorists Freud, Jung, Adler and Horney. Rather, study the behavior of the child. Let the conceptualizations of children be specified in behavioral terms.

Finally, the Skinnerian, or behavior modification perspective, demands that attention not be limited to the child's behavior (or symptoms), but to the interaction of the child's behavior with his environment. The focus was shifted to the effects of environment, particularly the people in the child's environment, in eliciting and maintaining undesirable and maladaptive behaviors by means of reinforcements. Now it is no longer adequate to diagnose what is right or wrong about a child; one must analyze the interaction which occurs between variables in the environment and the child. This is a critically important emphasis, as there are many sources and types of reinforcers capable of affecting any particular child. Children, strange beasts that they are, often have strange tastes in incentives. The analysis of the individual child and his surroundings will often lead to the discovery that there is a reinforcer more potent than that which is assumed on an a priori basis. One student teacher, for example, reported that a child participating in a learning project selected for a reinforcement to have a parakeet sit in her hair.

Moreover, the characteristics of the person who administers the reward may have a great effect upon the nature of the reinforcement. In a recent study, Midlarsky, Bryan and Brickman (1973) reported that when an adult praised an act which she herself would not commit (donating money to the March of Dimes), the praise served as punishment to the child. The praise decreased the occurrence of behavior on which it was contingent for most children.

The implications of a systematic approach are profound for the remediation of learning problems. There are implications for the direct change of academic achievement as seen in the Camp (1973) study and for the change of the many behaviors defined as undesirable in children. This approach thus has direct value for altering inattentive, hyperactive, disruptive behaviors and for increasing the degree to which a child learns to read. Because of the obvious potency of this approach, a description of the way in which a program is set up and a discussion of research relevant to learning disabilities follows.

The greatest extension of behavior modification principles into the classroom has been through the introduction of the token economy. Many of the children displaying learning problems in the classroom are those who have not responded to the usual techniques employed by teachers to control classroom behavior.

Remediation

Some children have not been affected by praise or reproof, stars or grades, peer or parent pressures. To meet this challenge, investigators instituted the now prevalent token economy program. These programs exploit the fact that children will behave in a manner which will get them something they want. If teachers provide desirable rewards, most children will literally "shape up" and perform in accordance with the teacher's desires. In token economy programs, teachers give children a token contingent upon the commission or approximation of a desired behavior. When the child accumulates a sufficient number of tokens, he may select to buy or exchange his tokens for one of many valued objects.

The hallmark of the token economist, or the operant conditioner, is sensitivity to the effects of reinforcements upon behavior. It is not just the institution of the token that marks these programs, but the preoccupation with the impact of all reinforcements, positive and negative upon children. These workers have focused not only upon the effects of the token, but the degree and nature of many forms of reinforcements which might maintain a child's behavior or misbehavior. Thus, the types of reinforcements given a child might be altered in light of the influences of the peer groups supporting the child. Teacher attention which is elicited by a child when he misbehaves is eschewed, although most forms of punishment are discouraged, particularly when teacher-child interactions are involved (Kazdin and Bootzin, 1972; O'Leary and Drabman, 1971).

Can the judicious use of a token economy program ameliorate problems associated with learning-disabled children? The answer seems to be yes. For example, the reinforcement of non-disruptive behaviors has been demonstrated to greatly reduce the occurrence of the disruptive behavior and increase the occurrence of studious behavior and academic achievement (Kazdin and Bootzin, 1972; O'Leary and Drabman, 1971). It might be predicted that academic skills would be immune to alteration by tokens because of the new learning demanded; nonetheless, gains have been reported to result through the use of token economy systems. Wolf, Giles and Hall (1968) introduced a token economy into a remedial program for elementary school children who had low academic achievement. Tokens were given to the children contingent upon correct academic performance in reading, language and arithmetic. Gains were made in all areas of performance associated with the reinforcement procedures. Hewett, Taylor and Artuso (1969) found that 8–11-year-old emotionally disturbed children's academic performance in arithmetic, but not reading, could be improved when they were exposed to a token economy program. The effects of token economy programs have been positive in controlling aversive behaviors and in improving academic performances.

There is every reason to be optimistic regarding remediation efforts which are based upon principles of behavior modification, at least those using token economies. Children do have to sit in their seats or at least attend in order to learn, and they are by and large well motivated to do so through incentives. Numerous studies reviewed by O'Leary and Drabman (1971) and Kazdin and Bootzin (1972) amply documented the utility and power of the appropriate use of reinforcements within the classroom setting. Of course, teachers, adults and even children have long recognized the power of a carrot, and yet their use of the carrot often appears to be less than optimal. The token economists have given us many useful suggestions as to how to implement the power of the carrot. Relying on the above-cited reviews, the following procedures should be considered.

A target behavior must be determined. Without a clear understanding of the behavior to be changed, it is likely that reinforcements for that behavior or its approximations will be sporadic and elicited for nontarget responses. In addition, without a careful specification of the behavior to be changed, it would be impossible to assess the effectiveness of the program.

Appropriate reinforcements must be determined and the "purchasing power" of the token reinforcements must be made clear to the children. The children must know that the token can purchase something they desire, a so-called backup reinforcer. In setting up a token economy, care should be taken to provide a sufficient number and variety of backup reinforcers so that all the participating children will have an incentive worthy of effort. Reinforcers may be chosen on the basis of the most frequently

engaged in activity of the child. If he likes it a lot, he will probably work to do it more often. Hence, backup reinforcers may
include excuses from the class, watching television, helping the
teacher, running errands and obtaining candies or toys. The selection of reinforcing reinforcers can be accomplished by asking the
children what they want.

Care should be taken in determining the type of token to be
employed. Tokens have included activities and objects like
teacher ratings, plastic chips and stars. The nature of the token
is critical only in the sense that suggestions are particularly helpful. These authors indicate that the following characteristics of
tokens be considered. The value of the token should be easily
understood by the child. The exchange rate and the contingency
of obtaining tokens should be understood. It is probably better
to dispense rating marks than plastic tokens. The token should
be easy for the child to manage and yet not distract him from his
usual academic routing. Tokens should not be toys, but symbols.
Finally, they should be easy for the teacher to dispense.

The critical feature of the token economy is that the token
be administered contingent on the occurrence of the desired behavior. No desired behavior—no token. Programs are generally
set up so that reinforcements are contingent upon an individual's
performance, not the performance of the group. This differs from
procedures currently used in the U.S.S.R. in which children are
rewarded on the basis of the group's allegiance to standards
(Bronfenbrenner, 1970). The current practice in the U.S. is to
reward individuals for their own rather than the group's appropriate behavior. There have been few studies of the impact of
token economies on a collective and no studies which have compared a group-oriented procedure to those currently in vogue in
the U.S. (O'Leary and Drabman, 1971).

Typically, when a child performs the target behavior, he
receives a token. What other events might mitigate or facilitate
the effectiveness of a token economy? It is now generally believed
that teacher attention, whatever its nature, might serve to increase the very behavior the teacher wants to eliminate. It is
generally recommended that teachers ignore disruptive behavior,
while reinforcing appropriate behaviors through rewards. This is

not always easy, sometimes it is not possible. In order to inhibit disruptive behaviors, programs have included time-out procedures (i.e., absence from the room and from the token economy), quiet verbal scoldings and deductions or fines in the form of removal of already earned tokens (O'Leary and Drabman, 1971). It has been claimed that each procedure has some success in altering disruptive classroom behavior.

Techniques aside, attention must be paid to the characteristics of the teacher and child which may facilitate or inhibit the impact of the token economy. If the teacher fails, the program fails. But relatively little work has been done on training teachers in the use of token economies or molding teacher attitudes toward such systems. There is some evidence that teachers who believe that the program does not work find that the program does not work. There is little evidence to indicate what type of training would be best for teachers, although one investigator indicated that having program operators rehearse the behaviors in training led to better performance than the usual lecture training method (Gardner, 1972). Kazdin and Bootzin (1972) reviewed investigations which suggest that even if the initial training of the teacher is adequate, repeated training sessions may be necessary to maintain the original level.

Young lower-class children who may have had below-average intelligence have been the subjects for most token economy programs. It is likely that the effectiveness of the behavior modification program will depend on the academic level of the children. No amount of tokens, no matter how skillfully administered, can teach a child who cannot count to understand set theory. If the child does not have the necessary skills within his repertoire, no amount of reinforcement will elicit more complex skills. The success of the token economy is thus dependent upon a careful diagnosis of the child's achievements and a careful task analysis of the behavior to be required of him. It would seem that within this context the learning disability specialist will be particularly able to make a significant and unique contribution to the child with problems.

Although the token economy strategy has been very successful for classroom management, the problems and limitations of this method should be recognized. One obvious issue is the durability of the effects of such programs. As things stand today, the use of token economies is short term and children are withdrawn from them. What happens when the token economy program is discontinued? The bulk of the literature suggests that the reinforced behavior will decrease in frequency unless it gets some occasional reinforcement. As long as the token economy is in operation, the teacher can expect to maintain rather good control of classroom behavior. When the program is discontinued the "good behavior is under environmental control as long as there is a token in it for him" (O'Leary and Drabman, 1971).

A major concern is the degree to which behaviors learned in the token economy room will generalize or be evidenced in other situations, with other teachers or some other time. If a child will sit still for tokens in one room, will he sit still in another classroom or in the same class with a substitute teacher? O'Leary and Drabman sum up the situation at present:

Those investigators who have assessed the generalization of behaviors reinforced in the token programs to those same behaviors when the token program is not in effect, in different situations and at different times, have not found generalization. (1971, p. 394.)

Other problems have been noted if not systematically studied. One common concern of the public regarding the instruction of token economies has been the issue of bribery. Some people argue that by having a token economy one is bribing the child to behave. Although this concern is not usually explicated further, the concern reflects an interest in the impact of tokens upon the attitudes and expectancies of the child. It would be naive to assume that such programs do not have effects upon attitudes and expectancies; surprisingly these effects have not been subject to systematic study. On the basis of anecdotal evidence, it has been suggested that children will model the "if-then" position of the token economist. Bushell, Wrobel and Michaelis (1968) reported that children negotiated contracts with peers in which pay-offs would accompany requested behavior. These behaviors might have occurred on a nonreciprocating basis prior to the initiation of the token economy program. Meichenbaum, Bowers and Ross (1969) reported that adolescent female delinquents turned the tables on the investigators. The girls were on a part-time token economy and blackmailed the investigators to extend the token periods. They were not going to work unless there was a pay-off.

It is our opinion that behavior modification programs offer considerable power of control to the teacher over a child's classroom behavior. The child with learning disabilities demonstrates many behaviors which have been shown amenable to the effects of token economies (Bryan and Wheeler, 1972; Bryan, 1974d). On-task behavior has certainly been shown to be influenced by token economy programs. Moreover, there is evidence that academic skills can be improved through the use of proper incentives (Hewett, Taylor and Artuso, 1969; Drass and Jones, 1971). The fact that such programs lead to little generalization of good behavior to other teachers, classrooms or similar behaviors should not be of great concern. Most studies concerned with generalization have focused upon social or deportment behaviors. They have not evaluated the durability of academic skills produced by behavior modification procedures. Social behaviors are most likely to be affected by the power of reinforcement contingencies available within the environment. It is quite another matter to think that academic skills would be lost under the condition in which reinforcement is terminated. The motivation to continue to achieve may cease, but it is highly unlikely that past learning somehow disappears from the child's repertoire (Underwood, 1954). It would be desirable if behavior modification procedures could be developed so that their application would result in a generalization of their effects to other situations. But to criticize these attempts and the success of these programs on these grounds would seem quite unjust. Parents and educators attempt to train children's "character," to develop a child who will show a desirable behavior across a variety of situations for a lengthy period of time. But those factors which facilitate this development are not well known. To criticize these techniques on the basis of this particular limitation is to condemn all known techniques used to influence children. It is an achievement of considerable magnitude and importance that control of behavior can be obtained on a predictable basis within the classroom. As to the attitudinal and expectancy effects of such programs, little can now be said concerning their nature or desirability. Perhaps the direction taken in research on token economies in the future will be to systematically study and evaluate such effects. In the meantime, anecdotal reports do not indicate that such effects would warrant the discontinuation of token economies. Even if token economies produced a reciprocal orientation toward interpersonal and academic relations, one must ask whether these effects are worse than those produced by continuing school failure and side effects of low self-esteem, social rejection and parental anxiety. All students interested in the remediation of learning disabilities, either within the context of classroom, resource room or clinic, must be concerned with developments in the field of behavior modification.

CHAPTER
12
CONCLUDING
STATEMENTS

To the Teacher of Learning-Disabled Children

There are currently a number of popular alternative intervention programs for learning-disabled children. The self-contained classroom is a segregated setting in which the learning-disabled child is programmed with a small number of other similarly handicapped youngsters. Many children are serviced through itinerant or resource room arrangements in which they obtain remedial help on a part-time basis while remaining in their regular elementary school setting. Some children attend private schools and others are served through university or hospital clinic programs. The mainstreaming concept of intervention is the most recent approach. This involves retaining the learning-disabled youngster in the regular classroom, with the learning disability teacher either working directly with that child in that room or helping the classroom teacher to provide appropriate materials for that child. Needless to say, we do not yet know which of these many programs the child should receive, nor which program is most effective for which child. We can say, happily, that a study of tutoring vs. classroom instruction (Bousell, Moody and Walzl, 1972) as well as other studies of the effectiveness of intervention (Balow, 1965) have shown that special help does make a positive difference.

While teacher training and experience have not been found to be related to achievement of children, we think that teachers of learning-disabled children need a number of unique qualities. There are no empirical data of which we are aware, so this represents an indulgence in espousing our personal feelings.

The success of any type of educational program for learning-disabled children rests on the success of integrating this child into regular settings. A single major goal is maintenance of children in home and school settings or reintegration of the child into these settings. To maintain a child with severe academic and behavioral problems in his home environment is not easy. Data have been cited on the rejection of learning-disabled children by teachers and peers and on the differences in feelings of parents. Maintaining problem children in the elementary school system, or reintegrating them, requires financial and institutional support from school administrators; it often requires special help from secretaries, lunch room attendants and building engineers. Their support is critical. To obtain acceptance and help requires great skills in interpersonal relations on the part of the learning disability specialist.

Ombudsman. The learning-disabled child needs his own lobbyist. The learning disability specialist needs to interpret for others the learning and behavioral problems of the child. These problems are often misunderstood if not ignored. The absence of a physical defect or obvious mental retardation often results in the child's problems being misinterpreted. We have seen instances where a child has developed his own way of compensating for his learning problem (auditorizing to work through a visual motor problem) only to have school personnel interpret his "talking out loud all the time" as crazy; or a teacher saying the family should not keep the child so drugged, when it was that treatment which allowed the child to attend school. The learning disability teacher has to explain to others and interpret for others the learning problems the children have, as well as be available when the teacher or parents are having problems dealing with the child.

The learning disability specialist should also be responsible for coordinating all the special and not so special services rendered the child. Parents are too often subjected to fragmented services from many professionals. Someone needs to integrate findings from various professional sources for the parents and for the school personnel.

Courage. Part of being the learning-disabled child's representative involves obtaining the needed resources from the school system. When resources are in short supply, or when there is resistance to developing a learning disability program, the learning disability specialist needs to represent (vigorously) the institutional needs of the disabled children. Enlisting community/parent help is an honorable means of dealing with this problem. This is probably the most difficult kind of role for learning disability specialists to play, because they are basically sympathetic, agreeable, nice people. Fighting is antithetical to such characteristics. But sometimes it is necessary to keep uppermost the needs of the children and make a stand for the resources they deserve.

There are no cookbooks for solving the problems of learning-disabled youngsters. The answers are not there; not even the questions have been asked yet. The children make progress, but it is often slow, and some children do not seem to make progress. The learning problems are severe and require sustained assistance. The learning disability specialist operates in a field which requires great flexibility, the ability to work when progress is slow and maybe limited, and in a situation of great ambiguity. Are we doing the right thing? Is there another way? To work with a limited technology, to experience the consequences and the frustrations by so doing, requires courage as well.

More courage. We are well trained to be accepting and understanding of the learning and behavioral problems of children. But learning disabilities are associated with many aversive behavioral characteristics, and it is the responsibility of the learning disability specialist to help the child stop engaging in obnoxious behaviors. Sometimes this can be done through a loving approach, but sometimes it is much more effective to directly and actively inhibit such behaviors. For instance, learning-disabled children sometimes engage in insulting others ("You're fat, not fat like him but fat"). Training in "making friends not enemies" is in order, and this may require toughness.

Data collecting. Keeping records is not one of the joys of teaching, but good record keeping has a number of important benefits. It is suggested that lesson plans be developed so that the teacher collects daily records on the specific material covered, the child's daily progress and the test and retest data. This provides a continuous record of specifically what the child achieved. One incentive is that carefully kept records of learning permit a continual analysis of the effectiveness of the educational program. In addition, this material provides the means to defend the program should it be challenged. The teacher is all too often "one down" on multidisciplinary team approaches to child assessment; having the data should increase the status of the teacher by making the critical information the teacher offers more specific for others.

No hardening of the categories. This field is young and the problems difficult to solve. Keeping an open mind . . . and . . . not throwing the baby out with the bath water are two clichés to keep in mind. It may not be easy to live with ambiguity as to the "rightness" of selected educational programs, but in this field we cannot promise the teacher a rose garden.

Finally, some comment on the future of the field of learning disabilities. A major problem facing this field is the definition of learning disabilities. On the one hand we have turned our back on the specification of brain damage as a criterion for labeling a child minimal cerebral dysfunction; on the other hand we may dissolve our identity as a field entirely by taking in every child with very minimal learning problems. Will we swallow general education or will general education swallow us? That is the question. It is our opinion that we must confine our concerns to children who demonstrate moderate to severe learning problems, and advise and consult on lesser difficulties. While the brain-damage approach was sufficiently limited so that we cannot return to this, we can specify the learning disability on the basis of demonstrated severe retardation in critical growth areas.

To make progress in defining learning disabilities requires more labels, not fewer; labels which describe behaviors in very specific terms. Rather than saying a child has a perceptual motor problem, let us describe that problem (*e.g.*, the child has difficulty writing cursive letters, or the size and shape of letters are correct but the child cannot sustain writing efforts for more than a few minutes). To get beyond overused, meaningless, generic terms (*e.g.*, hyperactivity) requires that we collect a great deal of specific information on learning-disabled children. Ultimately, we should have the clinical knowledge base, buttressed by empirical studies, to categorize learning problems and to trace effective interventions.

Meanwhile, it is necessary to not fall prey to fads either in our notions as to what causes or what will resolve learning problems. Careful consideration of new ideas and methods, retention of what seems to work and evaluation of both will in time help us sort out this thing called learning disabilities.

We have been highly critical of the ideas, methods and practices of the field of learning disabilities. We hope this critical stance will not be interpreted to reflect a lack of sympathy. If we lacked sympathy with the goals, efforts and concerns of the fraternity of learning disability specialists, we would not have bothered writing this text. But for a field to grow scientifically and conceptually, critical evaluations are needed, and practioners free of dogma need to be developed. It was not our intention to tell you how to do it, whatever the "do it" might mean, nor was it to give some direction to your efforts so that you will not feel at loose ends. Indeed, our conception of this text was quite other than providing you with a therapeutic experience; rather it was to provide information and challenges so as to prepare you to be critical and thereby more effective in the professional field which will soon absorb you. In the last analysis, an unthinking and uncritical practitioner is more dangerous to the field and the clients that he will serve than one who challenges dogma and is ultimately proven wrong in so doing. This is how technology grows.

REFERENCES

Ackerman P. T., Peters, J. E. and Dykamn, R. A. "Children with Specific Learning Disabilities: Bender Gestalt Test Finding and Other Signs." *Journal of Learning Disabilities,* 1971, vol. 4, 437–44.

Adams, G. R. & Hamm, N. H. "A test of the 'contiguity' and generalized imitation theories of imitation learning." Paper presented at the meetings of the Society of Research & Child Development, 1971.

Ames, L. B. "A low intelligence quotient often not recognized as the chief cause of many learning difficulties." *Journal of Learning Disabilities,* 1968, 1, 45–48.

Anastasi, A. *Psychological Testing.* New York: The Macmillan Co., 1961.

Aronfreed, J. "The concept of internalization." In D. A. Goslin (ed.), *Handbook of Socialization Theory and Research.* Chicago: Rand McNally, 1969, 263–323.

Baker, C. T., Sontag, L. W. & Nelson, V. L. "Individual and group differences in the longitudinal measurement of change in mental ability." In L. W. Sontag, C. T. Baker & V. L. Nelson (eds.), "Mental growth personality development: A longitudinal study." *Monographs of the Society for Research in Child Development,* 1958, 23, No. 2, 11–83.

Baker, H. J. & Leland, B. *Detroit Tests of Learning Aptitudes.* Indianapolis, Ind.: Bobbs-Merrill, 1935.

Bakwin, H. "Reading disability in twins." *Journal of Learning Disabilities,* 1973, 6, 439–440.

Balow, B. "The long-term effect of remedial reading instruction." *The Reading Teacher,* 1965, 18, 581–586.

Bandura, A. *Principles of Behavior Modification.* New York: Holt, Rinehart & Winston, 1969.

———, Grusec, J. & Menlove, F. "Observational learning as a function of symbolization and incentive set." *Child Development,* 1966, 37, 499–506.

———& Kupers, C. A. "Transmission of patterns of self-reinforcement through modeling." *Journal of Abnormal and Social Psychology,* 1964, 69, 1–9.

Bangs, T. E. *Language and Learning Disorders of the Pre-academic Child.* New York: Appleton-Century-Crofts, 1968.

Bannatyne, A. "Diagnosing learning disabilities and writing remedial prescriptions." *Journal of Learning Disabilities,* 1968, 1, 242–249.

Barsch, R. H. *Achieving Perceptual Motor Efficiency.* Seattle, Wash.: Special Child Publication, 1967.

References

Bartel, N. R., Grill, J. J. & Bartel, H. W. "The syntactic-paradigmatic shift in learning disabled and normal children." *Journal of Learning Disabilities*, 1973, 6, 518–523.

Bateman, B. "Learning disabilities—Yesterday, today, and tomorrow." *Exceptional Children*, 1964, 31, 167–177.

———."Reading: A controversial view." In L. Tarnopol (ed.), *Learning Disabilities*. Springfield, Ill.: Charles C. Thomas, 1969.

Bausell, R. B., Moody, W. B. and Walze, L., "A Factorial Study of Tutoring vs. Classroom Instruction." *American Educational Research Journal*, 1972, 9, 591–598.

Bayley, N. "Consistency and variability in the growth of intelligence from birth to eighteen years." *Journal of Genetic Monographs*, 1949, 75, 165–196.

———."Development of mental abilities." In P. H. Mussen (ed.), *Carmichael's Manual of Child Psychology, Vol. 1*. New York: John Wiley and Sons, 1970.

Becker, H. *Outsiders*. New York: Free Press, 1963.

Beery, K. & Buktenica, N. *Developmental Test of Visual-Motor Integration*. Chicago, Ill.: Follett, 1967.

Bender, L. "A visual motor Gestalt test and its clinical use." *American Orthopsychiatry Assoc. Res. Monograph*, 1938, No. 3.

Benton, A. *Right-Left Discrimination and Finger Localization*. New York: Hoeber-Harper, 1959.

Berko, J. "The child's learning of English morphology." *Word*, 1958, 14, 150–177.

Berry, M. F. *Language Disorders of Children: The Basis and Diagnoses*. New York: Appleton-Century-Crofts, 1969.

Bersoff, D. N. "Silk purses into sow's ears: The decline of psychological testing and a suggestion for its redemption." *American Psychologist*, 1973, 28, 892–899.

Birch, H. & Belmont, L. "Auditory-visual integration in normal and retarded readers." *American Journal of Orthopsychiatry*, 1964, 34, 852–861.

Birch, H. L., *Brain Damage in Children—The Biological and Social Aspects*, Baltimore, Maryland: Williams and Wilkins, 1964.

——— & Lefford, A. "Intersensory development in children." *Monograph of the Society for Research in Child Development*, 1963, 28, serial #89.

Birch, H. G. & Belmont, L. "Auditory-visual integration, intelligence, and reading ability in school children." *Perceptual and Motor Skills*, 1965, 20, 295–305.

Blank, M. & Bridger, W. "Deficiencies in verbal labeling in retarded readers." *American Journal of Orthopsychiatry*, 1966, 36, 840–847.

———, Weider, S. & Bridger, W. J. "Verbal deficiencies in abstract thinking in early reading retardation." *American Journal of Orthopsychiatry*, 1968, 38, 823–834.

Bliesmer, E. P. & Yarborough, B. H. "A comparison of ten different beginning reading programs in first grade." *Phi Delta Kappan*, 1965, 500–504.

Boder, E. "Developmental dyslexia: Prevailing diagnostic concepts and a new diagnostic approach." In H. R. Myklebust, *Progress in Learning Disabilities, Vol. II*. New York: Grune & Stratton, 1971.

Bond, G. L. & Dykstra, R. "The cooperative research program in first-grade reading instruction." *Reading Research Quarterly*, 2 (Summer 1967).

Borstelmann, L. J. "Review of Gesell Developmental Tests." in O.K. Buros, ed.,

References

The Seventh Mental Measurement Yearbook. N.J.: The Gryphon Press, 1972.

Bortner, M., Hertzig, M. E. & Birch, H. "Neurological signs and intelligence in brain damaged children." *Journal of Special Education,* 1972, 6, 325–333.

Brackbill, Y. "Extinction of the smiling response in infants as a function of reinforcement schedule." *Child Development,* 1958, 29, 115–124.

Bradway, K. P., Thompson, C. W. & Cravens, R. B. "Preschool IQ's after twenty-five years." *Journal of Educational Psychology,* 1958, 49, 278–281.

Braine, M. D. S. "On learning the grammatical order of words." *Psychological Review,* 1963, 70, 323–340.

Broadbent, D. E. *Perception and Communication.* New York: Pergamon, 1958.

Bronfenbrenner, U. *Two Worlds of Childhood: U.S. and U.S.S.R.* New York: Russell Sage Foundation, 1970.

Brooks, L. R. "Spatial and verbal components of the act of recall." *Canadian Journal of Psychology,* 1958, 22, 349–358.

Brown, R. *A first language: The early stages.* Cambridge, Mass.: Harvard University Press, 1973.

Browning, R. M. "Effect of irrelevant peripheral visual stimuli on discrimination learning in minimally brain-damaged children." *Journal of Consulting Psychology,* 1967, 31, 371–376.

Bruinincks, R., Glaman, G. & Clark, C. "Prevalence of learning disabilities: Findings, issues, and recommendations." Research Report, June, #20, Department of Health, Education, and Welfare, 1971.

Bryan, Q. R. "Relative importance of intelligence and visual perception in predicting reading achievement." *Calif. J. Educ. Research,* 1964, 15, 44–48.

Bryan, T. "The effect of forced mediation upon short-term memory of children with learning disabilities." *Journal of Learning Disabilities,* 1972, 5, 605–609.

———."Peer popularity of learning disabled children." *Journal of Learning Disabilities,* 1974a, Vol. 7. 261–268(a).

———."Social factors in reading disabilities." Paper presented at the meetings of the American Educational Research Association, Chicago, Ill., 1974b.

———."Peer interactions and sociometric choices." Unpub. manuscript 1974c.

———."An observational analysis of classroom behaviors of children with learning disabilities." *Journal of Learning Disabilities,* 1974d, 7, 26–34.

"Peer Popularity of Learning Disabled Children: A Replication." *Journal of Learning Disabilities.* In Press.

"Stranger's Judgements of Children's Social and Academic Adequacy: Instant Diagnosis." Unpublished manuscript, 1974 E.

——— & McGrady, H. J. "Use of a teacher rating scale." *Journal of Learning Disabilities,* 1972, 5, 199–206.

——— & Wheeler, R. "Perception of learning disabled children: The eye of the observer." *Journal of Learning Disabilities,* 1972, 5, 484–488.

Bryant, N. D. "Some principles of remedial instruction for dyslexia." *The Reading Teacher,* 1965, 18, 567–572.

Burns, G. W. & Watson, B. L. "Factor analysis of the revised ITPA with underachieving children." *Journal of Learning Disabilities,* 1973, 6, 371–376.

Bushell, D., Wrobel, P. A. & Michaelis, M. "Applying 'group' contingencies to the classroom behavior of preschool children." *Journal of Applied Behavior Analysis,* 1968, 1, 55–63.

References

Butler, K. G. "Review of the Utah Test of Language Development." In O. K. Buros (ed.), *The Seventh Mental Measurements Yearbook, Vol. II.* New Jersey: The Gryphon Press, 1972, 1366–1367.

Bzoch, K. R. & League, R. *Assessing Language Skills in Infancy.* Gainesville, Fla: The Tree of Life Press, Inc., 1972.

Cameron, J., Livson, N. & Bayley, N. "Infant vocalizations and their relationship to mature intelligence." *Science,* 1967, 57, 331–333.

Camp, B. W. "Psychometric tests and learning in severely disabled readers." *Journal of Learning Disabilities,* 1973, 6, 512–517.

Carder, W. O. "Effects of physical education on the intellectual, physical, and social development of educable mentally retarded boys." *Exceptional Children,* 1966, 32, 357–364.

Carlin, J. B. "Intensive reading instruction." *The Reading Teacher,* 1970, 23, 422–435.

Carroll, J. B. "Review of the Illinois Test of Psycholinguistics." In O.K. Buros (ed.), *The Seventh Mental Measurements Yearbook, Vol. II.* New Jersey: The Gryphon Press, 1972, 7, 819–823.

Carver, R. P. "Two dimensions of tests: Psychometric and edumetric." *American Psychologist,* 1974, 29, 512–518.

Cattell, P. *The Measurement of Intelligence of Infants and Young Children.* New York: Psychol. Corp., 1947.

Chalfant, J. & Scheffelin, M. "Central processing dysfunctions in children: A review of research." NINDS Monograph No. 9. Bethesda, Md.: U.S. Department of Health, Education, and Welfare, 1969. (Task Force III).

Chall, J. *Learning to Read: The Great Debate.* New York: McGraw-Hill, 1970.

Chase, C. I. "Review of the Illinois Test of Psycholinguistics." In O.K. Buros (ed.), *The Seventh Mental Measurement Yearbook, Vol. II.* New Jersey: The Gryphon Press, 1972.

Chissom, B. S. "Review of Frostig DTVP." In O.K. Buros (ed.), *The Seventh Mental Measurements Yearbook, Vol. II.* New Jersey: The Gryphon Press, 1972.

Chomsky, N. "Review of Skinner's verbal behavior." In L. A. Jakobovits & M. S. Miron (eds.), *Readings in the Psychology of Language.* Englewood Cliffs, N.J.: Prentice-Hall, 1967.

Christoplos, F. & Renz, P. "A critical examination of special education programs." *Journal of Special Education,* 1969, 3, 317–379.

Clements, S. D. "Minimal brain dysfunction in children." NINDS Monograph No. 3, Public Health Service Bulletin #1415. Washington, D.C.: U.S. Department of Health, Education, and Welfare, 1966.

Cohen, S. A. "Studies of visual perception and reading in disadvantaged children." *Journal of Learning Disabilities,* 1969, 2, 498–507.

Cohn, R. "Dyscalculia." *Archives of Neurology,* 1961, 4, 301–307.

Connors, C. K., Kramer, K. & Guerra, F. "Auditory synthesis and dichotic listening in children with learning disabilities." *Journal of Special Education,* 1969, 3, 163–170.

Corder, W. O., "Affects of Physical Education on the Intellectual, Physical and Social Development of Educational Mentally Retarded Boys." *Exceptional Children* 1966, 32, 357–36.

Cratty, B. *Perceptual-Motor Behavior and Educational Processes.* Springfield, Ill.: Charles C. Thomas, 1969.

References

Critchley, M. *Developmental Dyslexia.* London: Heinemann, 1964.

Cronbach, L. J. *Essentials of Psychological Testing.* New York: Harper and Row, 1960.

———. "Individualization of instruction." In M. D. Merrill (ed.), *Instructional Design: Readings.* Englewood Cliffs, N.J.: Prentice-Hall, 1971.

Cruickshank, W. M. "Review of the Vineland Social Maturity Scale." In O. K. Buros (ed.), *The Fourth Mental Measurements Yearbook.* New Jersey: The Gryphon Press, 1953.

———. "Some issues facing the field of learning disability." *Journal of Learning Disabilities,* 1972, 5, 380–388.

———, Bentzen, F. A., Ratzeburg, F. H. & Tannhauser, M. T. *A Teaching Method for Brain-injured and Hyperactive Children.* Syracuse: Syracuse University Press, 1961.

——— & Halloran, D. P. "Alfred A. Strauss: Pioneer in learning disabilities." *Exceptional Children,* 1973, 39, 321–327.

Curry, F. "A comparison of left-handed & right-handed subjects on verbal and nonverbal dichotic listening tasks." Unpublished doctoral dissertation, Northwestern University, 1966.

Curtis, B. A., Jacobson, S. & Marcus, E. M. *An Introduction to the Neurosciences.* Philadelphia: W. B. Saunders Co., 1972.

Czudner, G. & Rourke, B. P. "Simple reaction time in brain damaged and normal children under regular and irregular preparatory interval conditions." *Perceptual and Motor Skills,* 1970, 31, 767–773.

Dale, P. S. *Language Development.* Hinsdale, Ill.: Dryden Press, 1972.

Dechant, E. V. *Improving the Teaching of Reading.* Englewood Cliffs, N.J.: Prentice-Hall, 1964.

de Hirsch, K., Jansky, J. & Langford, Q. *Predicting Reading Failure.* New York: Harper and Row, 1966.

Delecato, C. H. *The Diagnosis and Treatment of Speech and Reading Problems.* Springfield, Ill.: Charles C. Thomas, 1963.

———. *Neurological Organization and Reading.* Springfield, Ill.: Charles C. Thomas, 1966.

Della-Piana, G. M. "Review of Gates-McKillop Reading Diagnostic Tests." In O. K. Buros (ed.), *The Sixth Mental Measurements Yearbook.* New Jersey: The Gryphon Press, 1965.

Denckla, M. B. "Research needs in learning disabilities: A neurologist's point of view." *Journal of Learning Disabilities,* 1973, 6, 441–450.

Deno, E. "Review of Slingerland's Screening Tests for Identifying Children with Specific Language Disability." In O. K. Buros (ed.), *The Seventh Mental Measurements Yearbook, Vol. II.* New Jersey: The Gryphon Press, 1972.

DiCarlo, L. M. "Differential diagnosis of congenital aphasia." *Volta Review,* 1960, 62, 361–364.

———. "Auditory discrimination test." In O. K. Buros (ed.), *The Sixth Mental Measurements Yearbook.* New Jersey: The Gryphon Press, 1965.

Diederich, P. B. II. "Research 1960–1970 on methods and materials in reading." ERIC Clearinghouse on Tests, Measurement & Education. Princeton, N. J.: Educational Testing Service, 1973.

Dienes, Z. *An Experimental Study of Mathematics Learning.* London: Hutchinson, 1963.

Dion, K. K. "Physical attractiveness and evaluation of children's transgressions." *Journal of Personality and Social Psychology,* 1972, 24, 207–213.

References

Division for Children with Learning Disabilities Newsletter, 1973, *iii,* No. 1.

Doehring, D. "Visual spatial memory in aphasic children." *Journal of Speech and Hearing Research,* 1960, 3, 138–149.

———— & Rabinovitch, M. S. "Auditory abilities of children with learning problems." *Journal of Learning Disabilities,* 1969, 2, 467–475.

Doll, E. A. *Vineland Social Maturity Scale.* Minneapolis: Educational Test Bureau, 1947.

————. *The Measurement of Social Competence.* Vineland, N.J.: Educational Test Bureau, Educational Publishers, Inc., 1953.

Doman, R. J., Spitz, E. B., Zucman, E., Delecato, C. H. & Doman, G. "Children with severe brain injuries: Neurological organization in terms of mobility." In E. C. Frierson and W. B. Barke (eds.), *Educating Children with Learning Disabilities.* New York: Appleton-Century-Crofts, 1967.

Downing, J. "A cross-national investigation of cultural and linguistic mismatch in fourteen countries." Paper prepared for the World Federation for Mental Health Conference, Tucson, Arizona, November 1972.

Drass, S. D. & Jones, R. L. "Learning disabled children as behavior modifiers." *Journal of Learning Disabilities,* 1971, 4, 418, 425.

Dunn, L. M. *Peabody Picture Vocabulary Test.* Minneapolis, Minn.: American Guidance Services, Inc., 1959.

————. *Exceptional Children in the Schools.* New York: Holt, Rinehart and Winston, 1973.

———— & Markwardt, F. C. *Peabody Individual Achievement Test.* Circle Pines, Minn.: American Guidance Service, 1970.

Durost, W. M. (ed.). *Metropolitan Achievement Tests.* New York: Harcourt, Brace & World, Inc., 1961.

Dykman, R. A., Ackerman, P. T., Clements, S. D. & Peters, J. E. "Specific learning disabilities: An attentional deficit syndrome." In H. R. Myklebust (ed.), *Progress in Learning Disabilities, Vol. II.* New York: Grune & Stratton, 1971, 56–93.

————, Walls, R., Suzuki, T., Ackerman, P. & Peters, J. E. "Children with learning disabilities: Conditioning, differentiation, and the effect of distraction." *American Journal of Orthopsychiatry,* 1970, 40, 766–781.

Edgington, R. & Blackmon, L. "Helping children with reading disability." Child Guidance Study Unit. Univ. of Arkansas Medical Center, Little Rock, 1962.

Entwisle, D. R. "Socialization of language behavior and educability." in M. Maehr & W. Stallings (eds.), *Culture, Child and School,* in press.

Ernhart, C. B., Graham, F. K., Eichman, P. L., Marshall, J. M. & Thurston, D. "Brain injury in the preschool child: Some developmental considerations." *Psychological Monographs,* 1963, 77, 17–33.

Estes, R. E. & Huizinga, R. J. "A comparison of visual and auditory presentations of a paired-associate learning task with learning disabled children." *Journal of Learning Disabilities,* 1974, 7, 35–42.

Ettlinger, G. "Analysis of cross-modal effects and their relationship to language." *Brain Mechanisms Underlying Speech and Language.* New York: Grune & Stratton, 1967.

Falik, L. H. "The effects of special perceptual-motor training in kindergarten on second grade reading." *Journal of Learning Disabilities,* 1969, 2, 325–329.

Farber, B. *Mental Retardation.* Boston: Houghton Mifflin, 1968.

References

———— & Jenne, W. C. "Family organization and parent-child communication: Parents and siblings of a retarded child." *Monographs of the Society for Research in Child Development,* 1963, 28, 63–78.

Farnham-Diggory, S. *Cognitive Processes in Education: A Psychological Preparation for Teaching and Curriculum Development.* New York: Harper and Row, 1972.

Ferinden, W. E., Jr. *Educational Interpretation of the Wechsler Intelligence Scale for Children (WISC).* Linden, N. J.: Remediation Associates, 1969.

————. *Educational Interpretation of the Stanford-Binet Intelligence Scale Form LM and the Illinois Test of Psycholinguistic Abilities.* Linden, N. J.: Remediation Associates, 1970.

Fernald, G. M. *Remedial Techniques in School Subject.* New York: McGraw-Hill, 1943.

Flavell, J. H., Beach, D. R. & Chinsky, J. M. "Spontaneous verbal rehearsal in a memory task as a function of age." *Child Development,* 1966, 37, 283–299.

Forness, S. R. & Estveldt, K. C. "Classroom observation of learning and behavior problem children." Graduate School of Education, University of California, L.A., 1971.

Frank, G. H. "The measurement of personality from the Wechsler tests." In B. A. Maher (ed.), *Progress in Experimental Personality Research, Vol. 5.* New York: Academic Press, 1970.

Franklin, B. "A dietary key to child behavior." *Prevention,* 1973, 25, 93–100.

Freeman, F. S. *Theory and Practice of Psychological Testing.* New York: Holt, Rinehart and Winston, 1962, 227–228.

Freibergs, V. & Douglas, J. I. "Concept learning in hyperactive and normal children." *Journal of Abnormal Psychology,* 1969, 74, 388–395.

Freides, D. "Human information processing and sensory modality: Cross-modal functions, information complexity, memory and deficit." *Psychological Bulletin,* 1974, 81, 284–310.

French, J. L. "Review of Peabody Individual Achievement Test." In O. K. Buros (ed.), *The Seventh Mental Measurements Yearbook.* N.J.: The Gryphon Press, 1972.

Friedland, S. J. & Shilkret, R. B. "Alternative explanations of learning disabilities: Defensive hyperactivity." *Exceptional Children,* 1973, 40, 213–214.

Friedlander, B. Z. & Cohen de Lara, H. C. "Receptive language anomaly and language/reading dysfunction in 'normal' primary-grade school children." *Psychology in the Schools,* 1973, 10, 12–18.

Fritsch, G. & Hitzig, E. (1870). Cited by R. F. Thompson, *Foundations of Physiological Psychology.* New York: Harper and Row, 1967.

Frostig, M. *Frostig Developmental Tests of Visual Perception.* Palo Alto, Calif.: Consulting Psychologists Press, 1964.

————."Visual perception, integrative functions and academic learning." *Journal of Learning Disabilities,* 1972, 5, 1–15.

———— & Horne, D. *The Frostig Program for the Development of Visual Perception.* Chicago, Ill.: Follett, 1964.

Fry, M. A., Johnson, C. S. & Muehl, S. "Oral language production in relation to reading achievement among select second graders." In D. J. Bakker & P. Satz (eds.), *Specific Reading Disability.* Netherlands: Rotterdam University Press, 1970, 123–159.

Fygetakis, L. J. & Ingram, D. "Language rehabilitation and programmed conditioning: A case study." *Journal of Learning Disabilities,* 1973, 6, 60–64.

Gagne, R. M. & Paradise, N. E. "Abilities and learning sets in knowledge acquisition." *Psychological Monographs,* 1961, 75, No. 14.

Gardner, J. M. "Teaching behavior modification to nonprofessionals." *Journal of Applied Behavior Analysis,* 1972, 5, 517–522.

Garrin, R., Veroff, J. and S. Feld, *Americans View Their Mental Health.* New York: Basic Books, 1960.

Gates, A. I. & McKillop, A. S. *Gates-McKillop Reading Diagnostic Tests: Manual of Directions.* New York: Teachers College Press, 1962.

Gattegno, C. *Teaching Reading with Words in COLOR.* New York: Xerox Corporation, 1968.

———. *Teacher's Guide: Words in Color.* Chicago: Encyclopedia Britannica Press, 1963.

Gatz, A. J. *Manter's Essentials of Clinical Neuroanatomy and Neurophysiology.* Philadelphia: F. A. Davis Co., 1966.

Gazzaniga, M. S., Bogen, J. E. & Sperry, R. W. "Observations on visual perception after disconnection of the cerebral hemisphere in man." *Brain,* 1965, 88, 221–236.

Gearheart, B. R. *Learning Disabilities: Educational Strategies.* Saint Louis: C. V. Mosby Co., 1973.

Gerstmann, J., "Syndrome of Finger Agnosia: Disorientation for Right and Left, Agraphia and Acalculia." *Archives of Neurology and Psychology,* 44, 389.

Geschwind, N. "Neurological foundations of language." In H. R. Myklebust (ed.), *Progress in Learning Disabilities, Vol. I.* New York: Grune & Stratton, 1968.

Getman, G. "The visual-motor complex in the acquisition of learning skills." In J. Hellmath (ed.), *Learning Disorders, Vol. 1.* Seattle: Special Child Publications, 1965.

Gewirtz, J. L. "Mechanisms of social learning: Some roles of stimulation and behavior in early human development." In D. A. Goslin (ed.), *Handbook of Socialization Theory and Research.* Chicago: Rand McNally, 1969.

Gibbs, F. A. & Gibbs, E. L. *Atlas of Electroencephalography.* Mass.: Cummings Co., 1941.

Gibson, J. J. and Gibson, E. J., "Perceptual Learning: Differentiation or Enrichment?" *Psychological Review,* 1965, 62, 32–44.

Gibson, E. J., Gibson, J. J., Pick, A. D. & Osser, H. "A developmental study of the discrimination of letter-like forms." *Journal of Comparative and Physiological Psychology,* 1962, 55, 897–906.

Gillingham, A. & Stillman, B. *Remedial Training for Children with Specific Disability in Reading, Spelling, Penmanship.* Cambridge, Mass.: Educators Publishing Service, 1960.

Glaser, G. H. *EEG and Behavior.* New York: Basic Books, Inc., 1963.

Goffman, E. *Asylums.* New York: Anchor Books, Doubleday & Co., 1961.

Goldstein, K. *Language and Language Disturbances.* New York: Grune & Stratton, 1948.

Goldstein, R., Landau, W. M. & Kleffner, F. R. "Neurologic observation in a population of deaf and asphasic children." *Annals of Otolaryngology, Rhinolaryngology and Laryngology,* 1960, 69, 756–767.

Goodenough, F. L. *Measurement of Intelligence by Drawings.* Tarrytown-on-Hudson, N.Y.: World Book Co., 1926.

Goodman, L. & Wiederholt, J. L. "Predicting reading achievement in disadvan-

References

taged children." Unpublished manuscript. Dept. of Special Education, Temple University, Philadelphia, Pa., 1972.

Goyen, J. D. & Lyle, J. G. "Effect of incentives upon retarded and normal readers on a visual associate learning task." *Journal of Experimental Child Psychology*, 1971a, 11, 274–280.

―――――."Effect of incentives and age on the visual recognition of retarded readers." *Journal of Experimental Child Psychology*, 1971b, 11, 266–273.

―――――. "Short term memory and visual discrimination in retarded readers." *Perceptual & Motor Skills*, 1973, 36, 403–408.

Graeme, S. C. & Harris, M. B. "Improving word recognition in retarded readers." *The Reading Teacher*, 1970, 23, 418–421.

Graham, F. K., Matarazzo, R. G. & Caldwell, B. M. "Behavioral differences between normal and traumatized newborns: II, Standardization, reliability, and validity." *Psychological Monographs*, 1956, 70, 17–33.

―――――, Ernhart, C. B., Thurston, D. & Craft, M. "Development three years after perinatal anoxia and other potentially damaging newborn experiences." *Psychological Monographs*, 1962, 76, (No. 3).

Grassi, J. "Auditory vigilance performance in brain damaged, behavior disordered, and normal children." *Journal of Learning Disabilities*, 1970, 3, 302–304.

Gray, B. B. & Fygetakis, L. "Mediated language acquisition for dysphasic children." *Behavior Research & Therapy*, 1968, 6, 263–280.

―――――, Baker, R. D. & Stancyk, S. E. "Performance determined instruction for training in remedial reading." *Journal of Applied Behavior Analysis*, 1969, 2, 255–263.

Greenspan, S. B. "Research studies of visual and perceptual-motor training." Optometric Extension Program, Duncan, Oklahoma, 1972.

Gruber, J. J. "Implications of physical education programs for children with learning disabilities." *Journal of Learning Disabilities*, 1969, 2, 593–599.

Gurren, L. & Hughes, A. "Intensive phonics vs. gradual phonics in beginning reading: A Review." *Journal of Educational Research*, 1965, 58, 339–346.

Guthrie, J. T. & Goldberg, H. K. "Visual sequential memory in reading disability." *Journal of Learning Disabilities*, 1972, 5, 41–46.

Hammill, D. "Training visual perceptual processes." *Journal of Learning Disabilities*, 1972, 5, 552–559.

Harris, A. J. "Individualizing first grade reading according to specific learning aptitudes." Office of Research and Evaluation, Division of Teacher Education, City University of New York, 1965.

Harris, D. B. *Children's Drawings as Measures of Intellectual Maturity: A Revision and Extension of the Goodenough Draw-a-Man Test.* New York: Harcourt, Brace & World, 1963.

Hartman, R. T. & Richards, G. B. "The effect of using a black light apparatus to reduce attention scatter in brain injured children." *Journal of Learning Disabilities*, 1969, 2, 391–394.

Hartup, W. W., Glazer, J. A. & Charlesworth, R. "Peer reinforcement and sociometric status." *Child Development*, 1967, 38, 1017–1024.

Hay, J. & Wingo, C. *Reading with Phonics, Teacher's Edition.* Philadelphia: Lippincott, 1960.

Hebb, D. O. *The Organization of Behavior.* New York: John Wiley and Sons, 1949.

379

References

Helveston, E. M. *The Role of the Ophthalmologist in Dyslexia.* Dayton, Ohio: Institute for Development of Educational Activities, Inc., 1969.

Hermann, K. *Reading Disability.* Copenhagen: Munksgaard, 1959.

Hewett, F. *The Emotionally Disturbed Child in the Classroom.* Boston: Allyn & Bacon, 1970.

———, Taylor, F. D. & Artuso, A. A. "The Santa Monica Project: Evaluation of an engineered classroom design with emotionally disturbed children." *Exceptional Children,* 1969, 35, 523–529.

Hindley, C. B. "The Griffiths scale of infant development: Scores and predictions from 3–18 months." *Child Psychology and Psychiatry,* 1960, 1, 99–112.

Holliday, F. B. "Title III Program in Early Childhood Development" (Evanston Screening Program), Timber Ridge School, Skokie, Ill., 1972.

Hollingsworth, P. M. "An experiment with the impress method of teaching reading." *The Reading Teacher,* 1970, 24, 112–115.

Honzik, M. P., Macfarlane, J. W. & Allen, L. "The stability of mental test performance between two and eighteen years." *Journal of Experimental Education,* 1948, 17, 309–324.

"Hotdogs and Hyperkinesis," *Newsweek,* Jul. 9, 1973, 57.

Huelsman, C. B., Jr. "The WISC subtest syndrome for disabled readers." *Perceptual and Motor Skills,* 1970, 30, 535–550.

Hughes, J. R. "Electroencephalography and learning disabilities." In H. R. Myklebust (ed.), *Progressing Learning Disabilities, Vol. II.* New York: Grune & Stratton, 1971.

Huizinga, R. J. "The relationship of the ITPA to the Stanford-Binet Form L-M and the WISC." *Journal of Learning Disabilities,* 1973, 6, 451–456.

Hunter, E. J., Johnson, L. C. & Keefe, F. B. "Electrodermal and cardiovascular responses in nonreaders." *Journal of Learning Disabilities,* 1972, 5, 187–197.

Hutson, B. A. "Language factors in reading disability." Paper presented at the American Educational Research Association, Chicago, Ill., April, 1974.

Hyman, H. H. *Interviewing in Social Research.* Chicago: University of Chicago Press, 1954.

Ilg, F. L. & Ames, L. B. *School Readiness: Behavior Tests Used at the Gesell Institute.* New York: Harper and Row, 1965.

Impellizzeri, I. H. "Auditory perceptual ability of normal children aged five through eight." *Journal of Genetic Psychology,* 1967, 111, 289–294.

Jackson, J. H., 1864. Cited in H. R. Myklebust (ed.), *Progress in Learning Disabilities, Vol. 1.* New York: Grune & Stratton, 1968.

Jackson, P. "Life in classrooms." In E. Hollander and R. Hunt (eds.), *Current Perspectives in Social Psychology.* New York: Oxford University Press, 1971.

Jakobson, R. & Halle, M. "Fundamentals of language. Part 2: Two aspects of language and two types of aphasic distrubances." 'S—Gravenhage: Mouton, 1956.

Jamison, C. B. "Review of The Purdue Perceptual-Motor Survey." In O. K. Buros (ed.), *The Seventh Mental Measurements Yearbook.* New Jersey: The Gryphon Press, 1972.

Jastic, J. F. & Jastic, S. R. *The Wide Range Achievement Test.* Wilmington, Del.: Guidance Associates, 1965.

Jensen, A. R. "How much can we boost I.Q. and scholastic achieve-

References

ment?" *Harvard Educational Review*, 1969, 39, 1–123.

Johnson, D. J. "Educational principles for children with learning disabilities." *Rehabilitation Literature*, 1967, 28, 317–322.

———— & Myklebust, H. *Learning Disabilities: Educational Principles and Practices*. New York: Grune & Stratton, 1967.

Jones, R. "Labels and stigma in special education." *Exceptional Children*, 1972, 38, 553–564.

Kagan, J. "Reflection-impulsivity and reading ability in primary grade children." *Child Development*, 1965, 36, 609–628.

————. *Change and Continuity in Infancy*. New York: John Wiley and Sons, Inc., 1971.

Kalaski, L. "Arithmetic and the brain-injured child." In E. C. Frierson & W. B. Barbe (eds.), *Educating Children with Learning Disabilities*. New York: Appleton-Century-Crofts, 1967.

Kanner, L. "Early infantile autism." *Journal of Pediatrics*, 1944, 25, 211–217.

Kass, C. E. "Introduction to Learning Disabilities." *Seminars in Psychiatry*, 1969, 1, 240–244.

————, Hall, R. E. & Simches, R. F. "Legislation in Minimal Brain Dysfunction in Children. Phase Two: Educational, Medical and Health-Related Services." *Public Health Service Publication*, No. 2015, 1969, 44–50.

Kawi, A. & Pasamanick, B. "Prenatal and paranatal factors in the development of childhood disorders." *Monographs of the Society for Research in Child Development*, 1959, 24, #4.

Kazdin, A. E. & Bootzin, R. R. "The token economy: An evaluative review." *Journal of Applied Behavior Analysis*, 1972, 5, 343–372.

Kender, J. P. "Is there really a WISC profile for poor readers?" *Journal of Learning Disabilities*, 1972, 5, 397–400.

Keogh, B. K. "A compensatory model for psychoeducational evaluation of children with learning disorders." *Journal of Learning Disabilities*, 1971, 4, 544–548.

———— & Hall, R. J. "Functional analysis of WISC performance of children classified as EH and EMR." Technical Report SERP 1973–A9 Graduate School of Education, University of California, Los Angeles, 1973.

————, Tchir, C. & Windeguth-Behn, A. "Teachers' perceptions of educationally high risk children." *Journal of Learning Disabilities*, 1974, 7, 367–374.

————, Wetter, J., McGinty, A. & Donlon, G. "Functional analysis of WISC performance of learning disordered, hyperactive, and mentally retarded boys." *Psychology in the Schools*, 1973, 10, 178–181.

Kephart, N. C. *Learning Disability: An Educational Adventure*. West Lafayette, Ind.: Kappa Delta Pi Press, 1967.

————. *The Brain-Injured Child in the Classroom*. Chicago: National Society for Crippled Children and Adults, 1963.

————. *The Slow Learner in the Classroom*. Columbus, Ohio: Merrill, 1971.

Kershner, J. R. "An investigation of the Doman-Delecato theory of neuropsychology as it applies to trainable mentally retarded children in public schools." Bureau of Research Administration and Coordination, Area of Research and Development, Department of Public Instruction, Commonwealth of Pennsylvania, May 1967, p. 105 (mimeo.). Cited in Richard L. Masland, "Children with minimal brain dysfunction—A national prob-

References

lem." In Lester Tamopol (ed.), *Learning Disabilities*, Springfield, Ill.: Charles C. Thomas, 1969.

Kiloh, L. G. & Osselton, J. W. *Clinical Electroencephalography*. London: Butterworths, 1961.

Kinder, E. F. "Review of the Vineland Social Maturity Scale." In O. K. Buros (ed.), *Mental Measurements Yearbook, Vol. 1*. N.J.: The Gryphon Press, 1938.

Kinsbourne, M. "Perceptual learning determines beginning reading." Paper presented at the meeting of the Eastern Psychological Association. Philadelphia, Pa., 1973.

Kirk, S. A. & Kirk, W. P. *Psycholinguistic Learning Disabilities: Diagnosis and Remediation*. Urbana: University of Illinois Press, 1972.

Kirk, S., McCarthy, J. J. and Kirk, W. D., *Illinois Test of Psycholinguistics Abilities:* rev. ed. Urbana, Il.: University of Illinois Press, 1968.

Klima, E. S. "Negation in English." In J. J. Fodor & J. A. Katz (eds.), *The Structure of Language*. Englewood Cliffs, N.J.: Prentice-Hall, 1964.

Kohlberg, L., "Stage and Sequence: The Cognitive Developmental Approach to Socialization." In D.S. Goslin, ed., *Handbook of Socialization Theory and Research*. Chicago, Il.: Rand-McNally, 1969, 347–480.

Knobloch, H. & Pasamanick, B. "Syndrome of minimal cerebral damage in infancy." *Journal of the American Medical Association*, 1959, 170, 1384–1387.

Koppitz, E. M. *The Bender Gestalt Test for Young Children*. New York: Grune & Stratton, Inc., 1964.

Kosc, L. "Developmental dyslexia." *Journal of Learning Disabilities*, 1974, 7, 165–177.

Kravitz, H. & Boehm, J. J. "Head banging is OK." *Northwestern Reports*, Winter/March 1973, 13–14.

Krieg, F. J. & Windsor, M. M. "Visual factors in reading disability." Paper presented at the Conference of the American Education Research Association, Chicago, Ill. April, 1974.

Landis, D. "Review of The Purdue Perceptual-Motor Survey." In O. K. Buros (ed.), *The Seventh Mental Measurements Yearbook, Vol. II*. New Jersey: The Gryphon Press, 1972.

Langer, S. K. *Philosophy in a New Key*. Cambridge: Harvard University Press, 1957.

Lapouse, R. & Monk, M. A. "Behavior deviations in a representative sample of children: Variation by sex, age, race, social class and family size." *American Journal of Orthopsychiatry*, 1964, 34, 436–446.

Lawson, L. J. "Ophthalmological factors in learning disabilities." In H. R. Myklebust (ed.), *Progress in Learning Disabilities, Vol. I*. New York: Grune & Stratton, 1968, 147–181.

Lee, L. L. "A screening test for syntax development." *Journal of Speech and Hearing Disorders*, 1970, 35, 103–112.

———. *Developmental Sentence Analysis*. Evanston, Ill.: Northwestern University Press, 1974.

Lenneberg, E. *Biological Foundations of Language*. New York: John Wiley and Sons, 1967.

Lerea, L. *The Michigan Picture Language Inventory*. Ann Arbor: University of Michigan, 1958.

Lerner, J. W. *Children with Learning Disabilities*. Boston: Houghton Mifflin, 1971.

References

Levin, J. R. "Inducing comprehension in poor readers." *Journal of Educational Psychology*, 1973, 65, 19–24.

Levin, J. R., Devine — Hawkins, P., Kerst, S. M. and Guttermann, J., "Individual Differences in Learning from Pictures and Words: The Development and Application of an Instrument." *Journal of Educational Psychology*, 1974, 66, 296–303.

Lewis, M. "Infant intelligence tests: Their use and misuse." *Human Development*, 1973, 16, 108–118.

Lewis, R. S., Strauss, A. & Lehtinen, L. *The Other Child*. New York: Grune & Stratton, 1960.

Lindamood, C. H. & Lindamood, P. C. *Auditory Discrimination in Depth*. Boston, Mass.: Teacher Resources Corp., 1969.

Lindzey, G. & Byrne, D. "Measurement of social choice and interpersonal attractiveness." In G. Lindzey and E. Aronson (eds.), *The Handbook of Social Psychology*, Second Edition. Reading, Mass.: Addison-Wesley, 1968, 452–525.

Littell, W. M. "The Wechsler Intelligence Scale for Children: A review of a decade of research." *Psychological Bulletin*, 1960, 57, 132–156.

Liverant, S. "Intelligence: A concept in need of re-examination." *Journal of Consulting Psychology*, 1960, 24, 101–110.

Lohnes, P. R. "Evaluating the schooling of intelligence." *Educational Researcher*, 1973, 2, 6–11.

London, P. *The Modes and Morals of Psychotherapy*. New York: Holt, Rinehart & Winston, Inc., 1964.

————. "The end of ideology in behavior modification." *American Psychologist*, 1972, 27, 913–920.

Loutt, C. M. "Review of the Vineland Social Maturity Scale." In O. K. Buros (ed.), *The Third Mental Measurements Yearbook*. N.J.: The Gryphon Press, 1949.

Luria, A. *The Role of Speech in the Regulation of Normal and Abnormal Behavior*. London: Pergamon, 1961.

————. *Higher Cortical Functions in Man*. New York: Basic Books, Inc., 1966.

Lyle, J. G. "Reading retardation and reversal tendency: A factorial study." *Child Development*, 1969, 40, 833–843.

———— & Goyen, J. D. "Visual recognition, developmental lag, and strephosymbolia in reading retardation." *Journal of Abnormal Psychology*, 1968, 73, 25–29.

————. "Effect of speed of exposure and difficulty of discrimination upon visual recognition of retarded readers." Unpublished manuscript, 1974.

Lyman, H. B. "Review of Peabody Picture Vocabulary Test." In O. K. Buros (ed.), *The Sixth Mental Measurements Yearbook*. N.J.: The Gryphon Press, 1965.

Maccoby, E. E. & Konrad, K. W. "Age trends in selective listening." *Journal of Experimental Child Psychology*, 1966, 3, 113–122.

McCall, R. B. "IQ pattern over age: Comparisons among siblings and parent-child pairs." *Science*, 1970, 170, 644–648.

————, Appelbaum, M. I. & Hogarty, P. S. "Developmental changes in mental performance." *Monographs of the Society for Research in Child Development*, 1973, 38, No. 3, 1–84.

————, Hogarty, P. S. & Hurlburt, N. "Transitions in infant sensorimotor devel-

References

opment and the prediction of childhood I.Q." *American Psychologist,* 1972, 27, 728–748.

McCandless, B. R. "Environment and intellectual functioning." In H. A. Stevens & R. Heber (eds.), *Mental Retardation: A Review of Research.* Chicago: The University of Chicago Press, 1964.

McCarthy, J. J. "Review of the Early Detection Inventory." In O. K. Buros (ed.), *The Seventh Mental Measurements Yearbook.* New Jersey: The Gryphon Press, 1972.

———. & Paraskevopoulos, J. "Behavior patterns of learning disabled, emotionally disturbed, and average children." *Exceptional Children,* 1969, 35, 69–74.

McClelland, D. C. "Testing for competence rather than for " 'intelligence.' " *American Psychologist,* 1973, 28, 1–15.

McFie, J., Piercy M. F. & Zangwill, O. L. "Visual-spatial agnosia with lesions of the right cerebral hemisphere." *Brain,* 1950, 73, 167–190.

McGahan, F. E. & McGahan, C. *Early Detection Inventory.* Chicago: Follett Educational Corporation, 1967.

McGrady, H. J. & Olson, D. A. "Visual and auditory learning processes in normal children and children with specific learning disabilities." *Exceptional Children,* 1970, 36, 581–589.

McGrady, J. J. "Language pathology and learning disabilities." In H. R. Myklebust (ed.), *Progress in Learning Disabilities.* New York: Grune & Stratton, 1968, 199–233.

McKee, P., Harrison, L., McCowen, A. & Lehr, E. *Reading for Meaning Series.* Boston: Houghton Mifflin, 1963.

McNeill, D. "The development of language." In P. H. Mussen (ed.), *Carmichael's Manual of Child Psychology, Vol. 1* (3rd ed.). New York: John Wiley and Sons, 1970, 1061–1161.

McNemar, Q. "On WAIS difference scores." *Journal of Consulting Psychology,* 1957, 21, 239–240.

———."Lost: Our intelligence? Why?" *American Psychologist,* 1964, 19, 871–882.

McReynolds, L. V. "Operant conditioning for investigating speech sound discrimination in aphasic children." *Journal of Speech and Hearing Research,* 1966, 9, 519–528.

Mann, L. "Review of Frostig DVTP." In O. K. Buros (ed.), *The Seventh Mental Measurements Yearbook, Vol. II.* New Jersey: The Gryphon Press, 1972.

Masland, R. L. "Children with minimal brain dysfunction—A national problem." In L. Tarnopol (ed.), *Learning Disabilities.* Springfield, Ill.: Charles C. Thomas, 1969.

Mecham, M., Jex, J. & Jones, J. *Manual of Instructions: Utah Test of Language Development* (rev. ed.). Salt Lake City: Communication Research Associates, 1967.

Meichenbaum, D. H. "Examination of model's characteristics in reducing avoidance behavior." *Journal of Personality and Social Psychology,* 1971, 17, 298–307.

———, Bowers, K. S. & Ross, R. R. "A behavioral analysis of teacher expectancy effect." *Journal of Personality and Social Psychology,* 1969, 13, 306–316.

Menyuk, P. "Syntactic structures in the language of children." *Journal of Child Development,* 1963, 34, 407–422.

———."Comparison of grammar of children with functionally deviant and normal speech." *Journal of Speech and Hearing Research,* 1964, 7, 109–121.

———.*Sentences Children Use.* Cambridge, Mass.: MIT Press, 1969.

References

Mercer, J. R. "Sociological perspectives on mild mental retardation." Paper presented at the Peabody—NIMH Conference on Socio-Cultural Aspects of Mental Retardation, June 1968.

————.*Labeling the Mentally Retarded*. Berkeley: University of California Press, 1973.

Merklein, R. A. & Briskey, R. J. "Audiometric findings in children referred to a program for language disorders." *Volta Review*, 1962, 64, 294–298.

Merwin, J. C. "Review of Wide Range Achievement Test." In O. K. Buros (ed.), *The Seventh Mental Measurements Yearbook. Vol. 1.* New Jersey: The Gryphon Press, 1972.

Meyers, C. E. "What the I.T.P.A. measures: A synthesis of factor studies of the 1961 edition." *Educational and Psychological Measurement*, 1969, 29, 867–876.

Midlarsky, E., Bryan, J. H. & Brickman, P. "Aversive approval: Interactive effects of modeling and reinforcement on altruistic behavior." *Child Development*, 1973, 44, 321–328.

Miller, S. A., Shelton, J. & Flavell, J. H. "A test of Luria's hypotheses concerning the development of verbal self-regulation." Paper presented at the meeting of the Society for Research in Child Development, 1969.

Milner, B. "Laterality effects in audition." In U. B. Mountcastle (ed.), *Interhemispheric Relations and Cerebral Dominance*. Baltimore: Johns Hopkins, 1962, 179.

Mountcastle, V. B. (ed.), *Interhemispheric Relations and Cerebral Dominance*. Baltimore: Johns Hopkins, 1962.

Muehl, S. & Kremenak, S. "Ability to match information within and between auditory and visual sense modalities and subsequent reading achievement." *Journal of Educational Psychology*, 1966, 57, 230–239.

Munk, H. "On the functions of the cortex (1881)." Cited by H. Schuell, J. J. Jenkins & E. Jimenéz-Pabón in *Asphasia in Adults*. New York: Harper and Row, 1965.

Myklebust, H. R. *Auditory Disorders in Children: A Manual for Differential Diagnosis.* New York: Grune & Stratton, 1954.

————. & Boshes, B., Olson, D. & Cole, C. "Minimal brain damage in children." Final Report. U.S.P.H.S. Contract 108–65–142. Evanston, Ill.: Northwestern University publications, June, 1969.

————. *Pupil Rating Scale.* New York: Grune & Stratton, 1971.

Nunnally, J. C. *Popular Conceptions of Mental Health, Their Development and Change.* New York: Holt, Rinehart & Winston, 1961.

O'Donnell, P. A. & Eisenson, J. "Delecato training for reading achievement and visual motor integration." *Journal of Learning Disabilities*, 1969, 2, 10–15.

O'Leary, K. D. & Drabman, R. "Token reinforcement programs in the classroom: A review." *Psychological Bulletin*, 1971, 75, 379–398.

Orton, S. *Reading, Writing and Speech Problems in Children.* New York: W. W. Norton, 1937.

Osgood, C. E., Suci, G. & Tannenbaum, P. *The Measurement of Meaning.* Urbana, Ill.: University of Illinois Press, 1957.

Otto, W. & Koenke, K. *Remedial Teaching: Research and Comment.* Boston: Houghton Mifflin, 1969.

Owen, R. W., Adams, P. A., Forrest, T., Stolz, L. M. & Fisher, S. "Learning disorders in children: Sibling studies." *Monographs of the Society for Research in Child Development*, 1971, 36, No. 144.

References

Painter, G. "The effect of a rhythmic and sensory motor activity program on perceptual motor spatial abilities of kindergarten children." *Exceptional Children*, 1966, 33, 113–116.

Palermo, D. S. & Molfese, D. L. "Language acquisition from age five onward." *Psychological Bulletin*, 1972, 78, 409–428.

Palkes, H., Stewart, M. & Freedman, J. "Improvement in maze performance of hyperactive boys as a function of verbal-training procedures." *Journal of Special Education*, 1971, 5, 337–342.

———, Stewart, M. & Kahana, B. "Porteus maze performance of hyperactive boys after training in self-directed verbal commands." *Child Development*, 1968, 39, 817–826.

Park, G. E. "Ophthalmological aspects of learning disabilities." *Journal of Learning Disabilities*, 1969, 2, 189–198.

Pavio, A., *Imaginary and Verbal Processes*, New York: Holt, Rinehart and Winston, 1971.

Pease, D., Rosauer, J. & Wolins, L. "Reliability of infant developmental scales during the first year of life." *Journal of Genetic Psychology*, 1961, 98, 295–298.

Peck, B. B. & Stackhouse, T. "Reading problems and family dynamics." *Journal of Learning Disabilities*, 1973, 6, 506–511.

Peisach, E. C. "Children's comprehension of teacher and peer speech." *Child Development*, 1965, 36, 467–480.

Penfield, W. & Rasmussen, T. *The Cerebral Cortex of Man*. New York: Macmillan, 1950.

——— & Roberts, L. *Speech and Brain Mechanisms*. Princeton, N.J.: Princeton University Press, 1959.

Piaget, J. *The Child's Conception of Numbers*. New York: Humanities Press, 1952.

———. *The Construction of Reality in the Child*. Translated by M. Cook. New York: Basic Books, Inc., 1954.

Pope, Lillie. "Motor activity in brain-injured children." *American Journal of Orthopsychiatry*, 1970, 40, 783–794.

Poppen, R., Stark, V., Eisenson, J., Forrest, T. & Wertheim, G. "Visual sequencing performances of aphasic children." *Journal of Speech and Hearing Research*, 1969, 12, 288–300.

Rabinovitch, R. D. & Ingram, W. "Neuropsychiatric considerations in reading retardation." *The Reading Teacher*, 1962, 15, 433–438.

Rake, E. F. "Appendix A—Neurological Evaluation." In *Task Force II. Minimal brain Dysfunction in Children*. Public Health Service Publication No. 2015, 1969.

Rappaport, D. *Diagnostic Psychological Testing*. Chicago: The Yearbook Publishers, Inc., 1946.

Reese, H. W. & Lipsett, L. P. *Experimental Child Psychology*. New York: Academic Press, 1970.

Reichstein, J. & Rosenstein, J. "Differential diagnosis of auditory defects: A review of the literature." *Exceptional Children*, 1964, 31, 73.

Rimland, B. *Infantile Autism*. New York: Appleton-Century-Crofts, 1964.

Rist, R. C. "Student social class and teacher expectations: The self fulfilling prophecy in ghetto education." *Harvard Educational Review*, 1970, 40, 411–451.

Roach, E. & Kephart, N. C. *Purdue Perceptual-Motor Survey*. Columbus, Ohio: Charles E. Merrill, 1966.

Robinson, H. B. & Robinson, N. M. *The Mentally Retarded Child: A Psychological*

References

Approach. New York: McGraw-Hill Book Co., 1965.

Robinson, N. A. "Review of Metropolitan Achievement Tests." In O. K. Buros (ed.), *The Sixth Mental Measurements Yearbook.* New Jersey: The Gryphon Press, 1965.

Rogan, L. L. & Lukens, J. E. "Education, administration and classroom procedures." *Minimal Brain Dysfunction National Project on Learning Disabilities in Children Phase Two, Public Health Service Publication,* 1969, No. 2015, 21–30.

Rosen, C. L. "An experimental study of visual perceptual training and reading achievement in first grade." *Perceptual Motor Skills,* 1966, 22, 979–986.

Rosenhan, D. "On being sane in insane places." *Science,* 1973, 179, 250–258.

Rosenthal, R. *Experimenter Effects in Behavioral Research.* New York: Appleton-Century-Crofts, 1966.

——& Jacobsen, L. *Pygmalion in the Classroom.* New York: Holt, Rinehart & Winston, 1968.

Rosner, J. "Language arts and arithmetic achievement, and specifically related perceptual skills." *American Educational Research Journal,* 1973, 10, 59–68.

Ross, D. M. & Ross, S. A. "The efficacy of listening training for educable mentally retarded children." *American Journal of Mental Deficiency,* 1972, 77, 137–142.

Rothney, J. W. M. *Review of the Vineland Social Maturity Measurements Yearbook.* New Jersey: The Gryphon Press, 1949.

Rourke, B. P. & Czudner, G. "Age difference in auditory reaction time of 'brain damaged' and normal children under regular and irregular preparatory interval conditions." *Journal of Experimental Child Psychology,* 1972, 14, 527–539.

Rowitz, L. "Socioepidemiological analysis of admissions to a state-operated outpatient clinic." *American Journal of Mental Deficiency,* 1973, 78, 300–307.

Ruben, R. & Balow, B. "Learning and behavior disorders: A longitudinal study." *Exceptional Children,* 1971, 38, 293–299.

Rugel, R. Q. "WISC subtest scores of disabled readers: A review with respect to Bannatyne's recategorization." *Journal of Learning Disabilities,* 1974, 7, 48–61.

Sabatino, D. & Streissguth, W. "Word form configuration training of visual perceptual strengths with learning disabled children." *Journal of Learning Disabilities,* 1972, 5, 435–441.

Samuels, S. J. & Anderson, R. H. "Visual recognition memory, paired-associate learning, and reading achievement." *Journal of Educational Psychology,* 1973, 65, 160–167.

Scheff, T. J. *Being Mentally Ill: A Sociological Theory.* Chicago: Aldine, 1966.

Schevill, H. S. "Longitudinal kindergarten-first grade perceptual study: Temporal ordering and first grade reading." Paper presented at the annual meeting of the American Educational Research Association. New Orleans: February 1973.

Schmidt, F. L. & Hunter, T. E. "Racial and ethnic bias in psychological tests: Divergent implications of two definitions of test bias." *American Psychologist,* 1974, 29, 1–8.

Schulman, J. L., Kaspar, J. C. & Throne, F. M. *Brain Damage and Behavior.* Springfield, Ill.: Charles C. Thomas, 1965.

Schuell, H., Jenkins, J. & Jimenez-Pabon, E. *Aphasia in Adults.* New York: Harper and Row, 1965.

References

Schwartz, T. & Bryan, J. H. "Imitation and judgments of children with learning disabilities." *Exceptional Children,* 1971, 38, 157–158.

Seaver, W. B. "Effects of naturally induced teacher expectancies." *Journal of Personality and Social Psychology,* 1973, 28, 333–342.

Sechrest, L. "Incremental validity." In D. N. Jackson & S. Messick (eds.), *Problems in Human Assessment.* New York: McGraw-Hill Book Co., 1967.

Senf, G. M. "Development of immediate memory for bisensory stimuli in normal children and children with learning disorders." *Developmental Psychology,* 1969, 1, 1–28.

———& Freundl, P. C. "Memory and attention factors in specific learning disabilities." *Journal of Learning Disabilities,* 1971, 4, 94–106.

Shatz, M. & Gelman, R. "The development of communication skills: Modifications in the speech of young children as a function of listener." *Monographs of the Society for Research in Child Development,* 1973, 35, No. 5.

Skinner, B. F. "Pigeons in a pelican." *American Psychologist,* 1960, 15, 28–37.

———*Beyond Freedom and Dignity.* New York: Vintage Books, 1971.

Slingerland, B. H. *Screening Tests for Identifying Children with Specific Language Disabilities.* Cambridge, Mass.: Educators Publishing Service, 1964.

Smith, C. M. "The relationship of reading method and reading achievement to ITPA sensory modalities." *Journal of Special Education,* 1971, 5, 143–149.

Solomons, G. "Guidelines on the use and medical effects of psychostimulant drugs in therapy." *Journal of Learning Disabilities,* 1971, 4, 420–475.

Sperry, R. "Neurology and the mind-brain." In R. Isaacson (ed.), *Basic Readings in Neuropsychology.* New York: Harper and Row, 1964.

Spitz, R. "Hospitalism: A follow-up report on investigation described in Volume I, 1945." *The Psychoanalytic Study of the Child, Vol. II.* New York: International Universities Press, 1946.

Spivack, G. & Swift, M. *Devereux Elementary School Behavior Rating Scale.* Devon, Pa.: The Devereux Foundation, 1967.

Stephens, T. M. *Directive Teaching of Children with Learning and Behavioral Handicaps.* Columbus, Ohio: Charles E. Merrill, 1970.

Strag, G. A. "Comparative behavioral rating of parents with severe mentally retarded, special learning disability, and normal children." *Journal of Learning Disabilities,* 1972, 5, 631–635.

Strauss, A. & Kephart, N. *Psychopathology and Education of the Brain-injured Child.* New York: Grune & Stratton, 1955.

———& Lehtinen, L. *Psychopathology and Education of the Brain-injured Child.* New York: Grune and Stratton, 1947.

Sullivan, J. "The effects of Kephart's perceptual-motor training on a reading clinic sample." *Journal of Learning Disabilities,* 1972, 5, 32–38.

Tanner, J. M. "Physical growth." In P. H. Mussen (ed.), *Carmichael's Manual of Child Psychology (Vol. 2).* New York: John Wiley and Sons, 1970.

Task Force II, "Minimal brain dysfunction in children." Public Health Service Publication No. 2015, 1969.

Teagarden, F. M., "Review of the Bineland Social Maturity Scale." in O.K. Buros, ed., *The Fourth Mental Measurement Yearbook*, N.J.: The Gryphon Press, 1953.

Templin, M. C., "Certain Language Skills in Children", *Child Welfare Monograph,* No. 26, Minneapolis: University of Minnesota Press, 1957.

References

Terman, L. M. and Merrill, M. A., *Measuring Intelligence.* Boston: Houghton-Mifflin, 1937.

Thorndike, L., "Review of Wide Range Achievement Tests." In O.K. Buros, ed., *The Seventh Mental Measurement Yearbook,* N.J.: The Gryphon Press, 1972.

Travers, R. M. W., ed., "Research and Theory Related to Audio-Visual Information Transmission." *U.S. Office of Education Interim Report Contract,* No. 3-20-003: Salt Lake City: Bureau of Educational Research, University of Utah, July, 1964.

Trimble, A. C., "Can Remedial Be Eliminated?" *Academic Therapy Quarterly,* 1970, 5, 207-213.

Uhl, N. P. and Nurss, J. R., "Socio-economic Level Styles in Solving Reading Related Tasks." *Reading Research Quarterly,* 1970, 5, 452-485.

Underwood, B. J., "Speed of Learning and Amount Retained: A Consideration of Methodology." *Psychological Bulletin,* 1945, 51, 276-282.

——."Degree of Learning and the Measurement of Forgetting." *Journal of Verbal Learning and Verbal Behavior,* 1964, 3, 112-119.

Vande Voort, L. and Senf, G. M., "Audiovisual Integration in Retarded Readers." *Journal of Learning Disabilities,* 1973, 6, 170-179.

Vellutino, F. R. "Psychological factors in reading disability." Paper presented AERA, Chicago, Ill., April, 1974.

——, Steger, J. A. and Pruzek, R. M., "Inter- vs. Intra-Sensory Deficit in Paired Associate Learning in Poor and Normal Readers." Canadian Journal of Behavioral Science, 1973, 5, 111-123.

——, Pruzek, R. M., Steger, J. A. and Meshanlon, U. "Immediate Visual Recall in Poor and Normal Readers as a Function of Orthographic-Linguistic Familiarity." *Cortex,* 1973, 9, 368-384.

——, Steger, J. A. and Kandel, G., "Reading Disabilities: An Investigation of the Perceptual Deficit Hypothesis." *Cortex,* 1972, 8, 106-118.

——, Harding, C. J., Phillips, F. & Steger, J. A. "Differential transfer in poor and normal readers." *Journal of Genetic Psychology,* in press.

——,Steger, J. A., De Setto, L. & Phillips, F. "Immediate and delayed recognition of visual stimuli." *Journal of Experimental Child Psychology,* in press.

Vernetti, C. J. & Jacobs, J. F. "Effects of music used to mask noise in learning disability classes." *Journal of Learning Disabilities,* 1972, 5, 21-24.

Vogel, S. A. "Syntactic abilities in normal and dyslexic children." *Journal of Learning Disabilities,* 1974, 7, 103-109.

Vuckovich, D. M. "Pediatric neurology and learning disabilities." In H. R. Myklebust (ed.), *Progress in Learning Disabilities, Vol. I.* New York: Grune & Stratton, 1968, 16-38.

Vygotsky, L. S. *Thought and Language.* Cambridge, Mass.: MIT Press, 1962.

Walberg, H. "Models for optimizing and individualizing school learning." Ontario Institute for Studies in Education, University of Toronto, Canada, *Interchange,* 2, 1971.

Waugh, K. W. and Bush, W. J., *Diagnosing Learning Disorders,* Columbus, Ohio: Charles Merrill, 1971.

Webb, E. J., Campbell, D. T., Schwartz, R. D. & Sechrest, L. *Unobtrusive Measures: Nonreactive Research in the Social Sciences.* Chicago: Rand McNally, 1966.

Wechsler, D. *The Measurement and Appraisal of Adult Intelligence* (4th ed.). Baltimore, Md.: Williams & Wilkins, 1958.

References

Wechsler, D., *Wechsler Intelligence Scale for Children: Manual,* New York: The Psychological Corporation, 1949.

Weinstein, R. & Rabinovitch, R. D. "Sentence structure and retention in good and poor readers." *Journal of Educational Psychology,* 1971, 62, 25–30.

Wender, H. *Minimal Brain Dysfunction in Children.* New York: Wiley-Interscience, 1971.

Wepman, J. *Auditory Discrimination Test.* Chicago: Language Research Associates, 1958.

Werner, E. E., Honzik, M. P. & Smith, R. S. "Prediction of intelligence and achievement at ten years from twenty months pediatric and psychologic examinations." *Child Development,* 1968, 39, 1063–1075.

Werner, H. *Comparative Psychology of Mental Development.* New York: International Universities Press, 1948.

Wernicke, 1894. cited in Schuell, H., Jenkins, J. & Jimenéz-Pabón, E. *Aphasia in Adults.* New York: Harper and Row, 1965.

Wiig, E. H., Semel, E. M. & Crouse, M. A. B. "The use of English morphology by high-risk and learning disabled children." *Journal of Learning Disabilities,* 1973, 6, 457–465.

Willows, D. M. "Reading between the lines: Selective attention in good and poor readers. *Child Development,* 1974, 45, 408–415.

Wolf, M. M., Giles, D. K. & Hall, R. V. "Experiments with token reinforcement in a remedial classroom." *Behaviour Research and Therapy,* 1968, 8, 51–84.

Wood, N. E. *Verbal Learning.* San Rafael, Calif.: Dimensions Publishing Co., 1969.

———."Auditory perception in children." Social and Rehabilitation Service Research Grant (RD-2574–5), University of Southern California, Los Angeles, Calif., March, 1971.

Woodrow, H. A. "The ability to learn." *Psychological Review,* 1946, 53, 147–158.

Worth, C. & Chavasse, B. "The reflex development in the child." In T. Lyle & G. Bridgman (eds.), *Squint.* London: Baillieve, Tindall & Cox, 1959.

Yarrow, M. R., Cambell, J. D. & Barton, R. V. "Recollections of childhood—A study of the retrospective method." *Monographs of the Society of Research in Child Development,* 1970, 35, No. 5.

Zigler, E. "The nature-nurture issue reconsidered: A discussion of UZGIRIS' paper." *Proceedings of Peabody–NIMH Conference on Social-Cultural Aspects of Mental Retardation,* June, 1968.

Zigmond, N. K. & Cicci, R. *Auditory Learnings.* San Rafael, Calif.: Dimensions Publishing Co., 1968.

———."Intrasensory and intersensory processes in normal and dyslexic children." Unpublished doctoral dissertation, Northwestern University, 1966.

INDEX